'As a travel book I would rate it very highly, I would even place it in the same category as Graham Greene, Evelyn Waugh, Paul Theroux — it is full of the most splendid, perceptive and often highly entertaining portraits' — Peter Mansfield, BBC Radio 4, *Kaleidoscope*

'. . . a very coherent and sympathetic account of a journey through the modern Arab world' — Ian McEwan, *Observer*

'With an eye for the striking scene and entertaining incident he combines a perceptiveness of deeper realities that makes *Arabia Through the Looking Glass* more than an amusing traveller's journal' — Martin Moore, *Daily Telegraph*

'His Odyssey through Arabia, incomplete and impressionistic, has a visual impact which brings instant recognition to those who are familiar with the background, and a kaleidoscope of images to those far away' — *Gulf Mirror*

'. . . immensely readable book' with a 'flair for bringing people and places alive' — Dilip Hiro, *New Society*

ARABIA THROUGH
THE LOOKING GLASS

Jonathan Raban was born in 1942. He lectured in English and American literature at the University College of Wales, Aberystwyth, and at the University of East Anglia, then became a full-time writer in 1969. His books include *Soft City*, published by Fontana in 1975. He has written more than a dozen plays for radio and television, and a stage play, *The Sunset Touch*, was produced at the Bristol Old Vic in 1977. He has contributed numerous articles, short stories and reviews to a number of publications, including the *New Review*, *New Statesman*, *New Society*, *Listener*, *Times Literary Supplement*, and he writes regularly for the *Sunday Times*. He is a Fellow of the Royal Society of Literature. He lives in London.

ARABIA THROUGH THE LOOKING GLASS

Jonathan Raban

FONTANA/COLLINS

First published by William Collins Sons & Co. Ltd
1979
First issued in Fontana 1980

Copyright © Jonathan Raban 1979
Set in Monotype Baskerville

Made and printed in Great Britain by
William Collins Sons & Co. Ltd, Glasgow

Contents

'You can just see a little *peep* of the Passage in Looking-glass House, if you leave the door of our drawing-room wide open: and it's very like our passage as far as you can see, only you know it may be quite different on beyond . . .'

Lewis Carroll, *Through The Looking-Glass*

Arabia on the Earls Court Road

He was wearing a grubby shift and plastic sandals: he'd pulled his head-dress close round his ears, and had a shiny jacket of the kind sold on market-stalls to keep off the dank cold of a London January. Its seams had split under the armpits. Outside Earls Court station, where touts and hustlers hang around in the entrance alert for likely victims, he looked half-frozen, frightened, and too far from home.

She was a business girl from Nevern Square; an urban savage, all lipstick and gristle, in a belted leather coat that gave her the air of a fat little stormtrooper lording it over an occupied territory.

'Coming home with me, dear?' She blocked his way, an unlit cigarette pouched in the corner of her scarlet mouth. He stared, half-raised his hands from the windy folds of his robe.

'Come on, darling – '

Her worn professional patter, at once intimate and impersonal, streamed out of her, too fast for a bystander to follow. There was, though, an edge of avaricious excitement in her talk. She had cornered an Arab. The usual customers of the ladies of Nevern Square are small businessmen, up in London for a conference or a meeting with the sales manager; they put up for a couple of nights in one of the warren of second-rate hotels around Earls Court, and study the postcards in tobacconists' windows – 'Massage . . .', 'Girl Student Seeks Employment . . .', 'Miss Tress . . .'

She clearly knew about Arabs. His cheap sandals, the rents

in his jacket, the week-old grime of his robe and head-dress, simply were not visible to her. Looking at him, all she saw was a figure of contemporary legend, a creature of rumour and newspaper headlines. Her head must have been awash with them. *Arabs* had bought the Dorchester; *Arabs* owned half of Holborn; *Arabs* tipped business girls with Cadillacs and solid gold watches; *Arabs* closed down the whole of Harrods for an afternoon, just so that their wives could shop in decent privacy. If they wanted to take a little perfume back to their palaces in the desert, *Arabs* purchased a couple of suitcases first, then instructed the assistant to load them to the brim with Dior, Givenchy, Paco Rabanne. When *Arabs* were caught shoplifting in Marks and Spencers, they were invariably found to have thousands of pounds in cash distributed in secret pockets in their robes.

She was close to his robe now, scenting money.

'It's only round the corner . . .'

He was lost in the rapid babble of her spiel. He blinked at her, studying her mouth, like a rabbit transfixed by a stoat. Then a sudden hopeful means of escape occurred to him. He groped among the folds in his shift. Her eyes followed his hand, as if she was intent on the mechanics of a conjuring trick.

Eventually his hand reappeared. She bent towards it. He was holding a soiled little booklet of limp matches. There were just three left. He tore one off and held it to the strip of emery-paper on the bottom of the packet.

'You like . . .?' he said.

'Oh, sod off, for Christ's sake – ' she said, dislodging herself into the current of the crowd. He was left holding the single unstruck match in the air, in a gesture of bewildered benediction.

Earls Court is usually a reliable, if seedy, barometer of the changes in social and political pressure in the world beyond. When anything really important happens on some outcrop of the globe with an unpronounceable name, it will show up a few months later on the Earls Court Road. The street swarms with Europe's latest arrivals: refugees, hopefuls, the new rich, the new poor, people in transit between an old life and a problematic future. Cambodian evacuees, Asians in flight from tyrannical black masters, newly-sturdy Japanese; after the murder of Allende, there were the Chileans; as the pound sank against the dollar, the crowd grew swollen with American teenagers humping backpacks, and when the Arabs raised the price of oil in 1973, it was on the Earls Court Road that one first saw the strange, beak-shaped foil masks of Gulf women and the improbably white dishdashas of husbands who walked exactly four paces ahead of their wives.

It was the masks I noticed first. They made the women look like hooded falcons, and they struck me not as symbols of Islamic female modesty so much as objects of downright menace. It happened in a summer; one day Arabs were a remote people who were either camping out in tents with camels and providing fodder for adventurous photographers, or a brutish horde threatening the sovereignty of the state of Israel; the next, they were neighbours – neighbours whose oddity far outclassed even that of the professional vagrants and wild men who find a natural asylum in Earls Court. Round every corner, one came upon the black-and-gold glint of those masks, and the black silk sheaths that encased the women as if they were corpses risen in their shrouds. The men were hardly less peculiar. Dressed for the desert, on the streets of west London they looked like a crew of escaped film extras, their head-dresses aswirl on the wind of exhaust fumes.

These people were not the oil sheikhs of the newspaper stories which had begun to break round the heads of Arabs in London. They ate from takeaways. They set up little transient stalls of junk in the street. They kept up a kind of aimless progress around Earls Court Road, Gloucester Road, Cromwell Road, Queens Gate and the Boltons, as if they were in a state of prolonged clinical shock.

They were not paupers, either. They hung in clusters round the hi-fi and photographic shops. Their Japanese cameras dripped with intricate accessories. They carried portable stereo cassette-recorders, and kept themselves company with a grossly amplified caterwauling which sounded repetitive, maudlin and unearthly. Sometimes I caught fragments of their language – an impenetrable labyrinth of consonants which sounded more musical to my ear than the noise which came out of their tape-recorders. As neighbours, they were uniquely inaccessible: it was much like having a family of Martians moving in next door.

My new neighbours were, I supposed, the family servants and hangers-on of the people who were getting into the papers in such tiresome quantity. There were, I read, whole collegefuls of Saudi students terrorizing quiet villages in the Cotswolds with their Lamborghinis and 1000cc Harley Davidsons. There were sheikhs in helicopters who landed on country-house lawns in the middle of lunch and evicted England's landed gentry with their chequebooks. Someone pointed out a vast stretch of the Kentish Weald through my car window and announced that 'Arab money' had purchased every last sod within sight of our native soil.

There were the jokes: barbecued goat at the Hilton; a muezzin calling the faithful to prayer from the roof of the Dorchester; the camel that got a parking ticket outside the Playboy Club . . . It was at least a change from the staple diet of jeers against the Irish and the Pakistanis; and 'The Arabs' were so evidently rich, so patently fair game, that they somehow seemed to be beyond the scope of the Race Relations Act. British xenophobia – which had lately been somewhat bridled under threat of prosecution – relieved itself in a great breaking of racist wind in the faces of the Arabs.

Whatever their effect on the economy of the West, the sheikhs and their doings were certainly adding to the general gaiety of the nation. They began to form a kind of gilded frieze populated by brilliant cut-out figures engaged in a wild dance for our snobbish entertainment. No one I ever met actually knew a sheikh, which was convenient since it allowed everyone the licence of gothic fiction when it came to talking about sheikhs. The amount of money that they splashed around was, everyone delightedly agreed, simply appalling. And their taste was, everyone said, utterly deplorable.

'I mean, what on earth can one do,' said Sally B. who is in interior decoration, 'with a man who points to this *hideous* sofa . . . really the worst . . . sort of Heals 1958, can you imagine? . . . and says, "I want four of those because I have a great love of the antique"?'

'Do you know what those houses are filled with? Giant lampstands, in *foul* yellow coloured glass, in the shape of bunches of bananas! And white rugs, with pile about a *foot* thick, made of some sort of ghastly polystyrene fur!'

These were pieces of brave imaginative guesswork, since the houses themselves remained firmly closed to all comers. With names like 'Zayed Villa', on streets like Bolton Gardens, they stood – empty for most of the year, as far as one could tell – like bank vaults. One could not even see through their windows, since the view was obstructed by dense, burglar-proof, aluminium zig-zag shutters.

Writers of gossip columns were marvellously informative about the sheikhs: they reported their liaisons, their newly-installed swimming pools, their late-night parties, the internal horrors they had wreaked on masterpieces of British nineteenth-century architecture. Yet not even the gossip columnists appeared to have succeeded in gate-crashing whatever inside-life was going on among the London Arabs. Aside from a few doubtful sightings in Annabel's and the Mayfair gaming clubs, the columnists were tacitly admitting defeat, with formula-phrases like 'neighbours complained . . .', 'neighbours have recently observed . . .', 'Penny Troublesome, a close friend of Bin Shaqiq, comments . . .'

My own Arab neighbours were quite different. I was getting used to hearing names like Aqhmed, Ali and Mohammad called across the square, and hardly noticed the calligraphic revolution that was going on in the Earls Court Road. A Halal butcher's opened up, its window a pretty conundrum of red squiggles and dots. Kebab- and kofta-houses followed. Then there were Arab doctors and dentists, then elegant Arabic graffiti at the foot of film posters, then instructions in Arabic on borough-council litter bins. The all-beef-frankfurter kiosk outside the Tube station went Arabic, and even the English shops along the road began to sprout Arabic notices. It was only when this process of decorative linguistic imperialism had nearly reached saturation point that I realized how suddenly different Earls Court Road had become; everywhere one walked, one was surrounded by those stylish, looping letters, a script of ripples and flourishes in which even the most cursory graffito takes on the air of something executed with deliberate artistry.

Earls Court tends to the squalid and the thievish: this summer-blossoming of Arabic signs gave it a touch of missing grace. Yet it also put the neighbours even further out of reach. One had only to stand on the street to see that they were living behind the veil of a language in which not a single sound was decipherable by us outsiders. All I knew of Arabic was that, like mirror-writing, it worked back to front. Staring at the signs, taking pleasure in their meaningless elegance, I couldn't make out where one letter stopped and another began. A word was a continuous brushstroke, resiliently abstract. Cyrillic lettering, or Greek, yields all sorts of familiar footholds, but Arabic gives up absolutely nothing.

I bought a copy of the Koran. In English, it manages to be boring and frightening in equal parts. Much of it is taken up by lists of bloodcurdling threats and prophecies of what will happen to unbelievers. In the curious nudity of translatorese, these imprecations sound more thuggish than godlike; there is a dull, cumulative bathos in their succession of burnings, hangings, and dismemberments. The English Bible (and the Old Testament is even bloodier than the Koran) comes with the authoritative crust of 400-year-old ceremonial language on it; translators of the Koran usually steal much of the vocabulary of the Authorized Version, but lapse, frequently and uncertainly, into the idiom of the newspaper crime report. This gives the book an unfortunate flavour of lurid piety. Its practical instructions (how to wash yourself with sand after intercourse, for example) sound eminently sensible. Its descriptions of paradise (fountains, virgins, goblets of wine, gold jewellery, silk and brocade robes, soft couches and large numbers of carpets) are enjoyably worldly. But as the sacred book of Islam, it is hardly more comprehensible in English than the Arabic signs on the shopfronts of Earls Court. The stories of Abraham, Noah, Joseph, Jonah and Mary are far more movingly told in the Bible than they are in the translated Koran; its morality seems infinitely cramped compared with the spacious eloquence of Christ's words in the New Testament. One catches no more than the vaguest glimpse of the inspirational force of a book which created a religious empire within a hundred years: all the richness, beauty and ambiguity, and most of the wisdom, which all introductions to the Koran claim as its essential features, are lost or clouded over in the English version. Reading it, I found my neighbours growing even more distant and inaccessible than they had seemed before.

Years before, I'd read *Seven Pillars of Wisdom* by T. E. Lawrence; I went on to C. M. Doughty's *Arabia Deserta*, Wilfred Thesiger's *Arabian Sands* and a clutch of books by Freya Stark. Along with Richard Burton and St John Philby, these are the classic 'British Arabists' – the writers who have done most to create a vivid, affectionate special relationship between the English and the Arabs. It was hard, though, to pick out Doughty-Arabs or Lawrence-Arabs or Thesiger-Arabs among the new nomads of the Earls Court Road; harder still to find them among the brisk millionaire-businessmen who were flying in and out of Heathrow and Kennedy and propping up the sagging economies of the West with petrodollars.

British Arabism is an old romantic love affair in which a faint glimmer of the perverse is never far from the surface. As a historical movement, it coincides exactly with that period when England was a rich country in the first flush of its dependence on industrial technology. For Lawrence and Thesiger, Arabia was an alternative kingdom; a tough utopia without either money or machines. In the bedu tribesman they professed to find all the simplicity, the powers of personal endurance, the stoic independence, which they feared the Englishman was losing. They loved him for his poverty, his spiritual leanness, his ignorance of the 'soft' life from which they themselves were on the run. In his desert they found a perfect theatre for the enactment of a heroic drama of their own – a drama whose secret subject was not really the desert at all but the decadent life of the London drawing-room.

In the prologue to *Arabian Sands*, Thesiger writes:

Men live [in the desert] because it is the world into which they were born; the life they lead is the life their forefathers led before them; they accept hardships and privations; they know no other way.

Looked at coldly, these are odd grounds for approval. They are qualities which, as Thesiger records with some testiness, the tribesmen themselves found it hard to recognize or applaud.

Thesiger's heroic Arabia is recent; it belongs to the 1940s and 1950s, when the importance of oil and the changes it was bound to make in Arab society were already clearly visible. Thesiger saw them, and his horror at the prospect is cruelly frank. The bedu people whom he had lived with were, he wrote, 'doomed'; with the coming of oil they could expect only 'degradation'.

Thesiger's writing (much more than Lawrence's) has enormous power: his portrait of desert life is so loving, so rich in detail, that one would be a clod not to be moved by it. Yet I felt tricked when I read *Arabian Sands*: Thesiger was making me fall in love with an abstraction – with a version of the Arabs which was impossibly constricting for the Arabs themselves; a version whose roots were in England and English life, and not truly in Arabia at all.

In the jeering tattle which followed the London Arabs like a ship's wake, there was a detectable note of perverse resentment: the Arabs had betrayed an essentially English dream of what Arabs ought to be. We had learned to love them for being heroically simple and poor; now, with their multi-national investment corporations, their Concorde-flying businessmen, their English country houses, their expensive cameras, cars and hi-fi equipment, they were flinging our sentimental illusions back in our faces. Back came *Arabia Deserta*. Back came *Seven Pillars of Wisdom*. Back came *Arabian Sands*.

In the place of these shapely and coherent masterpieces, all that was left was an impenetrable confusion. There were people who looked as if they might have stepped out of Thesiger, but who wore cufflinks and wristwatches which together would have accounted for a year's substantial English salary. There were Kuwaiti businessmen in Turnbull and Asser shirts; veils and foil masks; wild-looking men with gold teeth and dirty skirts; and the newspaper stories, a ceaseless rumble of gloating distaste. It was not just that the Arabs were richer than us; it was that they were a people whom the English thought they knew, and who had suddenly turned into bewildering strangers.

The English responded in the usual way, with a mixture of mockery and envy.

If I was going to pay the most perfunctory of courtesy-calls on my neighbours, I was obviously going to have to travel further than the Earls Court Road. I had been curious about the Arabs for a year; during that time I had actually met one – a mild man from Kuwait, who'd just returned from a salmon-fishing holiday in Ireland. I'd seen Arabs; I'd read about Arabs; I'd listened to endless speculative gossip about Arabs; but it was, apparently, impossible to meet them.

As a ritual preliminary, I tried to learn Arabic, taking a crash-course of a dozen lessons with a lovely Egyptian girl who had a voice that sounded like spring rain and a Ph.D in Linguistics. We stared solemnly at each other's uvulas; she inspecting mine to find out why it wasn't making the right noises; I inspecting hers for the sheer pleasure of looking at a piece of apparatus which was capable of producing such enchanting sounds. There is a letter in Arabic, beyond the range of the English palate and the English alphabet, which is usually represented in transcription by a *g*. To make the right noise, one has to tie one's vocal cords into a sort of reef-knot, then instantly release them, so that for a split second, in the middle of a word, one sounds like someone being strangled. We struggled for hours over the *gayn*; gurgling together into a tape-recorder.

'It comes,' said Fatma, 'from deeper in the throat.' I never found it.

What I did discover was the pure pleasure of the Arabic alphabet. Within a few hours the mysterious dots and ripples began to sort themselves out into recognizable letters. The pretty calligraphic abstractions on Earls Court Road suddenly resolved into words like 'hummus' and 'shashlik' and 'mansaf'. The fog started to clear over one small stretch, at least, of my local Arabia.

It is an alphabet of perfect economic logic. A single little wave-shaped mark does multiple service. With a dot underneath it, it is a *b*; with a dot above, it's an *n*; with two dots above it's a *t*; with three dots above it becomes a *th*-sound; and with two dots below it turns into a *y*. The strange symmetry of Arabic writing comes from using a small repertoire of intrinsically elegant shapes – uprights, ripples, waves and simple curves – and giving them identity by annotating them with a nearly-mathematical system of dotting.

The words themselves opened the door far wider for me than I had anticipated. Each word is a tight bundle of consonants; vowels are spoken but not written. Every bundle is related to a 'root' – a key word which acts as father-figure to an extended linguistic family of words and meanings. The root-word of everything to do with writing, for instance, is *ktb* – to write. By small variations on the root, one can derive the words for document, bookseller, Koranic school, booklet, penmanship, biblical revelation, desk, office, library, bookshop, correspondence, registration, dictation, novelist, typewriter, secretary, newspaper reporter, predestination (what is written as one's fate), subscriber, and, obscurely, cavalry detachment.

It is a language of inherent, logical ambiguity. Behind every word one uses lie the ranked shadows of all the other words in its family, crowding insistently in to give body and depth to the most casual utterance.

'*Ana haktb ktab*,' I said. 'I am going to write a book.'

'You must be careful,' said Fatma. 'It can mean "I am going to write a book". But people may think you're saying "I am going to get married" . . . you see, you are going to write the contract of marriage, you understand?'

I was very careful about saying that I was going to write a book.

Months later, someone in the British Embassy in Amman told me to look up the word for 'child' in the Wehr Dictionary – the treasure-house of Arabic roots. I did. The word is *tifl*, and it derives from the root *tfl*, meaning:

to intrude, obtrude, impose (upon); to sponge, live at other people's expense; to arrive uninvited or at an inconvenient time, disturb, intrude; to be obtrusive.

The linguistic family includes the words for softness, potter's clay, parasites, sycophants, initial stages and dawn. No richer or more sceptical definition of childhood has, as far as I know, ever been made.

As a conversational instrument, my Arabic is useless. I am limited to greetings, street directions, words for food and thank-yous. Yet the Wehr Dictionary, and the comprehension of the alphabet, seemed to shed far more light on the Arabs I saw in London than either Thesiger, Lawrence or the Koran. To live in Arabic is to live in a labyrinth of false turns and double meanings. No sentence means quite what it says. Every word is potentially a talisman, conjuring the ghosts of the entire family of words from which it comes. The devious complexity of Arabic grammar is legendary. It is a language which is perfectly constructed for saying nothing with enormous eloquence; a language of pure manners in which there are hardly any literal meanings at all and in which symbolic gesture is everything. Arabic makes English look simple-minded, and French a mere jargon of cost-accountants. Even to peer through a chink in the wall of the language is enough to glimpse the depth and darkness of that forest of ambiguity. No wonder the Koran is so notoriously untranslatable.

My short sightseeing tour around Arabic was the best possible preparation for a spell of six weeks during which I seemed to do nothing except live in the waiting-rooms of embassies. Originally, I'd thought that I would be able to visit Arab countries as one visits any others: a filled-in form, a couple of photographs, a visa and a stamp at the other end. It wasn't so. With the exception of Bahrain (where I didn't even need a visa), North Yemen, Egypt and Jordan, the countries I wanted to go to turned out to be like family houses at the end of long, guarded gravel drives. In central and south Arabia nationhood is still a novel concept: the tribe and the family are much stronger and more real ideas, and the nation is thought of as a big family in which the visitor is either a guest or an intruder. I was clearly a *tifl*; I was inviting myself at the wrong time, disturbing, sponging and being obtrusive. I found myself arguing on the doorstep with housemaids and butlers, the family dogs snapping round my ankles.

Like families, though, the countries were utterly different from one another when I made it through to the drawing-rooms. Qatar, for instance, was charming: the woman attaché was the nicest sort of hostess, inviting me to a delightful party.

'We shall enjoy having you,' said Qatar. 'You will like it. February is the best month. It is spring in Doha. Everything is green. There is no humidity. The temperature is cool. I think you will have a very good time.'

I remembered these sentences later, and my sprinkling of Arabic helped me to decode them. Their truth turned out to be more symbolic than literal. I *did* have a very good time in Qatar, and my hosts were infinitely more kind than any *tift* could have dared to hope. But the statements about the greenness, the temperature and the humidity were essentially Arabic. There was a little green; the temperature was in the high eighties; and the humidity varied between seventy and ninety per cent. Yet the general image, of a gaily hospitable springtime, was perfectly accurate. Whenever one hears what sounds like a catalogue of flat facts in Arabia, one must listen for the under-tone of metaphor.

By contrast, my encounters with Saudi Arabia made me feel like an inept housebreaker. First, I was shunted to the Saudi Press Agency, where a surly man took my letter of application and slid it carefully into the bottom of a steep pile of papers on his desk.

'Who is your sponsor in Saudi Arabia?'

'No one. I'm an independent writer.'

'You must have sponsor who invites you.'

'But I haven't a sponsor. I simply want to visit your country.'

'Who asks you?'

'Who asks writers?'

A small, mean glitter of victory lit up in his eyes. 'The Ministry of Information asks writers,' he said.

'But will they ask me?'

'Who knows? *Inshallah*. Maybe I make it easy for you and send telex.'

'I would be most grateful if you did.'

'But you must write letter first.'

'I've already written a letter. It's in that pile there. You just put it at the bottom of the heap.'

'Write another letter. A *long* letter. All details. Then perhaps I send telex.'

After a fortnight of appointments which he didn't keep, and telephone calls in which he claimed not to know who I was, I tried another route, through an English public relations man representing the Saudi government in London. He was friendly, and gloomy about my chances. Frankly, he could not hold out much hope. He would send a telex on my behalf. It was possible that he might get a reply. But I was anxious to leave as soon as possible, I said.

'A year is as a grain of sand in the eye of Allah.'

Why, I asked, was it so difficult to get a visa?

'They had a lot of trouble with Miss Linda Blandford.'

'But that was three or four years ago. It was just one book.'

'They are a very sensitive people,' he said.

But he did succeed in getting me an appointment at the embassy. Being able to walk past the man on the door at their Belgrave Square offices felt, by this stage, like touching down in Riyadh.

Saudi Arabia was in his office, sorting through his mail. On the desk in front of him was a leather-bound rack of pens, a box of Kleenex, a packet of boiled sweets, three sticks of chewing-gum and a pack of Peter Stuyvesant king size cigarettes. I watched in silence while he juggled in slow motion with these accessories. He would unwrap a boiled sweet, pop it in his mouth, wipe his fingers with a Kleenex, take a cigarette, induce a king-size spurt of flame from his leather-covered desk lighter, then begin to unpick the foil from around a stick of chewing-gum. Eventually his mouth was occupied in an astonishingly complex series of movements; simultaneously sucking, chewing and inhaling, while his hands played with a silver paper-knife. His mail finished, he picked up a pile of illustrated magazines and leafed through them. I coughed; I waved a synopsis of my book at him; I pulled faces; I lit my pipe, making as big and smoky a bonfire of the business as I could. After nearly fifteen minutes of this silent circus, he put down the last of the magazines.

'I am sorry to have kept you waiting . . .' he said, and broke into a surprising, steady flow of cold charm. He foresaw no special difficulties. He himself would send a telex. It was merely a question of confirmation from Riyadh, a simple matter which might be accomplished by tomorrow. I would hear from him by next week at the latest.

A fortnight later, I was telephoned by the public relations man. He had heard from Saudi Arabia. The Minister of Information himself had seen the synopsis of my book. A visa was certainly possible; but I should try to obtain it in one of the Gulf states. It would be easier there, he said.

Two months after this, when I was roasting in a Cairo hotel room, a letter arrived at my London flat. It came from the Saudi Arabian Embassy, and said:

> Dear Sir, Kindly contact Mr Naji Mufti at this embassy Monday–Friday between 9 a.m.–3 p.m. to arrange an appointment. Mr Mufti wishes to discuss with you matters of interest to yourselves. THE SECRETARY.

I once received a threatening letter, composed from bits of type cut out from newspapers and signed A FRIEND. The two have a curious similarity of tone. When I did return to London, Mr Mufti was out. Since it is hard to make contact with Saudi Arabia, may I say here – to Mr Mufti, to Mr Sami Badr, to Mr Farouk Tawfik – that all I wanted to do was to stay, at my own expense, in Jeddah for a week. I would have liked to have visited Riyadh and seen the desert. It would have been nice to be able to sail from Jeddah to Suez up the Red Sea coast. If you want your family to continue to be the victims of Western rumour, legend and gossip (much of it, I agree, quite unnecessarily spiteful and ill-informed), then your current policy of slamming the door in the faces of strangers is by far the most effective way of ensuring more misunderstandings and more slanders.

Like Qatar, the United Arab Emirates welcomed me as a guest. They would pay my hotel bills in Abu Dhabi and Dubai, and they would arrange for me to be driven into the desert to meet the bedu. It is, though, difficult to behave like a house-guest when a whole country is your host. Neither Qatar nor the emirates put any conditions on their hospitality; and all I offered in return was to send finished copies of this book to their embassies in London. I did feel rather easier in mind in those countries where I was footing my own bills; yet the system by which Qatar and the emirates admit writers to their countries is a revealing one. It wasn't simple kindness (though I met a lot of kindness among individuals). Nor was it merely done for motives of national propaganda, on the grounds that I was likely to write more acceptable things about the country if I was having my bills picked up than if I was paying my way. It is much more, I think, a survival of tribal custom, a reminder of the stubborn *familiness* of even the most bureaucratized and technologized Arab nations. It was in the Qatar national museum, in the section devoted to bedu history, that I found the best explanation of my own mildly embarrassing position.

> A traveller wishing to pass through the territory of a tribe approaches the chief of the tribe and requests his goodwill. If a man had to travel through territory not controlled by his tribe he would need by custom to be accompanied by a *rafiq* from the area in which he was travelling, under whose protection he would be.

The card went on to explain that the host tribe were under an obligation to provide the traveller with food and drink, and to accommodate him within their tents for the duration of his journey. Chiefs and *rafiqs* and killed camels and bedu tents have been supplanted by ministries of information, official drivers and rooms in Intercontinental hotels; but the habit of mind clings on. To be the guest of a tribe is an honourable privilege: Burton was one, so were Doughty and Thesiger. To be the guest of a government is to be instantly suspected of being a bribed hack. (And no authors of recent books about the Gulf states which I have read have come entirely clean about the way in which their expenses were paid by the governments of the countries.) In Arabia the division between the two positions remains blurred, especially in those countries where bedu traditions are still vivid, as they are in the Gulf and in Saudi Arabia. At any rate, two of these patriarchal tribal houses were generous to me; offering food, shelter and the services of a *rafiq*. I was glad to accept.

*

A few days before I left London, I spotted a new nightclub in Clifford Street called the 'El Nile'. Its window was a collage of more different brands of credit card than I knew existed. It promised Arab dancing and Oriental music. It looked a good deal more fun than the waiting-rooms in which I had recently completed a cover-to-cover reading of *Hard Times*, as well as filling thirty pages with copybook exercises in Arabic calligraphy and dozing over back-numbers of *Middle East* magazine. I had a dim notion that at last I might meet some real, off-duty London Arabs on neutral ground.

It proved almost as hard to get into as Saudi Arabia itself.

'This is not the old club,' said the doorman.

'I can see that – '

'This is new club. Oriental club. Oriental music.'

'It says that outside.'

'You will not like.'

'I like Oriental music,' I said, lying through my teeth.

'It is expensive. Not like old club. Old club, you pay two pounds. New club, costs six. Then you pay for drink.'

'Fine,' I said grandly, thinking that Barclaycard Ltd would have a hard time tracking me down in the places where I was going.

'You cannot dance.'

'We don't want to dance. I've got a limp.'

'The floorshow is not for one hour.'

'We'll wait.'

'You would not like other club, with dancing?'

'I like the look of yours.'

'You are very welcome. Most welcome,' he said, in a mysterious gearshift of tone.

We sat for a while at the ground-floor bar, where a group of Algerian hostesses were painting each other's nails. The only English in the place were an odd crew of matronly-looking girls with green Harrods carrier-bags and heavy tweed coats. Every so often one of them would amble to the door and get into a waiting chauffeur-driven car. They looked Roedean, class of '58. When they spoke, they had gymkhanas and lacrosse-rackets in their voices. They were, said my friend, exactly what one would expect.

'Of what?'

'Arabs,' she said. The 'El Nile' was not her idea of a night out.

We went downstairs to the blood-coloured barn of a basement. At first it looked quite empty, except for a tableful of hostesses; then one noticed occasional figures dotted in corners, like churchgoers at a badly-attended evensong. There were orange-juice men and whole-bottle-of-whisky men; no compromisers. At, I think, £2.50 for a single measure, whisky must have been far cheaper by the bottle.

It took a long time to liven up. Men drifted in in threes and fours. A surprising number of married couples arrived just before midnight, and distributed themselves around the room at separate tables. Then the floorshow began.

Belly-dancing is a peculiar art. For the most part it consists of long periods of almost total immobility in which one gets hypnotized by a single muscle twitching to music in the pelvic zone. Then, for a few seconds, the girl goes into a stamping, gyrating manic spell, before returning to that statuesque position, with the muscle going twitch, twitch, twitch, twitch, to a sort of tuneless moan on the violins.

Even my friend was moved to grudging admiration. 'There is something in it, you know. I couldn't do that with my tummy-muscles.'

'It's not her tummy-muscles that she's doing it with.'

'Well, whatever.'

More interesting than the belly-dancing, though, was the routine which came at the end of each act. The girl would step off the stage, and visit each table in turn, doing a lazy, overtime version of her stage performance. While she was thus engaged, the customers tucked currency into the numerous bits of elastic which kept her costume in place. By the time the first girl reached our table, she was looking like a walking money-changer's stall, festooned in dollar bills, rials and sterling. The going rate for her bra-strap seemed to be around five dollars; for the top of her bikini-pants it went up to £10. Sensitive to other people's supertax problems, I didn't contribute.

Yet the procedure seemed oddly devoid of any sexual charge. The money was purchasing nothing; it was simply, in that company, the only kind of applause which had any meaning.

Wives looked approvingly on while their husbands forked out, and at one table, a portly gentleman in a brilliant white robe persuaded the dancer and his wife to stand together on the tabletop while he took a whole reel of flash photographs.

In the gentlemen's lavatory, an attendant beat me to the taps in the washbasin, turning them on and testing the temperature of the water before I was permitted to wash my hands. For this service he was tipped, or so his plate seemed to claim, only in paper money, with £5 notes on prominent display. I gave him 10p, for which he thanked me, I thought, a shade unctuously.

We left. It was all alarmingly close to stereotype. It was the kind of scene which belonged to the gossip and jokes I had wanted to avoid. At embassy after embassy I had assured the appointed representatives of the family that I wanted to see the real Arabia, to visit the new cities, to see what contemporary Arab life was like, to try to begin to understand my neighbours.

The 'El Nile' club presented a real difficulty. Beggars without shoes see only a world of shoes and food. They must watch the street with the monocular attention of a footwear fetishist, seeing an endless procession of polished leather going by while the rest of the world doesn't bother even to look down. Something of the same problem afflicts the European who tries to write about Arabs: he sees their money with the same diverted and exclusive attention. It exerts a diseased fascination. Finally, like the vice which it so much resembles, it makes him go blind.

Full of pious resolutions about easy moralism, I took off for the Gulf.

2

Island Labyrinth

Jet travel makes a twisted nonsense of geography. In time, Bahrain is a good deal closer to London than Aberystwyth is, and the seemingly motionless speed of the Boeing 747 renders all the small, crucial distinctions of climate, culture and topography illegible. Europe slides by like a giant suburban golf-course; one can almost see the monotonous circulation of the sprinklers on the greens. It isn't until one crosses the Bosphorus and is over Turkey that one gets into the rough – a landscape of red boulders, creased and furrowed like badly wrapped parcels. Asia Minor begins as it means to carry on, with a sudden rude surge of rock, then shale, then sand. After the barbered green of Europe, Turkey comes as a peremptory reminder that the earth is really just a crust of cooled lava on which our own native patches are no more than happy, untypical geological accidents.

Behind me on the plane, a Lebanese was chatting up an English nurse who was going out to the Middle East for the first time.

'Believe me, England has my curiousness. I like England. I like English women. American women are *horrible*. I make you a promise: in fifteen years, America will be *trash*!'

Then there was a brief flash of green again; the Mediterranean, ribbed and viscous like boiling tar; and Beirut, steaming fast towards us across the sea, a toy city of baby skyscrapers and wide tree-lined promenades. Our Middle Eastern Airlines flight stopped at Beirut airport just long enough for us to grab a drink and undergo a body-search for bombs, and we were off again, casting a tiny sharp shadow on the Syrian desert. The shadow moved steadily ahead of us, lengthening and softening into sudden night. As the blackout hit us, I finished writing a book review of Uwe George's *In The Deserts of this Earth*. The desert, says George, if one includes the arid arctic zones, already composes nearly half the earth's continental surface, and it is steadily encroaching on us at a rate of forty square miles a day. Looking out of the plane window at that fading stretch of pink-and-grey sand, I was in a good position to believe him.

Cities are always best approached at night when they are at their prettiest and most full of secrets – especially Arab cities. At night the lattice (architecture's equivalent to the veil) takes over, casting mellow labyrinths of light on streets and courtyards; minarets turn rainbow, tricked out with fairy-lights like Christmas trees; the moon, twice as big and bright as the tarnished satellite that hangs in the European sky, silvers the palm trees. There's a humid bathroom-warmth and an old nursery-smell of eucalyptus. Breezeblocks and stressed concrete and parking lots can wait till morning; indeed by day one will be able to see little else in most modern cities in Arabia. At night time, though, even the brashest new bungalows and flats retire behind their veils, and the city becomes a welcoming maze of yellow lights and chocolate shadows.

Riding into Bahrain along the causeway connecting Muharraq Island to Manama, I saw two cultures in crisp silhouette. The fleet of camel-necked dhows in the harbour stood out against the sharp angles of dredgers, cranes and earthmovers immediately behind them; and far to the south a flare from the refinery was putting up a show of competition against the enormous moon.

A car in Arabia is a fine and private place. It is an eight-cylinder estaminet in which you can sleep, eat, drink, and conduct your social and business life. Houses tend to be left bare; plain little boxes of mud and brick. Cars bring out all their owners' genius for lavish interior decoration. Every one is different, decked out in colours unknown to nature, draped, cushioned, filled with ornaments and trinkets.

My taxi was furnished like a tart's bedsitter. Heavy red

brocade curtains hung on its windows. Furry puppets with big eyes danced from its roof. Every ledge and shelf revealed an open box of Kleenex; and the whole interior of the vehicle was done out in what looked like shell-pink mohair. The dashboard was covered in the stuff, so that the instrument-dials peered out through cute candyfloss fringes. The roof was padded in it, the seats upholstered in it, the floor carpeted by it.

The proprietor of this mobile oedipal fantasy was remarkably impassive. Perhaps he needed no expression, since his car spoke for him with such lurid eloquence. He turned up the cassette-player and submerged me in a flood of stereophonic lovelorn wailing.

The best Arab singers can drag out a song to make it last for upwards of ninety minutes; and the most popular singer of all is a dead Egyptian woman, known throughout the peninsula simply as 'The Lady'. She was so expert at this peculiar, un-endurable art that she never came to the end of the one song I heard her embark on. The noise that started in a Bahrain taxi was to wind its deafening way round the entire edge of Arabia. She moaned. She sobbed. She pleaded. She bawled. In Bahrain, she was merely distraught; in Qatar, inconsolable; in Abu Dhabi she was at her wits' end; and by Dubai she had entered a state of suicidal frenzy which she maintained, without remission, through Yemen, Egypt and the Hashemite Kingdom of Jordan.

We were only half-way across the causeway, a bare mile from the airport, when she ceased to become a novelty. Screened by curtains, cushioned in fur, with The Lady howling that her heart was breaking for me, that she ached for my return, that she would give her whole life for one night in my arms, I got to Manama.

We turned left, and left, and left again, through streets of bulging walls and latticed balconies. In Arabic, one of the many synonyms for 'desert' is also the word for 'labyrinth': desert people, looking for protection in the city, instinctively construct mazes around themselves – rectangular warrens of alleys and dead ends and tunnels and courts, in which a stranger gets lost within seconds of entering the system. I had never expected to find in an oil town such sandy, woody narrowness and intricacy. The taxi squeezed past donkey-stalls and little lock-up shops on streets that seemed to open just wide enough to admit our passage, then close as soon as we had gone by.

Then, at the heart of the labyrinth, we found Ralph Izzard's house. I'd heard about Izzard in London – how he was a journalist, a mountaineer, a wartime naval officer, a famous and convivial drinker, who had tucked himself away in the Arab quarter of Manama and was still, at seventy, roving up and down the Gulf as the correspondent of a clutch of news agencies and papers. Knowing only that I was an acquaintance of an acquaintance, he had offered me a room to stay in; a characteristically kind and open-handed gesture.

I went through a bleached wooden door in a steep wall of solid mud and found myself in a small, lamplit, private kingdom. It was a further labyrinth. Rooms opened on to a half-covered courtyard of flagstones strewn with threadbare Persian carpets. A parrot strutted on a beam. The wind rustled dryly in the leaves of a eucalyptus tree, and in a long, narrow, white-washed room Mr Izzard was at home. Big, with the face of a grizzled boy, he was folded untidily into a chair that was too small for him, his shirt-tails leaking from his belted trouser-top.

Would I, he asked, care for a splash of the Old and Gold? Stooping, carrying his height carefully like a house of cards, he hunted through his kitchen for a glass. Had I read *Under the Volcano*? Wasn't it the best bloody novel about hangovers in the world? Did I want ice? He'd been in Qatar last week, and was off to Kuwait to report a motor rally next week; so this week he was having a drink. He and Lowry had grown up together, did I know? At the Leys School, then Cambridge. Lowry played the ukelele, he played the banjo.

Solitary people in out-of-the-way places can afford to keep only the best company. Wherever there are long humid nights with crickets and fireflies, where lamps burn behind mosquito-netting and whisky is drunk from tin mugs, men on their own develop such a talent for recollection that every evening turns into a kind of ghostly party. Ralph Izzard's shadowy room in Manama, with its framed prints on the walls, its battered library, its long divan of cushions, was not as remote as that;

but he had the exile's gift for making it float free in space and time and filling it with companions.

We made friends over Malcolm Lowry. 'No one here much reads him, I'm afraid.' As the level in the bottle sank, we gathered in an amiable gang of enterprising loners. St John Philby and his son Kim – an old Cambridge friend of Izzard's. Jan Morris. 'Billy' Maclean. Freya Stark. Wilfred Thesiger. Gavin Young. 'Little Willy', son of Kaiser Bill. ('I used to go skiing with Little Willy at Cortina . . .') The living and the dead were all generously toasted.

There were few gatecrashers. When they did elbow their way into the conversation, Ralph ousted them in the purest Leys School fashion. 'Don't you think that chap is really rather a tick?'

It was a good party; Ralph Izzard's floating world was infectiously airy and tolerant, a superbly habitable place. I said, a little muzzily, that I'd like to read his books.

'Oh, they're not much – '

But he fetched them for me, walking with craggy delicacy through the shadows in the courtyard, saying a polite good night to his parrot.

He came back carrying three somewhat foxed first editions from the 1940s and early '50s.

'The Collected Works of Izzard.'

One was about the Everest expedition of 1953, on which Ralph had scrambled up in the wake of Sir John Hunt; he'd gone out and come back in the same pair of torn tennis shoes. One was on mountains and mountaineering; and one was on the search for the abominable snowman.

Ralph shook sand from the pages of his Everest book, and flipped over the frontispieces of the others: he looked a little baffled at their very existence.

'Jesus Christ. You know, I've had an awful lot of fun in my life.'

He drained the last few drops of whisky into my glass.

'D'you remember the Sudeten in – what was it? 'Thirty-eight?'

'Well . . . not exactly . . .'

'God, don't tell me you weren't even born then!'

'I was born in 'forty-two.'

'Do you know when I was bloody well born? *Nineteen-ten.* Good God. And I thought you were my contemporary.'

I had not expected much of Manama – it had struck me merely as a convenient jumping-off point from which to explore other bits of the Gulf, and I had assumed that it would be reassuringly dull. In the event, I found myself in a bewildering honeycomb, cell built on cell, full of interest and contradiction.

A half-mile walk without a map or any particular destination proved the point. I drifted into a maze of streets on which mine was the only European face in sight. One narrow alley was full of carpenters and the smell of freshly sawn pine; another was a dazzling canal of brilliant Hong Kong cottons; another, the car repair zone, was loud with lines of men banging shapeless bits of metal with hammers. It was all utterly unlike the tired 'Westernization' that I had expected of Bahrain: the protective labyrinth, in which every trade has its own allocated quarter fixed by use and tradition, is Arabia's strongest bastion against monoculture. Things are kept separate – gold and meat, vegetables and clothing, spices and hi-fi sets . . . every category has at least one street to itself. This separation of objects keeps people apart too; at each turn in the maze one notices a distinct difference in skin-colour and style of dress. You cannot go more than a hundred yards without trespassing across a clearly defined boundary. A blind man could find his way through the labyrinth by smell alone: machine oil gives way to turmeric and coriander, sweet sawdust to the acrid barnyard odour of live chickens, roast coffee to the oddly musky scent of cheap plastic.

In one step at the end of a street I crossed from a world of mud and wood to one of marble, glass and concrete. I had been threading my way through a long, rustling procession of black veils; suddenly there were only business suits and sharkskin document cases. The line of banks on Government Road was taller and wider than the lines of spice-sellers and carpenters; but it had the same air of being a single specialized component in a labyrinthine system. Hypertensive men with clumsily drawn Texan faces were paying off their double-parked taxis.

International money has a smell just as distinctive as that of coffee – a subtle blend of under-arm deodorant, dry-cleaning fluid, Havana Coronas and exhaust fumes. Like all the other smells in the bazaar, it marks just one route within the city. Stray a few yards from the route, and the smell is instantly displaced by the scent of another pattern of life altogether. When I crossed the street and walked behind the back of a great glass investment-company building, money gave way to wood-shavings and resin, and two men on a makeshift platform caulking the hull of a dhow.

I was a lucky trespasser. Most visitors to Bahrain have routes and purposes; I had none. Travelling salesmen and consultants put up at the Gulf Hotel; they take taxis to the business quarter, they lunch at the Ramada Inn, spend the afternoon lounging by the swimming pool, dine at the Delmon, and see a monotonously uniform city. Their Manama is expensive, plagued with piped music, a two-street, forty-eight-hour stopover. From their arrival at the airport, they are fed into one channel of the labyrinth – so successfully that many of them never realize that they are in a labyrinth at all. The air is cooled and conditioned for them; Dutch flowers and frozen Australian beef are imported for them; their Arab clients visit them in the conference rooms of their hotels. Everything has been arranged to ensure that there is no point at which their route intersects with any other route in the city. The presiding genius of the place who decreed that spice-sellers should be *here*, and carpenters *there*, has created a special vacuum for visiting businessmen, and nearly all of them keep meekly to their appointed path. They are permitted to take optional turnings into the gold-market and the dhow harbour; the rest of the town is effectively out-of-bounds. Unposted, unmapped, without names on its streets, it is open only to those who are prepared to take pleasure in getting lost.

I wanted to get really lost. I found my way back to the street full of mechanics by listening for the sound of hammering, and hired a very old, very thoroughly hammered Toyota from an Indian who demonstrated to me what an excellent car it was by walking round it and kicking its wings. I pointed out that two of the tyres had large triangles of torn rubber projecting from them, revealing pink glimpses of inner tube, so he took a couple of flying kicks at the tyres as well.

'Damn good tyres. Not to worry.'

'How many accidents do your customers usually have?'

'We never have no accidents.' It seemed probable that he was speaking the truth, since he was standing in a small graveyard of wrecked cars, in which only the Toyota looked as if it stood any chance at all of making it on to the road outside. Still, his charges were about a quarter of those of more conventional car-hire firms; and the Toyota gave me no trouble at all during the week that I drove it. When I returned it to the garage, I had the suspicion that I'd broken some long-standing record, since the Indian's astonishment at my expression of complete satisfaction was innocently frank.

I found my way out of Mud City and into breezeblock country. Everyone in suburban Manama that morning seemed to be either up a ladder or down a hole. Grey eggboxes, sheathed in scaffolding, dwarfed the minarets. Along the shoreline, dredgers were hauling sand out of the Gulf and piling it on to the island. Bahrain was getting visibly bigger by the minute, growing upwards and outwards in a frantic, last-minute dash to make the most of its diminishing oil revenues. Windy, unfinished skeletons announced themselves as hospitals, secondary schools, sports centres and department stores. Truckloads of Korean construction workers, looking like prisoners of war in their green uniforms and forage caps, hurtled round roundabouts, *en route* to some wild multi-lingual adventure playground of swaying steel girders and pools of wet cement.

In England, firms like to boast of their reliable longevity: 'Established 1826'. Manama did not seem keen on history. The words 'New' and 'Modern' apparently were regarded as surer guarantees. A pick-up truck with a cement mixer in tow belonged, I saw, to 'The Skylab Trading & Construction Company'; and all the local firms communicated a faintly hysterical sense of haste and imminence by collapsing their names into impossible mouthfuls of initials and abbreviations. *Aramco. Bapco. Darweeshconcorp. Manneitradco* . . . Language itself gets squashed and hammered in the urge to demonstrate that everyone is on the move and going places fast.

It was impossible not to be infected with the excitement of this headlong plunge into modernity; it was like stumbling through a time-lock into the heyday of the Industrial Revolution, and it required a nineteenth-century cast of mind to appreciate it. I remembered Henry Adams at the Chicago Exposition of 1893, standing in the ecstatic trance of a worshipper before the great dynamo. He, I thought, would have warmed to Bahrain. He would have loved the refinery and the brand-new aluminium smelter, which imports the raw metal from Australia, distils it in baths of hellish heat, converts it into something that the Oxford Dictionary describes as 'white, sonorous and ductile', and sells it back, half-way across the world, to Japan. He would have enjoyed the fish-processing plant, and he might even have found a small corner of his heart with which to embrace the plastics factory.

It was all angles, breezeblocks, gleaming pipes, a vaunting tangle of construction on an improbable landscape of sand and shale. Bahrain is just a little bigger than the Isle of Wight, but it seems carelessly defiant of its own geography. Its towns are little ones, as towns go: Manama has about the same population as Bournemouth. Its desert is, on the map, a handkerchief-sized scrap of wilderness. Yet the city has the labyrinthine diversity of a metropolis, and the desert feels as large and unending as the Empty Quarter. No one, though, appears to have bothered to consult the map: the limits of the place have been the limits set by money, machines, and the capacity of the chargehands and foremen – who are the real princes of Bahrain – to exploit that enormous, footsore army of cheap Pakistani and Korean labour.

My tedious hours in London embassies, spent leafing through copies of *Middle East* magazine, had supplied me with a cartoon-outline of the economy of the oil state. In every country on the Gulf, a clock is slowly winding down; some have thirty years before their oil runs out, some twenty, some, like Bahrain, are already down to the last dregs of their reserves. Either they can invest their revenues and live like Victorian gentry on interest and rents, insuring their futures with giant national pension schemes; or they can risk their money on a tantalizing dream of 'diversification', setting up industries which will go on producing wealth long after the oil fields have been pumped dry.

The word itself had sounded dull. I had found the graphs which always accompanied it incomprehensible. But on the ground, this idea of diversification took on a kind of insane vigour. Wherever I looked, Bahrain was diversifying. Buckets of concrete were being hauled up and down on winches; steel piles driven deep into the sand; whole sides of houses swung across the sky by cranes; convoys of container trucks delivering raw materials to factories which were as yet no more than rough outlines of stakes marked out on a strip of reclaimed waste land. Much of this diversification went no further than the words on a signboard erected over a few oil drums and a tangle of barbed wire; yet it seemed oddly probable that the Hilton would, indeed, be there by teatime and the school up in time for lessons tomorrow morning at the very latest.

Adrift in my hired car, I felt carried along by the sheer exuberance of this philistine poetry of change for change's sake. Sea was being turned into land; oil into gasoline; prawns into frozen packets; base metal into shiny tubes and pipes; and along the sides of every road, men were bashing at pavements with pickaxes and sledgehammers for no apparent reason. Nothing, it seemed, was being allowed to remain in any one state for any extended period of time; everything had to be dug up, frozen, moved about, reconstructed, smelted, refined.

Diversification is a heady principle; it makes its own momentum, and once under way it sweeps logic triumphantly to one side. No one ever succeeded in explaining to me why it was actually a sensible idea to ship huge quantities of alumina from the Pacific to the Gulf in order to smelt them and then return them to the Pacific as aluminium. Why Bahrain? Because it was diversification, and Bahrain needed diversification because its oil was running out. Was that not sufficient reason? Isn't it, I asked, rather expensive to take all this alumina 9000 miles out of its way just to boil it in vats or whatever you do in your smelter? Ah well, I was told; the economics of diversification are extremely complicated. A lot of factors are involved. I am easily impressed by the way in which 'factors' always seem to get 'involved'; and should perhaps have pursued the argument, but did not dare. Not understanding economics, I found the logic of the process baffling; what I did understand was the pure bravura of the enterprise, the simple excitement of watching all those girders and sheets of glass and pre-stressed concrete miraculously assembling themselves against a dazzling sky.

The city was in a state of delirious flux. Sometimes I caught its babble of different languages: a snatch of Hindustani, a bellow of pidgin-English across a building site, a rapid interchange in Arabic, a burst of Chinese. I realized why the roundabouts were so important. One meets them every few hundred yards on all main roads in Manama: trim, circular gardens of turf, palms, cacti and vivid flowers whose names I didn't know – still centres in a world of change, they provided the only splashes of natural shape and colour in sight. Men in turbans poked about in their foliage with garden watering cans and balls of twine. In the swirl of Datsuns and Fords, they looked happily displaced in a private elysium of grafting, seedlings, pruning, repotting and rubber gloves. They reminded me of my Wiltshire aunts, always busy about the herbaceous border with hoe and trug; except that my Wiltshire aunts are notably lacking in that strange imaginative facility for making a few square feet into an exclusive island which seems to be the chief property of almost every resident of every Arab city.

A roundabout is not a feature of the road-system; it is a space in its own right, a miniature park which just happens to be surrounded by automobiles – and in Manama the roundabouts are altogether prettier and more useful places than most English civic parks. People sleep through the afternoons under their palm trees; at night they hold card games and picnics under their sodium street-lights, oblivious to the traffic at their elbows. A screen of green, or a screen of light, makes a ready-made lattice or veil; however public the situation – even when it's in the middle of a thundering dual carriageway – an ingenious man can improvise a private world within it, as far adrift from its immediate surroundings as the long, white, sociable room in Ralph Izzard's house in the medina.

I had noticed the clubs. On some streets, every other house seemed to be a club. There were clubs for Armenians, clubs for Americans, clubs for rugby players and employees of Gulf Air;

every nationality, trade and hobby apparently had its own club. My morning as a trespasser had made me want to become a member of something; in this honeycomb of privacies I was already beginning to feel lonely, envious of the card-players on the roundabouts and the impenetrable banter of the bazaar.

I found the British Club up a sandy lane on the outskirts of the city. By now, I was used to sudden jolts in the texture of reality, and hardly noticed as I strolled past the guard on the gate that I was walking into a little imaginary England, a pretty, watercolour world where the roses are always in bloom and the year is always 1935. There were indeed roses, and hollyhocks too, mixed in with the tangle of flowering hibiscus. A nut-brown tennis girl was just about to serve ('Yours, partner!'), and a large lady in a floral dress was standing over a very small dachshund which was peeing on the crazy-paving.

I went through into the bar. It was dark, half-timbered, with a stag's head mounted on the wall and horse brasses and pewter mugs winking in the soft, Home Counties gloom. Most mock-Tudor does no more than cursorily ape the real thing. This was different. It was pungent with homesickness. Someone had laboured nostalgically over every detail, down to the last cracked willow-pattern plate on the last plastic beam. Even the light was right. Outside, the Gulf sun was whiting-out every-thing it fell on; in the bar, it was absorbed and scattered by fat pillars of rough brick, so that at midday it took on the warm yellow colour of a Surrey evening.

The expats were on Draught Bass and Worthington E.

'Just out from Youkay?' Without the article, it sounded like a remote suburb of Tokyo. 'We're going back to Youkay on leave next month.'

Youkay, Youkay. The bar was a memorial shrine to Youkay – the country of the rambler rose, the thatched cottage and the Ploughman's Lunch. Yet the drinkers themselves were not thatched-cottage men at all. They were technicians, builders, 'advisers', men with craft apprenticeships and evening classes behind them; in England, they would probably have lived on purpose-built industrial estates on the outskirts of some grey Midlands city. But Youkay isn't England: it is a country in a cherished legend. In Youkay, there are no drizzly ringroads, no tower blocks, no miles of corrugated iron and chimneys, no crowded sandwich bars, no standing-room-only rush hour trains.

Here in Bahrain, it was necessary to dream up Youkay in order to make sense of an impossible paradox. Most of the men at the bar were doing appalling jobs and dying young. 'Diversification' meant sweating through long mornings of hot, salty, sandy fog, working a six-day week, living with the linguistic Babel and incessant mechanical noise of the construction sites. The hands of the 'advisers' were blistered and ribbed with cuts and grazes. The advice they gave was clearly of a thoroughly practical kind. In return, they had villas, houseboys, eight thousand pounds a year tax-free and titles which put a polite gloss on the rough work they were actually doing. They had inherited the slang and the manners of a dead class of colonial administrators, a hill-station genteel breeziness. They were really chargehands, skilled labourers whose job it was to supervise the migrant proletariat of casual workers. In the idea of Youkay, they reconciled some, at least, of the anomalies of their position. *England* would clip their wings, return them to a cramped and humble place in the pecking-order of wages and social standing: *Youkay* gave their somewhat fragile dignity roots and support. Its vintage language was borrowed from happier days, 'before the war'. Its capital wasn't London but The Club.

A man with the faintly paranoid sideways blink of the provincial intellectual sidled over to my stool. A bristly toilet-brush beard circled his mouth.

'We ought to have a natter some time,' he said. 'Maurice-Whale's the name.'

He gave me a business card. It read:

> Bahcon Ltd.
> Building Contractors.
> Eng. Contractors.
> Manfrs. Agents.
> N. J. Maurice-Whale Manager.

'Nick Maurice-Whale.' In a whole barrage of blinks, he searched the bar for possible enemies. 'And by the way, while we're about it, if you're coming into the Club and want to get in touch with me, always remember to ask for *Maurice*-Whale. No good just saying "Nick Whale"; no one will know who you're talking about. You see, I'm known as Maurice-Whale. With the hyphen. Got it?'

It was clear that behind the hyphen lay a long history of border-incidents and skirmishes. With his balding skull, his studied diction and his portly figure, Maurice-Whale might have been at least fifty; he was in fact in his late twenties.

It was a heavy, humid, dog-day afternoon in the old city. I sat in the sun on an upturned crate drinking lukewarm Pepsi-Cola through a straw, idly decoding the Arabic lettering on the rusty signs over the shop. Logos so familiar that in England I hadn't noticed them for years took on a new life in Arabic. The 'Cola' sign was a zig-zag swirl – *Kola*; 'Craven A' was two elegant swoops followed by an upright – *Krfn Aleph*. 'Pepsi' was a bilious stammer: *B-bsii*.

In the gold-market, I watched a beggar counting his day's takings. He wrapped his bowl up in an old cloth, hoisted himself on to his crutch, and went swinging up the street. At the corner, fifty yards on from his own post, he reached another beggar who was missing both legs: without slowing his pace by a fraction, the first beggar flipped a pair of coins into the second beggar's plate. Alms-giving is one of the most strictly enjoined duties of the Muslim; even the destitute are bound to make a show of charity to each other. I wondered if this peculiar chain of philanthropy extended down to a single wretched man – the one beggar in Manama too desperate and too appallingly crippled to be able to give alms to another. All day I had been noticing the way in which everything and everybody in the Islamic world is separated, ordered, categorized. Was there a corresponding hierarchy of fine discriminations in rags and deformities?

In Western cities, the whole business of giving money to people on the street is incriminatingly personal. The transaction involves both parties in a dirty little piece of theatre, with faked generosity on one side and faked gratitude on the other. In Manama, it was altogether different. There were no thanks, not even a glance of recognition. One was giving coins not to a person but to a stump or a hump. The relationship was between things, not people; a purse on one side, a disease on the other. Begging was an established social function, just as giving was an established social duty. Seeing the remote, indifferent faces of the beggars, I thought of the most famous of all C. M. Doughty's remarks about the Arabs: 'The semites are like to a man sitting in a cloaca to the eyes, and whose brows touch heaven.' While I donated dutiful pennies to the rags and stumps, their owners were away and somewhere else; it would have been impolite – uncharitable – for them to have condescended to notice me in the performance of an ordinary religious duty. The process of keeping things separate extended to drawing a veil between a man and his own misshapen limbs. To my weakly Christianized sensibility, this seemed at once chilling and admirable.

Ralph Izzard's house had filled with shadows. A record was on the gramophone: *An Evening of Victorian Gems*.

'Do you like this sort of thing?'

Home, Sweet Home. Excelsior. Won't You Buy My Pretty Flowers?

'I love it,' said Ralph. 'Absolutely bloody marvellous, don't you think?'

As the city darkened and the moon came up, a baritone sang:

> . . . my brave Arab comrades come at my command –
> It's freedom I love, though the world be obscure;
> None so dauntless and free
> On land or on sea –
> For a son of the desert am I!

'Wilfred Thesiger.'

'C. M. Doughty.'

'T. E. Lawrence.'

'Have a Scotch.'

Was there anywhere in Bahrain, I asked, where the island actually came together? Was it really as much of a labyrinthine patchwork as it seemed?

The Yacht Club, Ralph said. The very rich did mix at the Yacht Club. Its vast annual subscription made it into a kind of social Fort Knox, but there one might find sheikhs and European and American businessmen mingling with one another. No sheikh would be seen in the bar of the Gulf Hotel, for instance; roustabouts from the rigs could afford to drink there. The British Club, too, was a narrow enclave. For every British resident who couldn't get in because he was lacking in the required social tone, there was another who wouldn't join because the Club was altogether too *déclassé*. One would find no sheikhs there. But the Yacht Club was different; Bahrain's only real social melting pot – if one happened to be a millionaire.

'The Arabs like to keep very much to themselves.'

'So does everyone else, it seems.'

Jumbled together on this tight little island, every group lived inside its own protective social network. The sheer quantity of these intricate divisions struck me as baffling: male and female, Sunni and Shia, Bahraini and expatriate, meat, vegetables, and gold – from these basic distinctions of kind, the islanders had constructed a fantastic maze of walls and discriminations. Perhaps, though, an English village would seem as complex and impenetrable to a visiting Gulf Arab. What appeared to be unique to Bahrain was the way in which so many nationalities had landed up on one small patch of ground, coming together to create not a cosmopolitan city but a multitude of tiny provincial hamlets. Few expatriates ever bothered to learn more than a word or two of Arabic; they had no Arab friends; they were comfortably ignorant of the lives of the people with whom they shared this meagre acreage of land. The same was true, apparently, of the Arabs themselves, the Iranians, the Indians, the Pakistanis. The different groups exchanged contracts, employed one another, purchased things at each other's shops, were each other's landlords and tenants – but they didn't mix. They had chosen to live, Ralph said, in a communally agreed system of apartheid. The Pass Laws were not actually written down, but they were there.

It occurred to me that the whole idea of British influence in Bahrain might have been an illusion: in a day, I had not seen a single piece of evidence to support the notion that the place was 'Westernized'; it seemed rather that the English – and everyone else on the island – had been thoroughly and effectively tribalized by the Arabs. Breezeblocks, Cadillacs and earthmovers mean very little when set against the way in which people actually inhabit the places they've built for themselves. All the exclusiveness and constraint of the old Arab city seemed to have been transmitted to successive waves of immigrants. Even I was rapidly finding my apportioned place in my own tribe.

At the British Club, the tennis was continuing under floodlights which gave the leaping, brown-legged girls the air of performers in a mime troupe. They served, and returned, and carolled to one another over the net, too brilliant and remote for me, glooming invisibly in the shadows. Maurice-Whale was waiting in the dining-room, ritzy with potted palms, brown tablecloths and hanging lamps. I said I'd been watching the tennis outside.

'Wink-wink, nudge-nudge, say-no-more,' said Maurice-Whale.

We sat down at a table under a long shelf of cups and trophies. The squash cup. The rugger cup. The shooting cup. The tennis cup. Perhaps there were darts and cribbage cups too. It reminded me of boarding school, but the recollection was fleeting and irrelevant. As a fag, I'd been made to clean those cups, scouring the etched copperplate lettering which said that Castle House had won the bloody thing in 1933, and School House had kept it from 1934–8, before it had gone to Creighton House in 1939. It was the first echo of school on my trip, and I remembered it later, when half of Arabia seemed to turn into a giant boys' boarding school, with fagging, ragging and compulsory games.

Maurice-Whale waved his tankard of Bass at me. 'You take the ugliest single girl on the island. Fattest old bag you can think of. Know how often she gets asked out? Twenty times a day. She's got chaps asking her out from breakfast time to how's-your-father. Fact.' He bulged with irritation at the prospect. 'Have you heard about the Gulf Air hostesses?'

'No – '

'There's forty of them on the island, right? They're one of the chief amenities of this place, like the Gulf Hotel. They all go to this particular beach, so the sheikhs can inspect them through binoculars. Fact.' He blinked his way around the dining-room. 'Do you know how much a Gulf Air hostess *costs*? A thousand dinars. Fact.'

Maurice-Whale was a married man himself, he told me.

'How does your wife feel about living in Bahrain?'

My question evidently struck him as a dumb one. He stared at me, crumbling bread irritably between his fingers. '*She* wouldn't come out *here*.' He sounded indignant at the mere idea of it. 'Of course she wouldn't.' He saw his wife on his annual leaves; but for forty-six weeks of the year he lived alone in his villa. He listened to records a lot, he said, and he was writing a pornographic novel.

'I suppose one has to put them through several drafts, does one?'

'What?'

'Books.' Abruptly, he switched tack. 'Where were you?' He sprayed the tablecloth with crumbs. 'At university?'

'Hull.'

'I'm a London man. SOAS. Sometimes I think it causes a bit of aggro – especially in the Club . . . having a degree. Have you noticed anything of the sort? Wisest course I've found is to keep one's BA under one's hat. Can cause aggro, you know. I've run into a good deal of aggro in my time here. Of course, the 'tash and beard don't help.' He sounded curiously cheered by this.

I said that I imagined that a degree in Arabic Studies must be an unusual qualification in the building trade. Maurice-Whale said that he thought he was pretty much unique.

'It must be useful, though,' I said, 'to be able to talk Arabic to the people you're working with – '

I had clearly been stupid again. Maurice-Whale blinked furiously at me.

'Never use it,' he said. 'You can't go round talking Arabic to chaps you're employing. If you talk Arabic, they think they've got you where they want you. Take my assistant. I was a bit green when I started. Talked Arabic to him for a bit, and he didn't do an honest day's work in a year. You can only frat up to a point, you know; frat too much with an Arab, and he thinks that if he feeds you up to the eyeballs with one plate of *mansaf*, he's got you eating out of his hand. If you want these buggers to actually do any work, you've got to order

44

them about in English; it's the only way.'

'That sounds like a piece of good old-fashioned racism.'

'*I* don't live in cloud-cuckoo land,' said Maurice-Whale. '*You* ought to read a book called *The Arab Mind*.'

The dinner table seemed like a miniature minefield. For a good ten minutes, we steered clear of further 'aggro' by devoting our exclusive attention to our grouper steaks. Our fish-knives and fish-forks clicked away, conspicuously noisy.

'If you don't mind my saying so,' said Maurice-Whale, 'you strike me as a bit naïve.'

'I could hardly be anything else. I've only been here twenty-four hours. Of course I'm naïve.'

'Oh, well that's all right then. Want a spot of broccoli?'

We made a truce over the remains of the vegetables; we ratified it on the happy topic of The Causeway – Bahrain's most ambitious flight of diversification so far. When it's finished, it will carry a trunk road twenty miles across the Gulf, linking the island with Dharhan in Saudi Arabia.

'It's going to be the salvation of this place,' said Maurice-Whale with a pitch of optimism in his voice that struck me as quite uncharacteristic of him.

'How?'

'Well, it's going to turn Bahrain into the brothel of Saudi Arabia, isn't it?' He unrolled for me a utopian dream of Scotch whisky and Egyptian whores. 'It'll be just like Singapore. Only *worse*,' he said happily. 'You know they're going to build a hotel under the sea? Underwater bars . . . underwater swimming pools . . . underwater casino . . . Place'll be *swimming* with Saudis chucking the old rials all over the bloody place. Twenty minutes from you-know-where . . . it'll be a ruddy paradise. Of course, most of the buggers will probably fall in on the drive back, but that's another story. The thought of what the Causeway's going to do to Bahrain drives half the people on the island absolutely hairless.' His blinking had stopped. His forehead had uncreased. For the first time since I'd met him, Maurice-Whale looked like a happy man.

'And the other half . . . ?'

'Wink-wink, nudge-nudge, say-no-more,' he said, tapping his nose contentedly.

At the end of dinner, he gave me the name and address of

someone he knew in Qatar. 'But if I were you,' he said solemnly, 'when you're in Qatar, I wouldn't mention Nick; I wouldn't mention Maurice; I wouldn't mention Whale. You see, I'm rather afraid that Nick Maurice-Whale is p.n.g. in Qatar.'

I was up at sunrise, awake before the parrot. It was a lovely hour. At that latitude there is a spell just after dawn when the empty blue of the sky is miraculously cold. The steambath heat of noon seems as if it must be months away; it is pure luxury to shiver over a mug of coffee, watching the ragged shadows on a courtyard shorten. By evening, the Arab city will smell as old as sin – rancid, like the bits of flyblown meat left in the street for the dogs to quarrel over. Every day, though, starts with a clean slate, glistening under a film of salty dew.

I had arranged to visit the Falconry Centre at the other end of the island, and I took the road south out of Manama, along another causeway which carries it through a flat, watery landscape of salt marshes and palm groves. The sea was dead calm, and the heavy sun had spilled all over it, leaking a dull gold on the oily grey which slurped and sucked at the piles of the causeway as if the sea was turning in its sleep.

The road veered inland, into an undulating desert of broken rock and scree. Every few hundred yards there were brightly-painted seesaws which rocked up and down. One end of each one was cut in the shape of a large disc, and these had been painted with diagrammatic human faces and horses' heads like lurid crayon-drawings. The road was empty, except for these grinning cartoons, which kept on popping up over banks of shale and disappearing again. They were – I found out later – oil pumps, and they marked the course of a pipeline; at the time, they just seemed companionable toys, put there to decorate the desert and keep the lone motorist amused. I liked their frizzy heads and huge teeth. Their lunatic humour was nicely in keeping with what appeared to be the general spirit of the island.

The Falconry was up a lane in a coastal swamp of palms and eucalyptus trees, a very new, red and white building which looked like an improbable cottage hospital. I was met by Dr Platt, an American who ran the centre. He was carrying a

bucket and wore a hawk on his wrist. With the kind of red
hair which leaps from the scalp in kinks and curlicues, he
strongly resembled the seesaw men who'd kept me company
on my drive across the desert.

He was a Mormon from Idaho, who'd been to Brigham
Young University at Salt Lake City, then Cornell, where he'd
been a member of a research team which was working on the
problem of breeding peregrine falcons in captivity in order to
reintroduce them into the Great American Desert. Sheikh Issa,
the ruler of Bahrain, had heard of the Cornell project and had
commissioned Dr Platt to set up the first falcon-breeding station
in Arabia.

I spent the morning tailing Dr Platt on his rounds. He
opened the beaks of flapping birds and peered into their
gullets. He put out trays of chopped quail for them in their
solitary chambers – airy, unfurnished rooms the size of large
student bedsitters. He searched in their feathers and peered
into their staring pebbly eyes. Most of the birds sulked indifferently on their perches, occasionally swivelling their
heads to catch one with a single direct glance of surly menace.
With their brown and white herringbone plumage they had
the air of choleric retired colonels, their heads full of plots and
coups. There seemed to be no sentimental attachment between
Dr Platt and his charges.

For the Bahrainis themselves, though, these birds were
passionately cherished symbols of a way of living; vivid, much-
exercised mementoes of the time before oil, breezeblocks and
telex machines. In the desert, the bedu tribes had used hawks
to kill the Houbara Bustard, a kind of migratory wild chicken
which half-flies, half-runs, and can outpace the Saluki, the
Arab hunting-dog. Every winter, as the bustards crossed the
Gulf on their way from the steppes of Russia and Persia to the
Saudi Arabian desert, they were hunted with falcons and
cooked in scoops in the sand. Now falconry is a sport. Every
Friday, the Range Rovers and beach-buggies go out to the
desert with hawks on perches in their rear windows, and city
people who man telephones in offices turn bedu for the day.
The past they are trying to recapture is not so distant; a few
decades at most – well within the memory of the older men.
The Houbara Bustard, however, is turning into a rare species;

on the Gulf it has been hunted to the verge of extinction. Hawks, too, are increasingly expensive; a good peregrine falcon is an important symbol of status. The rich now travel in hunting parties to Syria and Pakistan – the only places where the Houbara Bustard is still common. Dr Platt's experiments in breeding both hawks and bustards were being treated as an important investment in Arab culture; for a people who had good reason to fear that they were irretrievably losing their past, falconry had become a symbolic bridgehead.

Dr Platt's concerns were abstemiously practical and scientific. The main trouble, he said, was that the peregrine falcon goes off the whole idea of sexual intercourse the moment that it is put into captivity. Its courtship routines are athletic in the extreme, and take up vast amounts of airspace.

'The female is rather larger and stronger than the male, and when they get frustrated, the female usually just eats her mate. Even if they do manage to get together, and she lays eggs, she tends to eat the eggs; and if the eggs hatch, she just eats the young.' He spoke with weary professional detachment, evidently used to living in a world with lower moral standards than his own. 'It's something of a problem-situation. But I suppose that ten thousand years ago they were running into much the same headaches with chickens.'

The falcons glowered malignly on their perches. They did not look like willing suitors. Dr Platt was chopping up quail with a penknife.

'With the Houbara Bustard, you get on to a whole different parameter. The bustard is a monogamous bird, never lays more than four eggs in a year, lacks sexual drive . . . Prefers food. So you get a diet-problem. In the wild, a Houbara'll eat lizards, alfalfa, barley, mice, insects and quite a number of the smaller vertebrates; that's a tough diet to reproduce. But if they don't get it, they don't show any interest in sexuality at all.'

He seemed remarkably patient in the face of these boring and selfish traits in the avine character; a large, placid man for whom problems existed only in the form of temporarily-absent solutions. He finished feeding his moody hawks, and we drove out to the Game Park, where he had to pick up some crates of quail to show to Sheikh Khaled, the ruler's cousin and private secretary.

It did not look like a Game Park. A long barbed-wire fence divided the desert into two. On one side of it there were notices prohibiting unauthorized persons and threatening trespassers with prosecution; on the other there was just more desert, and in the middle of the desert, what looked like an aircraft hangar. Dr Platt gestured at this unpromising tract of white sand and scrub. There were going to be oryxes here, he said; and Houbara Bustards, and gazelles; they were thinking of importing some African animals – elephants, for instance. All I saw was stones and a few balding wisps of desert grass.

'We're bringing in a hundred thousand trees and shrubs.'

They would look lost, I thought, in that waste; and, in any case, surely they would die?

'We're irrigating the whole area with underground pipes.'

For Dr Platt, the future seemed as good as here already. Where I saw shale, barbed wire and barren and uncooperative falcons, he saw a leafy shade filled with stalking animals and hatching eggs. It was almost enough to have conceived the idea; money – and a little time – would make the fiction come true. Dr Platt's function was simply to iron out a few troublesome details in the conception. To me, it was a quite alien attitude, this casual confidence in the notion that things can be made to happen according to plan. In the Gulf, it was an instinctive habit of mind. Dr Platt talked of *will* and *shall*, and didn't muddle his tenses; later I was to meet people who would talk about plans for whole cities which had barely reached the drawing-board stage as if they were already built and populated. I got used to seeing in the desert things that weren't there – things which, because they had been postulated by someone, had to be referred to as accomplished actualities.

The quail were there, cheeping feebly in stacked crates. We loaded a couple of boxes of them into the boot of the car and went to see Sheikh Khaled.

The ruler's fort was in the middle of the island, on a bump of ground which is the nearest that Bahrain comes to having a commanding hill. Guards with machine-guns helped us to unload the quail. Inside the fort, we waited in an anteroom where a sergeant brought me cigarettes and nips of cardamom-flavoured coffee; Dr Platt, whose religion forbade both cigarettes and coffee, stood holding the crates of quail to his chest. The ruler's falcon-warden arrived, a solemn man with furrowed cheeks, a frosty beard and strangely large lips. He bowed formally, like a celebrant priest. We were shown in to Sheikh Khaled.

He was surrounded by telephones, most of which were ringing. A Saudi prince was arriving for lunch; his plane had been delayed at Riyadh; arrangements were being changed; he was sorry to have kept us waiting. A telex machine began to chatter at the side of his desk; he glanced at it, tore the message off and passed it to an under-secretary.

'She is still sick,' he said to Dr Platt. 'You know, the white one? Very beautiful. I like that bird. She is my favourite. But she has the disease. I feed her, she eats – she eats all I give her, but in the morning she is again thinner . . . like this, you know?' He cupped his hands tenderly around the shape of a wasted falcon. 'Last night I was up very late. I give her Pepsi-Cola. She takes a little Pepsi. Perhaps she is better – I hope. She is a very beautiful bird. Very white.'

'Yes,' said Dr Platt. 'Hypoglycaemia. You'd better keep her on Pepsi for the sugar content.'

The sheikh took another phone call from Saudi Arabia.

'I am full of worry for that bird,' he said when he'd finished.

'Just keep up the sugar,' said Dr Platt briskly.

'She is my favourite. I stay up all night. I have very little sleep.'

'What are you using? An eyedropper?'

'A bottle for babies – '

'Try an eyedropper.'

'I think that now she has the disease, she will die.'

'Try and make her take a couple of tablespoons of Pepsi every hour.'

'I do not know,' the sheikh said sadly. 'She is so very white.'

He received two supplicants with papers in their hands. Courtesies were exchanged. He signed the papers. The supplicants went out, bowing.

'About these quail – ' Dr Platt said.

'I see them . . . ?'

Dr Platt showed him the crate. Sheikh Khaled wanted it opened.

'I'm worried about your carpet.' With its deep maroon patterning, it was one of the most beautiful Persian carpets I had ever seen.

'No worry. We open the box.'

Quail ran everywhere. They fled, with shrill squeaks, under the desk. They stumbled and flapped in the thick pile of the carpet. We all got down on our hands and knees and tried to marshal them.

'I don't know if you have a knife?' said Dr Platt. 'I'd like to open one up for you, show you the flesh.'

I was glad that the best Sheikh Khaled could produce was an ivory paper-knife, too blunt to open up a quail. He took a bird in one hand and stroked its head with his forefinger.

'There's no fat on them. You ought to take a few home with you, have them for supper.'

The sheikh seemed a little puzzled by this suggestion. I suspected that he was rather further out of touch with his own kitchen arrangements than Dr Platt was with his.

We eventually got the quail back into their crate, and the falcon-warden took charge of them. Sheikh Khaled went back to his rack of telephones. As we left, he looked up from the mouthpiece.

'I will keep feeding her Pepsi,' he said.

'Right,' said Dr Platt. 'You do that.'

We went back to the Falconry. Across the desert, the rolls of barbed wire which marked the perimeter of the Game Park looked as if they might belong rather more plausibly to a Mongolian concentration camp. I asked if the fences were there mainly to keep people out or wildlife in.

'That's one problem we've just got to solve,' said Dr Platt. 'How to orientate people out here into a conservation-attitude. They're just not educated up to it. You build a game park; the locals think you've made them a free larder. Give them half a chance, they'd be out hunting with machine-guns.'

'You'll need the whole Bahraini army to guard it. Sheikh Issa won't like that.'

'The conservation movement's got a lot of headway to make up. It's an alien concept in the Gulf.'

'You think it'll catch on?'

'Education,' said Dr Platt, enviably American in his belief

in the perfectibility of man. 'We've got to hit them in the schools. Throw the lot at them: film shows, field trips, radio broadcasts . . . Yes, give them time, they'll get conservation-minded.'

I peered through the windscreen. With a little less humidity fogging the landscape, I might have seen the future: an elephant trumpeting in a grove of rhododendrons, a herd of white oryxes at pasture, flocks of Houbara Bustards on the run, and an orderly crowd of conservation-orientated Bahrainis with binoculars and wildlife guides. But the haze gave nothing away. There was just shale, and barbed wire, and notices with round pockmarks in them that looked as if they might well have been caused by bullets.

Returning to Manama, I took a minor road which looped round the top of the island, through nondescript mud villages in which the cars were bigger than the houses and where women brushed their veils across their faces as I passed. One of these villages hung on the horizon more importantly than the others, under a mushroom-cloud of blue smoke. Here men squatted in front of blazing kilns cut into the sides of ancient burial mounds. They piled old doors, window-frames, bits of discarded latticework into the mouths of the tombs. Grinning, blackened, their dirty robes full of singed holes and tears, they looked like djinns. Djinn-children played in the smoke on the mounds, and howled for baksheesh when I went by, while their fathers fed all the combustible junk left behind after re-building and diversification into the flames. It seemed rather a good way of using history. In England, antique dealers would have rescued the fuel, and archaeologists would have got up petitions to save the mounds; here graves and lattices found their rightful place in the natural economy of improvisation and make-do-and-mend.

I tried to ask what kind of pottery was being fired, but my Arabic was not up to phrasing an intelligible question. Mistaking my meaning, the man held my hand and led me to a sickly-green pool of stagnant water, where he took a lump of white china clay and kneaded it in one fist, splashing drops of water on it with his other hand. He gave me some clay too. The water was lukewarm, and made me remember my doctor's warnings about bilharzia snails. The clay disintegrated between my fingers into a pale sludge, which pleased the man. He showed me his: it was soft and elastic. He rolled it out between his palms, making an uncoiling snake of the stuff fall into his lap. He laughed, shrugged and chucked it into the pool.

Walking away, I saw some of the pottery fresh from firing in the graves – a heap of cheap dinner plates. I was cheered by the sight of them; I had feared souvenir ashtrays and folkware coffee-jugs looking as if they had been dipped in a glaze of All-Bran and treacle.

A mile beyond the smoking tombs, a concrete villa stood alone in a flatland of sand and telegraph poles. It had been transformed into a fantastic arabesque, in pastel pinks, blues, oranges, browns and whites. Its walls and windows made up an enormous geometrical doodle of lozenges, trefoils, flowers, stars and targets. The exuberant painted house stipulated its own terms: there was no bargaining with it. It was like a great multi-coloured ego, thumbing its nose at the desert which blew fretfully round the skirts of its walled courtyard. I should have found out who its owner was. Was he a dinner-plate entrepreneur? A housepainter, sick of the conservative tastes of his clientele? Whoever he was, his heroic cheek earns him a special place among the moving spirits of the Gulf. Brazen, dauntless, full of good humour, his house epitomizes the place.

During the afternoons, the bar of the Gulf Hotel turns into a kind of bourse: well-heeled drifters in Dacron suits go on the scrounge for contracts; there is the murmur of money in the air, indefinite and allusive; business cards are swapped like stamps; the small-time sharks hang around the telephone on the bar counter while the bigger ones huddle in pairs in the alcoves. It's a place where loose ends get tied up, and jobs and deals and easy pickings are floated out on the buzz of gossip, there to be snatched by anyone lean and eager enough to take them. The smallest, most freely negotiable unit of business currency is the 'agency'. If you sell washing machines, or steel brackets, or fibreboard sheeting, you need a local 'agent' to butter your contacts in the area; and these agencies are being continually collected, exchanged, sold and haggled over among the small fry of the business community. In the Gulf Hotel bar, agencies move as fast and invisibly as sharped cards. One can hear them travelling if one listens carefully; they make a very, very faint rustle as they pass.

This commercial volatility rubs off on people, giving them curiously provisional, temporary and easily acquired (and as easily discarded) identities. A man who on Monday was something in frozen meat might well turn, by Thursday, into a construction manager or a breezeblock-importer. Drinking at the Gulf Hotel is a hazardous business; one cannot count on coming out of the bar as the same person who went in.

I drifted into conversation with an Englishman who appeared to be living out of an overnight bag festooned with labels of obscure airlines that I'd never heard of. On our second Carlsberg, he offered me a job – as Gulf correspondent of a trade paper connected with the building industry. I explained that I was hardly qualified for the post. I knew nothing about building. I'd been in the Gulf for barely two days. I would be leaving the Gulf within a month.

'It's easy enough to pick up.'

'But I'm just passing through.'

'That's what lots of people say.'

I had a premonitory flash of life in a shared villa, consumed by dreams of unattainable air hostesses, relieved only by Scotch and light-classical music on the stereo system. It was not a welcoming vision.

'Sorry, I'm afraid I'm not your man.'

'Pity about that. You would have done nicely.'

Ralph Izzard turned up, looking like the Old Man of Hoy, and the job was cast out again, this time in the direction of an amiable blonde girl who turned out to be an undertaker. She nosed warily at the bait, looking for the hook; she was evidently used to having jobs dangled in front of her in the Gulf Hotel. She said she'd think about it; the Englishman said that there wasn't much time, he had to be going on to Kuwait, Teheran and Muscat. His suit looked as if it had already made the trip in advance of him. He rummaged in his bag for documents.

'You're an *undertaker*?' I asked.

'I do other things too.'

'How on earth did you land up doing that?'

'I came out to start a nursing agency. It ran into difficulties. The business had to be owned by a Bahraini; undertaking was easier. There weren't so many restrictions. I only bury expats.'

'What do they usually die of?'

'Coronaries. Drink. Cigarettes.'

'What's the age of your average corpse?'

'Oh, about fifty, fifty-five . . .'

I looked round the bar; on those terms, it looked like an undertaker's paradise. I tried to imagine this wistful, smoky-looking girl laying the afternoon-drinkers out on their slabs and rouging their faces. I supposed, I said lamely, that being a trained nurse must help her in her job. She said that burying people she liked did rather tend to get her down, but she helped to run a courier-service as well, so that brightened things up, and she had another job in an office, and she wrote the occasional article for the *Gulf Mirror* . . .

'The trouble is, people always remember the undertaking bit,' she said with an edge of resentment in her voice; and went on to tell me about an Irish labourer who had died on a building site in Saudi Arabia. She had flown his corpse to Bahrain (his body had gone Economy Class, lolling in a safety belt in a rear seat), where she'd had him cremated, and a good half of him had been returned to Ireland, securely corked in a brass candlestick.

'I wish people thought of me as a journalist or something,' she said. 'I don't know why they always batten on to the undertaking.'

She left the hotel as the Gulf Correspondent of the construction paper, but the title was like a stamp with too little gum on it; however hard one tried to make it stick, it kept on fluttering off while images of caskets and cadavers remained obdurately visible and pasted-down.

'You see,' said Ralph, 'how easy it is to land up in Bahrain.'

In the Gulf Hotel, though, I had seen only the shoal of tiddlers fighting for crumbs. The crumbs are large ones, and there are plenty of them, but they are just the leftovers from a long-running picnic which goes on elsewhere. All over Manama, on shops, warehouses and building sites, I had noticed names like 'Mannei' and 'Darweesh' – the names of the great trading families of the Gulf, the Borgias and Medicis of their world. Most of these families had been rich before the oil strikes of the 1930s and 1940s. They had been merchants dealing in pearls and gold; they had owned fleets of trading dhows and had dominated the commercial traffic between ports from Persia to the Indian Ocean and the Red Sea. The rulers of the Gulf states – the emirs and sheikhs – were bedu tribesmen from the desert; the merchants formed a rival aristocracy, based on sea trade. Oil did not so much transform their lives (as it did for some of the bedu sheikhs) as expand their field of operations. From gold and pearls and dhows, they moved into construction, department stores, aviation and international shipping. All down the Gulf coast, from Basra and Kuwait, through Bahrain, Doha, Dubai and Muscat, their names recur. They intermarried. They mixed Persian and Indian culture with their own Arabian stock. They represent an alternative cosmopolitanism to the Mediterranean cosmopolitanism of the Levant; and in the recent explosion of wealth on the Gulf, the trading families have been immensely important. They have had the experience of dealing with riches before. They have been traditionally city people. They have understood how to manage markets and finance and how to keep afloat on the veering tides of international trade.

I was given an introduction to Mohammed Mannei. He had, I was told, shops and offices all over the city; he arranged to meet me in the back room of a little jeweller's shop on Government Road. By the standards of Sheikh Khaled's office, it was a barely-furnished cubbyhole, and Mannei himself I took for a secretary. It was only after a minute or two that I noticed what a perfect foil the plain white robe was for his single diamond-crusted ring and for the flattest and narrowest of rolled-gold wristwatches. When he spoke, he talked softly; when he gestured with his hands, the gestures were tiny movements of the wrist, as if he was trying to economize on the air in which he was moving. There was a moral element in his restraint: he seemed determined to be a single-handed contradiction of the mythical rich Arab.

I said that few Europeans, fed on stories of Arab wealth, would believe that a Gulf millionaire would have such an office as his.

'They think three things about the Arabs. They think all Arabs are very rich. They think that they do everything in the *1001 Nights* and have many womens. And they think that the Muslim religion tells the Arabs to kill or conquer everyone who is not of their faith. It is sad, this not understanding. Sometimes it is funny. I was in a plane, you know, and this American woman is sitting beside me. I read a magazine, in Arabic. She stares a long time at this. Then she says, "What is that – is that Arabic? You are an *Arab*?" I say yes, I am an Arab. She leans to me and says, "Tell me, do you have many wives?" That is how they think of the Arabs.

'But this *rich*. *Rich* is just a sound. What is *rich*? *Rich* is education . . . expertise . . . technology. *Rich* is knowing. We have money, yes. But we are not *rich*. We are like the child who inherits money from the father he never knew. He has not been brought up to spend it. He has it in his hands; he doesn't know how to use it. If you do not know how to spend money, you are not *rich*. We are not rich.

'Without this knowledge, this understanding, we are nothing. We import *everything*. The bricks to make the houses, we import. The men who build them, we import. You go to the market, what is there that is made by Arabs? Nothing. It is Chinese, French, American . . . It is not Arab. Is a country rich which cannot make a brick, or a motor car, or a book? It is not rich, I think.'

When, I asked, did Mannei expect to see the first Arab automobile rolling off the first Arab production line?

'Never. Yes, I would like to see it. But I do not expect it.'

'In your own businesses, do you employ and train Gulf Arabs?'

'I have to admit to you, no. I will hire a Palestinian, an Egyptian, an Indian . . . These men have the skills. They work hard. If they are not skilled already, they learn quickly. If I hire a Bahraini or a Qatari, it is difficult. He is not used to work, he will not learn. So I choose the Egyptian or the Palestinian.'

'But then you're encouraging the very weaknesses in the economy that you are complaining of.'

'We are talking of business, and the needs of business. Whether it is good or bad is another thing. No, it is not good. This is not what I wish. This is what I do.'

'What about the Americans and Europeans that you deal with? Do you think that there's a lot of misunderstanding between Arabs and Westerners at present?'

'There is difficulty, yes; but it is not the difficulty of culture, it is more the difficulty of age. A vice-president of a corporation, for instance, comes here from America. He is – what, sixty? He is an old man. He meets the Arab, and the Arab is perhaps twenty-five, twenty-six; he is young enough to be the man's son, even his grandson. They must do business as equals, and I think the Westerner does not understand how to do this. In the Gulf, the businessmen are young men; the Englishman, the American, is old. There is the gap of the generations. It is more big than the gap of the countries, I think.'

'And the English? Have they adjusted to the new power of the Arabs? Or do they still come with the old condescension of colonials?'

'They have changed. A man cannot wear the same suit forever. But the Englishman still is wearing a very English suit, yes. It is perhaps more difficult for him. The English have been here too many years to change easily. They try . . . perhaps not hard enough.'

While we were talking, the Bahraini ambassador to Saudi Arabia came into Mannei's office for a cup of coffee. Mannei introduced us, then went into the shop at the front of the building to call the Indian assistant who was serving at the counter. He too was given a formal introduction to the ambassador. The immigrant servant and the ambassador bowed to each other as equals. I remembered Maurice-Whale's strictures about 'fratting', and shuddered. The Indian went back to the shop to deal with a customer.

After the ambassador had left, Mannei talked about Islamic law.

'Western people do not understand. They read the Koran in bad translations. The God respects *every man* as an individual.

That is how he is judged. Not as poor man, rich man, Muslim, Christian, Jew . . . He is judged as an individual.'

But, I said, it was the harshness of man, not the harshness of God, which Westerners found shocking in Islam — the public executions and amputations. These were what people in England thought of as the consequences of Islamic law, not the attitude of Allah on the Day of Judgement.

'In Saudi Arabia, yes, they cut off the hand of a thief. So, every year, they cut off — what, six, seven people's hands? And what is the population of Saudi Arabia? Seven million? In Saudi Arabia, people do not steal. Is that worse than in America, where there are not these "brutal" punishments, and fifteen people get killed or banged on the head or something every week in Park Avenue? Which is the more important? The lives of the people who get murdered there? Or the hands of the people they punish in Saudi Arabia? The one is the price you pay to avoid the other. I do not know. Perhaps you prefer to see the dead men on the streets in New York? Perhaps that is not so offensive to you?'

He took a gold ballpoint pen from the breast-pocket of his robe and put it on the table between us.

'You see, it is not just the punishments. That is not why. For the Muslim, there is always this other door that he must go through when he dies. He must keep his eye always on this other door. He comes into this room. He is alone. No one sees him. So — he will steal this pen? God sees. He will have to walk through that other door. If he takes this pen, it will not be forgotten, it will be written down. That is why you do not need to lock your car in Bahrain. Even bad men are thinking of that other door they will go through, of what will be written and remembered.'

He smiled — an economical twist of the lips.

'The other door, I think, is more important than the cutting of the hand.'

In Ralph Izzard's house the light was the colour of whisky, and the whisky itself winked in tumblers. Beyond the courtyard, with the shadow of the parrot's cage falling on the flagstones, the sleeping labyrinth was silver and black.

'The funny thing,' said Ralph, 'is you hardly ever meet an Arab who's an unbeliever. He may take a drink or two, of course, and go around in a London suit, and meet you down at the Flying Boat – but he never even begins to think of himself as not being a Muslim. I've got friends . . . been travelling with them for weeks . . . we've been sharing jokes . . . drinking out of the same bottle; and suddenly I've found them praying. There's this chap you think you know, down on his knees in the dust; and you wonder if you really know him at all.

'You ought to meet the local Catholic priest. Lovely man. Quite often drops in here for a drink. Scholar. He's made a study of Islam. I think he envies them, you know – their . . . unshakeability. Not like us at all. They don't make a great palaver about Doubt, like Christians do.

'Old Philby went in for it, you know. A bit like poor Kim and his communism, except that I think St John got much the better of the bargain. He was happy as a Muslim. I don't suppose Kim has much fun in that bloody Soviet flat, do you?'

After Ralph had gone to bed, I stayed up, with moon-shadows playing on the whitewashed mud walls of my room. I was reading Lévi-Strauss's *Tristes Tropiques*, and feeling suitably chastened by his prefatory remarks on the inanity of 'travel writing' – that pabulum of 'useless shreds of memory' and 'pitiable recollections'. I plodded humbly after the great cham of anthropology as he talked to Bolivian Indians in their local dialect about their marriage rules. Then, by one of those coincidences in which books swim into sudden focus, I came across Lévi-Strauss's encounter with Islam in what is now Pakistan:

I rediscovered in Islam the world I myself had come from; Islam is the West of the East. Or, to be more precise, I had to have experience of Islam in order to appreciate the danger which today threatens French thought. I cannot easily forgive Islam for showing me our own image, and for forcing me to realize to what extent France is beginning to resemble a Moslem country. In Moslems and French people alike, I observe the same bookish attitude, the same Utopian spirit, and the stubborn conviction that it is enough to solve problems on paper to be immediately rid of them.

I scribbled a wiggly line in Biro down the side of the paragraph, wrote the word 'Bahrain' followed by an exclamation mark in the margin, and fell asleep. For a moment at least, the island labyrinth had seemed intelligible. In the morning, seeing my own shaky, late-night handwriting on the book, I took it as a cue to move on.

3

The Day
Before Tomorrow

The bus which took us out across the airport to the plane for Doha was full of women and children. The women, in beak masks and black robes, might have been dead for all the noise or movement that they made, while the children were teeming and loquacious in brilliant cotton prints and woollen shawls. I had a conversation in flirtatious pidgin with two girls aged about eleven or twelve. Was I an American? Did I want to take their picture? They had been to London: London was very nice, Paris was also very nice. *Sura*, they said, pointing to my camera; *sura*, and giggled coquettishly. The glinting gold foil on their mother's mask gave nothing away; nor did she make any move to deter her daughters from making these distinctly fast advances to me. They had, I suppose, just a few months more before they too would disappear into silence and black. It seemed both improbable and sad.

Just before we reached the plane, the only other European on the bus pushed his way to the front and tapped the driver on the shoulder.

'Excuse me,' he said. 'This *is* the flight for Kuwait, isn't it?'

'No, Doha,' said the driver.

'Ah, good, that's all right then.'

He caught my stare. 'Just checking,' he said. 'I find in these countries you have to give them a question that'll make them think. They always tend to agree with anything you say, you see: so if I'm on a flight to, say, Abu Dhabi, I always ask "Is this the right plane to Teheran?" You might find it a useful dodge yourself.'

He gave me his card. His name was Roland Moon, and he was the Gulf representative of a firm of electrical engineers in London. Everything about Mr Moon was mild and economical. He had a small, squirrel-like face, full of sharp little creases which ran for half an inch or so, then stopped abruptly. They suggested that Mr Moon had contrived never to do anything to excess. He had evidently laughed – up to a point; he had had his sorrows – up to a point; and the lines on his face indicated that Mr Moon was, all in all, a very tightly run ship.

We settled into our seats. 'If you want despair, go by air,' said Mr Moon. 'That's one of my slogans.'

'I loathe flying too.'

'Whenever I'm on the ground and see a plane going over, I think, well at least there's one consolation – I'm not on *that* one. I think it's a good thing to count one's blessings, don't you?'

He spent, he said, 154 nights a year in hotels, working month and month about between his office in London and his string of agents down the Gulf coast. It was 'a bit of an unsatisfactory compromise'. He'd tried living in Iran, then in Africa; then had tried to settle down in England.

'I took a train every day from Crouch Hill to Dagenham, change at Barking . . . After three weeks, the man in the ticket office saw me coming and had my ticket ready for me. The next week, I packed in the job. I knew it wasn't for me.'

The plane's engines took a giant deep breath for the long, bumpy sprint up the airstrip.

'Funny, isn't it? Twenty-five years of flying, and it still gives me the willies.'

When I told him that I had come to Arabia to write a book, all the neat creases on his face went tight at once, as if some small seismographic implosion had taken place inside his skull.

'Oh, dear,' said Mr Moon. 'You won't understand, you know. People who come out here never do. They come in the winter . . . just like you. Notebook. Camera. They take one look at the place, and think everyone's working an easy ticket. You know, knocking off at lunchtime, down to the swimming pool, round to the British Club . . . Christ, bloody good life this is, they think; no income tax, hardly any work, lots of sunshine. They ought to come here in August. *Then* they'd see.

'When you write your book, please don't say we're all in it just for the money, will you? That's what they always do say. But we're not, you know. *I*'m not.'

I asked Mr Moon what had drawn him to the Gulf.

'People here aren't disillusioned like they are in England. You respect what they want to do; they respect what you can offer . . . there's a dignity in doing business with the Arabs – you don't get that in England any more. I'm not a cynical man,' said Mr Moon. 'Not like some of the short-term contract boys. Now, if you want to write about *them* . . . I don't know what they get out of it at all. They come out here to save a bit of tax-free money; they don't have anything at all to do with the Arabs – they've heard back in Youkay that they're a greasy lot of little bastards, so they don't bother. Then the drink gets them. End of two years, they find they haven't saved a ruddy penny. They're the ones who give the English a bad name.'

The Gulf had been his territory for fifteen years, and he was jealous of it. He disliked the new wave of brash young men, the freeloaders, the quick operators who got contracts signed during refuelling stops and who could be in and out of a dozen Middle Eastern countries in a week. Mr Moon's Arabia was a gentle, courtly place, and he was watching it going to the dogs.

'They've spoiled Abu Dhabi, you know. It's all spoiled, Abu Dhabi.'

But he liked Qatar.

'The Qataris never do anything too fast. They're a nice people; they don't go overboard about things. I always look forward to Doha – it's like going home. It isn't all change for the sake of change, like it is in these other places.'

Poor Mr Moon. Reluctant, sceptical of the consequences of his efforts, he was part of the avalanche of change which he deplored. With Mr Moon came power cables, electric light, air-conditioning, dynamos, turbines, lift-shafts, pylons: and the more Mr Moon watched his products fanning out across the Gulf, the sadder he became.

'You know, just a year or two ago, if you were doing business with an Arab, you'd know that he'd be in his formal robes; there'd be a morning of coffee and maa-salaaming . . . all the courtesies. You'd feel that you were really dealing with some-one with power – an aristocrat. You'd probably never mention the actual business on the first morning. Then you'd go and see him again . . . and again. You'd learn about his family, and he'd ask you about yours. You'd talk about everything under the sun – except the contract. You'd sort of sidle up to it, then move away as if you hadn't noticed it was there. It was like chess.'

Mr Moon moved his glass and empty lager can in a stately *pas de deux* across the flip-top Economy-Class table. It seemed that the lager can was Mr Moon and the glass was the Arab client.

'Now you go and see the same chap; he's probably in jeans and a sports shirt. He's not wearing a head-dress any more, so you can see he's got a crew-cut. Totally different fellow altogether – you can't have the same conversation with him at all. Chances are that you'll be in and out of his office in five minutes flat.'

Wrinkling his pointed face sadly at the decline of Arab manners, Mr Moon peered out of the plane window over the glittering wilderness of sand and sea and aluminium. As the undercarriage came down with an intestinal rumble, Mr Moon asked me if I was a gambling man. 'Thirty-three to one we don't crash,' he said, and closed his eyes tight shut. When we hit Doha, still intact, he opened them. 'I used to say a million to one, but the odds get shorter every time you fly. At the rate I'm going, they'll be down to evens in a year or two.'

Both Mr Moon and I had reservations at the second-best hotel in Doha. The best hotel has a speak-easy. Its near-neighbour has an overbright 'coffeeshop' where one can drink Evian water with one's fish-and-chips, and look out over a dried-up fountain and a palm grove decked with fairy-lights. Until recently, said Mr Moon, the Oasis had been the best hotel in Qatar, but like so much in Mr Moon's Arabia, it had gone downhill. For him, it was an object of compassion rather than complaint. When no one brought him the sandwiches he asked for, when no one shifted his bags, when his telex messages went astray, he shook his head and pulled one of his little rodent-like smiles, as if he was witnessing the slow deterioration of a sick old friend. A new crack had appeared in the brickwork since his last visit: he pointed it out to me with melancholy satisfaction.

'Give it a year or two, it'll just be a heap of rubble in the sand.'

I went to my room. The sound of ocean surf breaking on a rocky shore turned out to be only the bronchitic air-conditioner at work. When I turned on the hot tap of the bath, it spat gouts of what appeared to be blood. The colour television was showing an old episode of *The Brothers*. The procession of graceful Arabic subtitles across the screen gave a spurious dignity to the banal dialogue. How on earth had they translated it? Perhaps it had been transformed into heroic epic, in which the dreadful brothers, unobserved by their original creators, now lived in a world of vengeance, honour and bride-prices. I didn't know then that *The Brothers* is probably the most popular television programme in the whole of Arabia; its version of fraternal enterprise has accidentally struck some deep cord in the Islamic world. Shops and companies are named after it. Dubbed, subtitled, in black-and-white and colour, it was an inescapable affliction in every country that I visited.

Sometimes it was presented as an international bond. 'We like very much your *Brothers*.' It was not really hard to see why. However falsified and crude its portrait of British life, it makes the West uniquely accessible. *The Brothers* shows a society in which the close-knit family is the most powerful unit, where women remain in the background egging their menfolk on to ever greater achievements, where fraternity and business success are the two highest moral goods. To an Arab audience, it manages to suggest that the only difference between Britain and Arabia is a small matter of dress; translation, no doubt, has brought the language into line with Arab manners and business practices. Like *The Forsyte Saga*, another huge success on the Gulf, *The Brothers* preaches a beguiling untruth about cultural change and adaptation.

'Look, Mother . . . ' Brian was saying on the screen, and the camera framed the old goose surrounded by her collection of expensive, tasteless gew-gaws. A veil would have done her no harm at all; and a dishdasha would have been a considerable improvement on Brian's verdigris-coloured business suit. The lovely calligraphy unrolled from right to left. *Umm*. The root-word for 'mother' includes the meanings 'origin', 'source', 'illiteracy' and 'ignorance'. Perhaps the Arabic version was not so untruthful after all.

The Brothers limped to a temporary ending, leaving the Arab world in suspense for another week about the outcome of a takeover bid, a threatened divorce and a wage-claim by the maintenance men. As I laid out my stock of books about Qatar on the bed, the news came up. People in gold-trimmed robes stepped off aeroplanes and were embraced by similarly robed officials who stood in waiting on the tarmac. Moments later, they were filmed getting back into their aeroplanes again. This sequence, enacted by slightly different-looking characters each time, was repeated over and over again. The news in Qatar that day was that a lot of dignitaries had come, kissed, and gone away again. There was a shot of the Emir, Sheikh Khalifa. Stocky and plump-cheeked, he had an air of well-fed good humour which contrasted sharply with the cadaverous dignity of the official visitors. He looked like the sort of man who might be given to party games and winking. There was a touch of Mr Pickwick about him: for a father of the state, he seemed both oddly innocent and genial.

His face was there in the books too, looking out through formal, scrolled frames with ill-concealed jollity. It was a face worth studying. One would learn very little about any Western country from a portrait of its king, prime minister or president. In Arab countries, especially small ones, it is different. They are run so much like families that the personality of the father is probably the most important single factor in determining the character of the state. A hint of meanness in the face of an emir, and one will see starving beggars in the street. A down-turned lip may be the first warning one will get of public executions in the city square. The whole cast of Sheikh Khalifa's face, though, was one of chubby indulgence. It suggested that his family might be one of those untidy affairs with lots of courtesy-aunts, overgrown lawns and rowdy behaviour in the nursery.

The books themselves made Qatar sound a very odd place indeed for an oil state. There were, of course, the mandatory glossy pictures of shipping terminals, refineries, flare-offs and pipelines; but these were outnumbered by photographs of the museum, of fishermen mending nets, of ruins, dhows and old doors. Most Gulf propaganda emphasizes the modernity of the country concerned, the speed of the social changes taking place there, the 'Western' facilities, the ease and rapidity with which it has escaped from its tribal past. Qatar, however, appeared to find its oil something of an embarrassment; diagrams showing metric tonnage and thousands-of-barrels-per-day were hastily followed by pages of reverential description of the national literary magazine, the infant national theatre and orchestra and the television and radio archives of bedu folklore. Nor did this seem to be merely pious window-dressing; the prose was altogether too intense, too full of obvious yearning, for that. Qatar, it appeared, craved for a Culture of its own, and was openly fearful of losing its past. Unlike the brochures issued by the Ministries of Information in other Gulf states – in which all was invariably for the best in the best of all possible worlds – these books and pamphlets were evidently touched by anxiety, self-consciousness and uncertain hope. They pleaded with the reader to recognize Qatar as an individual nation with an important history and a serious-minded present, with roots firmly embedded in a rich and singular past.

The maps and statistics explained much of this. Finding Qatar at all on a map of Arabia requires a certain amount of perseverance: it is hardly more than a vestigial limb sticking out into the Gulf from the giant torso of Saudi Arabia. On the atlas, even its national boundary is in doubt – a broken shading in mauve across thirty miles of dunes. It looks as if it could be swallowed as an afterthought by its enormous neighbour. It is not only Saudi Arabia either which muscles up against the frail-looking little promontory of Qatar. The other independent emirates down the Gulf – some of them much bigger than Qatar – sit heavily, haunch to haunch, along the Trucial Coast. When they joined together as a single political unit in 1971, and became the United Arab Emirates, Qatar seceded from the arrangement at the last moment. There was a religious difference at stake: Qataris belong to the Wahabi sect of Islam, while the other emirates are Sunni Muslims. There was a touchy question of family precedence: the al-Nahyans of Abu Dhabi, the al-Maktoums of Dubai and the al-Thanis of Qatar were all afraid of losing their power and prestige in the new conglomeration. Qatari pride finally won, and the country backed out, clinging nervously to its independence.

It was vulnerable on too many sides. Its neighbours' properties bulged powerfully around it; but almost more importantly, perhaps, its own internal population was in danger of being swamped by expatriate outsiders. Qatar as an economy needs about two hundred thousand residents to keep the business in working order; but there are barely fifty thousand native Qataris in the country. The rest are Pakistanis, Sudanese, Palestinians, Egyptians, Lebanese, Jordanians, Syrians, and a few Europeans. The administrative middle class is Arab, but it is not predominantly Qatari. Civil servants from Beirut, Jerusalem, Damascus, Cairo and Khartoum, with their Western clothes, their liquor allowances and their easygoing approach to religious practice, come from a world so remote from that of the pearling dhow and the bedu encampment that they might just as well be Londoners or New Yorkers. The Qataris – a minority in their own country – have good reason to be frightened for the survival of their culture. Beside them, other small, half-swamped nationalities (the Welsh, for instance) look like great powers, their identities beyond question.

In my reading, there was a further complicating strand. Qatar, on paper at least, was a theocracy. Its law (unlike that of many Arab countries) was Koranic law, and its supreme court was the religious court of the 'Sharia'. Its version of Islam was stricter and more puritanical than that of any other Gulf state. Like the Saudis, the Qataris belong to the Wahabi sect, who practise a stern fundamentalism. They interpret the Koran more literally than any other group within Islam. Even their calls to worship from the minarets are made on a single note, to avoid profane decoration of the words of the Prophet. (To an infidel ear, these Wahabite summonses make a noise of extraordinary monotony, an aural version of the water-torture, relieved only when the muezzin, as occasionally happens, has a bad cough.) In Saudi Arabia, Wahabism has meant the imposition of a cold, totalitarian religious orthodoxy. It seemed hard to understand how Qatar could reconcile its official religion with the determined and prickly individualism which appeared to be the dominating feature of the national character. The books spoke of literature and painting and music, of the achievements of the Department of Culture and Arts; but what sort of culture was possible in a nation of water-drinkers and one-note singers? Wahabism seemed an unlikely ground for an Arab renaissance. Yet the effects of a religion on a small country are different from those on a big one; and in Qatar, the Wahabite teaching in the mosques turned out to be just another element in the insistent – and often contradictory – iconoclasm of the place.

I joined Roland Moon over a Wahabite Pepsi-Cola, and tried my new knowledge out on him.

'It's all news to me, too,' he said. In ten years of visiting Doha, he'd never heard of the national theatre, the national literary magazine, the national orchestra, or the new Qatari school of painters.

'I know where the museum is. Never been there myself. You don't do things like that when you're on a job like this.'

I asked him what changes he'd seen in the country since he first came.

'I'm afraid,' said Mr Moon, 'that I'm rather an unobservant man. I've only really noticed one thing – the flyover.'

I went out to look at the place for myself. It was at that moment in the evening when the low sun goes squashy in the Gulf and coats everything with a soft thick light the colour of broom. It gilded the wailing six-lane highway. It gilded the sandy roadside where I walked. It gilded the long trail of garbage – the crushed Pepsi cans, discarded Frigidaires, torn chunks of motor tyre, cardboard boxes, broken fan-belts lying in the dust like snakes, the building rubble, polystyrene packing-blocks, and a rather long-dead goat. So many cars had been junked at the side of the road, and reared, rusting, on their axles, that it seemed legitimate to wonder whether people here threw Pepsi cans out of cars or cars out of Pepsi cans. There were ruins, but they were not picturesque: squalid little rectangles of mud whose walls had fallen out, leaving a pathetic detritus in view – a few stained and ripped cushions, a child's graffito, a wrecked tricycle. A very pregnant, yellow, vulpine bitch – a degenerate descendant of the Saluki family – bared its teeth at me from the heap of rubbish which it was defending; and a rat the size of a domestic cat ambled coolly through a pile of fluttering multi-coloured rags.

It looked more like the scene of a recent civil war than a utopian city-state. Yet there was something about it which I recognized – the careless absentmindedness of the very rich. No one leaves more squalor in his wake than a passing millionaire: some hireling will clear up the mess afterwards, and to be tidy is to reveal a streak of mean thrift. Really lavish waste is one of the most certain of all signs of wealth. The man who can afford to create stinking eyesores, then negligently turn his back on them, is displaying his money just as arrogantly as the man who furnishes his house with solid gold doorknobs and diamond-crusted coffee tables. In a poor country the junked cars would have been either stripped or restored; the Frigidaires lovingly salvaged; even the cardboard boxes would have been dragged away to make improvised dwellings. Here they were simply litter – the overspill of some vast and smelly garbage bag. As the corpulent rats had evidently discovered, this was a handsome treasury of filth.

Down over the hump of Mr Moon's flyover I could see the bits of the city that one was supposed to notice. They looked as if a rich man had been making a hobby of them. The national museum was a castellated wedding-cake, creamy and toothsome in the sunset. The Qatar Monetary Agency was a giant gold ingot, its tinted windows taking their colour from the hammered sea. Around the harbour-front, the Corniche looped in a wide sweep past the moored yachts, the fishing dhows, cranes, container trucks and ships' funnels. It was, if one squinted a little and held one's nose, a lovely little golden city on the sea; and as the fairy-lights came up on the minarets, Doha gleamed and twinkled as prettily as if it had quite forgotten where it was and had mistaken the Gulf for the Riviera. The word 'Corniche' alone, of course, assisted in the illusion; it tried to nudge one into remembering that other city on a bay, where Regine's, the Casino and the Royal Palace glitter in a tideless mirror of sewage and suntan oil.

The 'Corniche', though, had come to Doha at fourth-hand. Beirut had borrowed it from Monte Carlo long ago. Then Kuwait looked at the Corniche in Beirut, saw that it was good, and transplanted it to the neck of the Gulf. Doha heard about Kuwait's Corniche, and so Doha has one too. Nor did it stop there. Abu Dhabi was not to be outdone in this competition to summon up echoes of Mediterranean glamour, and built a Corniche of its own; but the message had become a little scrambled by the time that it reached Abu Dhabi, where the Corniche is a long, dull promenade which bears the initially bewildering title of 'The Cornish Road'.

The Gulf Corniches are the most attractive counters in an expensive game which all the emirs play against each other. The exact length of airport runways in each emirate is another important token; every year the airstrips grow longer, as the rival rulers peer over each other's shoulders to see who has the most impressive stretch of tarmac. Fishmeal factories have been part of the game; so have underwater tunnels and the heights of Gulf hotels. Whenever something is described as the 'tallest' or 'longest' or 'widest' or 'deepest', it is almost immediately outstripped by something taller, longer, wider or deeper in a neighbouring state. I have never understood the obsession that English gardeners seem to have with cultivating giant marrows; much the same passion for the tape-measure grips the Arabian Gulf, where need and utility have been left far behind in the pure pleasure of gambling over the last crucial metre of useless but prestigious concrete.

Doha did not look afflicted by such obvious gigantism. Its winding Corniche fitted its waterfront snugly, without affectation. Its buildings were not especially high, and they clung to the line of the bay as if someone was frightened that the town might grow out of touch with its seagoing roots. As the water darkened and the sun faded, so the town seemed to shrink prettily round its harbour. From where I stood, on my little Tuscan hill of junk and crap, it looked thoroughly improbable. Here was a place which had just recently come into a tremendous fortune; a parvenu prince in the league of the world's *nouveaux riches*. Certainly its wealth was visible, but there was both a carelessness and a restraint in it which didn't at all tally with my notions of an oil state. With dusk, the cars thinned out on the highway, the howling motor horns quietened, and Qatar took on a salubrious Sunday air. It did not feel like a place where anyone was having very much fun.

In the Department of Culture and Arts, there was a leather-bound octavo edition of Shakespeare's complete works in four volumes on the director's desk. He raised the cover of the uppermost volume and passed the deck of books to me: they contained Rothman's King Size cigarettes.

'It is important to make a balance between the old and the new,' he said. As I took a cigarette from somewhere in the middle of the fourth act of *The Tempest*, I thought that the balance he was making was a shade on the extreme side.

'We make a collection of the singings of fish-men – '

'Sea shanties,' I said.

'That is correct,' he said. 'Also dances and antiquated stories. The folklore. It is important to keep the forgotten things. We have experts in the department who talk to dying people to collect the folklore.'

The ruminant sound of a herd of concrete-mixers drifted through the window of his office.

'But you also encourage young writers and painters and musicians,' I said.

'That is also of importance.'

'How? Do you give them grants for their work?'

'They can be given offices in the department.' The director pressed a bell on his desk and spoke to a male secretary. Three gloomy young men came into the room a minute or two later. They all wore white dishdashas with gold-plated Parker ball-points in their breast-pockets. The tails of their head-dresses were flipped up over their ears. A servant brought coffee in little fingerbowls. The young men knocked back the draught of pale, sour cardamom in a single, synchronized gulp, and twirled their bowls between their forefingers and their thumbs.

'That,' said the director, 'is a painter. That is a playwright.

And he is a musician.'

The artists sat gravely in line without speaking, like exhibits in a museum.

'I'd very much like to be able to talk to you about the theatre here,' I said to the playwright.

'That will be possible,' said the director.

Floundering, I remarked to the air that it must be difficult to foster a genuinely contemporary culture in a society where the traditional way of life and the modern way of life had become so suddenly and violently separated.

'There is much tradition in Qatar,' said the director. 'All artists know the folklore.'

'Do most paintings and plays deal with life as it is today, or are they mostly about the past?'

'They speak of both present and past. It is of much importance to keep a balance.' The director fondled the green morocco of the collected works of Shakespeare. 'You wish to speak now with Mr Abdel Rahman? I am glad to be of assistance. You are welcome.'

The playwright and I went to another office down the corridor. I had heard of Abdel Rahman al-Mannai. He was the author of the most successful play ever to be performed in Qatar. It was called *Umm Ziin* – 'The Most Beautiful' – and had run for fourteen nights to audiences of two hundred people a night. The figures need a footnote or two. Qatar has a population of fifty thousand native Qataris at most; and the play was in Qatari dialect. So its total audience was equivalent to about six per cent of the entire population of the country. In Britain, a comparable turnout would have produced around two and a half million people, or a twenty-five-year run in the West End. *Umm Ziin*, on that reckoning, did roughly as well as *The Mousetrap*. It had turned Abdel Rahman into Qatar's national playwright.

He looked burdened by his laurels. He was barely thirty. His moustache drooped; his eyes had a melancholy glaze. When we reached his office, the phone was ringing.

'My mother,' he said, cupping his hand over the receiver. 'If I do not call her by eleven o'clock each morning, she calls the office to find out why I have not rung.'

'All mothers are the same,' I said.

'With Arab mothers it is especially so,' Abdel Rahman said, talking over the electronic burble of his mother's voice. 'In the West, I think it is different. Mothers do not so much use the telephone.'

'I'm afraid they do.'

'It is the close-knit family,' explained Abdel Rahman solemnly. '*Na'am . . . Na'am . . . Na'am . . .*' he said into the phone. He was evidently a dutiful and obedient son.

He picked up a Rothman's King Size cigarette from his desk, clicked the filter tip, and produced a spurt of flame from which I lit my pipe.

We talked about writing. Abdel Rahman shuffled the heap of foolscap on his desk, a play he had been working on for two years. The paper looked as if the rats had been at it.

'It is difficult. In this office . . .' he gestured at his opulent abyss of leather and knick-knacks, 'I do not write. I change words. I put in one, then I take it out. But it is not writing.'

He had completed his play several times already. Each time it had gone to 'The Committee' and he had been instructed to make revisions. Now he spent his days gloomily scratching at it.

'I think that now it is not so good. I write better before, perhaps, when I was younger. Once I write J. B. Priestley's *An Inspector Calls* in three days.'

'You *translated* it.'

'No, not translate. I make it happen in Qatar. It has a different plot. I make it into an Arab play. The characters are all Arabs; things go differently, you see? *An Inspector Calls* is some by J. B. Priestley, some by me.'

'But this play which the Committee keeps rejecting – it's a political play?'

'No, it is a very old story. It is folklore. It is about a princess who is very sick, and she is going to die, and her father, the king, is very unhappy, she gets so thin. He calls all the doctors in the kingdom; they can do nothing for her. She say to her father, only one thing make her good again: if a poor donkey-man songer makes songs to her. You know this story?'

'Yes – '

'So she fall in love with the donkeyman, and the king kill him, and the head go on singing. That story.'

'Yes . . . *The Arabian Nights*.'

'It is very old folklore.'

'So why do the Committee make you rewrite?'

'They say many things. They say people think that the king is the emir, and he spend too much money on the army, and the princess is the people, and he not take enough care of the people, and the donkeyman songer is the poor people . . . I do not see these things. I write it as an old story, as folklore. Everyone who reads sees different meaning . . .' Everything about him sagged as he contemplated the critical ingenuity of the Committee.

'I suppose it is the same in all places. In England, you have a Committee?'

'No. Most of our censorship is just commercial – if it doesn't pay, it doesn't get put on. Then there are laws of libel and obscenity . . .'

'But you could not write about the government?'

'Yes. People often do.'

'They will stop you writing of the Queen?'

'No. A lot of people might think it was in bad taste, but one would not be stopped exactly.'

'Then perhaps I think I go to England.'

'You wouldn't be nearly as well paid.'

'But they would put on my plays?' He dredged up a wan grin. 'You make joke, or is it true that you can write about the Queen?'

On my way down the stairs of the Culture and Arts building, I looked at the paintings on the walls. They were mostly glutinous oils in which the paint had been applied so thickly that its surface was wrinkling like an old man's skin. They were in very bright colours, and showed Qataris in traditional dress, dhows and mosques. They were, I think, unexceptionable pieces of folklore.

It was easy to jeer. Where I came from, folklore meant the tastefully expurgated hey-nonny-nonnyings of Cecil Sharpe; it meant vicars bullying reluctant villagers into dancing round maypoles and dressing up in the clownish costumes of Morris-men. For me, the word merely conjured up an irritating, sentimental nostalgia for a past that never really existed. 'Folklore' was a way of telling irrelevant lies about history. It was responsible for the tiresome banality of Merrie England and cosy, teashop-Tudor.

Out on the streets in Doha, I realized that folklore meant something quite different. Hot, lonely, half-deafened by the din of horns and motors, I found myself suddenly panicking. I was without bearings. The city offered no point of rest or perspective. It was an impossible jumble. Carved wooden doorways gave on to building sites of steel and concrete; at street level, neon signs clashed and bled into one another. The faces of the storekeepers were Pakistani; their goods, perspiring in cellophane sachets, came from Taiwan, Hong Kong, Japan, America. In the crowd on the pavement, other faces loomed – all of them displaced and temporary. Europeans looking sick with the heat swam by like fish against glass, followed by sallow Levantines, Sudanese Negroes and wild day-labourers from Baluchistan. It was like being caught in the middle of a vast, fatal, cultural car-crash. I leaned against the half-demolished remains of a mud wall, and tried to get my breath, taking in lungfuls of hot fog.

Everything I had seen of the Arab world up to that point had been obsessed by order and division: the arrangement of the souk, the separation of male from female, the intricate proliferation of lattices, screens, veils. On that street in Doha, the whole delicate structure appeared to have fallen disastrously apart. Objects, people, clothes, traditions and technologies were swirling about in an unholy stew. Nothing matched. Everything grated against everything else. There was a kind of fever in the air as if some violent chemical reaction was going on, creating a new and particularly nasty variety of toxic gas.

I tried to look at it as a Qatari might. What on earth would Abdel Rahman, his head full of princesses and singing donkey-men, make of it? It certainly didn't look like his – or any other Qatari's – city. One would have to be a lord of miscegenation to feel a citizen of this place. The Pakistanis did not look at home. The Europeans looked shipwrecked. The Palestinians and Egyptians and Lebanese looked as if they were gritting their teeth and making the best of a bad posting. There was hardly a Qatari to be seen. The few I did spot were in their cars, their palms locked solid on their horns, hooting their way

77

good-humouredly through the multi-coloured, multi-lingual mob who had taken over their city.

No wonder the Qataris needed to remind themselves of who they were. They were being overrun by their own employees. All their money and new power in the world was actually only putting them in more and more danger of being lost in the crowd. The bad paintings, sea shanties and old men's tales were genuinely vital symbols; without them, Doha might just as well be Babel. For me it was Babel already, and in the faces of other people on the street I caught the same confounded expression, the same look of sweat, bewilderment and hypertension. The Qataris were obviously in real need of all the folklore they could find.

Dodging shark-nosed Buicks, I escaped from the business centre of the town. There were still a few dusty streets of mud-housing left sandwiched between the grey utility blocks and the Gulf shore. They had been abandoned long ago by their original Qatari owners and had been taken over by indigent Baluchis and Pakistanis. Children dressed in cast-offs grubbed in the dirt. The women who watched them from low doorways were not wearing veils. Already I had become so accustomed to slits or, at most, a pair of give-nothing-away eyes, that seeing a woman's face seemed like being caught trespassing, and I turned my own face away sharply when I picked up the glances of these watching mothers. Islam conditions one alarmingly quickly to the Way.

Down on the Corniche, things suddenly steadied and Doha came into focus again. The deep crescent of the waterfront put a limit on the place and gave it back a purpose and identity. I came across a row of Juice Houses -- one-storey shacks which were painted in fluorescent rainbow colours on the outsides and bare as cupboards within. I stopped at the most garish one I could find for a pint of Juice and a chicken roll.

Juice is one of the happier inventions of the new Arabia; a by-product of prohibition and the electric blender. Raw fruit, sugar, powdered milk and crushed ice are churned and whirred into a lovely drink which is half water-ice, half milkshake. The Juice House itself works as a sort of drive-in pub. It comes into its own, as I discovered later, at night; but even by day it is a good, easy-going social institution which has the happy, unselfconscious grace of something which people have improvised for themselves in an impromptu burst of culture with a small *c*. In the daytime, it is a family place. Large, packed cars park side by side in line. You take a random place in whatever vacant slot you can find. Windows are wound down; the men buy Juice for their families; and the whole strip turns into a kind of attenuated reception room. Gossip drifts from car to car, while the men sit on folding chairs outside, watching the shot-silk colours of the water in the bay.

After dark, the tone changes sharply. The big family Cadillacs leave, and the Mustangs come. The young bloods sit along the waterfront in pairs, the tips of their cigarettes glowing. They stay parked there for hours. There is a discernible edge in the ripple of conversation as it passes from car to car; a sense of something brewing in the general boredom. There are no girls to meet. Black-market Scotch is vilely expensive (though large quantities of it are bought and drunk, and some of the seedier and more incautious expatriates are reputed to be making fortunes out of the liquor racket). Occasionally one catches the yellow flash of a whisky bottle passing, as the talk passes, through the car windows. The young Qataris on the Juice House line have the sullen cool of American teenagers in the 1950s; James Deans in their world, stepping on the gas and taking the roundabouts along the Corniche in a squeal of tyres as their sloppy cars roll on their frames. They have the dangerous look of unrelieved machismo: laundered, muscle-bound, their expensive wrists heavy with solid gold watches and solid gold cufflinks, they sit about like cougars behind bars, waiting for a break.

Sucking my Juice through a straw, watching the reflections of moored dhows and steam-yachts in the harbour shatter, I warmed to Doha. It seemed more like Brighton than Monte Carlo: white-painted mud, Regency stucco . . . the same small, self-contained prettiness with a saving hint of the corrupt behind it. I talked to the Pakistani who was wiping out his blender with a dirty rag.

He was a moonlighter. He had a job in a garage, a job in the Juice House and turned out at dawn most mornings to hang around the post office, where construction foremen took on day-labourers to dig holes and drive piles.

'How do you like Doha?'

'*Like* it?' He made a soundless *heh-heh-heh!* through his teeth which was half-laugh, half-sneer. 'How long you been here, mister? I like the money. The rest is hell.'

It seemed a pity to meet such disaffection at that moment.

'I make a pile of bloody money, then I go home. I would like to go to England, but no fuckin' visa. Fuckin' visa problem in England. Heh-heh-heh!'

The end of my straw gurgled in the pile of dry ice at the bottom of the glass.

'What a shit-heap,' said the Pakistani equably. 'Why they make it so fuckin' difficult in England for a boy to get a fuckin' visa? You tell me.'

It seemed impossible to explain why the Home Secretary should choose to exclude anyone with his remarkable command of English. I said that England was a poor country, quite unlike Qatar, with no piles of bloody money to be made by anyone. *Heh-heh-heh*, went the Pakistani, and started to savage a kilo of oranges with a butcher's chopper.

I crossed the Corniche and walked to the fish-jetty, where small groups of fishermen were making traps. They were shaped like conical beehives, taller than me, with funnels let into their sides. The fishermen showed me some old smashed ones, made of bamboo; the ones they were constructing now were steel wire. The wire came from Japan, an old man said; and the fishermen themselves had sailed up from Sharjah, nearly two hundred and fifty miles across the Gulf, in a diesel-powered dhow. The *hammour* fishing was good here. There were not so many *hammour* off the coast at Sharjah. Many fishermen there used big nets. Once they caught many *hammour*; now not so many. Along with diesel engines and Hiltons, seine-netting has come to the Gulf, and the old balance between fish and fishermen has been dangerously tipped.

Yet the quays here, as everywhere else on the Gulf, had been touched relatively little by the avalanche of economic and political change. The traders and fishermen were using the same dhows, even though they had stripped them of sails and installed engines. They were indifferent to the new boundaries, and untroubled by international maritime limits. The Gulf was still simply the Gulf, *El Khalij*, with the same harbours and markets that they had always used. They squatted round their traps, their backs indifferently turned to the stream of new automobiles on the Corniche and the great smoked-glass counting-house of the National Monetary Agency. Oil-rigs for them meant just another sort of reef to steer one's way round on dirty nights. One of them spat on his fingers before bending a sheet of steel netting; in an unthinking moment, he was still handling cane.

There were, curiously, more Qataris in the museum than any-where else in the city. It was a fine, quiet place of arches, turrets, gardens, balustrades; all on different levels and arranged with that instinctive architectural feeling for the labyrinthine. I sat on a bench, watching the drift of the afternoon crowd. Birds with names I didn't know sang among the cedars and eucalyptus trees. Roses, palms and flowering cacti were framed against black porches and walls of brilliant white cake-icing. It was a confectioner's masterpiece. Once it had been a fort; now it was a defence of another kind.

On a lawn, a bedu tent had been put up. The family, supposedly, had just moved on, leaving their clothes, their cooking gear, their embroidered bolsters and rusty muskets behind. A coffee-pot stood over the ashes of a fire. The whole scene accidentally managed to suggest that some cataclysm had taken place. In fact, the imaginary inhabitants of the tent were probably well taken care of, with jobs in the refinery, purpose-built workers' flats, and government-assisted summer holidays in Earls Court. My London neighbours, who looked as confounded on my local streets as I had felt in Doha, had perhaps once owned that coffee-pot and lived on those faded carpets. One would have to be no older than one's early twenties for one's life to have become a museum piece.

Inside the air-conditioned gloom of the old fort, there were waxworks behind glass illustrating bedu customs. But it was the people on my side of the glass who interested me most. Fathers went on ahead with their sons, busy with explanations. The masked women and their daughters were left behind with time to gaze and dawdle. They stood absorbed in front of waxwork figures who looked exactly like themselves. From the illuminated glass cabinets the same masked faces stared back;

they wore the same gold necklets and bracelets, the same black robes and shawls. *Women In Typical Qatari Costume. A Bedouin Wedding. A Sheikh's Family.* Their own everyday bangles had been laid out on beds of black velvet and softly backlit. Their waxwork counterparts had the same artificial brilliance as the characters in a 1930s drawing-room comedy playing to an audience of people with french windows in their houses and tennis courts in their gardens. Their authority existed by a trick of the light and a certain stiffness in their posture. Otherwise they were identical.

Did these women come each week to look in the mirror of the museum to reassure themselves that they really existed? The city outside had a quality of terrifying volatility; but the waxworks remained comfortably the same, the only genuinely stable figures in a world which was speeding too fast and too far, like a teenager's Thunderbird on the Corniche.

Roland Moon had told me that the electricity supply in Doha gets frequently overloaded and power cuts are common. I hope the museum has its own reserve generator. I was dogged by a vision of the waxworks melting on a hot night; of faces dribbling away behind their masks. I suspect that the same prospect, cast in a slightly different form, haunts the Qataris and is, in fact, the driving force which makes them repair in such numbers to their own museum.

At the far end of the building, a gallery was devoted to the oil industry. It was deserted. Diagrams and working models showed pools of crude oil trapped in folds of bedrock with miniature rigs and drills and a refinery laid out like a multi-coloured electrical circuit. Every case had buttons to push: at the pressure of a fingertip, the whole business was supposed to come alive, with oil flowing, gas bubbling, drills drilling and the refinery winking like a pinball machine as it rehearsed the entire process of the new alchemy. I would have liked to have been enthralled, although the inert exhibits did remind me of a manual I had once found in the glove compartment of a second-hand car – a book which I studied with appalled bewilderment and which came close to persuading me never to trust myself to have anything to do with an internal combustion engine again. I pressed all the buttons. None of them worked.

The oil stayed trapped in the rock, the refinery was dead: this section of the museum appeared to be rather over-eagerly anticipating the future.

Outside, antique dhows floated on an ornamental pool. They had been beautifully restored, with full rigging and furled sails. Next to them – more officiously guarded than anything else on display in the museum – were parked two 1940s Cadillacs and a British army truck. One Cadillac was labelled as being 'the first Cadillac in Qatar'; the other was, presumably, the second. They had been owned by the al-Thanis. Every culture, I suppose, has a certain point in history beyond which the past is simply the past – where all events seem to take place in the same unreal and unremembered span of time. In most cultures, that point is located several centuries before the present: in Qatar more or less anything that happened before 1950 belongs to legend. The dhows and the Cadillacs came from the same mythical period of antiquity; the venerable cars might just as well have been excavated from Tutankhamun's grave. They too were folklore.

Roland Moon and I were two of a kind. We dined together on fried junk from the hotel deepfreeze; we treated each other ceremonially to extra bottles of Pepsi-Cola. We watched the Boeing 747s roaring in over the bay and making the windows of the coffeeshop rattle.

'Won't make it . . . won't make it . . . won't make it . . .' said Moon, as each plane disappeared past his ears in a grotesque sigh of turbines. He was gloomily calculating how far his own odds were shortening.

From Moon, and from our fellow-guests, I caught the vacuous desolation of the Overseas Representative. In the mornings, he chased up his agents. In the evenings, he wrote up reports of his encounters while I committed mine to my notebook. I began to think of him as a rival, and tried to worm from him what he was writing.

'Do you put in details, like what the chap looks like, or how his office is furnished, or the kind of voice he speaks in?'

'Oh, they wouldn't want that kind of thing in London. No, it'll be about how a certain building is overloaded with air-conditioners . . . potential orders for switchgear . . . just technical stuff.'

'Don't you ever get tempted into writing the whole thing up quite differently?'

'No,' said Moon.

He was sceptical about his own value. 'The trouble with companies in England is they mistake movement for action. So long as they've got someone like me dashing up and down the Gulf, they're happy, they think they're doing business. But most of the time it wouldn't make any difference if I was here or in Nether Wallop. The real reason I'm here is just because some bloke in London wants to say the firm's "active" in the Gulf. I'm just a what-do-you-call-it . . . a symbol . . .' said Moon, ladling ketchup over a heap of soggy crinkle-cut chips.

'I suppose,' he said, 'that you'd call it rather a lonely life, really.'

I was luckier than Moon. Friday – the longest and loneliest day in Arabia for the unattached visitor – was spoken for. I had met the young British director of the aquarium, Peter Hannum, and he had invited me to come along on a fishing trip. It was a truant day. The team from the aquarium were there to catch specimens and survey the sea-bed; two stray bachelors who worked in a brick factory and shared a flat on the outskirts of the city were on the run like me; an American marine biologist from the FAO had dropped in on his way back to Iran. We loaded the workboat with oranges, aqualungs, crates of lager, rubber buckets, fishnets and sandwiches and headed out into a sea that looked like a great sheet of green cellophane until Doha was just a faint smudge among the dunes and salt-marshes which surrounded it.

On glassy days like this, the Arabian Gulf is an unreal sea; one might easily mistake it for an eccentric millionaire's aquarium. Even as much as three and four miles out from shore, the water is only about fifteen feet deep and as clear as a block of translucent quartz. We drifted over tuberose reefs of coral and long stretches of ribbed sand, dappled with wet sunlight, where crabs scuttled and giant starfish let their lazy arms sway and ripple in the currents. The shadows of fish passed over the sand before one saw the fish themselves: big, block-headed groupers rootling like pigs; rainbow shoals of angelfish;

cruising cat-sharks; convoys of tiddlers, bright as silver-filings. I saw a black and yellow stripey thing like a New Forest adder disappear under the boat, a long, zig-zag thread of pure muscle.

'Sea snake!' said Pete Hannum. 'We want sea snakes,' and crashed backwards over the side of the boat in a black wet-suit waving a fishing net.

I restricted my own part in these adventurous proceedings to fishing over the side of the boat with a borrowed rod and a hook baited with a rubbery strip of cuttlefish. When I pulled out a little sea perch which had taken a bait which was, if anything, slightly bigger than the fish itself, I was joined by Dave, one of the brickmaking bachelors.

'Fishing . . .' he said. 'You can't beat it, can you? I'm a roach man myself. Sunday morning . . . cycling off at six . . . There's nothing like watching a float . . . Then knocking off for a pint and a ploughman's lunch. There's a place I go near Nottingham – just a cut, but there are some bloody marvellous roach there . . . I've had some over two pounds out of there. There's this one spot, where it's all overhung with willows, and a deep pool where another cut comes in. There are bream there too, and tench – '

Someone came splashily aboard with a grouper. Dave watched it flapping on the duckboards; an exotic intruder gatecrashing his England.

'Nightfishing for carp,' he said. 'Did you ever do any night-fishing for carp?'

I had. We put together an anthology of secret places: lakes in the grounds of ruined country houses, spread with lilypads and haunted by pike as big as submarines; tiny Wiltshire chalk streams; acid brooks in the Yorkshire Dales where little trout have to be teased out from under stones; a certain lock-gate on the Oxford Union Canal; a rocky Derbyshire river where grayling shoal under a humpback bridge and rise to a fly only when the sun drops behind the squat church tower.

There was another sea snake, another chase, but Dave and I were lost in a world elsewhere.

'I'm a Dalesman. Another three, four years of this, and I'm going to go back to the Dales and put down my roots.' He stared gloomily over the edge of the boat. In his eyes one could

85

see that the lovely coral-coloured water of the Gulf had the repellent brilliance of a cheap picture postcard.

I wondered why he was here at all. Like so many expatriates he was a fugitive. His marriage to a Danish girl had smashed. He was denied access to his child, and had refused to pay maintenance until access was granted. The Danish authorities had pursued him to England; in the Gulf he had found a temporary, moody sanctuary. Didn't he, I asked, miss the company of women in this boarding-school world of solitary men?

'I gave up sex years ago, thank God. Haven't had a woman since 1975. I lost the taste. Saw too much of it in Copenhagen. I used to run a sex-circus, you see.'

'What sort of acts did you have in this sex-circus?'

'Oh, usual sort of thing. You know. Birds pulling Coke bottles in and out of their fannies to the tune of "I can't get no satisfaction". *You* know. I prefer reading, now. You get a lot of time for reading here. Have you ever read Adam Smith's *The Wealth of Nations*? I've been reading that lately, and Keynes; I'm getting interested in economics.'

Dave talked about the birth of his daughter in the Danish hospital. She was four now, but he hadn't seen her for nearly three years. 'They won't even send me photographs.' He had joined an organization which was called 'Families Need Fathers'.

'When she was born, the nurse did her bit, and then she gave me this little bundle, wrapped up, and said "Now it's your turn . . ." And I held it – ' He stood in the shade of the cabin, cradling the imaginary baby in his arms as he talked. 'And I just felt tears all over my face, just running down. The funny thing is, I'd never liked children before. I didn't know what it meant to have a child.' He wiped his forefinger across the bridge of his nose embarrassedly. 'Shit. That's the thing I like about the Arabs, you know. They really care about their children. You see an Arab father, he's fantastically proud of his kid. Always shows it to you . . . really proud. They'd do anything for their children, the Arabs.'

We reached the line of buoys where the aquarium people had laid their fish traps.

'I'm not lonely,' Dave said. 'I never get homesick. I've always been a traveller. To me, travel is a kind of compromise you make with death. I've thought about that a lot.'

The traps were hauled up on to the boat. The net on the deck was squirming with groupers. Close-up they had the riveting ugliness of creatures out of Bosch. Their wedge-shaped, hydrocephalic heads were complemented by popping frog-eyes. Their bodies were irregularly decorated with what looked like liver spots. The rows of spines on their backs had the gap-toothed appearance of old broken combs; and their gross lateral fins, on which they trod water while waiting for prey, were as big as saucers.

'One thing you can say for the Trent,' said Dave, looking at these horrors and thinking of his delicate, pink-tinged roach, 'is that you'd never find anything like that in it.'

They were shovelled into wooden tanks – some destined for the aquarium, some for supper. It was curious, and mildly disturbing, to have met what had recently become my staple food in person.

On the edge of the harbour, someone spotted the hump of a dugong taking a breather; a sea cow – placid, vegetarian and prosy, it did not look to my eyes at all like a mermaid. They are becoming rare now. Perhaps their own dwindling numbers have given them their fatal appetite for human company. At any rate, they seem to like the busy world of jetties, piles and boats. They seek out ports, and slumber in the cool shady water at the sides of dhows and tankers. Then the local fisher-men beat them to death, cut them up and sell them cheap in the souk. It is a peculiarly unkind fate for merpeople. I thought of Arnold's poem –

> When did music come this way?
> Children dear, was it yesterday?
> Children dear, was it yesterday
> (Call yet once) that she went away?

It stuck in my head for days like a jingle; perhaps because it seemed as right for Qataris as for mermen or dugongs.

I went back with Dave and Doug to their bachelor flat. It was on the ground floor of a block situated in a sandy tip of junked cars and mounds of rubbish. Newly installed street-lighting lent a surrealist brilliance to the place, picking out bits of twisted wreckage and the carcasses of dead animals as if they were on deliberate exhibition. Doug said that the government had just put the whole question of garbage disposal out to tender and that in a month or two Doha would be swept as clean as Montreux.

'When you get any sort of change here, it just happens overnight.'

Their flat was bare. The new plaster was cracking on the walls. The company had furnished it to a standard of minimum utility. It had a faint, familiar bachelor-smell of socks and towels and aftershave. In the living-room, there was a *Daily Telegraph* Map of the World on the wall and bottle of HP sauce on the table. We had mugs of tea, then cans of Tiger beer. Doug fetched some colour photographs of the brick-making machine. It coughed out 9000 bricks a day; and each brick was made to a strength of nine Newtons. In the first rash of building, apparently, the government had allowed contractors to use bricks of only four Newtons: four-Newton blocks of flats had a habit of collapsing in piles of grey dust.

Both Doug and Dave were being paid £8000 a year. Of this, they expected to save £2000, and with each year in the Gulf these savings took on a more and more exact pictorial shape, like a jigsaw puzzle gradually closing towards its centre. For Dave, the picture showed his roots in the Dales; the cottage with its vegetable garden and trellis of rambler roses, the smoke from its chimney swept flat by the wind; the pub at the bottom of the hill; the deep pool in the crook of the stream. For Doug, it showed a kennels. He wanted to breed beagles in Devon.

It all seemed almost as far away from the England I had left behind as Doha itself. There was no room in these pictures for inflation, the falling pound, the endless wrangle of industrial disputes, the winter power cuts, the steady erosion of the landscape by vast estates of buildings much like the one we were sitting in now. Yet the bareness of this apartment had its own function. There was nothing personal in it, no clutter of private associations to bring dreams back to book.

It was like a blank screen on which any picture might be projected, and if at first glance it had seemed empty it was actually full of shadowy green hills, beagles, stone cottages, church spires, showery weather. As each monthly deposit of £160 went into the bank, these shadows steadily solidified and grew in detail.

Dave showed me his library. There were the books on economics, a battered, much read complete Orwell in paperback, stories by De Maupassant and Roald Dahl.

'Have you ever read Roald Dahl? He's a bloody good writer. Do you know the story where the bloke keeps the eyes and brain of his dead wife in a saucer?'

I had read it. Dave had actually got it slightly wrong. In the story as I remembered it, it was a woman who, bullied in life by a pedantic, domineering and puritanical husband, devoted herself to torturing his remains by spending her widowhood sitting beside his brain where she tippled, chain-smoked, swore, and placidly watched his eyeballs dilate to bursting-point with inexpressible rage.

'That's my favourite. Bloody marvellous story.'

Several days later, I was having coffee with Marion Hannum in the office of the literary magazine where she worked as an illustrator. Without thinking, I mentioned the story of Dave's marriage and exile, assuming that in an expatriate community as small as that of Doha everyone's personal history was probably public property. It wasn't. Marion had known nothing of Dave's reasons for coming to the Gulf.

'No one here ever talks about their past; not to each other. It's something you never raise. You can talk about the future, but never the past – it's as if it was forbidden. Everyone tries to give the impression, *we're doing fine here, we like it* – no one talks about what they were doing before they came out to the Gulf. Doha is always supposed to be the *beginning* of whatever you're doing, not the result of something that you've done already. People may talk to you because you're an outsider, but they wouldn't talk to me. What I get is always the *nice* bit. *We're having a nice time.* It's like the news on television: have you noticed how *nice* it always is? There's never anything nasty on the news. It's as if everyone was involved in a conspiracy to make everything that happens in Qatar just *nice*.'

For expatriates, their two-, three- and four-year spells in Qatar were a way of breaking with the past; a time in which to turn over new leaves and clean balance sheets. On the streets of Doha, though, it was impossible not to become infected by the chronic national anxiety that the past was losable, and that if the past was lost then the present would turn into Babel. Yet none of the actual custodians of this past seemed to be Qataris. Ministers were Qataris, but directors were nearly all from northern Arabia: the Qataris had commissioned foreign experts to keep their own memories intact.

At the television centre, off a windy roundabout a couple of miles out from the city, with armed guards and barbed wire around its perimeter, I met some of the technicians of the national memory. Emil Kobrussi was a TV producer from Jordan; a harassed-looking man with a sweaty scalp, a Western suit and the air of someone living off coffee, nerves, cigarettes and overwork. He was making several programmes at once; all of them were designed, like the exhibits in the museum, to remind the Qataris of who they really were.

There was *El Süf*, 'The Sword', a thirteen-part serial about a feud between two bedu families.

'It is like your *Robin Hood* or *Elizabeth R*. It is a popular-historic series.'

'Do people living in urban flats in Doha really want to see stories about tribesmen in the desert? Wouldn't they prefer *Kojak*?'

'No. You see, it makes a talking point. The young people have not seen anything like this before, but the old people all remember. So *El Süf* brings the family more close together.'

'But surely for you and the people who make the programme, bedu life is about as romantically remote as it is for me?'

'I have lived with the bedu, not here but in Jordan. We have a common heritage. The life of the bedu is more secure than European life, much more secure. There is not the stress. One does not hear of bedu people with high blood pressure. There are no coronaries . . .' It was clearly a subject on which he himself knew rather more than was good for him. His office, a familiar jungle of scripts and contracts, was a world and a half away from the bedu encampments in which he insisted that his own roots were lodged. 'You go to a bedu family . . . they will welcome you, they will protect you. They will kill a camel – it is an important thing to kill a camel – '

'But *you*,' I said, 'you don't have camels to kill for your visitors.'

'If someone comes to my house, I cannot give him just a hamburger or a piece of steak; that is not a welcome invitation. If I give a lunch, then my wife kills forty chickens: that is an invitation you can accept. You know, my son is at school in Oxford, in the sixth form. One week, I write to him and say that we have given a lunch and fifty chickens were killed for this lunch. He writes back to me saying he cannot tell his friends at school this, they will think his mother is running a restaurant. At heart, you see, I am still a bedu.'

He told me about his other programmes. One was about traditional Arab medicine – the herbal remedies which were now banned in the new hospitals along the Gulf. Another was called *Yesterday's People*; a weekly series of interviews with Qataris in their seventies and eighties talking about fishing, pearling and the nomadic life.

'These are hidden stories. With television they can be found and kept so that people will not forget them again.'

Yet were he and his Egyptian, Palestinian and Lebanese colleagues in the TV centre really the proper custodians of the customs of this distant and singular country? Were they not practising a kind of cultural colonialism?

'We are training the Qataris. The assistants are Qataris. Soon, quite soon, we will go. Look,' said Kobrussi, irritated by my scepticism, 'your presence in this area dates back . . . what? Two hundred years? The British have been in the Gulf for two hundred years, and in all that time what have *they* done for the Arabs? What have they taught them? I will tell you. They teach the Arabs two things – drink and sex. The Turks at least brought some education to the Arabs – they would take clever young men, send them to university, then bring them back as provincial administrators and governors. What did the British bring? Fornication and the whisky bottle.'

*

A Qatari assistant showed me the studios. We passed a cutting-room which looked the liveliest place I had yet seen in Doha: it bulged with young men in white robes all of whom were in a state of perpetual vibration. Their giggles coalesced into a kind of sniggering symphony. My guide did a little jump to see over the tops of their heads, and giggled too.

'That,' he said, 'is where they take the sex out of Egyptian stories.'

We reached a studio where a variety programme was being recorded for the English language service. On the floor, an all-girl black rock group from London were doing each other's hair, while the Lebanese presenter was briefing them from his clipboard. For what was, apparently, the umpteenth time, the tapes rolled.

'Hi there, girls. Welcome to Doha. How you bin? How's the tour? What do you think of Reggae? Goes down big, right? Right . . . Right . . . So what are you going to sing for us tonight? *Vitamins?* Vitamins – just what I'll need after the show! OK, then, here are . . . BLACK GOLD and VITAMINS!'

'Sorry, Elias, let's try that again,' said the director.

The girls' keepers, two young Englishmen from an entertainment agency in Dubai, lolled against the wall of the control cubicle. One of them said that it was a pity that on the Gulf all-girl groups had to be locked into their hotel rooms for their own protection.

'Camera One! Camera One! Wahed! Close up!' shouted the director into his microphone. The camera wobbled, then made a running lunge for the group, ending with a shot that left the girls with their heads severed above the line of their noses. 'Wahed! *Shweyya! Shweyya!*' The image receded with a drunken lurch, and settled on a longshot of the top of the cardboard set.

'I said slowly,' moaned the director to no one in particular. 'Slowly.'

The group tidied each other's hair again.

'Hi there, girls! Welcome to Doha! How you bin? How's the tour? What do you think of Reggae? Goes down big, right?'

I left.

*

In Abdel Rahman's office I watched the tip of his pen as it covered a sheet of paper with a random scribble of circles and straight lines. He didn't look at it as he talked. It was an automatic, absent-minded labyrinth. He told me how he had been a Shell technician working on an offshore oil-rig. There he had worked twelve-hour shifts, and lived in a cupboard-sized cabin with just room enough for six bunks.

'It was not a room like this, you understand. They play the radio, they make jokes and shouts, you know? Always it was full of noise. I get the top bed, and I lie there and write, from perhaps eight o'clock to midnight, every night for a month. Then it is not difficult. Every time I think something new, I write. I have no time, no space, but I write. When I lie on this top bed, I write a play in one week, with the radio and the jokes and the shouts . . .

'Now perhaps I have too much time. I have a big office, big desk . . . they give me everything so I can write. But it is difficult. I cannot write. I only change words.'

His pen drew a series of bars over the top of his labyrinth.

'Then it was easy; now I do not know why it is so difficult.'

He called for coffee. A friend drifted into his office from the corridor: he had the same wan, over-tended moustache, the same preoccupied gloom.

'This is Hamud. He writes poems.'

I asked Hamud about *El Doha*, the literary magazine. A copy of the current issue was lying on Abdel Rahman's desk.

'It is a good magazine. They say it is the best magazine in the Arab world.' He said this with a melancholy emphasis on the word 'they'.

'Are your poems in it?'

'It is not for Qataris.'

'It's called *El Doha* — '

'Look.' He picked up the copy from the desk and opened it on the Contents page. He banged his forefinger down on the name of the first contributor. 'Egyptian. He is a writer from Cairo . . . Sudanese . . . Egyptian . . . Palestinian . . . Palestinian . . . Palestinian . . . Lebanese . . . Egyptian . . . Sudanese . . . one Qatari . . . Egyptian . . . It is not a Qatari magazine.'

'When I write my first play,' said Abdel Rahman, 'the director is from Jordan. Then I write another, the director is from Kuwait. They show these plays on the television, many people come, everyone knows about it. But then I write a play that I want to direct myself. They do not say anything about it on the television. Few people come. It lasts for only three days. You see, without the Jordanian, or the Egyptian, or the Lebanese, or the Kuwaiti, we are just young Qataris messing about. What we do is not taken seriously.'

'We need time,' said Hamud, using a phrase which had become an inevitable antiphon in almost every discussion in the Gulf. Time, which had hung so heavily on people's hands for several hundred years, was suddenly much more precious than money. Dazed and enervated by change, Abdel Rahman and Hamud put me oddly in mind of Wilfred Thesiger's companions in *Arabian Sands*. They had been obsessed with the discovery of gold, and Thesiger had lost his temper with their 'greed'. Abdel Rahman and Hamud were greedy too – for a manageable past on the one hand and for a foreseeable future on the other. Meanwhile they wasted time, as if their own regretful inactivity could bring Qatar itself to a standstill.

Hisham Gaddoumi didn't waste a second. He bit the ends off his Havana Monte Cristo cigars and spat them into the waste bucket. 'You read Marshall-*spit*-McLuhan?' Gaddoumi was the Emir's special adviser on town planning.

'When a technology is accessible and affordable, you can't resist it. The medium is the message.'

A great chart covered one wall of his office. It was headed, 'ACTION PLAN 1398'; by the Islamic calendar, which dates from Mohammad's flight from Mecca to Medina in 622, the Arab world is just entering the High Renaissance, poised on the brink of the Quattrocento. The Action Plan showed a series of steeply rising graphs: *Roadworks, Reclamation and Earthworks, Water Supply, Sewage. Roadworks* and *Sewage* were about to go straight up through Hisham Gaddoumi's ceiling.

'There are a lot of dreamers about,' Gaddoumi said. 'They like to talk about the Classical City: the city without cars . . . the organic city. Sure, it's nice to talk like this over coffee at the Club, but it is an unrealistic fantasy. The technology is there. We can afford it. You think we're going to say, "Sorry chum, thanks for the offer, but it's not for us"? No way. Of course the first onslaught of this affluence has produced a lot of horrors. Look out the window. But the existence of the horrors doesn't mean we've got to go out and smash the machines that produced them; it just means that we've got to learn to control the technology which is *in-evit-able*. Read Galbraith. You like cigars? Have a cigar. Sorry, no cutter; always use my teeth.'

Gaddoumi was a new kind of Arabian potentate. He came from Palestine. His cigars came from Cuba, his clothes from Paris, his shoes from Italy, his language from the Harvard Business School and the Massachusetts Institute of Technology. He was part of the diaspora of 1948 which, like the ancient diaspora of the Jews, has created a huge, highly mobile class of talented middlemen. Denied access to their own property, they live off their wits and education; temporary men moving fast and prosperously through the countries which have adopted them for as long as their foreign skills are needed. Everything about Gaddoumi was large, restless and canny. He looked as if he might well go off and build a dozen more metropolitan cities after he had finished with Doha – the kind of man who would make a light breakfast of the moody artists in the Department of Culture and Arts.

His office was littered with balsawood models of Gaddoumi's new world. I imagined that he frequently trampled them underfoot and ordered bigger ones. Aerial photos of Qatar pinned on the walls showed enormous tracts of sand and marsh – a *tabula rasa* on which Gaddoumi could paint highways, cities, sewage disposal farms and desalination plants. Even the sea was vulnerable: Gaddoumi was reclaiming it.

Doggedly, I pursued the line of thought which had so irritated the Jordanian television producer.

'If I was a Qatari, I don't know that I'd feel safe trusting my future to the hands of someone like you. Look at the mess we've made of cities in the West. London, Cairo, New York . . . they're all part of the same armpit; and aren't you just bringing to Doha the very experience which has made most cities in the West practically uninhabitable? Isn't the presence of people like you simply preventing the Qataris from discovering that there might be a special, new, essentially *Qatari* city which might be quite different from the sort of cities you and I know?'

As far as he could manage it with a cigar clenched in his

teeth, Gaddoumi assumed an expression of simple-minded piety. It looked like a face which had come in useful on television programmes, and when he eventually spoke I could very nearly hear him counting off half-second intervals between the words. It was not a style that suited him.

'We have a common identity. We have the bond of the Arabic language. We share the heritage of the same tradition. We have the force of the Islamic religion. We are one people.'

'I read the PR handouts.'

With evident relief, Gaddoumi took off his television face. 'Usually the people who come to my office just want to be told how many blocks of flats we're building and how many square miles of land have been reclaimed. I can generally get them out of the door in five minutes.' I warmed to the compliment. We went to lunch at the Doha Club.

Hamud had said that the Club, like *El Doha*, was 'not for Qataris'. Certainly a first glance round the dining-room suggested that the place was a north Arabian stronghold, with few head-dresses and lots of very expensive, very light-weight, very blue suits. Gaddoumi knew everyone, and passed through the maze of tables with one hand raised in perpetual, negligent salute. With things like escargots and cassoulet on the menu, we might have been at Claridge's, had it not been for the importunate jugs of iced water standing on each table. Nor did the diners, forgetfully tippling the stuff from wine glasses, look like men who went for very long periods without hock to start, claret to follow, and brandy to finish off with.

'. . . everything that's workable in the Arab city,' Gaddoumi was saying, 'of course we retain it. No one's going to take a bulldozer to the souk. I don't want a phoney souk either. Put in tiled ceilings and a marble floor and eliminate the dirt – that's a fake, not a souk. You just have to get some of the dirt out – '

'How much?'

'Just as much as is needed to stop it blocking up the air-conditioning.'

He demolished a salad at a stroke.

'When I came in two years ago, my main job was to slow things down.' It seemed a wildly unsuitable occupation for someone of Gaddoumi's speed. 'The pace of development was too fast, the building standards were far too low. Now we're getting it right. Of course there's an impulse to mindlessly replicate features of the Western city. Someone goes to London, sees Bond Street, and says, "Right, we want Bond Street on the Rayyan Road." They want the Rockefeller Center . . . they want the Arc de Triomphe . . . they want the Coliseum and the Bridge of Sighs and the Hollywood Bowl and the Grand Canal . . . They've got the money, they can afford it, so why can't they have these things? You have to curb that impulse, teach them that what is right for London or right for New York isn't necessarily going to be the cherry on the cake for Doha.

'We want the best features of the Western city; the ones that fit. Take participation in planning; that's coming in this year. We've set up a committee of five hundred people – nearly all of them very bright Qataris. They're going to vote on all the new housing development plans.'

'To any real effect? Or are you just giving them a chance to express their "views" before you go ahead and do what you were going to do anyway?'

'No. The plans change. If they say they need space to keep goats in their flats, OK, we make space for the goats. But we don't give them the Rockefeller Center.'

'Even if they all vote for it – '

'Of course there are limits. The important thing is, we've got participation.'

'It tends to be a pretty empty word usually.'

'It's not in Doha. These people are changing the way we're building the city.'

We talked about the unplanned bits of Doha's development. I said how much I admired the free spaces along the Corniche where people were able to improvise their own buildings and businesses.

'That line of Juice Houses,' Gaddoumi said: 'it would be anathema to some planners. They would want to tidy them out of existence. But the planner's job is just to make the skeleton, and then wait and see what kind of flesh the people grow on it. You see, now, a lot of the rich guys here, they want a farm outside the city as well as a house inside. It's not the English or Parisian thing so much as the bedouin thing. They want to move regularly between the two, like the old summer-winter quarters. So you drive outside the city now, all these farms are springing up. The city is actually creating the countryside around it. Just like Jane Jacobs.'

For all Gaddoumi's intelligence and charm, I was still haunted by the idea of something which wasn't just like Jane Jacobs. I didn't know what shape it had, but it was an Islamic city, unique to Arabia, where machines bought from the West would be assimilated into Eastern traditions and put to wholly Eastern purposes. The phrase 'Western technology' enshrines a chauvinistic untruth. Although the machines may have been invented in Europe and the United States, machines in themselves do not have national cultures. Machines are not Christian; they don't subscribe to beliefs in certain kinds of family structure or social organization. Surely the mere existence of telephones, automobiles, steel-frame buildings, electronic calculators, television sets and the rest does not of necessity convert the world into a giant suburb of Birmingham or Detroit? Isn't it Western vanity which makes the European or American visitor to Arabia take one look at a Dodge pick-up or a Hilton and instantly conclude that the place has been 'Westernized'? I only had to look round the dining-room of the Doha Club to see how at least one rich Arab city was covered in a shiny patina of *Western* plastic, *Western* leatherette, *Western* concrete, *Western* aluminium, *Western* facial tissues, *Western* double-glazing, all conditioned by *Western* air and lubricated by *Western* mineral water. Yet I couldn't get rid of the conviction that these things added up to a thin skin which was as relevant to the essential working of the place as the colour of the paint on the outside of a car.

'Suppose,' I said, 'that the Industrial Revolution had happened in an Islamic culture, not a Christian one. Do you think the social consequences would have been very different?'

'It could never have happened. But if it had, I think the results would have been much the same.'

'What about the sheer safety of the Arab city? The low crime rate . . . the way in which nobody needs to lock their car? Isn't that an example of a social tradition surviving in Arabia in a way that's unimaginable in Western Europe or the States?'

'The safety's temporary, I'm afraid,' said Gaddoumi. 'We need time.'

'You're a technological determinist.'

'No, I am not a determinist. I am a realist. Sure, I'd like to go along with the dreamers. OK, this is Utopia. How do you like it?'

'So you'll have to agree with the idea that building cities has to threaten Islam with destruction – that you yourself are partly responsible for creating an educated class of disaffected urban sceptics; and you're doing this in a theocracy. Isn't that living a little dangerously?'

'You mean, Islam as a religion, or Islam as a political instrument?'

'Surely they're inseparable?'

'As a political instrument, Islam is historically necessary.'

'All right then, by building cities are you effectively weakening one of the most powerful political instruments in the Arab world? If you argue that technology and urbanization must threaten religion and the structure of the family, then aren't you implicitly confessing to being an enemy of the state?'

Gaddoumi laughed. 'It's amusing to talk about these things.'

'Do you think Islam can survive the modern city?'

'What shall I say, "no comment"?' A hint of that earlier face of his came back. 'Yes. It will. Islam now is much stronger than Christianity was at the time of the Industrial Revolution. It is the people in the city . . . students, intellectuals . . . who lead the pan-Islamic movement. It's so different from Christianity, anyway. The line between supernatural belief and political commitment is a very thin one.'

I had been lent an ageing green Pontiac with a climacteric temperament. I nursed it gingerly out of the city on to an empty freeway and let it roll. Coasting past shale, chickenwire, pock-marked hoardings advertising cameras, cars and hi-fi equipment, and ragged Baluchi hitch-hikers with leaking bedrolls, I reached the desert. It was not much of a desert. It was not much of anything.

It was clear that I'd made a mistake and come at the wrong time. It was the wrong time of day, the wrong decade. Everything was either in ruins or in an indeterminate state of infancy. I went by a village which consisted of one desolate minaret, a couple of broken arches and a great heap of brown dust. No one, I think, had destroyed it: the buildings just seemed to have sunk to their knees and rotted to bits. The ribs of an abandoned dhow stuck out from a mud bank. The rusted hulks of cars stood in what might once have been streets.

A little further on, I came across another village. It was heralded by a mile-long triumphal avenue of eucalyptus trees and a large estate of handsome bungalows. But the trees were barely knee-high; not yet strong enough to face the world unprotected, they lived in rectangular cages of wood and wire. The bungalows were only frames with the sky for walls, like the bare bones of the wrecked dhow. The concrete mixers were unattended; the builders' signs were already going rusty in the salt winds.

The resemblance between these two villages took me back to Abdel Rahman, the blocked writer, glooming the time away in his office. The past was a mound of dust, the future a skeleton – too provisional, too much on paper, to believe in. Where was the present? Driving between ruins on one side and baby trees on the other, I thought that perhaps the present existed as a sort of station waiting-room where people gathered to waste an hour or two between changing trains. The future was late, not due until tomorrow; meanwhile the passengers were marooned among their piles of baggage.

At Al-Khor, I found a street of shops. No one was out shopping, though, and the storekeepers squatted in a circle under an awning, smoking and chewing nuts. The grocer asked me to photograph him inside his shop, a gloomy cupboard full of canned foods and packets of soap powder. Then the goldsmith showed me his establishment. He kept the things he'd made himself in a dusty drawer: hammered wristlets and fragile chain necklaces. I admired them, but his customers apparently didn't. Now his shop was stocked with dreary little bangles from Italy – the same cheap trinkets that fill the windows of the tourist clipjoints around the Pontevecchio. On a card were hung crosses, saints, flowers, stars-of-David; mass-produced symbols that had lost their meaning during the long trip from the Oltrarno to the Qatari outback. How long was it since the goldsmith had made his own goods? A long time. He counted five years off on his fingers and shrugged for the rest.

The grocer, the goldsmith and I grinned and gestured amiably at each other over bottles of Jolly Cola.

Up a mud alley, the rooftops were brilliant with little girls who looked like macaws in cotton-print dresses of purple, pink and scarlet. Wherever I went, they twittered over my head, hiding behind turrets, making sudden, unexpected swirls of colour among the TV aerials and drying washing.

'I love you! . . . I love you!' they carolled.

'I love you too,' I croaked back in a pederast's stage-whisper, thinking that the open letter from the Ministry of Information which I carried in my wallet might not make much impression on the fathers and brothers of Al-Khor.

'Darling! Darling!' they pealed, and their giggles followed me all the way out of the town.

Out in the desert again, I saw the 'countryside' which Hisham Gaddoumi had talked of. Money, determination and main force had created it against all natural probability. In the middle of nowhere a juvenile forest had been placed on the sand like a new wig. Rich men's 'farms', set a mile or more back from the highway, were walled enclosures of the virulent green that undertakers use when they cover graves with sheets of plastic grass. Their soil was imported, their water piped: every glade and flowerbed must have represented a triumph of biochemical engineering. There was a despotic grandeur in all this, but it was overshadowed by a sense of the frailty of the whole enterprise: a lapse of memory, a blocked pipe, and every stretch of green would burn to the colour of rust.

Not far from the Saudi Arabian border I got a distant glimpse of a bedu encampment. I mistook it at first for a used-car lot. It did not at all resemble the airy tent in the grounds of the museum. The carcasses of old automobiles had been hammered together to make temporary shelters, while new Range Rovers stood parked near by. Remembering Lawrence and Thesiger and the legendary hospitality of the bedu, I stopped the car. From somewhere inside this great scrapheap, dogs set up a ferocious yowling, and a young man waved his fist and shouted at me to go away.

At Umm Said, I came to the refinery. It was meaningless to me: a tangle of tanks, pipes, catwalks; a monstrous jungle gym of aluminium set among steep dunes. It was at the refinery, though, that I saw the first camel I'd seen outside a zoo. It was a poor, scrawny, moth-eaten creature, and it was grazing joylessly in the shadow of a gasometer. It looked as if it was all too well aware that its day had come and gone. None of its legs appeared to know what the others were doing, and it lurched about in the oily sand, grabbing forlornly at single blades of marsh grass with hairy, elephantine lips.

I had told my hosts that I would like to visit a Sharia Court and watch the exercise of Koranic Law in action. Although the legal system of Qatar is officially based on the teachings of the Koran, there are in fact two kinds of court. The majority of trials and disputes are conducted by professional lawyers who are trained (outside Qatar) in international law, and their courts are modelled on a mixture of French, British and American legal practices. The Sharia Court is largely reserved for domestic cases; it deals with trouble in the family and leaves most other questions to the secular system.

Fayez, a Palestinian who worked as a ministry driver, had been asked to interpret the proceedings for me. I had met him a few days before, when he had been brimming with good humour; on the morning when the Sharia Court was due to sit, he was a miserable shadow of himself. His voice had dropped an octave. He looked like a man beginning a prison sentence.

'Why they ask me, I don't know. You want to meet anyone, I'll go with you. You want me to introduce you to somebody? I'll drive you there. But I do not like this place. I have been in Doha ten years; never do I go near this building.' He visibly shuddered as he looked up at it. 'I have no wife, no family, I know nothing of the law. Why do they ask me? I am no good to you as an interpreter. The language they speak in here, I do not understand a word of it. All the words are religious words and law words; I do not know their meaning.' He was begging to be let off his assignment.

When we entered the courtyard, Fayez hunched his shoulders and lowered his head in the stance of a boxer who knows he is outclassed and is in for a beating. He stuck close to the shadows wherever there were shadows to be found. He made enquiries in a melancholy whisper, and I followed his skulking figure up stairs, along corridors, through narrow passages.

'I will never find the way out again.'

Women holding toddlers crouched in rows on the floors of anterooms. Fayez looked at them and said, 'I am not married; I know nothing of all this.'

We reached an office where half a dozen court officials sat around drinking coffee. We joined them. Fayez, in a remarkable breach of manners, demanded that we be given clean cups rather than take coffee from the communal ones which were being passed around the circle.

'These men speak in Qatari. Even I do not understand half the words they say. I am no good for this job. Why did they not send someone else?'

We sat for half an hour. Children were crying outside the door.

'Why do you want to know about this place?'

I said that if I was going to understand anything about Qatar, I ought to see something of the workings of Islamic Law.

'I live in Qatar for ten years,' said Fayez. 'I know everybody. I can tell you anything you want to know about Qatar – ' He paused with the sneakily triumphant look of someone about to lay an ace. 'But I know *nothing* of the Sharia.'

'It'll be an education for you then,' I said.

'Psssh – ' he said and shuddered.

Another official came into the room and made an announcement. I watched Fayez's face; it moved steadily from faint hope to pure joy. He was on his feet and half-way out of the door before the man had finished speaking.

'There is no court today! The man says that the sheikh is very tired!'

The dark corridors had turned into a playground: Fayez danced down them, chattering. On the street he took my hand and led me, in a series of terrifying leaps, through the traffic. It was evidently true that he knew everybody: in the course of a walk of fifty yards he had embraced ten people. He was in a state of manic good humour. One of his friends had a car for sale – a Park Lane Buick which was going for around £2000. Fayez felt the upholstery, stretched his legs against the pedals, tried the horn, and bought it on the spot.

'You like it? It is for a friend that I buy it. I have plenty of cars for myself.'

The deal was concluded with kisses. When all the endearments were finally over Fayez took my hand again and hauled me back into the crowd. We were on the same street where I had come near to crack-up just a week before; but for Fayez, the city was a hospitable club of which he was a popular member. We zig-zagged like minnows through the stream.

'That is my friend . . . that is my friend . . .' He pointed out the scribe who sat on the corner in front of an upturned packing-case surrounded by a noisy queue of people waving bits of paper: 'That is a man from Iran. He writes letters for sheikhs with no heads.'

I left him to enjoy his holiday. 'Please,' he said, 'if you go to the Sharia again, do not ask for me to interpret for you. I go with you anywhere else but, please, not the Sharia – '

I went on alone to the Industrial Training Centre, a complex of huts and hangars on the city outskirts where Qataris – along with students from the poorest Arab countries like the Yemen – were being taught skilled jobs. At present the country's carpenters, electricians, car repairers, welders and builders were nearly all foreigners, from Pakistan or north Arabia. The Industrial Training Centre, unglamorous in name, unglamorous in appearance, was designed to help return Qatar to the Qataris; just as much as the museum or the Department of Culture and Arts, it represented that yearning for a national culture which seemed to suffuse Doha with such wistful intensity. Yet its director was an Egyptian. Its chief instructor was a Scot. Its brochure announced that 'essential facility in Job English' was an obligatory requirement for graduation.

Mr Kaddouri, the director, received me in his office. Like so many of the Arab expatriates whom I had met, he had the troubled gravity of someone who has to live daily inside an insoluble paradox. He had been commissioned to perform miracles and the strain showed. Did he, I asked, really believe in the Gulf dream of industrial self-sufficiency?

'For a successful industrial economy, you need three things. You need a stable market, you need the human skills, and you need an easily available supply of raw materials. When one of these factors is missing, then it is dangerous. When two are missing . . .' his tired eyes wandered to the window and the landscape of telegraph poles and girders outside; '. . . it may be disaster.'

We discussed just one raw material – water. By drilling ever deeper under the desert to reach subterranean springs, one lowers the water table. When the water table goes down, salt water from the sea seeps through to replace the fresh water extracted from underground. The only alternative in a country like Qatar is desalinization – a process so expensive that one tomato reared on desalinated water would, if sold at a realistic price, cost a dollar or more. The desert, like the bank in roulette, cannot lose in the long run.

Yet Kaddouri was prepared to play against it with loyal determination on behalf of the Qataris. This was not his country. He would probably never be allowed to take Qatari citizenship. He had no facile optimism about the likely outcome of the process in which his own centre was a key institution; nevertheless he was committed to realizing the dream. Like Kobrussi, the television producer, his loyalty to the Qataris was fuelled by anger at the indifference he saw displayed by the European and American visitors to the country.

'The businessmen who come here from London and New York . . . they are one-track, you understand? They fly over, they talk to their agents. They spend all Friday on the beach under umbrellas. They sell, sell, sell. They fly back. They never talk to people here. They see only their agents and the people at the hotel. They never come to ask questions. They are not interested in the society here, in the people. They are only interested in what to sell, what to buy. Even if they come here to this centre, they never look at the training, they don't talk to the students, they don't care about the skills we are teaching. They only think "can I sell him this piece of equipment for his workshop?" '

An instructor took me through the warren of workshops. In the language laboratory, students with earphones clamped over their head-dresses were picking up Job English. The textbook they were working from struck me as a shaming example of the indifference that Kaddouri had talked of.

'Hello, Mrs Jones. Would you like some coffee?'
'Yes please, Mrs Smith.'
'Do you like sugar and milk in your coffee?'
'I want milk but no sugar please, Mrs Smith.'

No doubt the author of this cosy sludge is sitting in a tax haven somewhere. I hope he is troubled by the occasional twinge of conscience. He would probably, sadly, be reassured to hear that I watched a class of Yemenis and Qataris poring diligently over every word of his awful dialogue.

A happier hut housed a group of trainee draughtsmen learning to design arches. They were being taught by an enthusiastic Indian who explained that it was important to learn how to make arches in the Arab world; it was part of the tradition. The arches looked fine to me, and the Indian instructor had made up his own course based on a study of Arab architecture. He showed me plans of houses which adapted modern building techniques to the layout of the traditional Arab house with its courtyard, arches, male and female quarters. I said that I wished the writers of English textbooks had half his sensitivity to the needs of the people he was teaching.

'English,' he said, 'is a very important language. The people go to English; English is too important to go to the people.'

I interrupted another group of students who were being shown how to take television sets to pieces. The Qataris among them had all been to London. Where, I asked them, had they been?

They enumerated the places carefully.

'Earls Court. The Cromwell Road. South Kensington. Gloucester Road.'

'Cheltenham,' said an eccentric.

'When you were in England, did you meet English people and make English friends?'

'No. I see my cousins. They are staying in one hotel, I am staying in another.'

'Did you enjoy being in London?'

'I like London very much. Very good city. I go to London again in June.'

'But you will not meet Londoners?'

'No. Is very difficult.'

'What do you like most about London?'

'The pubs.'

'The girls.'

'The Museum of Science and Natural History.'

The Yemenis stood by shyly. Scholarship boys, living on grants from the Qatar government, they were out of this world of holidays in Europe. Smaller, frailer and much more untidy than the Qataris, the Yemenis wore frayed tweed jackets over their robes and had twitchy, ambitious faces. They were, I was told, much the most hardworking of the students.

'For most of the Qataris,' said the instructor, 'it really doesn't matter very much whether or not they have a job at all. They'll get allowances from the government and paid holidays. So why work? You get an awful lot of Qatari students here who just play along because it's a way of passing the time. They're very polite, very nice; they pretend to work to please you, but at heart they really don't care a damn either way. Sometimes they just seem to be dropping in here for the sake of the company.'

Lunching in a Juice House on the Corniche, I met a young Qatari with a strong reek of whisky on his breath, a fat deck of visiting cards in the breast-pocket of his dishdasha, and a brand-new red Thunderbird. I had in fact met him before, in the pages of novels by Thackeray and Trollope, where he appears as a cheerfully idle young rentier who, chastened by his experience, usually reforms a few chapters from the end and marries the nicest and prettiest girl in the book. In Trollope and Thackeray, he is called Johnny Eames and Pendennis. In the Juice House he introduced himself as Mohammad.

Mohammad had tried working in an office. The office was all right, he said; but the work had interfered dreadfully with his social life. He was a busy man – I was lucky to have met him at all, he was so busy.

Busy with what, I asked. 'Visiting,' he said, taking the cards from his pocket and making them waterfall from hand to hand. He had contrived to spend so much of each year travelling abroad that his spells in Doha were divided into two equal bouts of strenuous activity. For the first fortnight or so he raced around the town saying hello, he was back; and for the second fortnight he repeated the circle of calls saying goodbye, he was going away again.

He must, I said, be a rich man. No, he said, he was a poor man; he had no money to speak of at all. His life, he explained, merely required ingenuity in its arrangement. For instance, I knew about the government health scheme?

'Everyone who is sent to Europe to go to hospital is allowed to take a companion to look after them. Usually it is a relative . . . a father, a brother. But the regulations say only "a companion". So I have a friend who has to go for an operation at the London Clinic; I go as his companion. This is the journey I have just returned from. I go with my friend from Doha to London and from London to Doha: altogether, I visit twenty-six . . . no, twenty-seven countries.' His grin was full of charm and cunning. 'It just takes a little planning.'

Mohammad did not seem noticeably afflicted by any kind of identity crisis. He didn't look racked by a sense of the lost past. He wasn't bothered about the lowering of the water table, nor was he anxiously counting off the years before the oil ran out. Why indeed should he, when the city was jampacked with chain-smoking Egyptians, Palestinians, Lebanese and Jordanians, all giving themselves acid stomachs and high blood pressure as they wrestled with these distasteful problems on his behalf? Mohammad was enjoying his Grand Tour. The estate was in the hands of capable servants. He had the tastes of a nineteenth-century landed gentleman: a talent for languages, an amiable curiosity about foreign parts, a predilection for food, drink and ladies, and an eye for the occasional speculative bit of business.

He lazily drained off the last of his lemon juice.

'I visit everybody. You have a card? Perhaps I'll visit you when I'm in London.'

Roland Moon had left to make contact with his agents in Abu Dhabi. The hotel was full of members of an African brass band. Every time I stepped into a lift, I found a pigmy with an enormous drum whom I suspected of using the lift-system as a mobile rehearsal studio. At night I had expatrial dreams. I would wake from wild dinners in Soho restaurants, in which almost everyone I had ever known since my adolescence had mysteriously come together over quantities of asparagus, artichokes, veal chops, double Gloucester and buckets of chilled white wine. Muezzins calling at 3 a.m. were smuggled into the dream as rowdy Italian waiters. The monotonous surf of the air-conditioning turned into gossip from neighbouring tables. Night after night, I found myself back in England; morning after morning, replete from these imaginary feasts, I woke astonished, unrested, and quite unable to face the cold, watery eggs on my breakfast tray. I stirred them with a coffee spoon and emptied them into the lavatory bowl, where they curdled odiously.

It was still winter. By Gulf standards the weather was pleasantly cool. Yet by nine in the morning one could feel the damp heat building in the air for a tropical storm that never came. By ten, I was soaked in sweat. My room was littered with shirts that had gone stiff with salt. I was leading as leisured and sedentary a life as was conceivable. Like Mohammad, I was making visits. I was reading Evelyn Waugh. I was writing my notebook. All around me, the city was going up in an orgy of manual labour. I cannot imagine how the migrant construction workers who swarmed like locusts round the skylines of the city were able to keep going in that suffocating air. They probably suffered from expatrial dreams too, if they were not too exhausted even to dream. They would never be able to keep pace with the other kinds of dreams that were taking shape in the air-conditioned offices of luckier men – with Gaddoumi's balsawood models and accelerating graphs. In this climate the natural thing was to live a life of unpunctuality, idle conversation and frequent refreshment with the coffee ceremony; but now the Gulf was determinedly flying in the face of nature. Poor bloody Baluchis.

An Egyptian professor from an American university had been billed to speak on 'What is Islam?' at the Doha Club on Friday night. I went more for form's sake than anything else; later in the evening, Abdel Rahman was going to show me a videotape of *Umm Ziin, The Mousetrap* of Qatar. I was looking forward to the play and was trying to remember the repertoire of distractions that I'd once invented for surviving boring sermons in cathedrals. I plodded through sand, thinking that Sundays were in no way improved by the novelty of making them happen on Fridays. Trailing unwillingly to evensong was something I thought I had escaped from twenty years ago. The one significant difference was the position of the moon: it was stuck, like the outline of a saucer, on a sky of stripey ultramarine. I had never realized that the horizontal crescent of Islam wasn't a fiction made up by whoever designed the original symbol. The crescent moon in England is vertical; here it was just as it was on the flags – huge, yellow and improbable, hanging over the Doha Club like a neon advertisement for the professor's lecture.

The auditorium was an acre of scarlet plush. It held what theatre managers call a poor house. The north Arabians were there: I recognized Hisham Gaddoumi seated a hundred yards away from my corner at the back, as well as two delightful Sudanese lawyers who had explained to me the difference between civil and Sharia law. A couple of Indians in torn plastic sandals drifted in, looking as if they had come to enjoy the air-conditioning. The English brigade (from the embassy, I assumed) had occupied a strategic row in the middle. They were evidently anticipating the event with much the same enthusiasm as me; a tin of Meggezones was making its way up and down the line of whispering Sunday suits. The professor was late. On the speaker's table, a heavy gilt lampstand was placed on a pink-and-white tablecloth which hung in newly-laundered folds. I'd seen the same accoutrements at meetings of Christian Scientists. I think that they are meant to reassure prosperous and worldly people that they are not going to be embarrassed by too much talk about God and the supernatural; they fill me with the certainty that someone is going to hide a pill in a nauseating quantity of strawberry jam.

I disliked the professor long before he arrived. When he did show up, he satisfied my worst expectations. Barrel-shaped, in an electric-blue suit and silver tie, Dr Farouki looked like the sort of corporation vice-president one sees on television putting up implausible defences of his company after it has been charged with corrupt business practices.

It was a misjudgement. Dr Farouki's lecture made Islam more intelligible to me than anything else that I have ever read or heard. Before setting off on my trip I had waded through a book called *Understanding Islam* by Frithjof Schuon – a 'masterly classic', much admired, apparently, by T. S. Eliot, but which struck me as a numbing piece of existentialist philosophizing. I had talked to Muslims about their religion, but the imaginative force of Islam still seemed remote and theoretical. Dr Farouki at least brought Islam to within my own range of foggy visibility. I wish that my notes had been more detailed: what follows is a thumbnail sketch of what he said.

'Islam is a corrective version of semitic religion. Christianity emerged as a reformation of Judaism, and six hundred years later the initial force of Islam was as a purgative administered to the weakened systems of Judaism and Christianity. It is an evangelical, conversionist movement.

'Christianity and Judaism had both centred on moral law. They had stressed the importance of man's intentions over and above his actions. They were concerned to the point of obsession with motive at the expense of consequence. Islam insisted on a return to natural law rather than moral law. Man's relation to "morality" exists solely in his capacity to obey or disobey. It is in his obedience to natural law that he becomes a moral being, and not in the exercise and examination of his conscience.

'In Christianity and Judaism, man's destiny is essentially personal and actuated by conscience. In Islam, the destiny of man is the bridge by which God's will becomes actualized in History. The Muslim believes that the world is capable of being changed to actualize the divine pattern. For him, History is linear. It is not cyclical or predetermined. History is not regarded as dialectical necessity, as in Marxism; nor is it viewed as unnecessary, as in Christianity. Rather, History is the work and battleground of man.

'There is, therefore, an essential concordance between God's will, man's destiny and natural law. In Islam, there is no original sin. Man is innocent; his death is natural. God did not plant man in this world as a fallen creature in need of a saviour. The world, being innocent, needs no saviour. Death is both natural and innocent. It is not a punishment or a tragedy. Concern with funerary affairs is absent from Islam. The Prophet said: "You must not weep or cry over your dead."

'Man is the servant of God. His cosmic status lies in that service. Islam is a civilization-building religion. The initial triumph of Islam was in coming out of the desert and achieving the highest standards of civilization in the world within one century of the Hegira. It commanded that the desert not remain a desert, the mountain not remain a mountain. The world must be transformed into a semblance of the divine pattern, and it is that transformation which constitutes History in Islam.

'What is at issue is not the moral intention of man, but his *works*. "Faith" in Christianity is valued the more highly when it is a blind leap. In Islam, faith is a fully-conscious affair. It means an understanding of the divine pattern and a commitment to that pattern; it can only be made by one who is convinced of the veracity of the pattern.

'It is the responsibility of man to actualize the pattern in space and time. Islam requires man's powerful intervention in the course of nature. The personal communion with God, which is the essence of Christianity, is not enough; it is merely a prerequisite. The world must be changed and rebuilt. There is no room in Islam for the merely individual. Christianity lays all its stress on the widow's mite, on the personal gesture. Islam states clearly that the widow's mite is insufficient: the world will not be rebuilt with pennies; it needs the wealth and power of the strong.

'Islam is a societistic, not an individualistic religion. It is continually on the move towards a social ethic, towards the idea of Islam as a state – a federal union of communities built on Islamic Law. In the first century after the Hegira of the Prophet, the Sharia developed as an international system of law, a Pax Islamica which included Christian and other states – a kind of United Nations.

'Islamic art is a single song of praise. It is denaturalized, destylized. Unlike the representational art of the West, the arabesque has no limit. It conveys the limitlessness of the state of Islam, of the continuous process of civilization which is Islam in action.

'We come now to the Judgement, the Day of Reckoning. For Judaism and Christianity, with their visions of a hopeless world, riddled by original sin, the Day of Judgement marks the start of an alternative kingdom. Paradise and Hell are eternal kingdoms, for which man's temporary existence on earth tests and qualifies him. Islam utterly rejects that notion. In Islam, the Day of Judgement is seen not as the initiation of another kingdom but as the consummation of life on earth. Everything that man does is written; and on the Day, man is required to read that record. In place of Paradise and Hell, Islam substitutes Reward and Punishment. Whether man is rewarded or punished depends upon his record, but neither the reward nor the punishment is a kingdom; it is merely the summation of man's life on this earth.'

I thought of the great pyramid of labour in the city outside, the lavish investments of the rich, the farms, the desalinization projects, the reclamation of land from the sea . . . Were these all part of the 'actualization of the divine pattern'? I hadn't realized their theological significance. They were certainly 'powerful interventions in the course of nature'; and never, since that first century of the Hegira, had so much money and power been at the disposal of the Muslims to transform the world with works. 'The world will not be rebuilt with pennies,' said Dr Farouki, and I thought of the tinted glass windows of the National Monetary Agency, the models, graphs and the sweating Baluchis and Pakistanis, obedient in the service of the divine plan.

For the moment at least, it was like watching a code being cracked. Dr Farouki's lecture explained a great deal. It explained the unembarrassed wealth of the Gulf, the passion for change and construction, the bewildering optimism. More importantly, it explained a lot of my own failure to strike any sympathetic cord in what I saw. I was, in Dr Farouki's terms, a model Christian. My whole habit of thinking was rooted in the personal. I had the automatic pessimism of someone with an ineradicable, ancestral belief in original sin. 'God did not plant man in the world as a fallen creature in need of a saviour.' I had long ago abandoned belief in God and salvation; but I believed in the Fall, and the idea of an innocent world in which all change could be for the better had the force of wild novelty. I was an attender of funerals, a devotee of the representational, I suspected history of being cyclical, and I thought that individual conscience and motive were matters of supreme importance. In short, I was about as far away from being a Muslim as it was imaginable to get. No wonder I found Islam cold and theoretical. Dr Farouki had made it even colder and more theoretical than I had believed it to be before; but he had given it an intellectual substance, an extremely valuable ABC of its theology.

When his lecture was over, he answered questions from the floor. I said that I had read the Koran in English and had found it boring and crude; was there any English translation he could recommend in which some of the force and subtlety of the Arabic original survived?

Dr Farouki said that Carlyle had remarked that the Koran was the most boring book in the world, and that, as far as all translations into other languages were concerned, Carlyle was perfectly right.

'The Koran is untranslatable because it is sublime. Its form and its content are inseparable. The presence of the Divine is in the words themselves, and only in those words which were given to the Prophet. The Koran, which is the most beautiful book in the world, exists solely in those words. Therefore Islam commands its followers to read the Koran only in Arabic. If you wish to understand the Koran, you must learn Arabic. That is the only answer I can give you.'

His answer, like his lecture, had all the clarity and absolutism of Islam itself. I came out of the Doha Club in an odd mental state – highly elated at discovering more or less exactly why I was an infidel.

I turned left, and left, and left again through the back streets of the divine plan. The headquarters of Abdel Rahman's theatre group was up a lane opposite a building site. Its painted signboard had an amateur look, and the dingy concrete building was a place I'd been inside a hundred times before. It had the same draughty rehearsal room, the same tables ringed with stains from coffee out of plastic cups, the same cheerfully shoestring air as any London fringe theatre.

It smelled of painted canvas flats and spirit gum. Abdel Rahman was there along with two actors in their twenties, one of whom was on vacation from drama school in Kuwait.

I said that I felt at home here.

'It is a club,' Abdel Rahman said. 'Sometimes many people come in the evening. Today, no. It is Friday. You like the lecture?'

'Yes, surprisingly,' I said. 'It explained a lot.'

'This is a *Qatari* lecture?' said one of the actors.

'Egyptian,' I said. 'From America.'

'Egyptian,' the actor said, and the word itself was enough to make a gloomy joke.

'I think I would not like the lecture,' said Abdel Rahman. 'You'd know it all already. It was for ignorant people like me.'

'The Egyptians like very much to make lectures,' said the other actor. 'They make many, many lectures, the Egyptians.'

We all took turns in fiddling with the videotape machine. *Umm Ziin* eventually started running. It was a recording of a performance – one of the triumphant fourteen nights; and Abdel Rahman and the actors settled down to enjoy their own shares in what had already become a historical event. Nothing that they had done since (though Abdel Rahman thought that he had written better plays than this) had come anywhere near to *Umm Ziin* in creating an enthusiastic audience for theatre in Qatar.

'Umm Ziin is the name of a girl. It means she is the most-beautiful . . .'

The painted backcloth showed the swirling green-and-turquoise water of the Gulf, with ribs of foam breaking on the sand. A group of musicians playing gourds and one-string fiddles started up a slow lament, and the tune was gradually taken over by a chamber orchestra in the pit.

The play was set in a fishing village in 1936. The cardboard houses were in crumbling disrepair; the villagers were women, cripples and old men, since the young men had gone to sea, and the orchestra throbbed with rumours of storm and ship-wreck.

It was a *Romeo and Juliet* story. A brother and sister were in love with another sister and brother in the village, but their families were keeping them from marrying. The two girls were waiting for their lovers to come back from the sea. The Gulf was a casual killer, and it gave the villagers only the meanest of livings. It separated lovers more effectively than the most tyrannical of families, and regularly drowned the best of the young men.

Then oil came. An absurd figure in tropical kit strutted, bellowing, across the stage.

'This is a very red man,' whispered Abdel Rahman. 'He is an English – he is an American man.'

The audience, who treated the play as pantomime, cheering the characters they liked and hissing at the ones they despised, went into such a fit of derisive giggles that the performance had to stop for a minute or two.

'They think that the red man is funny.'

The red man was recruiting labour for the oil company. One villager went with him, and returned shortly afterwards as a changed character. He'd lost his head-dress and dishdasha, and was wearing Western dress. A silver hard-hat came down to his ears; the sleeves on his jacket barely came up to his elbows, and his tight trousers flapped high round his calves. The villagers laughed at him. The audience laughed at him. He found an obscure corner of the stage, where he sat on a ruined wall nursing his pride. Hamid, the hero of the play who was now back from the sea, laughed more loudly at him than anyone else.

But the father of Umm Ziin had set a high bride-price on her head, and it had risen even further after the news of the discovery of oil. The only way in which Hamid could hope to marry her was by taking a job on the oil-field. Torn between Umm Ziin and the sea, he chose Umm Ziin and the humiliation of a job with Shell.

In the next scene, a child rode a brand-new tricycle across the stage; the first symbol of an avalanche. One by one, the villagers left for the city, until the stage was deserted except for one man, who sat disconsolately on the ruined wall and raised the ghost of Neptune, or his Arab counterpart, from the empty sea. At the end of the play, in an improbable, fairy-tale coda, the villagers returned to dance among the ruins, as if it was possible to come back and pretend that the oil industry was an illusion. The play, it seemed to me, took an even more cyclical view of history than I did myself.

When it was over, Abdel Rahman talked about the research he had put into writing it.

'For one and a half years, I speak to old men. I go to the villagers and find old fishermen and divers. I ask them how was life then and what do they think of their life now. They all say, "Yes, the present is very nice, very easy. Now we have 'a.c.' and the car, that is good. But before was better. People now all stay inside their houses. They watch TV. Before, everyone goes in everyone's house. Peoples were very close. Now, is different. Easy, yes, but not as good." '

His play looked forward to the present with retrospective disillusion. The past he described was not a past that he himself was old enough to know. Abdel Rahman was a child of the oil age; so were most of his audience. *Umm Ziin* provided them with a romantic explanation of their present boredom and sense of disconnection. They could afford now to look back at the lives of their grandparents with more or less unqualified nostalgia. The dangers of the sea were heroic: death and poverty, in *Umm Ziin*, existed only as forces which united the community; while prosperity merely brought tricycles and alienation.

It was a familiar theme. If Wilfred Thesiger had ever written plays, he might have been the author of *Umm Ziin*, and I found it sad that a Qatari audience should subscribe so readily to this (I had thought peculiarly Western) mythology of their own loss and corruption. Where Dr Farouki had been chillingly blithe about social change and man's capacity to arrange his future, *Umm Ziin* was full of unhope; it was charged with – if not the doctrine of original sin – a pervasive sense of the intractability of human character. I had the sneaking suspicion, though, that its disillusion was as much an imported luxury as a new Cadillac. It is one of the privileges of the rich to idolize poverty from a safe distance.

Muddle-headed, I drove back through the city. Did the lecture give the lie to the play? Did the play give the lie to the lecture? It was late, and the wild dogs had come out from under the container trucks where they spent the day sleeping. The wide sweep of the Corniche was empty. If there were dugongs by the quays, they were safe for a few hours yet. The lights of the museum had been left on, and the fishing dhows floated in silhouette on their floodlit artificial pool. It felt lonely and unreal. By the time I reached the deserted flyover the nostalgia and disenchantment of *Umm Ziin* had got much the better of the argument.

4

Temporary People

It doesn't matter where one is going; there is always an exhilaration to be had from just moving on. Packing my bags in the early-morning blue, I felt that I'd joined the ranks of the lucky ones. There were a few lights on in other parts of the hotel, throwing the stooping shadows of Overseas Representatives on to the blinds. We were the men with planes to catch: self-important with our luggage and separate destinations, we gave the hotel lobby a faintly carnival air, leaving those less privileged than ourselves to turn in their sleep and dream of home. Riding to the airport, my head swirled pleasurably with the first pipe of the day. My only complaint was that even at this hour the Baluchis and Pakistanis had beaten me to the morning. The dawn chorus of growling cement mixers had started up long ago, and my last sight of Doha was of men up ladders working by lamplight while the stars faded out of the sky.

Flying from one Gulf emirate to another is travel in its most condensed – and for me most satisfactory – form. Abu Dhabi is only a little more than a hundred and fifty miles from Doha: between the surge of take-off and the sickening reverse-thrust of landing, there is an absurd pantomime interval in which hostesses have to move as fast and jerkily as Harold Lloyd in order to get coffee served down the length of the plane, in which 'No Smoking' lights go off then on again, and there is just time enough to decide that a crossword in a week-old Sunday paper is beyond one, before one is chucked out into the brazen glare of another country.

Abu Dhabi is another country. Its economy is based on oil, its language is Arabic, but there most resemblances to Qatar stop. Everywhere I went in Doha had had the untidy, equivocating atmosphere of a house whose owner is troubled by fits of conscience, haunted by the clutter of his family past and given to spells of introspection. No wonder that British businessmen in the Gulf had talked of Qatar as the 'nicest' of the emirates: in Qatar one is always catching odd, distorted echoes of England.

There were no such obvious footholds on the face of Abu Dhabi. It looked conscienceless. Steep cliffs of coloured glass and pre-stressed concrete rose over boulevards lined with palm, acacia and eucalyptus trees. I got my first proper view of it from a window high up in a ministry building in the city centre, and saw a sunny, miniature Manhattan. Someone in Abu Dhabi must have bought the idea of New York on the strength of getting picture postcards of the place from a holidaying friend: the entire city had the appearance of something obtained ready-made in bulk. Twenty-eighth to Fortieth Street, please, from Park Avenue to the East River Drive. The condition of Abu Dhabi was so evidently mint that it would not have been surprising to see adhering to the buildings bits of straw and polystyrene from the crates in which they had been packed.

The office in which I sat was as disconcertingly brand-new as the city outside the window. It looked as if it had been furnished that morning. The leather smelled new. The twin speakers of a new Japanese hi-fi system stood on either side of the desk; black, shiny, and tall as ten-year-old children. A portrait of the ruler, Sheikh Zayed, hung on the wall. It was a bas-relief, moulded in gold leaf, mounted on black velvet and framed behind dark-tinted glass. He looked like one of the more extravagantly handsome and temperamental of the Medici princes, and every time the light changed in the room with a passing shadow or an opening door, furrows crossed his gold features and his mouth would seem to clench and unclench among the whiskers of his gleaming beard.

The office was not an office in the English sense of the word. It was a divan. People drifted into it, took coffee from an attendant, chatted with their neighbours, and drifted out again. It was hard to work out whose office it was, or who I was supposed to be speaking to, since a succession of men sat behind the desk for a minute or two at a time, talked into the telephone, then resigned their post to someone else. I felt at a considerable disadvantage: I had been tucked away into a green grotto with large pot plants on either side of me, and my view of the desk was obstructed by a low crystal chandelier. The only person whom I could see clearly was Sheikh Zayed, grimacing behind the glass.

I helped myself to a paper handkerchief from the open box on the table. *Modern Tissues: Modern Tissues for Modern Life.* When I wanted to put down my glass of tea, my neighbour pushed across a brightly-coloured glass butterfly from behind the hedge of greenery which divided us. I was afraid of shattering it, but the man gestured for me to place my tumbler on it. When I did, the tea turned peacock, infusing the blues and scarlets of the coaster.

We talked through the foliage. He had been born in Abu Dhabi. Ten years ago, he said, the city was just 'sand . . . tents . . . burn hot . . . a few houses . . . little market . . .' It was an impoverished village, dependent on an ailing trade in pearls, dates and fish. 'The houses – not houses, not like this!' With pride and wonder he pointed to the city outside. It was indeed a marvel, and the man's pleasure in it was infectious. Like the gold portrait and the butterfly coasters, it had brilliance and nerve. A minute or two before, I had looked at it and seen an expensive fake; looking again, I caught the glory of the thing. That anyone should have the arrogance, optimism and imagination to create *this* on an obscure sandbar was genuinely awesome.

The man led me to the window; on the desert-fringes of the city, steel frames stood waiting to be coloured in with more glass, more concrete.

'One year . . . two . . . you see no sand!'

There was real magic in it. In the West, cities in general are in disgrace, and high-rise apartment blocks tend to be seen automatically as social evils. For this Abu Dhabian, though, the shimmering towers were innocent: they were wide open with the sheer possibility of urban life, still part of that dream city which New Yorkers and Londoners once believed in too. I envied him his obvious delight. As he ran through his small stock of English words, hunting for just one or two that would convey the splendour of the place he now lived in, he reminded me of James Boswell, brimming with incommunicable enthusiasm for his London.

> I was full of rich imagination of London, such as I could not explain to most people, but which I strongly feel and am ravished with. My blood glows and my mind is agitated with felicity.

That was in 1763, and the passage in Boswell's *Journal* was triggered by a ride through the Haymarket. I think it is roughly what the Abu Dhabian was trying to say to me.

I was carried along on a tide of high spirits. A Syrian taxi driver kindly pretended, at least, to understand my Arabic. I said that Abu Dhabi seemed a fine city. Yes, said the taxi driver, it was a fine city, but not as fine a city as Damascus. There were many tall hotels here, but none so tall as the Damascus Intercontinental. As conversations go, this one may sound a little threadbare; as a conversation in Arabic it was for me a highly successful raid on hitherto unexplored territory. Encouraged by the driver's willingness to decode my mangled pronunciation, I burst into a flood of confidences about myself. I was writing a book about Arabs. I wanted to meet as many Arabs as possible. It was, I said, essential to speak to people in their own language. I spoke very little Arabic, but I wanted to learn much more. At the end of this torrid confession, he looked across at me with pity and disbelief. This book you are writing, he said, it is written in Arabic? No, I said, it would be in English. The driver said that he thought my decision to write in English was, on the whole, a wise one; that, at any rate, was what I think he said, but he may have been remarking, with some justice, that he thought the whole enterprise ill-conceived and impertinent.

The hotel where I was staying turned out to have a cocktail bar. Just the word 'Bar' and the flashing neon arrow which pointed across the vestibule seemed a good enough excuse to feel elated by Abu Dhabi; and when I stood at the extreme end of the verandah of my room, craning my head to see over the top of an electricity generator and through the rusty skeleton of an infant skyscraper, I could just manage to snatch a glimpse of the sea.

I lunched on whisky-sours, my head full of kindly thoughts about Sheikh Zayed's family estate. After lunch, I went for a walk through the grounds. At the bottom of the hotel drive, a gang of Baluchis were planting turf from Mexico in soil which had been imported from the oasis at Al Ain a hundred miles deep in the desert. Another gang of men had a water-hose which they were chiefly directing at the turbanned heads of their colleagues. On the dunes near by, a large barbed-wire compound held what looked like a shabby gymkhana of flapping tents. It was guarded by a man with a machine-gun. There were no cocktail bars for the Baluchis, but they did have the better view of the sea.

I stumbled about in the deep sand at the side of the 'Cornish Road'. In broad conception, seen from an upstairs window or a passing car, the city was certainly fine; in the details of execution, it seemed afflicted by gimcrackery. In the random patches where there was a sidewalk, steel rivets stuck out of it. I tripped on one and fell, grazing my shins. The Corniche itself was just another imported good idea. It was dead straight. There was none of the improvised life of its namesake in Doha. Even as a long promenade it didn't work, since a flood-barrier obstructed the view of the beach beneath it.

The sand was continuously on the move, travelling at waist-height, making the road look like a muddy river. I waded through it, with the sand stinging my hands. This was only a breeze; when the wind gets up, the sand can take the paint off a car in minutes. It will scour the skin from one's face. It moves exactly like water, with rapids, whirlpools and slow deeps. After a hundred yards of walking through a mere zephyr of a sand-wind, I realized why I was the only pedestrian in sight, and I was grateful when a car drew up and the driver offered me a lift.

He was a big man with a face of clownish gravity. He smelled of hair-oil and appeared to have sublimated a passion for gardening by the intense cultivation of a magnificent moustache. Its points were waxed. It had been so combed and curled and trimmed that it seemed to have made some sort of declaration of independence from the face which had borne it. Major Barza himself looked tired and scruffy. Keeping his moustache in the style to which it was accustomed was obviously costing him dearly. He was a Jordanian serving in the Abu Dhabi Defence Force. He loved the English people, he said. The British Army was the finest in the world. He admired Sir John Glubb, and it was one of his great disappointments that he had not been able to go to Sandhurst.

'I would like to drink with you because you are an Englishman.'

'I'd like that too.'

'Only first I must see a doctor. I have many troubles.' He tilted his face to the rear-view mirror and gave the waxed tip of one end of his moustache a slight upwards nudge. The car continued at speed down the straight road. Major Barza occasionally glanced through the windscreen to make sure we were going in the right direction; but most of the time his eyes were engaged either with me or with his moustache.

I said that I hated being driven fast.

'You must have courage,' said Major Barza, gazing at himself in the mirror while he stepped hard on the accelerator. 'The English are a brave people.'

'Not me,' I said.

'You will drink with me?'

'That would be very nice.'

'We are friends.' I wasn't sure whether he was making a diplomatic statement about Britain and Jordan or a personal statement about ourselves. I found Barza's operatic manner a bit unnerving. I had met it before, though. Ordinary courtesies in Arabic take on a quality of Miltonic grandeur when translated directly into English. Most of the people I had met either spoke English so well that they had absorbed an Anglo-American casualness along with the language, or their English was so broken that they could not find the heroic phrases which they clearly would have liked to use. Major Barza was unusual in that he spoke English with great fluency, but the content of what he said was almost exclusively Arabic. It was a little like trying to hold a conversation with Tristan or Don Giovanni; and the interior of an ageing Datsun was a surreal location for such an encounter.

'When you drink with me, we shall talk the truth.'

We shook hands ceremoniously, and arranged to meet in the Wimpy Bar an hour later.

I walked round the souk. The old market had been torn down long ago and in its place there was a shopping precinct of purple concrete which looked as if it might be altogether more at home in Basildon or Levittown. Its pedestrian streets were too wide and windy. It had lost all the intricacy of a real souk, although its architect had clearly had some hazy idea in his head that a souk ought to be a complicated place with a lot of alleys and turnings. So he had created a rectangular grid which took its inspiration not from the labyrinth but from the squared pages of arithmetic exercise books. The only good thing that one could say for it as a piece of building was that the concrete was riddled with cracks and it looked as if a few more years of use would turn the place into a cheerful purple ruin.

Instinctive habits are, mercifully, much more powerful than bad architecture; and the residents of the souk were simply ignoring all the architect's designs on them. They had set up stalls in the walkways and constructed their own labyrinth in spaces which had been meant as routes of access. There were no straight lines to walk down; one had to zig-zag through a maze of one-man businesses which were conducted from upturned packing-cases under torn umbrellas. There were repairers of sandals and transistor radios, tailors sitting cross-legged in front of ancient Singer sewing machines, hawkers of clockwork junk and plastic carpets. Men on prayer mats were bent due west to Mecca, reliable in their way as compass needles; and under one umbrella an old man with a mouthful of gold teeth was crouched over the Koran. The book, which looked older than he was, was coming apart in his hands. Its pages were brittle and grey; the oldest, grimiest, most battered object in the whole of Abu Dhabi. The man's mouth moved as he read, making a kind of throttled, private incantation, the words rattling in his throat.

In the window of a hi-fi shop, I saw both of us reflected: a red-faced man in denim suit and Italian sandals, and this rapt, ancient reader. The image wasn't just a tourist snapshot: it was studded with clues about the nature of the absolute gulf between the two figures. For him ideas of 'the book' and 'the Koran' were indissoluble. Written language for him meant the language of scripture. It meant the revealed truth of God, and the printed words were there as objects of mystical contemplation. Had I told him that I was writing a book, his first thought would almost certainly have been that I was speaking a blasphemy.

Of course there were other books besides the Koran – mostly technical manuals and school textbooks. The language of these was not inspired, but it too was the Truth. It was impossible to tell the Truth about assembling an electronic calculator or building a desalination plant; just as the news on television, like the newspapers, told the Truth about events by avoiding any description of them. 'Today the Minister of Culture received the Under Secretary for Cultural Affairs of Saudi Arabia. Also today, His Excellency Sheikh Khazi Ibn Rashti Al-Tabanyi, Minister of Defence, flew to Bahrain, where he was received by . . .'

The printed or the broadcast word had a status of a kind which I found totally foreign. Either it was scriptural and divinely inspired, to be marvelled over and rolled around in the head in a state of religious trance, or it formed part of an inventory of the ascertainable, material world. Print was formal, public, and holy. Wherever I went I heard splendid gossip and argument, but this belonged to the realm of private language – to have printed gossip would have been unthinkable, because it would have meant confusing two categories as distinct and rigid as male and female or meat and vegetable. This, I think, was why Linda Blandford's book, *The Oil Sheikhs*, caused such fury in the Gulf: she had written what was only speakable, and her book was regarded as a betrayal because it was an outrageous contradiction in terms.

I had come up against this problem earlier in the day. In the Ministry of Information, a genial official had said that he hoped I would write a good book. I said that I very much hoped so too. He had then reached up to a shelf and picked out three or four 'good books' to explain what he meant by the phrase. A good book is very short and consists mostly of glossy photographs. Its text begins with a page or two of the kind of piously ornate prose of the kind which favours the word 'vasty' as an adjective for 'desert', and then goes on to become a catalogue of thinly disguised statistics. *Among the numerous social amenities enjoyed by the inhabitants is the flourishing Health Service, on which the Government spent five hundred zillion dollars in 1978.*

I looked politely through the good books, and said that, much as I admired them, I thought that mine would be rather different.

'What do they tell you to write?' asked the official.

I explained that no one had told me to write anything. I would write about what I saw and heard; it would be a personal view.

'They must tell you that you write something.'

'No. The idea for the book was mine. It was something that I wanted to do to satisfy my own curiosity.'

He was suspicious and uncomprehending. My claim that I was responsible for my own words struck him as insupportable arrogance. Words were public property. Islam's rejection of the personal, its insistence on sharing, its doctrine that society is always more important than the individual, have gone deep into Arab attitudes towards language. Had I been a poet, then God would have been responsible for my language (at first I mistook the enormous esteem in which writers are held in Arabia for a version of Romantic Individualism in which the artist is the supreme hero; in fact, the esteem is a species of religious feeling – the language of the poet is touched by divinity, it is a manifestation of Allah). As someone who was simply writing a book about Arabia, I wasn't responsible for my language; Society was, and Society was represented by the Ministry of Information. The logic was unanswerable. If I had tried to explain why the 'good books' on the table did not seem to me to be good books at all, I would have had to get into an impossibly complicated theological tangle. As it was, I said lamely that I wasn't trying to write a political book – a concessionary statement which was gratefully accepted by the official. We took coffee together with obvious relief on both our parts: we had come close to falling into the cultural divide which we were pretending did not separate us.

In the market, I felt I was a trespasser. It was all so deceptively close to home: the cracked shopping centre, the tall buildings, the Wimpy Bar, the photographic shops. The old man muttering over the Koran, and the arched backs of the praying figures gave the architecture a fierce ironical twist. I thought of the Gulf Arabs who were adrift in Earls Court, and of how lightly we were tiptoeing over the top of each other's worlds, travelling freely on passports of ignorance and misunderstanding. Old travellers grumpily complain that travel is now dead, that the world is a suburb. They are quite wrong. Lulled by familiar resemblances between all the unimportant things, they miss the brute difference between everything of importance. Abu Dhabi souk was as remote as an island in New Guinea – and its remoteness was accentuated rather than diminished by the banality of its appearance.

Major Barza was waiting in the Wimpy Bar.

'I trusted you,' he said. 'I believed that you would come.'

He made me feel like a girl on a blind date.

'I will take you to my room.'

He drove fast and dangerously out of the city. He had developed a singular technique for overtaking. He would accelerate furiously as he approached the rear of another vehicle; when he was within a few feet of it, he would slam on the brakes, hoot, slew the car into the centre of the road, and shoot past the other driver with his hand banging up and down on the horn.

'They do not know how to drive here,' he said. 'One must have courage.'

We passed a suburb of apartment blocks hatching out of chrysalides of scaffolding, and reached the barracks. Major Barza took me to the officers' mess.

'This,' he said, 'is like England, yes?'

It was. There were shelvesful of cups and shields, won at some desert Bisley. The dull click of cannoning billiard balls came from a further room, and a starchy Indian mess servant brought us cans of Pepsi-Cola on an engraved silver tray.

In the Jordanian army, Major Barza had held the rank of lieutenant-colonel. His pay had been £100 a month. Here in Abu Dhabi, with a drop in rank, he was earning £1100 a month. He laboriously inscribed the figures in dirhans in my notebook, and pointed to the difference between the rows of noughts. 'Jordan – Abu Dhabi.' It seemed a reasonable measure of the wild economics of Arabia, just as Major Barza's presence here a thousand miles away from home was a typical indication of how heavily the rich countries were dependent on their poor relations. There were few Abu Dhabians in the Abu Dhabi Defence Force. The officers came from north Arabia; most of the men were Yemenis and Omanis (a fact which struck me as curious, since the United Arab Emirates were then engaged in a border dispute with Oman). I asked Barza what discipline was like.

'Not like your British Army. It would not compare. I try to teach them to march in step . . . their legs do not listen.' He filled his pipe from a tin of Three Nuns tobacco which he patted affectionately before putting it back in his pocket. 'English,' he said. 'It is the best.'

One of his brother officers wandered into the mess and stood scratching his leg with a swagger cane. Barza ignored him. When he left, Barza said: 'That man is not my friend. He is an Egyptian.' There is a peculiar Arab expertise in twisting vowels to give a contemptuous inflection to unpopular words. 'Israeli' is universally pronounced 'Izrayee-ili', so that the word itself acquires a greasy, slithering nastiness; when Barza said 'Egyptian', he made the second syllable squirm in his mouth – 'Ijee-ye-ipshun'.

'We go now to my room. I show you how I live my life.'

I followed him through a maze of one-storey shacks. The smell of latrines was strong in the afternoon heat. Yemeni soldiers squatted in heaps outside their quarters. Slightly built, and short to the point of being dwarfish, they did not look as if they would make a very frightening army.

Barza's room was a bare concrete box. It contained a rumpled bed, an armchair which had fallen on hard times, a roll-top escritoire and a stereo system. A door at the back led to a shower and a cooking-stove. The entire apartment was about half the size of my hotel room. Its sorry, jail-like air was not much relieved by the pin-ups which Barza had stuck on the walls; although I felt a certain lift at the sight of them. Surely no one that addicted to black lace and suspenders could have designs on me.

He brought out a bottle of Scotch and two grubby tumblers. Then he fished under the bed and came up with an empty gin bottle.

'I drink all that this morning.'

'That's terrible – '

'Something did not work out with a friend. We have an argument. I feel sad, so I drink. I don't eat: I drink the bottle. I am not a happy man.'

He stared miserably into his whisky. 'Do you have a wife?'

'Once. I'm divorced.'

'I think you are a happy man.' He hunted through the mess of aerogram forms and shaving tackle on his desk, and gave me a dog-eared photograph. 'That is my wife. I do not love her, but I am not a selfish man, so . . .'

She was plump, with heavy jowls. Posing for the camera had made her adopt a bovine stare, with her head set deep in her shoulders. Beside her, a pretty little girl of eight or nine was as full of coquettish animation as her mother was stolid and weighty.

'My children I love. My wife . . . you would not love my wife.' He suddenly took fire from his own remark, and laughed delightedly. 'No, you would not love my wife!' He chinked his glass against mine. 'Cheers.'

'Cheers – '

'That,' Barza said authoritatively, 'is what they always say in England. Cheers.'

His face clouded again, and he held my eye with a long, melancholy stare.

'I want to ask of you a most personal question, which I do not know how to put.'

I tried to remember the ways in which nice girls were supposed to say no: none of them seemed appropriate to the occasion. Major Barza was working up courage to pop his question by knocking back half his tumbler of Scotch at a gulp. He tweaked the knees of his trousers and leaned forward.

'May I ask it of you, as a friend?'

'Yes, of course – ' I heard my voice come back to me in creaking falsetto.

'You think English girls find the moustache not sexy? Why

do German and English girls not like my moustache?' His expression was deadly serious. It demanded an answer of corresponding gravity. I said that I thought that the day of the moustache in England had come and gone with the Beatles and the cult of Che Guevara. As I talked, as solemnly as I could, about the declining fortunes of moustaches in general, I saw Barza passing his fingers protectively over his own as if what I said might be causing some injury to its pride.

'It is thought sexy no longer?'

'It's bound to come back into fashion soon.'

'I worry about it. It is something I do not understand. With English and German girls, I know there is something wrong – I think it is the moustache, but I do not have the courage to ask them.'

'I wouldn't let it prey on your mind.'

'Many officers of the British Army wear the moustache.' Barza looked mournfully into his whisky, reflecting on the injustices of the whirligig of fashion. 'In Arab countries it is thought sexy.'

He rummaged in a drawer and got out a photograph album. It was upholstered in cream-coloured plastic which had been got up to look like pigskin. A long time ago, the words *My Wedding* had been stamped on it in gold leaf; but nearly all the gold had flaked away, leaving dirty indentations where the letters should have been.

'You would like to see?'

'Please – '

He came and sat down on the bed behind my chair and turned the pages for me. The pictures were of girls, and they had the brutality of a certain genre of war photography. Flash-bulbs and over-exposure had burned out all but the harshest, most unsubtle of their colours. The succession of buttocks, thighs and breasts looked like the contents of a butcher's shop. One girl, her knees drawn up to her head to show her vulva to the camera, looked like a giant plucked chicken, trussed and ready for the oven. The major himself figured in many of the photographs. Even in these scenes of carnage he still looked sorrowful: his eyes told one story while his moustache and phallus told another.

'That one is Thai.' He flicked the page over. 'She is from

Morocco . . . Egyptian . . . Lebanese, from Beirut . . . that is an American girl . . .'

I found myself looking at the backgrounds of the pictures rather than the girls. In each of the rooms in which they had been taken, someone had made a futile and pathetic attempt to make it look like home. A poster of an Alpine scene had been tacked on the wall of one, with cows grazing under ice-cream mountains. In the photographs were other photographs, too small to make out, standing on bedside tables; I imagined stiffly posed family groups – fathers with rigid smiles, and younger brothers larking on the outskirts.

'Who *took* this one?' I asked, pointing to a picture of Barza and a girl in violent congress.

'Oh, another girl . . .' He turned back a few pages and pointed to the trussed chicken. 'That one, I think.'

I closed the book.

'You do not like them.'

'Not very much. They make me feel lonely and sad, more than anything else.'

'I am always sad and lonely. But I am old now. I am thirty-nine years old. I die soon. I drink, I smoke, I have sex, I am an old man. I die when I am forty-five.'

The photographs had made Barza's quarters even more oppressively solitary and displaced than they had seemed before. Across the sandy square of the barrack compound I could see some soldiers lethargically kicking a football about.

'It is easy for you,' Barza said. 'You live in England. In England, you have girls as friends. If you want to go to bed with them you just ask them because they are your friends. That is what they do in England. Here it is different. One must pay. They are not friends. I do not love them. But it is necessary to have sex. Without sex one becomes ill. I know what you are thinking when you look at the pictures.'

We gloomed over our drinks. Hoping to change the drift of the conversation, I told Major Barza about the Arabic lessons I had taken in London, and how inept and childish I felt in my struggles with his language.

'Who teaches you Arabic?'

'An Egyptian girl – '

'Never trust Egyptian girls,' Barza said. 'They are interested only in your money.'

I said that I wasn't complaining about the quality of the lessons; they had been excellent lessons and the fault lay entirely with me. Barza slowly shook his head from side to side. 'From an Egyptian girl, you will not learn *anything*. She cares only for what you pay. Look –' He sorted through a stack of old airmail letters. 'This is from an Egyptian girl. You can read Arabic? Look here!' There were greasy thumb marks all over it. It had obviously been read and handled many times. The rows of characters meant nothing to me. 'It says, "Please send me fifty dirhans." Fifty dirhans! You read! That is all she is interested in.'

'It's not very much.' Fifty dirhans is about seven pounds.

'No, *here* it is not much. Here it is nothing. But in Egypt fifty dirhans is a lot of money.' He took the letter back from me, screwed it into a ball and chucked it into a corner of the room. 'I don't reply. I never write to that girl again.'

'It really wouldn't hurt you to send her fifty dirhans. Perhaps she needs it, and you're the only friend she can ask who would be able to afford it.'

Barza angrily puffed a great cumulus cloud of Three Nuns tobacco smoke around himself. When his voice came out of this enveloping screen, it was woebegone. 'I want her to like me for myself, not for my money. You are my friend; don't you understand?'

I did. His raging solitude, with all its cruelty and unreason, was something that I had felt often enough for myself. Barza's room in the barracks was a place where one felt that only depression and loneliness could flourish. He had run out of the usual consolations of exile: for him there were no dreams of a new life of kennels or country cottages. He was down to the point where the one thing which he could take real pride in was his luxuriant moustache.

Later he took me to a happier bit of the barracks. He wanted me to meet his friend – a Jordanian sergeant. Country was more important than rank, and Barza preferred the company of Sergeant Qaweira who came from a village near Petra to that of the Egyptians and Sudanese who hung around the officers' mess. Qaweira shared a room with two other sergeants: one was playing a radio, one darning socks, and

Qaweira was writing an epic letter. Already he had covered twenty-four sheets of paper, and they lay all over his bed, each one a careful, tightly-spaced exercise in calligraphy. Qaweira himself had the slightly batty distraction of someone caught in the throes of literary composition. When Barza told him I was writing a book, he clasped my hand in both of his and said that writing books was one of the finest things that a man could do with his life. He himself had many books. He opened a cupboard to show me a heap of paperbacks and magazines. He loved reading and loved writing. I said that his letter was almost as long as a book.

'I cannot stop. I write *everything*.'

'Qaweira is a literary man,' said Barza. 'He reads too much. He will spoil his eyes. I ask him to come out with me for the evening, and he says no, he is reading or no, he is writing. I tell him that he will destroy his health.' He then spoke to Qaweira in Arabic.

'I say to Qaweira that Mr Jonathan is also a literary man, but he drinks with me.'

Qaweira cleared away the sheets of paper on his bed so that we could sit down.

'Is this a love letter?' I asked.

'It is to my wife. I love my wife.'

'Some men do not love their wives,' Barza said, and laughed.

Qaweira asked if he could look at my notebook which I had put on the floor at my feet. He measured it professionally, by length.

'You write many pages too. You write every day?'

'I try to.'

'Very good,' he said, weighing it in his hand.

'You will put Qaweira in your book?' asked Barza.

'I'm like Qaweira. Everything goes in.'

'You will say of Qaweira that he is a very handsome man, very tall, that he has a fine soul – he will be your . . . hero. What will you say of me? "Barza drinks too much." '

The bedu had been resettled. All over the emirate, the nomads who had been the companions of Thesiger, Philby and Bertram Thomas now lived on new breezeblock estates in the desert. I had asked to meet a bedu family, and it had been arranged for a ministry driver to take me out to Al Ain, an oasis town on the edge of the Empty Quarter. The car was late. Sitting in the hotel lobby at eight in the morning, I was conscious of the irony of the excursion. Through the window, I could see the Baluchis planting grass and their torn tents straining at their guyropes. If I wanted to meet nomads, they were a hundred yards away from where I was sitting. A Thesiger or a Lawrence, in search of people living lives of heroic privation, would, I was sure, have simply walked down the hotel drive and talked to the Baluchis.

I turned to the *Emirates News*. Its front page was dominated by a photograph of a Manhattan skyscraper. The headline read: NEW HOTELS GRACE THE SKYLINE OF NEW YORK. My skyline was similarly graced, and I was sure that this happy verb would prove useful in polite conversation. If I ever met an emir I could try it as an opening gambit: 'I see that a new office block graces your skyline.' The lobby filled with salesmen, some of whom I had seen before in Qatar and Bahrain. Their briefcases were fat with glossy promotional literature and duplicated technical specifications. Every one of them had designs on Sheikh Zayed's skyline.

The driver had brought a friend – a young man who sat in the back seat looking wan and disinclined to talk. The Lady wailed monotonously over the car stereo. She fitted in well enough with the landscape of wrecked cars and half-built houses. The highway to Al Ain gave a certain credibility to her recital of death and desertion. Drifting sand had buried sections of the tarmac, but the course of the road itself was clearly marked by a long, straight avenue of mangled trucks and automobiles. Burned-out, rusted, many of them torn inside out like socks, they made the desert look like some historic battleground, and they filled me with much the same depression as I'd felt a year before when I'd driven through the cemeteries along the Somme. It looked as if there wasn't a single patch of road on which someone had not been mutilated or killed.

Seeing me stare out of the car window, the driver said, 'Sheikh Zayed loves trees.'

I hadn't noticed the trees. No one else seemed to notice the wrecked vehicles. Our own car was travelling, at my insistence, at a hundred kilometres an hour – a speed which the driver clearly thought was annoyingly tame. Other drivers were leaving us standing, disappearing into the sand ahead with their horns moaning like cattle, totally indifferent to the long trail of accidents which staked out their route.

'All the trees are new. Sheikh Zayed orders them to be planted. Now the road is very green.'

I watched the sand blowing through the frames of the hulks on the roadside. We passed a village of squat concrete bungalows. A camel grazed in the shadow of the Range Rover which had superseded it.

The morbid singing on the radio was interrupted for a news bulletin. The young man in the back of the car leaned forward to listen. I caught little more than the words 'Israel', 'Lebanon', 'Palestine', and the gravity of the announcer's tone of voice. After the bulletin was over, I tried to find out what had happened. The driver and I traded our small vocabularies in English and Arabic, and it took some time to piece together the fact that Israeli troops had attacked Palestinian positions in southern Lebanon and had advanced six miles into Lebanese territory. In the middle of my dumb cross-questioning, I realized that the man in the back seat was sobbing.

'He is from Palestine,' the driver said. In Arabic the word is Fi'lastin'. Palestinians are Philistines.

The man's family were all safe on the Gulf; he was not crying because he feared for any of his immediate relatives in the fighting. Yet the war touched him with a degree of violence and distress which I found hard to understand. Coming from a nation without a territory of its own, he was able to take no consolation in distance. The invasion had taken place a thousand miles away, but they were meaningless miles to a people without a homeland. Like the Jews threatened by the Pale of Europe, the Palestinians have taken on the characteristics of a dispersed race. An injury in one part of the diaspora is instantly transmitted through the entire system like an electric current. Geography is no insulator. There are no spatial dimensions to Palestine any more. The man in the car was just as much 'in Palestine' as the El Fatah guerrillas on the Lebanese border, and he was feeling the hurt inflicted on his nation with a keenness that could probably be fully comprehended only by members of another diaspora. I was shocked by his pain. It occurred to me that there might be an element of propaganda in his tears. Later, though, I saw other Palestinians who were just as personally bruised as he was by the news. They might work in offices in Abu Dhabi or Dubai (or London, or New York), but the nation they belonged to was Palestine. There is no émigré status for citizens of a land which doesn't exist.

We dropped off the Palestinian on the outskirts of Al Ain. Hunch-shouldered under his flapping white robe, he plodded miserably down a sandy avenue of date palms and eucalyptus trees, bearing the mark of his people as clearly as any Wandering Jew.

At the Al Ain museum I met my interpreter for the morning. He was a Palestinian too, and was equally heavy with the day's news. When I found him in his office, he was dealing with a Jordanian television crew who had managed to lose an army tent while filming a serial about bedu life; they were in deep trouble. So, it turned out, was I. The letter I had brought from the Ministry of Information said nothing about meeting a bedu family; it stated that I was permitted to look at the museum and the historical sites.

'But I am not interested in either of these things. I want to meet a bedu family.'

'That is what is said in the letter.'

'Then my journey is wasted.'

I sulked extravagantly. Phone calls were made. More letters were written. I pleaded with the Palestinian who regarded me with a stare of cold, mourning gravity. I was made to feel that my presence in Al Ain was an irrelevance on this of all days. He never mentioned the events in the Lebanon, but they came between us like a wall of ice.

'I can visit the village without you.'

'That will not be allowed.'

'It was my only reason for coming to Al Ain.'

'I do what they write on the paper. They do not write on the paper that you go to a village. I take you to an archaeological site.'

'I don't want to *go* to an archaeological site.'

'That is what is on the paper.'

'Then the paper is wrong.'

'This is what the Ministry of Information say in Abu Dhabi.'

'Please – '

He relented, quite suddenly, with the same distant courtesy with which he had been obstructing me, and we drove out to the village with further news of the Israeli invasion coming in over the car radio.

'I am sorry,' I said foolishly.

He shrugged. 'For what? For the Balfour Declaration?'

The village looked deserted. Sand blew around a few acres of rectangular boxes. Sodium street-lights of a height that might have been appropriate for a metropolitan ring road made these houses look even squatter than they really were. The Palestinian knocked and called at several doors in turn and got no answer. At the fourth door, an old man said yes, we were welcome to come in and talk; he was only sorry that he could not offer us a meal as custom demanded.

I went through the door in the wall, and was met by a bewildering change of scale. The house I had looked at from outside had been no bigger than a slab-sided concrete garage. Inside, it was all air and space, sun and shade. We were standing in an open courtyard full of trees. A carpeted wooden platform stood on stilts in the centre, and a complete canopy of foliage allowed the sunlight to trickle through and fall in bright splashes on the blue and scarlet patterns of the carpets. The trees had created deep pools of shadow; beyond them lay lattices, windows and more doors. We were shown up on to the platform. It made a lovely outdoor drawing-room. Vines and acacias, set against white stucco, formed a kind of living wallpaper. It was as cool as any air-conditioned office, and the constant play of the light in the leaves gave it a brilliant under-water air, as if we'd stepped into an illuminated tropical aquarium.

The old man brought out a hammered brass goblet filled with incense and set it in the middle of the platform, then a box of Modern Facial Tissues for each visitor. In the shadows a group of veiled women stared at us through a trellis. The old man called to them to bring orange juice and coffee. A boy of eight or nine acted as go-between, carrying things from the women's quarters to the men's divan.

We settled down, cross-legged, to an elaborate diplomatic interchange of compliments. I said to the old man that I was proud to be a guest in his beautiful house; he said that a deep friendship existed between the English people and the Arabs and that he was proud to welcome an Englishman to his home. He was glad that I had called it beautiful, but he could take no credit for it; his house existed by the grace of Allah and the beneficence of Sheikh Zayed. Slowed by translation, we moved at a snail's pace through the ritual of introduction, using language as formal and figurative as that of the communion service. As we ascended higher and higher into the realm of metaphoric overstatement, the more we touched our hearts to indicate our sincerity. Anyone who has enjoyed the conceits of seventeenth-century English poetry will feel more or less at home in formal Arab conversation: it is an area where the truest statement is the most feigning, and all good structure lies in winding stairs. So we wound, upwards and further upwards, until there was nothing left to praise in each other's countries, their histories, rulers and the souls of their people. Having established perfect international amity between England and Abu Dhabi, we were at last free to actually talk. (The conduct of Middle Eastern political affairs follows exactly the same basic procedure, except that it usually works with insults rather than praise.)

The young men of the house – sons and nephews – were summoned to join us. They ranged themselves on either side of the old man, and spoke only when he indicated that they should. He was a mild, but wholly authoritative patriarch. His glassily pale skin was stretched around shrunken jaws, giving his face an odd resemblance to that of Joan Crawford; in old age, fragility and the habit of power had arrived at a perfect balance. Beside him his strapping juniors in their laundered gowns looked gross, too full of flesh, too callow in their manners, for this delicate world of carpets, incense and careful phrases. I hoped that the Palestinian interpreter was translating what I said into language that was fitting for the occasion.

'When I tell him what you say, I do not put it exactly as you say it; I say it in an Arab way, you understand?'

I thanked him. Inside the house, he had become more

helpful, and more patient with my own hesitant questions, than I could have hoped. Perhaps he was glad to be distracted from the news by the mechanical difficulties of translation; at any rate, I felt grateful and apologetic towards him.

Just six years ago, the old man said, counting the years off on his fingers, their life had been very different from this. They had spent the summers in a mud fort a few miles down the road – quarters they shared with many other families. Then, for the winter, they had driven their sheep and camels south to Muscat, where they lived in tents. It had not been like this at all: they had been very poor; there had been no television, no motor cars. Now – he praised Allah and Sheikh Zayed – they had this fine house; they had 'a.c.'; life was very good; they wanted for nothing. He remembered when Al Ain had been only an oasis in the desert: now it was a fine city, with a Hilton hotel. (It also had a hotel called the 'Rolex'; the names of famous wristwatches are potent symbols in this part of the world.)

In the shadow beyond where we were sitting, I saw a woman's face pressed against the mosquito mesh of a door-frame. When she saw me looking at her her face dissolved back into shadow.

Did he not, I asked, think that with the coming of the city there would come other, bad things? Could a close family like his own survive in a world of tall buildings and super-highways?

His family would always stay together, he said. His eldest son, who was not here today, was an engineer; he had trained in Beirut and London. When he was away, he had written home every week. When he returned, he was still obedient to his father. The power of the bedu family was very strong; I must understand that. The city was good, the motor car was good; how one used these things depended on the character of the people.

'But,' I said, 'you have a television – '

'Two!' he interrupted me. He had two televisions: one for the women and one for the men.

'On television you see what goes on in cities in the West, like London and New York. You see the violence in the streets, the break-up of families; aren't you frightened that something like that can take place here?'

Television, said the old man, was a great teacher. One learned much about distant countries from it. There was much to praise in England and America.

While the father talked, I looked at the young men to see if their faces showed any flicker of scepticism or dissent. I thought that I caught the occasional hint of a smile – but perhaps that was only because I expected to find one there. When I addressed questions to them, it was the old man who nearly always answered on their behalf, finishing sentences which they had begun. His youngest son wanted to be a doctor. I said that to be a doctor he might have to train far away: the boy said that he would come home to his family every Friday. *Every* Friday, said the old man; theirs was a close family, and it was unthinkable for anyone not to be home on Friday.

Sitting among the leaves, sipping coffee and smelling incense and eucalyptus, I tried to threaten them with another world of thuggery, isolation and family breakdown. The more I talked, the more unreal the words sounded in my own head. The men and the boys listened politely while I spoke of marooned wives in tower blocks and juvenile delinquency. Nothing like that, they assured me, would ever happen here. It was obvious that they thought I was telling improbable travellers' tales. Yet they had come much further than I had. Six years away from being desert nomads, they were talking confidently about careers in engineering and medicine; one member of the family had already worked in Europe and the Lebanon; they gave every sign of having adapted gracefully to a life in which Modern Tissues, the Range Rover, the twin-tub washing machine, two televisions, floral Thermos flasks, air travel and the local Hilton were taken perfectly for granted. The veiled women fluttered behind dark screens: I wondered how many more years it would take for them to emerge, and what the consequences would be then. At present their exclusion from this male domain of freedom, ambition amd machines was vital: the blithe way in which the bedu men were able to talk about the future depended on keeping the women in the past.

The old man said that he would like to show me his farm. He led me around the edge of the women's quarters – still inside the walled box – to a well. Beside the well, on a patch of earth just a few feet square, he was growing oranges, mangoes, dates, grapes and olives. They were clustered so thickly together that it was like standing in a shadowy greengrocer's shop, with fruits entwining with each other on their stalks.

I said that it seemed to me to be a miracle of intensive agriculture. He must be a very talented gardener to make so many things grow so richly in so small a space. He smiled self-deprecatingly, showing his two teeth, and said I must not compliment him: I should instead praise Allah and Sheikh Zayed.

As we drove away I looked back at the village through the car window. Its streets were just as empty, its dice-like houses just as small and squat, as they had seemed when we arrived. It gave away nothing to the world about what was going on inside. Its farms and leafy courtyards were well-kept secrets. The family I had met had gone through an extraordinary revolution. They had been suddenly exposed to the full blast of twentieth-century manners and things. Other people in other places had simply been smashed by the impact: half of Africa has been devastated by the gale damage. Here, though, it was different. The bedu had met the century head-on, but they had been able to deal with it in the family, protected by thick walls of breezeblock and cement. It seemed much the safest and most graceful way. On the road back to Abu Dhabi, passing the same villages which I had seen before as desolate places, I realized that I wasn't looking at soulless bungaloid estates, dormitory suburbs, the all-too-recognizable inter-national territory of the sleeping pill and the anti-depressant. These were decompression chambers. It didn't matter what they looked like from the outside; their bleakness was part of their point. Everything had been focused inwards: inside these boxes the unmanageable century had been reduced in scale so that it could be dealt with at a domestic pace in a domestic space. It *could* be coped with, if it was taken inch by inch.

We stopped for a meal at a Rest House. Hearing that I was English, a young man at a neighbouring table came over to talk. He was from a local bedu family, and in his own house he would probably have been as quiet and noncommittal as the sons and cousins I had met in the village. The Rest House was his club, full of men in their early twenties enjoying a long afternoon of unbuttoned talk away from their families. A year ago he had gone to Baton Rouge University in Louisiana on a government scholarship and had studied English there for four months. He had been frightened by America.

'I was not white. I was not black. I was between the two. They think I am from Puerto Rico. Some of my friends get thieved and beaten.'

He had made no close American friends. At Baton Rouge, the few Arabs had kept together in a beleaguered group, terrified of going out on to the streets after dark. ('I didn't went.') He had wanted to take his wife with him, but the government had not allowed that. Nor did he have much money to live on. His grant, of four hundred dollars a month, must have made him a pauper compared with many of his American fellow-students.

'When they know I am Arab, they think I must have aeroplane. But it is a treat for me to go to Howard Johnsons. I find this very hard to explain. But in USA, nobody knows anything about you if you are Arab. I come from Abu Dhabi. "Where is Abu Dhabi? We never heard of Abu Dhabi." In the school I go to here, I learn the Boston Tea Party, General Custer, The Gilded Age, The New Deal, Paul Revere . . . I learn the history of America, the history of Europe. I know of Queen Victoria and the Great War and Charlemagne. But in America, they know nothing of the Arabs. Israel, yes, they know *everything* about Israel. They want to live on the kibbutz and they read the book of Moshe Dayan. I wish that they know a little bit of my history; all they know is sand and camels and what they see in *Lawrence of Arabia*. So, you see, is hard to make friends.'

Yet he wanted to go back. America had scared and fascinated him. What he wanted most was to be able to take his wife.

'I tell her about Baton Rouge, but how can she understand? To her, I am talking of the moon. After I come back from America, I have seen all these things, but my wife has seen only the village. It is not easy for us. I want her to know what I know, or there is no talk between us.'

'Does she want to go to America?'

'Yes, she wants very much. She wants to see all these things that I see. She is intelligent, you know? Before I go to America, we talk about everything. But after America . . . is not so easy.'

He went back to rejoin his friends at their table. When I left, he waved. 'Have a good day,' he called, in a pure Louisiana accent.

Coming into Abu Dhabi we passed a huge desert lot filled with parked cars. Import labels fluttered on their windshields. Dust had dulled their livid colours of red, green, blue and gold; still clad in the protective film of grease in which they had left the production lines of Detroit and Tokyo, they stood like an army of raw recruits newly arrived on the battlefields. For every car which crashed, rusted to death, or just got junked out of pure boredom, there were ten more waiting to take its place, ready for a short, fast, dangerous life on the Abu Dhabi freeways. The average life-expectancy of a car in the Gulf is two years. Two years, in fact, is a key measure of time here. It is the period in which investments are reckoned to make a full return. Two years in the Gulf have roughly the same weight as a decade in Europe. They represent as much of the past as can comfortably be remembered; as much of the future as any sensible man would dare to anticipate. In two years, cars turn to scrap, contracts expire, investments come home, and the whole vastly accelerated cycle of life starts up again. This biennial whirligig gives an insistent edge of temporariness to everything. Only the trees are exempt. Toiling bands of Baluchi gardeners work day and night to make them grow faster, mollycoddling them with the latest in nutritious soil-substitutes, heaping their roots with fertilizers, spraying them continually with expensive desalinated water; but they rise at their own dogged, vegetable pace while all around them cars, buildings, people and projects boom and crash.

I sprawled uncomfortably on a barcalounger by the hotel pool. A fresh breeze was coming in off the Gulf. German businessmen and their wives were massaging suntan lotion into each other's brown backs. A crackly speaker relayed 'Tulips in Amsterdam' over the long line of charred bodies and undone bikini-straps, and a Pakistani waiter, who looked distinctly pale beside these ritually blackened Europeans, brought out trays of Heineken lager and Pepsi-Cola. I swam two feeble lengths of the bath and crawled out exhausted. I tried to concentrate on the heap of glossy propaganda which the Ministry of Information had given me; it was unalluring stuff and read like a brochure for a nondescript international hotel. Sitting on the premises of just such a hotel, I was well placed for scepticism.

Yet the analogy held. Abu Dhabi was like a hotel. Everyone was in transit. Some people, like myself and the travelling salesmen, were here for a few days, living out of suitcases and calling up sandwiches on room-service. Others, like Major Barza and Sergeant Qaweira, were out on two-year contracts; the Palestinians were here until that mythical day when Haifa and Tel Aviv would be liberated; the Baluchis, in their encampment on the sand, were passing through; even the bedu had been turned into guests of the state, *en route* from a nomadic past to a sketchy future.

Temporary people. Migrants. Passengers. I was myself beginning to get used to that hotel-life of casual acquaintance-ships and chance encounters where there are no long-term consequences and few responsibilities to the people whom one brushes past in one's journey. It's a life where one learns to become socially weightless, drifting among strangers like a spaceman in a bubble. In Abu Dhabi, I had lit on a society in which nearly everyone, to some degree, shared my traveller's uncommitment.

The state itself forced most residents of the place to remain travellers. It is immensely hard to become a citizen of any Gulf state; the privileges of citizenship (free housing, a personal stake in the oil revenues, membership of a health service which specializes in sending people on summer holidays abroad) are too generous to be squandered on Baluchis, too politically dangerous to be granted to Palestinians. Barely a quarter of the number of people who live in Abu Dhabi are natives of the region. Of these, half are women, sequestered behind lattices and veils. So for every eight people whom one sees on the street or working at a job, only one is a full citizen, and he is engaged on a journey of his own which turns him into just as long-distance a traveller as my fellow-guests in the Khalidia Palace Hotel.

Who seriously cares about the future of a hotel? One wants

the service to hold up for the length of one's own stay; and if it gets intolerable one checks out and moves on. Guests continually bump into each other and talk at the bar in a friendly enough fashion; but if the man you drank with last night turns out to be dead this morning, it is more a matter of curiosity than an occasion for grief. Indifference and egotism are embedded in the character of the chronic traveller; sitting at his train window watching the world roll by, fussing over his own creature comforts, his eye is engaged by the passing cavalcade of strangers' lives, but his heart is not seriously stirred by them. I had plenty of reason to feel this on my own account: it was unnerving to have arrived in a state where a very large proportion of the population were travelling almost as lightly as I was myself.

No wonder that Sheikh Zayed was obsessed by trees. No wonder, either, that the idea of the 'Indivisible Arab Nation', united in Islam, was so powerful and necessary a touchstone. No wonder that the tight, authoritarian structure of the bedu family – with all its suffocating consequences for Arab women – was held so sacrosanct. Without these things, Abu Dhabi might reasonably be expected to turn into the biggest, most indifferent Intercontinental hotel in the world.

Yet the Arabs here – Palestinians and Jordanians, as well as people from the Gulf – were much more seasoned travellers than me or the Germans who lounged round the hotel pool. All the traditions of the bedu had been evolved as means of regulating a society composed of wanderers and migrants. More than any other people in the world, the nomadic tribes of Arabia had equipped themselves for life spent continuously on the move, holding the family together and dealing easily and amicably with strangers. Their social code, with its ritual language and elaborate formalities, was a highly developed instrument for negotiating a passage through other peoples' territories. Their family structure, with its rigid roles and divisions, had been designed to withstand the stress of constant motion and the consequent threat of dissolution. In a sense, the bedu had been better prepared for a world of cars and skyscrapers and jet travel than anyone in Europe or the United States. Modern Abu Dhabi, with its migrant tribes of exiles, had not made the skills of the desert nomad redundant; rather, it was testing and straining them in a way that they had never needed to be so fully exercised before.

At the hotel desk I asked the clerk if he could recommend a restaurant in the city which served wine with meals. I wanted to take Major Barza and Sergeant Qaweira out to dinner.

'*Wine?*' The Pakistani stared at me for a moment. 'You want Yvonne's, I think.'

'Do I need to book in advance?'

Another curious glance. 'No need to book.'

When Barza and Qaweira arrived in the lobby I announced that I was taking them to Yvonne's. Barza, all in black, looking like Hamlet gone to seed, visibly brightened.

'I am worried that you spend too much money.'

Qaweira was splendid in a predominantly mustard-coloured check suit and orange tie. His hair was plastered round his temples. He raised each foot in turn to shake the sand off his black-and-white striped kid shoes. He, though, seemed rather less enthusiastic at the mention of Yvonne's.

'It is very expensive. I shall pay for you. I shall pay for everyone,' said Barza.

'It's my night,' I said, sounding, I hoped, more confident than I felt. I had put by £30 for the evening, and was trying to calculate whether I could afford to double it.

'We are friends. With friends, money is nothing. Qaweira asks me to tell you that he wants you to go to his village when you are in Jordan. They will make a feast for you. They will kill sheep, goats . . .'

'Thank you very much,' I said to Qaweira, who was standing on one leg, rubbing at a spot on the heel of his left shoe with a moistened finger. He beamed and wobbled.

'Qaweira will drive us,' said Barza, putting an arm round my shoulder. The hotel clerk watched our exit through the glass doors with the sniggering scepticism to which the Pakistani face lends itself with irritating facility. *Heh-heh-heh.* He gloated happily behind his telephone.

Yvonne's was a neon-lit barn on the Corniche. Its large parking-lot was occupied by two Range Rovers. The doorman asked us to pay an entrance fee of £7 a head, but Barza haggled with him in Arabic and he let us through free.

'I tell him we look first. If we like, we pay. If we don't like, we go. It is for you to choose.'

It was not much to my liking. The phrase 'a restaurant which serves wine' was clearly a well-known Abu Dhabi euphemism. The whores were ranged round a horseshoe bar like so many inflated rubber dolls. They were uniformly enormous, caked in kohl and rouge, and their sloppy breasts, laid out as if separately on sale on the bar counter, reminded me of jellyfish. At our entrance they switched on expressions of mechanical hunger and rippled their pectorals.

A group of men in robes and head-dresses sat at a table playing cards over a bottle of whisky. Not altogether surprisingly, they were studiedly ignoring the freak show which was going on over their heads. Barza made a swift circle round the horseshoe, came back, and started on a minutely detailed inspection of the goods on show.

Poor Qaweira was staring miserably at his beautiful shoes. 'I tell you before, I love my wife. I look at girls only. I not pay. I love my wife.' I felt that way too. Barza, making a brief pause in his shopping expedition, came over to us.

'It is not good to leave direct,' he said and winked. 'We stay fifteen minutes. That is polite.'

I suspected that the proprietor of this place was supplied with hostesses by some other crook who ran a hospital for mental defectives. The glandular size of the girls with their empty, protuberant faces made them seem barely human. They looked as if they were unconscious of where they were or what they were doing. I wondered how on earth they had arrived here. Were they shipped in crates? In shrouds? In strait-jackets? They appeared quite incapable of any volition of their own. The effort of making their rubbery flesh twitch on the bar counter totally absorbed whatever vestigial mental powers that they possessed. Barza pranced and twirled among them, a jack-in-the-box man, the waxed ends of his moustache glinting.

Qaweira and I left. 'I'm sorry,' I said to the doorman. 'I'm afraid I made a mistake.'

Qaweira, leaning against the bonnet of the car and gazing into the black space of the Gulf, said: 'My wife is in Petra.'

'Do you think we'll ever see Barza again tonight?'

'For Barza it is different. He does not love his wife.'

After twenty minutes, Barza came out, vastly pleased with himself. He was counting his conquests off on his fingers.

'I talk to three Egyptians, two Syrians and one girl from the Lebanon.'

'Did you make any dates?'

'They all want me.' He touched his moustache complicitly as if it was his ally in a joint campaign. 'But I will not buy them a drink. They say "Please, I come with you, I spend night with you, but first you buy me drink." ' He laughed. 'The drinks was too expensive.'

We drove back to the hotel. 'It is not good to go without sex,' Barza said gravely. 'You go ill.

'Here it is not like London or New York. I have been to those places. I know. Here it is different. You go to the beach, you see girls. You go to restaurant, you see girls. Everywhere, you see girls. You see, see, see. You see, but you cannot have. No chance.'

'So you pay – '

'One night only. Here and there.'

'Major Barza has many, many girls,' said Qaweira. Barza preened himself on the compliment.

'One girl there – an Egyptian – she is surprised. "You speak *Arabic*?" She thinks I am a Pakistani!' He laughed delightedly. 'I would not buy her a drink for one dirhan.'

We ate in the hotel dining-room, where we were served by a pretty girl from Alexandria. Barza spent much of the meal addressing remarks in rapid Arabic in the direction of her navel. She took this stream of rather-too-well-practised intimacies with surprising good humour, but declined when Barza suggested that she might like to stroke his moustache.

'I thought you didn't like Egyptian girls,' I said.

'That,' said Barza, laying his hand on my wrist, 'is my great trouble. You see, I like *all* the girls. Black, white, yellow, brown . . . no matter. I think that is why I die soon. For liking the girls. You see, I am not a happy man.'

Towards evening, for the lucky ones, Abu Dhabi turns into a dizzy floating opera. When the fairy-lights are switched on in the skeletons of the half-built office blocks and hotels and the whole place begins to wink in the sea like the reflection of a giant, gaudy carousel, one can feel the tide of feverish elation rising in the city. The surrounding desert darkens and disappears. The floodlit gardens on the roundabouts appear to hang improbably in space. Solitary Indians squat under the streetlamps reading engineering textbooks. On vacant lots, in the neglected shadows of brand-new skyscrapers, one stumbles on little impromptu markets: a maze of trestle tables lit by swinging Tilley lamps on sticks. It is a weird, peepshow world. Stacks of imported vegetables and fruits gleam blue and silver in the guttering light. One stall – which looked at a distance as if it was selling a tumbling heap of mercury – turned out to consist of a vast quantity of miniature plastic oryxes. Close-to, they were hideous. Their tiny, ill-made heads and legs stuck out at all angles; their bodies were covered with carelessly glued-on pelts of polystyrene fur.

The stall's Indian proprietor reached into this pile of quicksilver carnage and produced an oryx for me.

'It is very pretty. Very good for girls.'

It was so spectacularly repulsive that I nearly bought it. I was deterred, though, when I heard the price.

'It is traditional handicraft,' the Indian said, holding it up to his Tilley lamp and stroking its horrible fur to produce an unearthly viridian halo. 'You want elephants? Giraffes? I have gazelles – '

I stopped for a drink at a hotel on the Corniche. The bar was empty except for an Englishman who had a slightly shaky hold on his glass of vodka-tonic. He was sitting by a telephone, and every few seconds his eyes would flip round nervously to the dial. Hearing me ask for a lager in English, he introduced himself.

'Morgan,' he said. His hand felt charged with static. 'Awfully glad of a chance to talk, actually.' He was all tremor and glitter, like someone who has just sniffed a heavy charge of cocaine. He sneaked an anxious look at the telephone, set to cracking his knuckles, and told me his story in a frantic rattle of parentheses.

He had come out to Abu Dhabi with his partner six weeks ago to set up an import-export agency dealing in engineering tools and plant. They had sunk all their capital into the idea, and fallen on Abu Dhabi like a pair of Dick Whittingtons in search of their fortunes. Morgan had got what he called an 'in' with a sheikh. In the import-export business, apparently, one needs an in with a sheikh for the thing to have any hope of success. Three weeks ago, the partner had returned to London leaving Morgan in the hotel bar waiting to conclude the deal.

He gestured at the tacky, empty tables with their view of the flood-barrier on the Corniche. 'For three weeks this place has been my office. I spend every day just sitting here waiting for the phone to ring. Sometimes it does, and I go to see my sheikh. Sometimes it doesn't, and I think we're both going to land up on National Assistance, trailing along at the end of the dole queue every Friday morning. It costs me the best part of a hundred pounds a day just to sit here. I spend much of the day doing sums. I add the vodka-tonics together and work out whether I can afford to slip in a chicken sandwich . . .'

He talked about the agency, conjuring hundreds of thousands of pounds from thin air. As he spoke, machines were crated in the English midlands; forklift trucks took them to container lorries; ships and planes carried them half-way around the world to construction sites in the desert; and this trundling progress set up a whirlwind of paper – dockets, inventories, contracts, bills of lading, customs stickers, petro-dollars. In the talk, Morgan and his partner were rich men, zig-zagging the globe in their executive jets, masterminding this great caravan of steel as it wound its way from England to the Gulf. Then he remembered.

Today his sheikh had had his final meeting with his financial advisers. A decision should have been made. Morgan had expected a call at lunchtime; it hadn't come. Would I like another lager? He was going to stick to plain tonic.

Standing at the bar, he looked more like Eeyore than Dick Whittington, his nervous shoulders gathering themselves for disappointment.

It was, on the whole, a good thing, I thought, that factoriesful of men in Solihull and Wolverhampton were almost certainly unaware of how much their lives were dependent on Morgan. They were clocking on and off their shifts without giving a moment's thought to this man in a nondescript bar keeping his eye on the telephone with a mixture of dread and hope. When it rang, it might mean jobs, overtime, new washing machines, mortgages: or it might, just as easily, bring a small, sad addition to the unemployment statistics.

'Please talk about yourself,' Morgan said. It looked as if the muscles controlling his pupils were engaged in a tug-of-war against the magnetic pull of the image of the telephone. They kept on sliding a few millimetres to the side and jerking back to centre again.

I explained why I was in Abu Dhabi.

'That sounds *awfully* interesting,' Morgan said, hammering the line to give it a rather wan ring of conviction.

The telephone rang. Everything on Morgan's face went rigid. I watched him counting the rings. On the fifth peal, he picked it up. The conversation lasted for the best part of twenty minutes, during the course of which I bought him another vodka-tonic and placed it on the shelf by the phone. He didn't touch it. When he finished speaking he came back to the table wearing an expression of vastly calculated impassivity.

'It's on,' he said. Pure joy. Morgan was not a man to dance a jig in a deserted bar, but he was as near to dancing as anyone with both feet on the floor can reasonably come. When I got up to go, one delirious drink later, I left the happiest man in Abu Dhabi. He was so happy that I suspect that the odd housewife or machine-tool finisher in Solihull may well have been seized by a passing, inexplicable surge of elation at about five o'clock (Greenwich Mean Time) on 15 March 1978.

Coasting along on the tide of Morgan's high spirits, I drifted into an evening of grand opera. For a few hours I was admitted into the giddy overworld of the very rich. Before coming out to the Gulf, I had vaguely supposed that every 'oil state' swarmed with millionaires, and I had assumed that whatever social life I found there would have the flash and bravado of a new Gilded Age. It hadn't been so. The few millionaires I had met had exuded a remarkable measure of puritanical restraint in the way in which they betrayed their wealth; and most of the people I had seen and talked to had been no more than comfortably off by European standards – many of them, indeed, had been miserably poor by any standards except, perhaps, those of Bangladesh and Baluchistan. My first impressions of life in the oil states had not been of the lavish scale of their wealth but of their characteristic tendency towards the seedy, the gimcrack and the poverty-stricken.

That night, though, I saw the city from another angle. I took the elevator up to the penthouse flat of Zaki Nusseibeh, the special adviser to the Emir. It was an eyrie, perched high in the blue over Abu Dhabi, with books on the walls and a tiger skin on the floor. From the window, the surrounding buildings tapered downwards to the street, and the Gulf twinkled with ships' lights. It was West Side, Manhattan, but with more innocence and sparkle than one ever finds in modern New York. In the 1890s, possibly, before the skyscraper-city fell from grace, one might have caught the same heady grandeur in a view from an apartment overlooking Central Park.

Nusseibeh himself was a Palestinian with the rapid, allusive style of a New York intellectual, primed on Galbraith, McLuhan, Rachel Carson, Hannah Arendt. His room was high enough up from the street to float in that international airspace where the books one has read count for more than the climate outside the window or the language of the people down below.

'There are two things you have to understand about this city. One: don't get taken in by the vertical architecture. The real city is lateral. It's the hardest thing for a visitor, to see that Abu Dhabi is really a bedu town. You look at the way people visit each other, who they marry – the way they actually use the buildings. The secret infrastructure of this place is pure bedu. And you'll never really see it, because it's something that no one but an Arab can. The best you can do is to know that it's there. Everything you see here is a kind of optical illusion – it makes you see one kind of society while what you're looking at is really quite another. It's much, much more foreign than it looks.

'The second thing is this fantastic adaptability that the bedu have. They take change with such cool and self-possession. I'm getting used now to my own surprise at discovering that someone's whole view of the world has undergone a quiet revolution in a matter of just a year or two.

'Like, I'll give you an example. There's an old man in the Emir's household, a retainer. He's not educated. He was brought up in the desert. His whole life has been spent in knowing about things like camels and falcons, you know?

'You remember the first moonshot in – what was it . . .'sixty-nine? We were in Spain, and this old man came up to me – he'd seen the television pictures, and he was in a state of pure rage. He said the entire thing was a hoax, a put-on. It was a piece of American propaganda. They were just showing pictures of some desert and telling people it was the moon. Because it was impossible for a man to go to the moon. That was in the Koran. Allah would not have allowed such a thing. Why, he asked me, were so many people believing in this terrible sacrilegious lie that the Americans were putting about?

'Then, last year, when they did the Mars probe . . . The same old guy . . . We were talking, and he said, "Look, supposing they do find traces of oxygen in the rocks they bring back, do you think that means that there really is life on Mars?"

'Don't you find that something? How can you make predictions about a people who can move as fast as that? The whole inside of his head had changed, but he was still just the old family retainer . . . a typical bedu. And this was an old man. What do you think the young men will be like? – the ones who've already grown up with moonshots and jet travel? I think this power of accommodation is something that no one understands yet; and I think that people who catch even a glimmer of it tend to be frightened by it.'

Nusseibeh invited me to hitch a lift on his evening. He had nothing special to do that night: there were a few parties that he had to drop in on, a cousin he must visit . . . I was hesitant. Having been invited to none of these parties, would I not stick out as a *tifl*, an intruder? I had no need to worry, Nusseibeh said. These were parties that *everyone* went to.

It was much like being a pawn in a game of three-dimensional chess. Horizontal moves were made in Nusseibeh's Porsche, vertical ones in elevators whose doors kept on opening on the wrong party. For a few hours, the whole city seemed to consist exclusively of Indian waiters carrying silver trays of orange juice and cocktails, of ball-gowns, beefy American oilmen, and a deafening linguistic salad of Arabic, German, French,

English and Italian. As the lift-doors slid open on each identical *tableau vivant*, Nusseibeh, making a grave salute to the nearest braying group, would say, 'I think this is not the one we want', and press the button for another floor, another party.

There were villas at the end of gravel drives. Between sky-scrapers, Palladian country houses nestled in unlikely floodlit gardens, looking as if they had been uprooted some time earlier that day from manorial parks in Wiltshire, Kent, Hertfordshire or Somerset. There were ranch-style bungalows from California, pint-size Loire châteaux, alpine chalets on stilts to keep them proud of some freak Abu Dhabi snowdrift. I must have passed these places by day and never noticed them; in the sun perhaps they merged imperceptibly into the general tacky sprawl of breezeblock, lath and tarpaper which forms the lowlands of Abu Dhabi. At night though, with their façades brilliantly picked out by powerful spotlamps planted in the imported earth of their front gardens, they had the exaggerated reality of scenery in an old-fashioned theatrical production. I remembered going to *Chu-Chin-Chow* in Southport when I was seven: no trees that I'd ever seen before had been as intricately green as those painted cardboard flats, no sea so vividly, enticingly watery, no room so solidly inhabitable. I had sat with my grandmother in the back of the stalls, aching to be admitted to that enchanted social world of costume, rouge and cardboard, because it was immeasurably more real than the grindingly artificial place that my family and I lived in outside the theatre. In Zaki Nusseibeh's car, racing through avenues of trees which spread over us in heroic defiance of the climate, looking out at these dazzling architectural conjuring tricks, I felt something of the same lift, the same tug of the heart. There is nothing quite so marvellous as really expensive, really cunning artifice.

'This,' said Nusseibeh, a shade unnecessarily, 'is the rich quarter of town.'

Everyone went to the parties, Nusseibeh had said. In court life, anyone who isn't somebody is nobody – and the parties were all part of Sheikh Zayed's court. He wasn't to be seen, but his presence was imprinted on every noisy room. In some of the rooms his framed gold image hung, winking, on a wall; in others his person was distributed and extended through his apparently uncountable retinue of courtiers. The Commander of the Personal Bodyguard was there. The Advisers – on economics, agriculture, aviation, defence, sewage, telecommunications, trees – were there. The Official Historian was there. So were the Sheikh's Ministers – tidy men in brown silk robes trimmed with gold leaf at their hems, who moved from group to group sipping abstemiously from cut-glass goblets of orange squash, while their American guests rattled the ice in their Bourbon and drained their glasses at a gulp.

In one room I found an English banker and his wife, at bay in an inconspicuous corner. They had recently come to the Gulf and were talking about their newly rented house on the Corniche.

'The trouble is,' said the wife, 'we got it from a Lebanese, complete with furniture.'

'All glass,' said the husband. 'The tables are glass. The chairs are glass. There's a glass sofa, and the bed looks like some sort of aquarium. It's not really our thing at all, all this glass. Regency's more our thing, isn't it, dear?'

'But I'm afraid that Regency just wouldn't *do* in Abu Dhabi,' the wife said plaintively, with Pimlico all too clearly in her eyes.

'No,' I said. 'Abu Dhabi's definitely more Jacobean.'

'Glass,' said the husband, 'might be all right for a couple without children, but it definitely does not go with a family. One cannot –' and I saw him making a cautiously firm banker's point at a board meeting – 'have glass furniture and children.'

In another room a very thin man with a gentle, bemused face showed a batik picture he had just bought. He held it up against the wall and looked anxiously out from beside it.

'You do not like it. I know you do not like it. When I bought it, I knew no one would like it. Tell the truth, please. You *hate* it, don't you?'

With his fragile stoop and soft voice he looked like an obscure, passionate scholar of some very dead language. He was in fact an Arab economist on whose decisions smaller and poorer countries daily waited. He decided who should get aid from the oil states and who should be frozen out of the enchanted financial circle. But he was terribly, comically apprehensive about his batik picture.

'Please tell me. Honestly. I want your honest opinion. You think it is awful.

'Perhaps it would be better on another wall, no? Yes? Shall I try it on the other wall?

'It is by a woman artist from Kuwait. I think she is very talented. But perhaps . . . I don't know. Do you see *anything* in it?

'I cannot tell you how much I paid for it. You will laugh at me.'

In another room, much later, after more cocktails had come and gone than now seems decent to remember, an Indian butler wheeled on a series of silver trolleys laden with food. Some rooms, some houses ago, all women had disappeared. By midnight we were down to a dinner party of perhaps twenty men, with almost as many nationalities between us as there were guests, slumped in armchairs and sprawled on cushions.

'I have been going to London for twenty years,' said a Kuwaiti. 'I think something very bad has happened in the last five years or so.'

'The Arabs moved in,' suggested an American, honking over his bowl of salad.

'Once it was the friendliest city in the world. Now it is spoiled. It is rude and dirty. I do not know why this happens. You have lost something very precious. A change, I think, has come over the people – '

'Your success and our failure, perhaps – ' I said.

'They have lost their spirit. They have become *thugs*, like people in New York. It is very sad. I loved London once. It is very hard to love it now.'

Streaming through Abu Dhabi in the small hours, it was easy to see what the Kuwaiti meant. With its floodlit façades and illuminated skeletons of wonders yet to come, the city had all the vigour and likeability of an experimental society; it was a maze of more or less untainted social possibility. Two hundred years ago, the townships of New England must have had the same freshness – hopeful theocracies, ideal cities. Never in history had so much money, so much technical expertise, or so powerful a social and religious vision been at anyone's disposal to build a civilization from scratch as here and now in the Gulf. Compared to Sheikh Zayed, the Pilgrim Fathers were ill-equipped paupers. Only the great families of the Italian Renaissance could seriously bear comparison with the Gulf emirs.

Yet no Medici would ever have committed Abu Dhabi. Trees were growing where no trees logically could; buildings and frames of buildings disappeared upwards into the sky; the whole place was bursting at its unfinished seams with pride and hopefulness. At the same time it exuded a quite un-Italian, un-American anxiety. Its taste, for so rich and possible a place, was oddly tremulous. All its energy seemed to be in danger of being sapped by that sense that everything and everybody were only temporarily here.

We got it from a Lebanese, complete with furniture.
Please tell me. I want your honest opinion. You think it is awful.
Before, was just sand, tents, few houses, little market . . .
I am not a happy man.
Perhaps it would be better on another wall?

I stayed on walking in the city until dawn. In the empty concrete souk I came across a Baluchi with what looked like an antique blunderbuss slung over his shoulder. Perhaps he was out hunting for plastic oryxes; at any rate, he did not seem much interested in me. The moon was trapped in the steel frame of a skyscraper-to-be. It had no walls or windows, but its staircases had been already built – zig-zagging upwards between imaginary floors. On the sand under the stairs there were half a dozen badly wrapped parcels – sleeping men with not much more than a blanket to their name. Baluchi labourers, in this richest of all the world's cities, earned, so I was told, about £100 a month, and most of these meagre wages were being sent back to their families in Baluchistan. Women locked in their quarters . . . Baluchis under the stairs . . . these were the people who were really keeping the opera afloat. Plato's ideal city-state had its base in a slave-class, and so did Abu Dhabi.

At four in the morning, the recorded voices of the muezzins were switched on in the minarets. In wailing, unsynchronized stereophony, they multiplied over the city, loudspeakers calling to loudspeakers in an unearthly electronic concert. It was still an hour before sunrise, but cars were already beginning to show on the Corniche and the first of the Baluchis were shaking sand out of their blankets. I was dog-tired. The ultramarine landscape of towers and scaffolding, loud with mechanical muezzins, seemed like the sort of place which one should only visit in dreams.

By the Dawn and the Ten Nights; by that which is dual and that which is single; by the night when it comes!

Have you not heard how Allah dealt with Aad? With the people of the many-columned city of Iram, whose like has never been built in the whole land?

5

Quattrocento

The road to Dubai is long, straight, dusty, littered with wrecked cars and punctuated only by the odd windswept gas station. There are no villages, no oases, and the Gulf is hidden behind sand-dunes which look as if they are suffering from some sort of desert scurf or mange. It is the kind of road on which car crashes look like philanthropic gestures; they at any rate do something to provide a momentary relief in that monotony of sand and rusted oil drums. Skeetering Cola cans, blowing across the highway, make an ersatz wildlife; half-close your eyes, and you can imagine them as rabbits, surprised in a hedgerow on an English lane. On second thoughts, don't: they are just Cola cans, tumbling in the wind across the Arabian desert, their paint stripped, sandblasted down to bare metal. It is a road which instantly explains the Arab passion for fitting out the insides of cars like shrines, boudoirs and fun-palaces. There must, I suppose, be some stretches of desert which really do correspond to that romantic image of a kaleidoscope of changing moods and colours, a heroic emptiness in which man stretches his limbs, gazes on infinity, and finds himself. Most desert, though, is not like that at all. It is simply boring – hundreds and hundreds of miles of it, stretching away like a flat Sunday afternoon. The interior of the poorest taxi, with its dancing gew-gaws, Polaroid pictures and quantities of nylon fur, is immeasurably more interesting than the desert outside. The desert is the only conceivable place on earth where the camel could have earned itself a place in human affections:

no animal is more stolid, stupid and utterly unresponsive, but in the desert the face of a camel takes on an expression of astonishing animation in contrast to its surroundings.

Fortunately I was sharing the taxi with a Jordanian television journalist whom I had met in the hotel bar, and we contrived to blot out the desert with talk. He was another member of the northern Arabian diaspora: educated at an English boarding school, he was based in London and spent half the year making films in the Middle East. He had just come back from filming a forty-day hunting trip in Pakistan with Sheikh Zayed and his retinue.

'In the city, you would never guess the real bedu simplicity of the man. There, you meet the head of state, always closeted with his ministers in offices . . . a natural politician, perfectly urbane. On this trip, though, he is another man altogether. For six weeks we live on Houbara Bustard – they cook it in charcoal in scoops in the sand. He flies his hawks. In the evening, he sits in the circle round the fire, talking with people you would think were just servants. But they are his real friends, these bedu who have been with his family for years; round the fire, there is no sense of difference between the Emir and his men. It was like a club in which everybody was a full member. Everyone was living very rough in tents: Sheikh Zayed was absolutely at home. It was not a pose. It wasn't like one of President Carter's fishing trips. This was how he liked to live. I think, somehow, that explains a lot about Abu Dhabi.'

We were still within the Emir's domain. A tree or two would have made no end of difference to that blight of useless dust and shale. An angry Tanzanian engineer had assured me that the penalty for killing a Baluchi on the roads was less than that for knocking down a tree. ('They don't have human rights in this country. No one will say this. They don't have fucking human rights. Will you say this in your book?') Looking out of the car window, I saw a momentary glimmer of reason in this peculiar hierarchy of justice. In a green country it is almost impossible to communicate the extraordinary price which is put on vegetation in the desert: a single splash of dusty foliage really is a treasure, extravagantly loved, meticulously cared for. Here, though, there wasn't even an anaemic blade of grass in sight.

'We've got a house in Surrey,' said the Jordanian, following my gaze.

In Surrey, spring must have started. Beech trees, daffodils, rhododendron glades ... we were a day or two away from the opening of the trout season, and I thought of pussy-willows overhanging chalk-stream pools. Until that moment I had not felt any serious twinge of homesickness on my trip; suddenly I found myself longing for that imaginary, expatriate's England which I had found half-touching, half-comic when I had glimpsed it in the British Clubs or the dreaming conversations of Doug and Dave in Qatar. In six weeks, I'd fallen too for that jigsaw-puzzle picture of hollyhocks, sweet peas and cottage roses, with all its attendant oak beams, ale-from-the-wood and labrador dogs with short breath and lolling tongues. The whole silly, bogus image made my eyeballs prickle. I wondered what image of Arabia suddenly tugged at the heartstrings of Arabs in London, and decided that one thing at least was certain: it was not a picture of this bit of desert.

'Last year,' the Jordanian said, 'we went to Crete on a package holiday – my wife and I and our baby daughter. We flew from Gatwick, and, you know, there were long delays then. We were a whole day in the airport before our flight took off. Everyone on the package made friends, and because we had our baby with us we were a kind of focus of attention, almost a mascot, you know? All these old ladies cooed over her ... it was fantastically warm and friendly. And, of course, because people had got to know each other during this long wait, they started to ask questions. Our new friends were very interested in our accents. "What are you – French?" they said. Someone – a big sophisticate – decided we were Italian. "Actually," I said, "I'm a Jordanian Arab" ...

'You, perhaps, can mask the feelings on your face: you can go on smiling when really you are shocked. But these people were not like that. They were very straight, quite simple – package tourists. Their faces couldn't conceal what they felt. When I said the word "Arab" they just gaped, and you watched their faces freeze. You know, they didn't speak to us again once. There we were ... on the same plane ... staying at the same hotel ... and after I had said "Arab", not one word. Not a single word. It hurt my wife, but I really found it funny, that. It was too impersonal to cause proper hurt. When we came back from our holiday, our friends asked us how it had been. I said it had been . . . quiet – a quiet holiday, you know?'

He laughed – a much more generous laugh than I would have been able to manage if I'd had the same story to tell.

'I think there is nowhere in the world that you could go and get quite the same response to the word "English", is there? Not even in Africa. And yet England's my home. I never feel disliked for myself there. "Arab" is a word that people learn to hate when they hear it on the television; they never connect it personally with you. At Gatwick, I made the connection, and people just couldn't take it. "Arab" either means "terrorist" or it means "millionaire"; it means you are not a human being.' He beamed at me. 'By the way, that suitcase I put in the back – there is a bomb in it.'

The desert petered out into a no-man's-land of barbed wire, Baluchi tents and idle concrete mixers. Some fine filigree work on the skyline turned out to be Dubai's new port and dry dock. Soon it was to be the biggest, most expensive, most modern thing of its kind in – I cannot remember whether it was in the Gulf or in the world, for I was rapidly losing any sense of distinction between the two terms. At present, though, it was just a pretty, distant winter forest of unfleshed girders, caught in a low sun, their shadows stretching out across the sand. We passed the Dubai Hilton. It looked to me like a Hilton, but it too was marked by one of those singular honours which count for so much and seem – to an outsider – so numbingly unimportant. At that particular moment it was The Tallest Building In The Gulf, and Sheikh Rashid of Dubai was apparently doting on it like a favourite child. Next week or next month the Dubai Hilton would probably be topped by one of the rising frames in Abu Dhabi; but on that afternoon it was basking in evanescent glory. Looking at its smug, slab-sided cliffs of glass and concrete, I hoped that it would not be allowed to enjoy its pre-eminence for too long.

A shanty town, a bridge, a glimpse of dhows and cargo steamers, and we were in the thick of the city. It swirled with acrid, chocolate-coloured dust of the kind that takes at least a century to accumulate. It had settled on the buildings, the streets, the people, and given Dubai the instantly-recognizable gravity of a place with a history. There is something very reassuring and comfortable about old dirt. After the strain of living with the temporary and the brand-new in Abu Dhabi, coming into Dubai was like easing oneself into a well-worn tweed jacket. It didn't reek of new paint. The smell that came through the taxi windows was of carbon, sweat and cinnamon – a good, rank, big-city smell which had substance and experience in it.

'You wouldn't see that in Abu Dhabi,' said the Jordanian, pointing out a woman walking alone in a backless dress past a hoarding plastered with posters advertising Indian films. The afternoon crowd bulged on the sidewalks – a grubby, cosmopolitan swarm. There were Hindu caste-marks on the foreheads of some of the women, while the men were a rag-tag-and-bobtail lot, in threadbare shifts, in shiny Hong Kong fashion-wear, in home-made trousers with rolled-up ends. I decided that I was going to like Dubai.

We turned the corner of a narrow, flyblown street and suddenly the city unveiled itself. It was as legible as a relief-map. We had arrived at the Creek – a twisty inlet, rather wider than the Thames at London, which at once divides Dubai into two halves and is the main artery of the city's life. The Creek gives Dubai a shape, a direction and a certainty of character which I have seen in no other Arab town. Dubai is not labyrinthine: it is logical and worldly, a city with both feet firmly on the ground. And this oddly rational quality is rooted in the Creek. To get anywhere, you have to go up the Creek, or down the Creek, or across the Creek; and the whole intricate social geography of the place could be charted by keeping a close watch on the patterns of movement made by people on the waterway. There's a bridge over the Creek at one end of the city, and a tunnel under it at the other, but all the vital motion of Dubai takes place on and around the water itself – water which is, mysteriously, obstinately pure and lucid. In colour, it is milky, green and crystalline, full of small fish which flash and wink in the sun, several feet down. Its clarity is the clarity of Dubai as a city, banked so intelligibly around the long, clear, lazy *S* of the Creek.

Our taxi had arrived at the Creek just at the right moment. The sun had set, leaving a darkening orange afterglow over the city. In the dhows, which were double-parked all down the wharfside, small groups of men were crouched in pools of lamplight, cooking things on stoves. Twenty or so water-taxis – narrow boats with paraffin lanterns swinging from their prows – were cutting zig-zag paths across the Creek, making the air thick with the chug of little marine diesels and catching the last feeble rays of the sun with their wakes. It was a lovely, commanding image to have happened on. The self-absorbed busyness of the Creek gave it a beauty of a kind which European cities have lost. Venetians, for instance, know all too well that they are 'picturesque'; in Venice one never loses the sense that life is being staged for the onlooker. The gondolier is always posing for an imaginary camera, the *vaporetti* have caught the indolent complacency of mere pleasure boats – they idle round the city as if they were wearing straw hats and striped blazers. The nice thing about Dubai was that it was obviously getting on with what it always did. It hadn't yet fallen victim to some Arab Canaletto.

I checked into a hotel and got myself a room with a hawk's-eye view of the Creek; it was on the top floor, and so high that they were still finishing the roof over my head. The corridor outside was a tangle of plasterboard and electric cables, with bits of sky poking through the part-built ceilings. I sat mesmerized at my window, looking down on this water-world of dancing lights and tiny, preoccupied people. It was the first symptom of a kind of traveller's coma, in which I was to spend the best part of the next week.

Momentarily roused by the ticking of my watch – a sound I've never usually been able to hear at all – I took myself down to the overbright coffeeshop on the ground floor. There was no service to be had: the Lebanese waiters were all in an anxious cluster around the crew of a Middle Eastern Airlines plane which had just arrived from Beirut. There had been more fighting, more shelling in the suburbs; everyone was trying to get news of his own district in the city, and I caught the rush of names ... Baabda, Aley, Damour ... the hapless Wimbledons and Hampsteads of Beirut. In Europe, events on the other side of the continent remain comfortably remote; in Arabia, where almost every country has been stirred up and dispersed over the peninsula in a stew of different nationalities, a raid, a coup, a border-clash on the far Mediterranean fringes is immediately felt fifteen hundred miles away where people wait in a climate of continual rumour. Radio, television and newspapers tell one little or nothing: real news is still passed by word of mouth. Travelling businessmen and aircrews are seized on and questioned; impressions of impressions of impressions ripple through the cities in widening and increasingly distorted circles. One hears strange things. During my trip, I heard that the Israelis had sacked Cairo, also that Palestinian guerrillas had taken control of Jerusalem. This dependence on whispers and rumours gives all news a peculiarly extremist flavour – everything turns into either a victory or a catastrophe. There is already a tragic quantity of blood being shed in northern Arabia: if one happens to be on the far side of the desert, the amount of blood turns into an appalling, unprecedented torrent. Nor is the magnifying power of rumour at all modified by the language in which it is transmitted: Arabic, with its habitual overstatements and poetic flourishes, confers a degree of wild gothic elaboration on everything it touches. The political world quickly comes to resemble that of Marlowe's *Tamburlaine* – a domain of totalitarian metaphor in which satanic evil and godly heroism clash in an unending orgy of blood and guts.

Going hungry in the Carlton Tower coffeeshop, I watched rumour hatching at the table across the room. At one level, one was being jolted back into the 'real' world of grisly international affairs; at another, one was witnessing the Byzantine unreality which is such a major characteristic of Middle Eastern politics. I suppose that the aircrew really were able to communicate a few shreds of first-hand truth about Beirut; but on the faces of the waiters, pale as cheese, frightened for their families, I just saw that burning sense of extremity which is the inevitable consequence of living by hearsay. The official version of events on television would be discounted automatically – with reason; but a chance whisper from someone who'd seen or heard someone who'd seen or heard . . . that would be believed implicitly, and anxiously embroidered on.

I had the uneasy feeling that it would not be beyond the capacity of a mad cabin steward to provoke a full-scale war.

There was not much about Beirut in the *Emirates News* the following morning; a bare little paragraph at the bottom of a page which was dominated by a massive story about the official opening of the Dubai Hilton. It was easy to drift back into the self-contained world of the Creek. I had grown tired of asking questions, and was getting impatient and uncurious about the answers. I was sick of having to play Alice.

'I can't believe *that*!' said Alice. 'Can't you?' the Queen said in a pitying tone. 'Try again: draw a long breath and shut your eyes.' Alice laughed. 'There's no use trying,' she said: 'one *can't* believe impossible things.' 'I daresay you haven't had much practice,' said the Queen. 'When I was your age, I always did it for half an hour a day. Why, sometimes I've believed as many as six impossible things before breakfast.'

I had not had much practice either. I swapped my notebook for a copy of *The Moonstone* and dropped out of the whole business of making appointments and trying to be observant and believing impossible things. At the door of the hotel, I fed myself into the moving crowd and for six days I just went where the swarm went, carried along on whatever thermals and currents the city had to offer.

An Arab crowd is a very hospitable vehicle. It is a travelling warren of talk, full of that easy sociability which comes from men -- and only men -- doing almost everything in life in public. A Muslim's relation with God is public: he prays in the street without any consciousness that to some eyes there might be an embarrassing contradiction in this casual crossing from the mundane to the sublime and back again. His relations with other men have the same unshy, unguarded quality. This openness can easily strike the visiting Westerner as merely an unnerving disrespect for one's own privacy. In London, people go about like so many stuffed birds in glass domes, encased in invisible armour consisting of ten cubic metres or so of inviolable body-space. The crowd in Dubai had things quite differently organized. A space was immediately made for me, but it was a very small space; one moves hand-to-hand and haunch-to-haunch even on the widest sidewalks where there is plenty of spare room for people to unglue themselves from this curious, impersonal intimacy.

I fell into step. Anywhere else on the Gulf, I would have been clearly marked as an outsider; but Dubai was different. The crowd absorbed strangers easily: Indians, Iranians, Pakistanis, Arabs congealed into the careless cosmopolitanism of an old port which has always been used to beaching the tidewrack of the Gulf and the Indian Ocean. European faces do not stick out with any special prominence from that dun-coloured mass of different skins and styles of dress. The noise of the crowd, too, was a muted Babel, an indecipherable mutter of Hindustani, Urdu, Persian and Arabic. My own language seemed to melt in freely enough; I had precious little occasion to use it, and after a day or two I began to feel that its loss was no particular burden. It was the language of the book I was carrying, and every so often I would read a paragraph or two of Wilkie Collins, just to remind myself of who I was.

Finding this ability to abandon oneself to the crowd seemed precious. I had been frightened when it had nearly happened to me in Qatar; I welcomed it in Dubai. I felt pleasantly empty-headed and adrift. Things happened for no special reason and in no special order; I relapsed, happily, into being an accidental man.

We wound slowly through the souks – long, dark, makeshift corridors of stalls from which the sun was kept out by slap-happy roofs of cardboard, corrugated iron and old doors. I bought a kilo of mangoes to eat as I went along. Some lemon trees turned out to be made of plastic, and so were the toy models of the Concorde. We swarmed through the fabrics – bolts of pure rainbow. In the gold souk, I stayed for a while catching my own reflection in a window which framed a waxwork bride surrounded by a battery of powerful electric bulbs. Braids of gold hung from her forehead; a big, knobbly bangle of gold hung in the cleft between her breasts; and an even bigger gold star hung over the bulge of her pelvis from a golden rope around her waist. Her eyes, dark and dreamy under their enormous plastic lashes, gazed vacantly skywards as if she was quite innocent of these chains of expensive metal into which she'd been trussed – a golden martyr ready for a golden stake. She looked nice, too; like someone's famously pretty sister. But the crowd moved on, and I went with it through the meat souk and out into the sun of a crumbly square of mud and coral where I drank a glass of black tea and read about Rachel Verinder and the Indian jugglers.

It was very easy-going, this casual crowd-life. Someone offers you a cigarette; you proffer a light in return. They buy you a glass of tea; you buy them a glass of tea back. These gestures of ritual good humour are almost sufficient in themselves – indications that you are welcome in the fraternity and that, in your turn, you are glad to be a member of the club. Indeed, club life in London frequently has little more communication in it than that; it consists, for the most part, in a kind of amiable nuzzling. The inside of White's is much like this street-café society of Dubai – as contentedly animal as a field of friendly grazing cattle. The great difference lies in the fact that the Dubai crowd make no fuss about membership; the only qualification is that you have to be male.

We got on, as clubmen do, with jokes instead of conversation. Since practically anything can be seen to be funny between friends, the jokes were easily made. A man carrying a large cardboard box was a good joke; so was my dropping my teaspoon out of my glass; so was a dog which stopped to bare its haunches and deposit a large turd at our feet. We laughed a lot and clasped each other's wrists over a Pakistani falling off a bicycle. That was undoubtedly the best joke, but the world was infinitely seamed with happy ironies, and it was a pleasure to enjoy them in such good company. When I drifted off into the crowd again, I was content with the thought that I must make an even better joke than the unfortunate Pakistani.

With the crowd, I crossed and recrossed the Creek on the convoy of chugging longboats at twopence a ride. We saw the carcass of a dead dog hanging in the brilliant water, and laughed a lot about that. I grew adept at making the jump from the bobbing prows of the boats on to the wharves, and sat on the wharf steps delighting in the prospect of a veiled lady who stood dithering on the deck of one of the boats making little jumping motions which never quite materialized into the leap which was going to carry her to the safety of the shore. Living idly, out of language, I found myself in a state of very nearly continual mindless mirth. I giggled a lot, drank large quantities of tea and lemon juice, munched at chicken legs, smoked, and spat into the Creek.

At night, falling asleep over Sergeant Cuff and his roses, I heard the shrill honk and peal of bagpipes coming from the far side of the Creek. They were playing some Fling of the kind that Scotsmen like to march to and which sounds like an awakened graveyard of souls in torment. It didn't seem particularly odd at the time – I vaguely supposed that Dubai at midnight was quite probably full of Scottish pipe bands. Later someone told me that the band belonged to a Scot who was chief of police: apparently he dressed his men up in kilts and marched them, whooping and skirling, through the streets at all hours. The crime rate in Dubai is tiny, and it might repay the time of a researcher into the penal system to investigate whether nightly doses of 'The Campbells Are Coming', 'Scots Wha Hae' and 'The Banks and Braes o' Bonny Doon' on the bagpipes are not as effective a deterrent as hanging, amputation or the lash.

In an alley café I met a man who owned a rowing boat – it bobbed at our feet in the floating debris of wooden spars, lumps of polystyrene and dead cats; a long time ago, the man had obviously made the boat himself. It was a roughly-carpentered patchwork of bits and pieces salvaged from the tidewrack. After we'd drunk three glasses of tea together, the man made a proposal: for the equivalent of about £5, he would spend the entire day rowing me around the Creek. In a city where one pays £5 for a ten-minute taxi-ride, £50 for a hotel room, £25 for the barest meal in an ordinary restaurant, this seemed an embarrassingly measly sum; but the world of the Creek is a generation or two away from the Dubai of the oil boom and the visiting businessmen. It's as if the two cities floated one on top of the other, each living in nearly perfect ignorance of the conditions of the other's existence. Falling into the crowd, I had drifted into that other city – a nice, relaxed, idle, improvident place. Sitting on a shady bench under a crumbling mud wall, one can look out on the indulgences and pretensions of the new Dubai and enjoy them in exactly the same way as one enjoys the prospect of Pakistanis falling off their bicycles. *Maalesh. So it goes.* And giggle. In that deep reserve of philosophical good humour which is so constant a feature of Arab talk, wealth itself turns into a joke. You see it, you shrug: it provides yet more evidence of the universal irony in which all the details of this world are steeped – and it becomes an object of innocent laughter.

We ambled over the water. The boatman seemed pleased that I was not trying to go anywhere in particular. We crossed to the south side – my side – of the Creek, and sidled up the long line of banking houses. For half a mile they made a solid wall of marble and money; Dubai's treasure chest, as cold and impregnable as the Medici Chapel and its tombs. The Arab Bank, the National Bank of Dubai, the Commercial Bank of Dubai, the Dubai Bank . . . banks from Iran, London, New York, Saudi Arabia and the other Gulf states – everyone with a finger in Dubai's business seemed to have their own towering slab of marble. Set end to end they made a great mausoleum of cash, and the presence of all that money radiated a kind of refrigerated shade in which we drifted in the boatman's home-made skiff, glad of the cool which the banks spread over the wharves.

The boatman and I traded a few small shreds of language. He had always lived in Dubai. He shrugged at the banks; they were of no special interest to him. He had had a boat on the Creek for thirty . . . forty years – he couldn't remember. Yes, once Dubai was smaller; now it was bigger. But it was a big city even when he was a boy. He had none of the excited civic pride which I had met in people in Abu Dhabi. The Dubai which had changed in the great oil boom wasn't his city. It was an abstraction on the horizon.

Tugs were hauling a lumbering rig up the Creek for servicing. 'Oil,' said the man, and laughed. *Zayit*. It wasn't a very interesting word.

What he liked best was to thread his boat through the avenue of dhows. We slid between them; the wood of their hulls had been bleached to a pale whisky colour, speckled like butterflies' wings by the play of the sun on the water. Sleepy men leaned over their sides, and we politely maa-salaamed our way through, with the boatman occasionally stopping for a conversation far too rapid for me to follow. Some of the dhows (a Westerner's generic term – none of these boats were really dhows; they had names like *jawwalla, sambuk, boom, bukari,* but they were dhows to me) had poops and forecastles which were obvious copies of Portuguese galleons. The galleons themselves had fallen into obsolescence hundreds of years ago; but in the design of dhows, these modish Western trimmings had dawdled into the twentieth century unchanged.

We crossed the Creek again, bouncing in the wake of a big, new coaster from Kuwait, and nosed up alongside a decrepit street of ancient houses. Their rough mud stucco had cracked, and was falling away from their walls in jagged lumps, revealing the coral rocks from which they had been built. They had wind-towers on their roofs – carved wooden turrets made to catch whatever breeze was going and funnel it down to the bowels of the house; a simple, elegant air-conditioning system.

The boatman pointed. He lived over there, behind those houses . . . From outside, they were inscrutable – cubes of burned pastry without windows. But here and there a bit of wall had fallen out, and I caught passing glimpses of court-yards, vines, stairways, lattices, carved doors and hanging balconies; all the essential ingredients of the inward-looking order of the Arab household.

These houses had in their time occupied the same symbolic position on the Creek as the line of marble banks did now. They had belonged to rich merchants, and fifty years ago or less they must have looked like fine *palazzi*, lining the waterside in a concerted display of wealth and power. The merchants had gone – their heirs now lived in California-plush in seaside suburbs like Jumeira; and the houses had a sunken-jawed look, now just a storm or two away from collapsing into total ruin. Longshoremen, jobbing carpenters and small stallholders from the near-by souk had moved in where – until just lately – the great gold- and spice-merchants had lorded it over the rest of the city.

I asked the boatman if he had television. No – he had no television, no motor car. But he did have a son who was training to be an engineer.

It struck me then that almost everyone I'd met around the Creek had been that contradiction in Gulf terms, a poor Arab. The men who sat and talked in the cafés with their feet tucked under the hems of their long skirts were all Arabs from Dubai.

On the streets, they were easily outnumbered by Indians and Pakistanis, who were all in far too much of a hurry for tea and conversation, moonlighting as they were at half a dozen jobs at once. The Arabs in the cafés, though, didn't belong to that rentier class of state-pensioners, of which I'd seen so much in Qatar and Abu Dhabi; for these men, the oil revenues had simply passed straight over the tops of their heads.

'Sheikh Rashid doesn't go in for the sort of handouts that these other fellows do – ' an English financial adviser had said. 'Dubai isn't like the other Gulf states: Rashid's a realist . . . believes in investing his money in infrastructure, not in some crackpot scheme in which everyone gets coddled silly from the cradle to the grave . . .'

So the boatman was still just a boatman. Rowing boats are, actually, a highly significant part of the 'infrastructure' of Dubai; but I don't think that they enter Sheikh Rashid's calculations very much. For the boatman, not being 'infrastructure' meant having an old house without television or a car, doing an old job in an old way, and having a son who was going to be an engineer – because training schemes *are* 'infrastructure', like banking licences, dry docks, Hilton hotels and fishmeal factories.

We stopped at another waterside alley where there were more friends sprawled on long pews and drinking tea. Finding myself out of the gossip, I busied myself taking snapshots of everything in sight, enjoying my dislocation from events. Watching the miniaturized, reflected image of the Creek swim prettily into focus in my viewfinder, I had the world exactly as I wanted it.

Occasionally I felt guiltily recalled from this cheerful, inconsequential life of the Creek, the souk and the café. Conscious that I was officially a guest of the state, I paid some duty calls at government offices. They weren't at all like Abu Dhabi offices; they were severely functional with bare 100-watt bulbs and metal utility furniture – more evidence of Rashid's 'realism'. My hosts were polite, gave me tea, and seemed a little puzzled as to why I had bothered to call at all. I invented some appointments that I would like to make: perhaps I could visit the ruler's daily *majlis*? (More than the other emirs,

Rashid was reputed to make himself unusually accessible: at his *majlis* people seeking oil concessions rubbed shoulders with men who wanted to grouse about holes in their roofs and aggrieved owners of goats killed in motor accidents. At the *majlis*, held most mornings of the week, Rashid listened to every application and complaint, and passed a summary judgement on it.) I was told that it would be impossible for me to attend a *majlis*: the Sheikh's public relations man would not allow it. A school, then? Could I visit a school? The Minister of Education would have to assent to that; it might take weeks to arrange.

Far from finding these rebuffs discouraging, I welcomed them, and escaped from the office each morning feeling that my truancy now had official blessing. Let off the hook, I resumed my Huck Finning existence round the Creek.

On Friday, I heard the Home Counties in full cry as I passed the hotel bar. The expats were in. There was Double Diamond on draught to remind people of Sunday lunchtimes in the pub at home, a roast-beef-and-Yorkshire buffet, and a general smoky mateyness in the air. From villas and bungalows in the desert suburbs, the Dubai English had packed themselves into their Range Rovers and come bumping into town. The hotels along the Creek all competed with each other to lay on a rough-and-ready impression of an English Sunday on the Muslim Sabbath, with pub-food Lebanese-style and lots of beer in tankards and saucers of soggy potato crisps on the tables. If one didn't look too carefully out of the window, Dubai at Friday lunchtime turned into a passable version of Putney-in-exile, right down to the Rovers and Rexes who dozed on the floor, tethered to chair-legs on their leads.

Even from the window, the Putneyfied air of the occasion wasn't wholly shattered, give or take a *sambuk* and a *boom* for a rowing eight and a fleet of Merlin Rocket racing dinghies. All it seriously lacked was a nip of cold and a brush of Putney river mist. I barged happily in, glad of the chance to practise my rusty English, bought a pint of bitter (thinking that my preference for the barman's speciality of Pimms might strike my compatriots as a bit unmanly), and did my best to become one of the crowd. I got very interested in the route of next week's car rally, and mustered a fair degree of enthusiasm over the power-boat race.

'Oh, you get a pretty full life in Dubai, all right. Of course, you have to make the effort for yourself. But then – ' said the man complacently, 'if a chap comes out here in the first place, it shows he's someone with a bit of spunk and initiative to his name, doesn't it? Take someone like myself . . . How you doing? What's that? Double-D? Another pint of Dirty Dick, Charlie!' All barmen in the Middle East are, for some reason, known generically as Charlie. 'No, take someone like myself . . . typical week: spin round the bay in the boat – darts match up at the Country Club (Been to the Country Club yet? You ought to) – get in a game of squash if I can – and rugger, of course, there's always rugger. Yes. I'd say that was a full life by any Youkay standards you could name . . . wouldn't you?'

Two conversations away, I heard a lady complaining about the quantity of 'dog-do' on her street.

The men were contractors, quantity surveyors, engineers. They lived in that well-heeled limbo of upper-servantdom, midway between stairs. On their sites, they were the ones who gave the orders, and for days at a stretch it was easy for them to believe that they were the natural ruling class of Dubai. But they all had Arab bosses, and on Fridays their masters were put more and more firmly in their place as the beer took hold.

'Of course, he hasn't got a clue as to what he really wants – '

'If I didn't run round like a nanny, picking up all his mistakes, the whole damn project would fall slap-bang into the bloody sand – '

'They're just like children, really, don't you think? Children with a lot of new toys – '

I was introduced to the Usherwoods. Merrick Usherwood was a building contractor from Leeds. His wife Elizabeth came from Barnsley. Her mouth was a rigid cupid's-bow of scarlet lipstick, and she spoke in a pained little-girly voice which sounded like the product of years of rather unsuccessful elocution lessons. In her red slacks and tank-top she bore a strong resemblance to a talking Post Office pillarbox.

The Usherwoods, said Elizabeth, loved the Arabs. They'd been out in Dubai for two years and never wanted to go back to England again. Never.

'You see, Jonathan, I'm sorry to say it, but I'm afraid that England's gone soft. They've just driven out,' her voice peaked, 'the people of initiative. There's no *incentive* any more. It's the Brain Drain, isn't it? I mean, all one's asking for is a fair day's pay for a fair day's work. But I'm afraid you won't find that in England any more, will you?

'*That's* why I respect the Arabs so much, you see. In *this* country, you take a man who doesn't do his fair whack, and what happens to him? He gets sent *home*, doesn't he? To Parky Starn. *That's* why things get done in *this* country. And, do you know, Jonathan, I wouldn't mind going out at midnight in Dubai, because Dubai's *safe*. They know what to do with delinquents here; they flog them. An eye for an eye . . . I mean, it's only *justice*, isn't it? And that's what England's lacking in, I'm afraid: we've lost our sense of fair play – '

Elizabeth's England was indeed a very terrible place. 'The Race Relations Board' had rendered the country uninhabitable for nice people like the Usherwoods. The police went in terror of the 'Race Act', and were forced to stand by while black muggers and rapists left a trail of blood and misery through the streets of London. Immigrants grew fat and lazy on National Assistance, while 'productive people' were bled dry by avaricious taxmen. The education system had collapsed: even the teachers now were hooligans. Elizabeth had ample evidence for every accusation. She had heard dreadful things from the taxi driver who had driven her to Heathrow airport on her last leave; and a friend regularly sent her clippings of new horrors from the *Daily Mirror*.

'It's not fair – I mean, it's not *right*, is it? You take our son, for instance. He had to go to a state school before we came out here, oh, it was terrible, I can't tell you. Do you know, Jonathan, he was diagnosed as educationally . . . well . . . *sub-average*? First thing we did when Merrick got his job, we entered Clifford for the best private school in Yorkshire. He's there now. He's captain of the rugby team – the Under Fifteens; and top in French – oh, his *French*!

'I mean, don't get me wrong, Jonathan. I'm saying all this because I love England. I think . . . well, the Dales and the Lake District – there's nothing to beat them in the world. It's a tragedy – what's happened to England. I'm not political, Jonathan, but I can tell you that there are people in England now who are *glad* that the country's being ruined. And ruin is the only word, you know. It's ruined. Spoiled. That's what they've done to England – '

She leaned tipsily in her chair. 'I've got a slogan for you, Jonathan. Do you want to hear my slogan?'

'Yes,' I said. 'What's your slogan?'

'It's "Put the 'Great' back into Britain". That's my slogan for you. Put-the-Great-back-into-Britain . . .'

For the Usherwoods, Arabia was the Promised Land of the far Right, a place where miscreants met the noose and the birch, where 'decent people' paid no taxes, where immigrants were repatriated the moment that they ceased to be useful, and where Usherwoods could eke out their days in peace and prosperity. If only Britain could adopt Sharia Law, it would turn into a land fit for Usherwoods. All the tact, good humour and courtesy that I'd seen in Arabia evaporated as Elizabeth extolled its ghastly virtues. As she drilled on, her voice rising in pitch and righteous indignation, I ached to get back to the Creek.

'But, Jonathan, do you see what I *mean*?'

'Yes. I see exactly what you mean.'

'It's only *fairness* that I'm after – '

'Fairness for whom, though?'

'Why,' she said shrilly, 'I want to be fair to everyone, of course!'

Perhaps in South America there is some small state, famous for its public executions, martial law and the lavish style of life enjoyed by its middle class, which is still going through a spot of difficulty in finding a dictator. If the praesidium there are still sighing over the memory of the great Eva Peron, I think I have an answer to their problems. She lives in Dubai. Her name, in fact, is not 'Elizabeth Usherwood', but a few discreet enquiries in that city will surely root her out.

By half past three the bar was almost empty. The Usherwoods had gone, leaving me, a scattering of bachelors and a Lebanese businessman called Mussa. Someone I hadn't noticed before, a little man in a dirty shift and carelessly tied head-dress, fell against me when I was ordering a final drink. His head barely topped the bar counter.

'You . . . me . . . we . . . drink – ' he said, bringing out each word with the dreadful labour of the very sloshed.

'I'm afraid so.'

'I . . . buy . . . you . . . drink – '

'Very kind of you, but no, thanks all the same.'

'I . . . listen . . . every . . . word . . . you . . . speak.'

'Good – '

'All words . . . I . . . understand.'

After a talking pillarbox, this was much like encountering a speak-your-weight machine with ambitions altogether beyond its mechanical powers. He leaned heavily against me, snuffling faintly.

'I listen to everybodies,' he said in a sudden premeditated rush.

'Do you?'

'Go . . . every . . . hotel . . . listen . . . every . . . word . . . English . . . very . . . good . . .'

'Oh, first rate,' I agreed politely.

'I – ' he said, drawing himself up as best he could into tottering erectness, 'hear what everybodies speak.'

'I bet you do.'

'I drink too much.' It seemed a frank enough admission. 'Why I drink? I am . . .' he fell into my pocket, '. . . detective.' I was afraid that he was going to be sick, and edged him carefully away.

'For my job, I drink. For detective. For to listen to everybodies speak.'

'Why don't you go home?' asked the Lebanese.

The detective looked at him, his eyes focusing with difficulty. Mussa was a good sixteen stone and bore a massive beergut. One could have fitted three or four detectives into him quite comfortably. The detective reached the door like someone walking gingerly on water. Once there, he held himself with precarious dignity.

'All what you say, I listen.'

'*Folie de grandeur*,' said the Lebanese, as we heard the man falling into an open lift.

In the evenings I took long walks along the wharves, where the dhow cargoes were laid out in heaps and bales. The laden dhows, set to sail at first light, looked like floating general stores, festooned with ironmongery and fancy goods. I tried

to make an inventory of what I could see on one dhow alone:
six Korean refrigerators, four Japanese washing machines,
three red Suzuki motorbikes, nine bicycles, five tricycles, a
green garden wheelbarrow, sacks of steel wire, some mesh
netting (for making fish traps, presumably), a Buick, two
dozen Taiwanese motor tyres and – Britain's only contribution
to this particular bit of international trade – a case of Tempest
hurricane lamps. There was much more that I couldn't see or
name. The ship's lifeboats were overflowing cornucopias of
interesting things in sacks; more stuff was lashed to the rigging.
All down the wharf, other dhows were similarly weighed
down.

Just about everything that comes into the Gulf from the
Indian Ocean gets to Dubai, where it is parcelled out and
shipped north to Abu Dhabi, Qatar, Bahrain, Saudi Arabia
and Kuwait. The oil boom has simply intensified Dubai's
traditional buzz of water traffic. The tankers and container-
ships dock at Port Rashid, at the mouth of the Creek; the dhow
trade, based on the Creek itself, is an intricate warren of
relatively small-time private enterprise. Every souk on the
Gulf depends on it. Independent merchants working out of
stalls and cubbyholes do most of their buying and selling
through it. If you want a washing machine, a set of spare
tyres, a tricycle or a wheelbarrow, it will most probably arrive
by dhow.

The dhows made up a small, self-sufficient, waterborne city
in themselves – a fine place to wander and pay calls. Invitations
were easily come by: I only had to pause in my walk, light my
pipe, and look hopefully in over the sides of boats whose crews
were crouched companionably round a paraffin stove. Hens
squawked in the scuppers, and goats were tethered to the mast.
There was always coffee going, and a turn on the hookah,
and that wordless amity of smiles and shrugs. A portable
Japanese television cast a cold blue flicker over the circle
where we squatted. An advertisement for soap powder came
up, starring two Egyptian actresses going through exactly the
same routine that I'd seen a hundred times before in England.
One was in despair over a pile of underclothes which were
muddy, bloody, streaked with grease and marked with what
are known in the advertising business as 'understains'. The

other housewife, smart as paint in her check shirtwaister, introduced her friend to the remarkable 'biological power' of her brand of powder. The vinyl kitchen in which they stood was pure Surrey, so was their pealing suburban brightness. The wording of the advertisement was Arabic, but its grammar was totally English. The crew of the dhow watched it with rapt attention. They showed every sign of being thoroughly impressed when the underclothes were finally taken from the spin-dryer and shown to be immaculately white. We all grinned happily at each other as if we were in on the satisfactory conclusion of some exotic conjuring trick, and the talk only started up again when the next programme came on – a display of local folk dancing. After five minutes or so this was broken for another ad, in English, for Hitachi radios.

'You'll never feel lonely, even when you're alone,' said the voice-over in husky pillowtalk.

'Ingleezi,' said the man next to me, his one gold tooth winking in the blue light of the television, and laughed.

'It says that the radio makes company,' I explained, pleased to find a chance to show off a word that I had just learned that morning. *Jima*. The man laughed again, this time clasping my arm in his enthusiasm at such a hilarious idea. I thought he was taking the joke a shade too far, and later I checked my usage with the dictionary. I had not been far wrong: at least the root was correct. The word I'd used in fact meant 'sexual intercourse'. With a slightly different inflection, it also means 'socialism'.

I did manage to make one or two more official encounters. I had wanted to meet Ayysha Sayyar, the Director of Social Services for Dubai. I had first heard about her in Abu Dhabi: she was famous for being the Gulf's token Emancipated Woman. I had seen her fleetingly on television, where she was much in demand for quiz shows and discussions. Curiously enough (considering the enormous fuss which attended the appointment of the first woman newscaster on British television in 1976) quite a number of Gulf women worked in radio and television – and many more worked as schoolteachers. In all the emirates, the news was just as likely to be read by a woman as by a man. But Ayysha Sayyar was different because she was a director of a ministry. She was responsible for drawing up schemes which would be executed by men. Whenever I asked anyone about the changing position of women in the Gulf (and whether, indeed, their position was changing at all, or was merely being entrenched still further in reaction to the frightening pace of other kinds of change), Ayysha Sayyar's name came up with solitary and monotonous regularity. No, there was no Women's Movement to speak of (unless one counted the Sheikha's sewing circle in Abu Dhabi); but there was Ayysha Sayyar. No, women were not, by and large, able to have administrative careers — except for Ayysha Sayyar. I soon learned to rephrase my questions in the form: 'Apart from Ayysha Sayyar . . . ?' When I succeeded in making an appointment to visit her at her office, I felt much as A. W. Kinglake did when he went to see Lady Hester Stanhope in the Lebanon:

> Up to the period of my arrival in the Levant, I had seldom even heard a mentioning of the Lady Hester Stanhope; but now wherever I went I was met by the name so familiar in sound, and yet so full of mystery from the vague, fairy-tale sort of idea which it brought to my mind.

The strain of Ayysha Sayyar's lonely prominence told vividly on her face. At first sight, she was all frown. Her forehead was clenched in a knot of tight creases above the bridge of her nose. The frown never relaxed, even when she laughed, and it conferred a stern and troubled intensity on the most casual of her remarks. Nothing that she said or did looked as if it could sneak out without being brought to book by that grave, unyielding frown.

We had to talk through an interpreter, and this exaggerated my feeling that I was interrogating a solemn and suspicious oracle; and at first she was only oracular and diplomatic.

'She says that the Koran grants equal rights to women, and that only misinterpretation of the Koran has denied women these rights.'

'She says that the family in Islam need not be weakened by changes in technology. She says that the mistakes of the West have been observed; and that the Arab world has learned a lesson from the West's failures.'

'She says that members of the Arab family still visit one another once a day, at least once a week . . . This is what keeps the family close. These old habits do not die just because people live in tall buildings.'

'She says that it is possible to keep the closeness of the Arab family even when women work.'

'She agrees that countries like the emirates cannot afford to waste half their educated manpower, and that it is inevitable that more women will work.'

'She says that all change must come gradually.'

It was obvious that I was asking her questions which she had had to answer a thousand times before. She finished each sentence with a small, tired, wooden smile. Her desk was full. I could see that I was wasting her time.

In Qatar, I'd met the Sudanese novelist, Tayeb Saleh. We'd been talking about Qatari writers at dinner, and he had remarked that if the Gulf was ever to acquire a genuine contemporary literature (and not just a greenhouse of subsidized forced blooms), it would be written by women, because women were the only people who were living under the kind of strain which produces serious poetry and fiction. Men, he said, had it too easy. If there was a 'Gulf Novel' in ten years' time, it would be a Women's Novel, written out of anger and distress. I asked the interpreter to put this idea to Ayysha Sayyar. Her answer was a long time coming, and when she did speak her voice had lost the measured, clockwork tone of her earlier pronouncements.

'She says that this is very difficult for a woman. Yes, a woman may write. But it would be permitted for her only to write poems in praise of the Koran – like your hymns; or poems about nature. These are the things she might show to her husband, or even have published in a magazine. She says that it is possible that there might be the kind of writing you talk about. But it is impossible to know whether it exists or not. If women are writing these things, they will be locking them up in boxes. They would not show them – not even to their sisters. It would be a secret writing – a hidden writing, in a box. She says perhaps this exists; she does not know. She says that she thinks it will be long time before she reads the novel that you talk of – perhaps ten years, maybe . . . perhaps more. But she thinks it possible.'

I wanted to ask her whether she had thought of writing such a book herself. But the question would have been a trespass, and in any case she had virtually given me the answer to it. Instead I asked her how she felt about being the only woman in Dubai with a job as important as hers; did she feel isolated and freakish, or did she feel that she would very soon be joined by other women occupying similar positions? As soon as I'd put the question, I regretted it – it seemed too dumb to elicit an interesting answer, but again Ayysha Sayyar started to talk in her quick voice, her hands making small darting gestures as she spoke.

'She asks me to tell you that you must first understand that she comes from a very good family. This is true. She is from a very old, very much respected family in Sharjah. It is because she is so well born that it is possible for her to do this job. If she came from a less respected family, she would not be allowed; people would not listen to her. Even if she had the same education, the same qualifications. People think of her first for her family, for her breeding; second, for her capacity to do the job. Because she is from this very good family, she is now pointed out as an example. Even in Sheikh Rashid's own family now, they speak of Ayysha Sayyar to show the girls what it is possible to do – '

At the mention of Rashid, Ayysha Sayyar nodded at me. This was true. There was a complicated mixture of pride and irony in her expression. She interrupted the interpreter.

'She says that if a woman doing a job can earn the respect of the girls in the ruling family, that is the most important thing. Then, perhaps, other families will follow. Women – particularly women with education – will only work if they can see that that is the correct thing to do in the best families. So she says that her example is very important; if *Ayysha Sayyar* does this job, then why should not *I*?'

We went back to the subjects that I'd raised at the beginning, this time with far more ease and fluency. Ayysha Sayyar agreed that there *was* a real paradox. In a country in which the natives were in a small minority, it was economically crazy to lock away half the indigenous population behind the lattice and the veil; on the other hand the secluded position of women and the extreme privacy of Arab domestic life provided almost the only element of continuity and reassurance in a society which was in all other respects in a state of hectic flux.

'She says that it is very important here to see the difference between Dubai and Abu Dhabi. You have been to Abu Dhabi, yes? There, the change is faster – so it is more difficult for a woman doing a job. In Dubai, it is different. The change is slower; so the possibility for women is greater. She asks – do you understand?'

Yes, I said, I understood exactly. The element of topsy-turvy in the statement went a long way towards explaining that scowl of furious concentration: Ayysha Sayyar was living inside a whole nest of contradictions. When I left her, all I could think of was the locked box and the stack of secret writing inside it. I suspect that it will not be very long before the box is opened, the manuscript published, and Arabia considerably shaken by the consequences.

I took to drinking in the middle of the day with Mussa, the Lebanese. He found me in the bar one afternoon poring over the Wehr Dictionary, mugging up new roots. In the morning, Syria had announced that she would provide covering air support for the Palestinians in the camps of southern Lebanon. Mussa picked up the dictionary and slapped it down on the bar.

'With a language like *that*, do you think that promise means anything at all? It means anything that anybody wants it to mean. It means damn all. It's just a noise in the air.'

He heaved his gut on to a stool and blew on his beer before drinking it. He had brought some more appropriate reading matter of his own – Andrew Lang's *The Yellow Fairy Book*.

'For my son,' he said. 'I want him to read some English. I spent the whole morning choosing it. Arabs understand fairy stories.'

It was full of pictures of princesses and severed heads. Mussa's son was thirteen, and I wondered whether *The Wind In The Willows* might not have been a more suitable choice.

'It's too English. He would not understand the manners.'

'Look,' said Mussa suddenly. 'You know English history. Where do you think these countries are now in English history? What century are we in here? Give me a date –'

'I don't know – 1880, perhaps? Somewhere in the middle of the second phase of the Industrial Revolution and the rise of the city . . .?'

'No, no, no – you're too damn polite. Earlier. Much earlier.'

'When?'

'I think perhaps we are in the time of your First Charles, or your James the Second. It took you hundreds of years to learn how to run a country without executing the opposition or the previous regime. Your Callaghan doesn't throw Mrs Thatcher or whoever in jail – but we are still in that kind of society. You take the way your Henry the Eighth behaved – cutting his wives' heads off and everything . . . he would get on here better than your Callaghan, I think.

'I read a lot of English history. I like the Tudors and the Stuarts – they are very . . . *Arab*, you know?'

'How do you like the prospect of Gaddafi as your Cromwell?'

'There is a difference. Cromwell knew that there were limits to his power; there were things he couldn't do. *That* man knows no limits.'

Mussa flipped over the pages of *The Yellow Fairy Book*. 'You see why I have to go to Florida,' he said.

He was leaving Dubai after ten years of profitless business in the city. He had arrived just after the first offshore oil strikes were made in 1966, and had set up a property development company with a Dubaian partner. He was going to build offices, hotels, apartment blocks, and make a fortune – one of that army of wheeler-dealers who had descended on the Gulf with a little capital, a talent for fast talking and a gleam in their eye. Mussa, though, had been elbowed out. I found it difficult to follow the technical details, and in any case they were unprintable. It seemed that he had bribed the wrong people; the bribes had not been big enough; the building permits had not been forthcoming; the land had been confiscated . . . the usual story, I suppose. No doubt property developers in London, Birmingham and Newcastle are constantly running into the same annoying snags in the practice of their profession; but knowing no property developers, I was innocently awed by this Byzantine tale of crooked millionaires and laundered petrodollars.

'Ten years,' said Mussa. 'And what do I have to show for it? I have less money now than I brought in.'

I said that I had heard worse hard-luck stories.

'It may not be exactly *heart-rending*; but it's not what anyone expects of Dubai.'

He told me how, a few months ago, he had been put in prison for two days after he had committed a minor traffic offence. He had been able to put up the money for his release, but the Indians and Pakistanis with whom he had shared his cell were still there – many of them had not even been charged yet, or so he said, and they had precious little hope of ever coming up for any proper trial. Their relatives brought food into the prison for them and waited for the day when they would have saved enough cash to buy them out.

'And this is for nothing! Nothing at all – some little bump in the car, not a crime. This is a country where if you are rich you have a very good time, and if you are poor you have no rights at all.'

The days hung heavily on Mussa's hands. He had wound up his affairs; in two months he would leave. At present, he was killing time in bars, glooming over the fortune he had failed to make in Dubai.

'You think I will make out in Florida?'

'What are you going to do there exactly?'

'I don't know. Buy a couple of hotels . . . I've got a cousin in Miami. He made out. He's in office blocks.'

He sank his fourth pint of the afternoon.

'When I get to the US, I stop drinking. Look at that! When I came to Dubai, you know how much I weighed? Ten stones. I looked like an athlete. *That's* all I've got out of this place – ' He fingered the lower buttons of his shirt. They were fighting a losing battle against the escaping tangle of black hairs and brown flesh. It looked as if Mussa had a baby orang-utan curled up in his lap under his clothes. Every so often it turned and shivered in its sleep. Mussa slapped it irritably.

'You know how my wife has kept her figure? – she has no friends. When we first came out to Dubai, we got asked everywhere. She was going off to these "coffee afternoons". Every afternoon, the women go to the house of some woman, a hundred of them at a time. There's fifty thousand dirhans' worth of food there. You can't see the damn room for food. And these fat bitches just sit there, eating their way through this mountain of cakes and stuff. Saturday, Sunday, Monday, Tuesday . . . it never stops. Eating crap. Every afternoon. That's Dubai social life. And every afternoon they walk in the door and price the joint: if Fatima puts out forty thousand dirhans' worth of shit, then Leila raises the ante to fifty on her afternoon . . . so it goes. My wife opted out. Who wants to pay five thousand pounds sterling – more than that – to have your friends round to tea and watch them stuffing their faces and making sex jokes? Thank God my wife doesn't. In Florida . . . we'll have just three or four people round to dinner . . . a couple of bottles of wine – but you can't do that in Dubai. It has to be a big banquet. You have to show the colour of your money. You have three, four people round to dinner here, and next day, what do you hear? "Mussa's finished. He's washed up. He's lost his money. He had *three* people to dinner." Then you try to buy a bit of property from someone, and he laughs in your face. *Sell to Mussa? The man who has three people to dinner?* Big joke. You might as well do business with your houseboy.

'Perhaps it will be just the same in Florida,' Mussa said. 'I've lived in Lebanon, Europe, the Gulf – and every time I think "people will be different here", but they're not. You know the way that the English always talk about the Arabs – that they're lazy, that time doesn't mean anything to them . . . all those things that everyone says? When I was a student in Leicester, I used to work in the town hall during the holidays, and people were exactly the same as here – lazy. No one wanted to work. We spent our time playing whist, and fiddling with our watches to make our tea-breaks come quicker. It's no different here. Laziness and inefficiency are part of the human character: they're not "Arab" or "English". Or do you think that when I was in Leicester I just taught all the people in the town hall how to behave like Arabs?'

I was leaving the bar when Mussa called me back.

'Did you ever hear the one about Enoch Powell going to

heaven? He gets to the pearly gates . . . knock-knock, knock-knock. And a voice comes back from the other side: "Who dat dere?" See you – '

'See you,' I said.

'In Florida,' said Mussa and laughed. ' "Who dat dere?" '

Mahdi means pure, sheer, unadulterated, downright. *Tajir* means merchant, trader, businessman. For once, Arabic is not ambiguous, and Mahdi Tajir really is a pure, sheer, unadulterated merchant, trader and businessman. Whether his name was a kind of totemic spell cast on him at birth, or whether he acquired it much later, as a simple description of what he had become, I do not know. I rather doubted whether he was a human being at all: his existence in the Gulf was institutional, like Tiffany's or the Ritz. I had once seen him interviewed on British television, when a reporter had asked him if it was true that he was the richest man in the world. 'That must be for other people to decide,' Mahdi Tajir had said: 'I do not know the secrets of other men's bank accounts. I can only say that it is a statement which it would be unwise of me to deny.'

I had an invitation to lunch at Mahdi Tajir's, and what chiefly preoccupied me was the question of my tie. I had two ties – a greasy black affair, bought for a friend's funeral two years before, and a green silk one which had been worn for too many scrambled-egg breakfasts. Neither seemed right for lunch with the richest man in the world. I spent the whole morning combing the men's shops of Dubai, most of which specialized in neckties which looked like flayed strips of the skin of a marmalade cat. Finally, I went back to the smallest and most expensive of the shops and said, please, I was going to lunch with Mahdi Tajir and wanted a tie.

'Lunch with Mahdi Tajir?' The Indian assistant took the phrase exactly as I had hoped he would – skipping his stock of beachwear, officewear, evening dress, safari gear, and getting straight down to his lunch-with-Mahdi-Tajir-wear. 'You want a Leonard of Paris tie,' he said. 'That is the right tie. Top tie. A1 – ' and produced a violent optical eyesore of narrow, zig-zagging silk stripes. It cost just a little more than £27, but since it said 'Leonard of Paris' on the front as well as on the back, I bought it, thinking that a man who had so evidently paid £27 for his new tie must have one thing at least in his favour at Mahdi Tajir's.

'This is the most expensive tie you sell?'

'Yes. There is no more expensive than Leonard of Paris.'

'This is an expensive shop, right?'

'This is very, very expensive shop. No cheap stuff in this shop, I can promise you.'

'But are there other shops where I could buy a more expensive tie?'

'On my honour, no, sir. That is very, very most expensive tie in town.'

I walked back along the Creek. At intervals I stopped, opened the paper bag, and inspected the tie in its wrapping of cellophane. Even in the shadow of the bag, it looked capable of blinding or maiming at any range up to about five yards. I began to suspect that the Indian had told me less than the absolute truth: was a man who came to lunch in a Leonard of Paris tie a potentially even greater scandal than a man who gave dinner for three people? I looked for Mussa in the bar, but he wasn't there. When I left the hotel, I tried to measure the effect of my tie on the desk clerk when I handed in my key – he didn't appear to notice it at all. I thought this, on the whole, was rather a bad sign. Surely the very, very most expensive tie in town deserved one brief flicker of admiring recognition? In the taxi I scanned the lines of clerks who were coming out of offices and filing on to the decks of the ferries. I looked at the beggars, and the moneychangers and the proprietors of juice stalls. None of them, to my considerable relief, was wearing a Leonard of Paris tie.

We crossed the bridge and drove into a bald patch of sand, tarmac and telegraph poles. Beyond that was Jumeira – Dubai's Los Angelean suburb where huge houses lie stranded in the desert, each one an unnecessary quarter-mile away from its neighbour. Shampooed dogs came to bark at armoured fences and Pakistani gardeners toiled away over lawns of imported turf. Mahdi Tajir's house was up a cul-de-sac on the Gulf shore. Its garden walls were higher than anyone else's, and its entrance was marked by a platoon of guards who cradled submachine-guns in their arms. For the moment, though, they wore expressions of oily subservience, nodding and grinning at the stream of guests who were getting out of chauffeur-driven cars. I got my taxi to stop well back from the house, and walked the rest of the way: I was not going to be seen arriving at Mahdi Tajir's in a '72 Dodge with a crumpled fender.

The lunch was an official reception. Later that afternoon, Sheikh Rashid was to open the Dubai Petroleum Company's new office complex. A whole raft of American oil millionaires had been flown over from the United States for the occasion; and as I joined the queue at the front door I saw them herding – red-faced, jet-shocked, prime beef in Dacron suits. They were making cattle noises.

'Say, isn't that just something? That's something. That really is something,' said a Texan bullock contemplating Mahdi Tajir's private army. Can one order custom-built packages of guards and submachine-guns from Sears, Roebuck?

We shuffled through in line, into the refrigerated cool of the house. Fountains played in a covered courtyard round a pool of deep, artificial blue, and brilliant terracotta frescoes lined the walls. Silent Indian servants funnelled our procession into a long, pot-pourri-smelling drawing-room where circulating trays of cocktails appeared to be moving in some complicated balletic sequence without any visible human intervention. It is possible, I think, that there may have been Indians underneath the trays; indeed, Mahdi Tajir may breed midgets specially for the purpose. At any rate, whenever a tray reached me there was no hand to be seen on it, and it glided away as soon as one removed a glass from its surface.

I found myself standing next to an American.

'Howard B. Nutcracker,' he said – or words to that effect, because I wasn't listening, I was looking at his tie. Ten stripes up from the bottom, in small blue letters, it said 'Leonard of Paris'. A heavy weight had been lifted from my mind, and I settled down to enjoying myself.

Mr Nutcracker was jingling the ice in his Bourbon and saying to a Mr Blauvelt that it was just great to see him, it was great that he'd been able to come, that the operation was going just great, that this was a great time of year to come to Dubai, that Mahdi Tajir's house was great –

'Everything's just great,' he said.

As far as I could see, Mr Nutcracker was perfectly correct in his assessment. Everything was just great. I was sandwiched between Mr Nutcracker and a life-size jade buddha, whom I at first mistook for a sickly green fellow guest. What looked like a large Christmas crib turned out to be the most intricate and elaborate piece of Chinese ivory that I've ever seen – a complete miniature city of polished bone figures engaged in a courtly party of their own. Bowing mandarins in the foreground were saying whatever mandarins say when Americans say 'Just great'. I wanted to study this scene in more detail, and put my drink down on a side-table. Its top was smoked glass, but beneath the glass there was a thick rime of what I took to be diamonds.

'The really great thing about Mahdi,' Mr Nutcracker was saying, 'is he's got Taste. You meet a helluva lot of Arabs with Money, but Mahdi's the only one I know with Taste. Take a look at that – '

'Just great,' agreed Mr Blauvelt.

My own eye skimmed a wall of masterpieces and came to rest on a tall window overlooking a swimming pool. On the ruffled mirror of chlorinated green floated a giant swan. It was roughly seven feet tall, made of inflatable plastic, and its big, round, black-and-orange eyes winked like those of a Cindy Doll. As I watched it turning and drifting in the wind, I wondered if it was the one object in sight which had not been vetted as a good investment; no expert had advised on it, no banker had calculated its percentage – the swan was Mahdi Tajir's very own. Did he come out here in the privacy of night, surrounded by his guards, and ride his swan from end to end of the floodlit pool, geeing it up and paddling with his feet?

A lot of cocktails had been clinked and drained before Mahdi Tajir himself arrived, like the Queen, in a sudden peremptory hush. The roomful of people split down the middle, opening up a royal pathway for the host. He was a small man, in a plain cream linen shift, and at a distance he looked like an escaped mandarin from the ivory tableau. There was a thriftiness about the way he moved; every nod, smile and handshake was nicely calculated, as if it would have to be accounted for later on the balance sheet of Mahdi Tajir's day.

His Indian secretary, Oscar Mandoodi, introduced me to him.

'This is Mr Raban. He is writing a book – '

At the word 'book', a passing squirm of distaste showed on Mahdi Tajir's powdery face, and he slid quickly past me into the waiting crowd of millionaires.

'He is not like Linda Blandford – ' said Mr Mandoodi, but Mahdi Tajir was gone. I always lose my biggest fish.

Someone pointed out 'the British consul' across the room – a pepper-and-nutmeg man in a shiny suit.

'You're the British consul here?' I said.

'Consul-*General*.'

'I'm sorry – '

'It really doesn't matter,' he said huffily. He had the tired air of a man who had grown used to being pestered by fools. While perfectly prepared to put up with people like me, he was not willing to go so far as to pretend to enjoy the experience.

He was an Arabist of the old school. He had read Arabic at Cambridge in the 1930s, and had spent his diplomatic career in the Middle East. I sensed that he felt that almost everyone in the room was a trespasser or a vandal. The oilmen and I were much alike: ignorant of the country's history, unable to speak its language, we existed in order to goad the Consul-General with stupid questions or, worse, to make known to him our even sillier opinions.

What did he think had happened, I asked him, to that traditional goodwill and understanding which was supposed to exist between the English and the Arabs?

It had been eroded, he said. There was little of it left.

'Do you think it'll help when English schools are offering Arabic at "A" Level, and more British businessmen can speak the language?'

'It's too late for that,' said the Consul-General. 'We're much too far behind. Look at all the Arabs who've got degrees – through the medium of English – at British and American universities. How many Englishmen have degrees – through the medium of Arabic – from universities in the Middle East? Name me one. You can't. The Arabs are too far ahead for us to ever catch up. Our only merit is our professional expertise.

It's the only thing we've got that the Arabs are remotely interested in. There's hardly a single Englishman alive who can carry on an intelligent conversation in Arabic; but the Arabs you meet here will have digested everything in the *Financial Times* by breakfast time. They're not going to give tuppence for your love of Arabia, or your fourth-year Arabic from SOAS; the only thing they want from you is your technical knowledge, your advice on investment or construction. The rest is simply flummery.'

'Do you think the Americans are any better at this than the British?'

'Worse,' said the Consul-General with a certain melancholy satisfaction. 'Far, far worse.'

Trolleys of food had been wheeled on at the far end of the room.

'*That*,' said one of the jet-shocked Americans, standing back from the display and judging it as if it was on exhibition at the Metropolitan Museum, 'is what I would call some spread.'

It was. I loaded a plate with caviare and slices of smoked salmon, and found myself a quiet corner overlooking the swimming pool, where I sat down to enjoy my spoils.

'What's that, smoked salmon?' An oilman with his mouth full of bread put his face into my plate. 'I guess it's a kind of an acquired taste.'

'Hi, *Howard*!' But this was a different Howard. Perhaps everyone was called Howard.

'Hey, great to see you! How are you?'

'Just great.'

'You live in Dubai too?' This was to me.

'No,' I said, 'I'm just passing through.'

'What business are you in?'

'I'm writing a book,' I said.

'Oh, Jesus Christ,' said Howard. 'The guy's writing a book. What sort of a book are you writing?'

'It's about American oilmen in the Gulf,' I said.

'You think I ought to call my lawyer?'

'I wouldn't think so,' I said. My confidence was rising fast. For Howard was also wearing a Leonard of Paris tie.

With two more hours to kill before the opening ceremony, I

wandered into Jumeira, a lone pedestrian on a long dull boulevard. After lunch at Mahdi Tajir's, I was not easily impressed by the houses of the rich: they were just Beverly Hills without the hills. I was primarily concerned to avert an incipient hangover by taking a good strenuous walk in the sun, and at first I didn't notice that I was actually strolling through two suburbs at once. The second suburb was too low in height, too close to the colour of builders' waste and dirty sand, to be immediately visible in the glare. Looking out of the window of one of those gimcrack Palladian villas, one's view might never be checked by the miserable shacks of one's neighbours.

They were barely even shacks. They were scoops in the sand with piles of junk for roofs: oil drums, car doors, bits of chicken-wire, cardboard boxes, torn strips of rush matting. That they were human habitations at all, and not heaps of garbage from the surrounding houses, was only proved by the animals tethered round them – dogs, goats and camels; creatures with moth-eaten fur stretched like drumskins around their pro-tuberant ribs. A woman was walking across this grisly wasteland, balancing a rusty oil drum full of water on her head. She was lost to sight in the black shadow cast by the gables of a brand-new fake French château.

A fine red carpet had been laid out for Sheikh Rashid, and three Pakistanis with long brooms were engaged in keeping it free of the sand which blew round the entrance to the Dubai Petroleum Company's new office complex. The waiting crowd around the carpet was mainly European and American, and everyone had brought their cameras. Company husbands were fussing over the lens apertures of their Nikons, Pentaxes and Yashicas, while their wives were busy snapping each other with Kodak Instamatics. I drifted into conversation with the company doctor, a kindly Englishman who reminded me not to forget to keep up with the course of malaria tablets which I'd been prescribed in London. 'There's a lot of it about.' We scanned our order papers for the day – an international goulash of the names of the companies responsible for the architecture, mechanics, electrics, interior design and landscaping of the building.

'I sometimes wonder,' said the doctor, working his way

through 'Bisharat . . . Szegezdy . . . Al Habtoor . . . Blake-down . . .', 'whether colonialism by contract isn't really just the same as colonialism by more traditional means.'

'At least it has a time-limit,' I said. 'In three years, five years, or whatever the term is, the land and everything reverts to being the exclusive property of the state.'

'Then the state signs more contracts – ' the doctor said, as Sheikh Rashid's convoy of limousines drew up at the entrance.

Everyone had said of Sheikh Rashid that he was 'shrewd'. He looked shrewd; a bearded Olivier in the role of Iago. He was small and quick on his feet, his black muslin robe with its trimmings of gold leaf blowing behind him in the wind. He had snipped the ribbon at the door of the building before anyone had had a chance to make a speech, and I was relieved to see a disappointed American hastily disposing of a voluminous sheaf of notes. I had been steeling myself for half an hour or so of windbaggery, but we were inside the complex within seconds, with the Ruler's entourage springing nimbly ahead for the elevators.

'Did you get your picture, Howard?'

'I couldn't, honey. He was just too fast – '

'Ellen got him – '

'The focus was all wrong. I thought there were supposed to be *speeches*.'

'Oh, that's too bad. Howard didn't get his picture.'

'Well,' said the doctor. 'What do you think of it?'

I hadn't even looked. When I did, I doubted the evidence of my own eyes. No wonder Sheikh Rashid had been in such a hurry to get in: it was a delirious funhouse, a lovely techno-logical wonderland. We were standing under the high dome of a night sky with a Milky Way of gold stars. Giant gold oil-drills spiralled down from this painted heaven towards sunken water-gardens of palms, ferns and tropical flowers. A labyrinth of marble walks led to other vast covered courts. On the wall of one, a whole dhow had been sliced in two from bow to stern and leaned out on a wild diagonal from its sea of rippling blue plaster. A cool brook glistened over pebbles at my feet, and I sat sipping orange juice under a glade of trees whose branches were lit by a hidden artificial sun. Far above my head, I saw Sheikh Rashid nipping in and out of office doors

along the catwalks which ran round the sky. A fountain played
at my elbow as I lounged, marvelling, on a prettily cushioned
stone bench; this was kitsch so magnificent and inventive that
it totally transcended the category – it was a triumph of
happy make-believe.

For those that fear the majesty of their Lord there
are two gardens (which of your Lord's blessings would
you deny?) planted with shady trees. Which of your
Lord's blessings would you deny?
    Each is watered by a flowing spring. Which of your
Lord's blessings would you deny?
    They shall recline on couches lined with thick brocade,
and within their reach shall hang the fruits of both
gardens. Which of your Lord's blessings would you deny?
    A gushing fountain shall flow in each. Which of your
Lord's blessings would you deny?
    Each planted with fruit trees, the palm and the pomegranate.
Which of your Lord's blessings would you deny?
    They shall recline on green cushions and rich carpets.
Which of your Lord's blessings would you deny?

The description of Paradise in the Koran serves pretty well as a
rough guide to the glories of the new office complex of the Dubai
Petroleum Company.

'You like it?' said an oilman whom I had met at Mahdi
Tajir's lunch.

'Wonderful,' I said, and babbled on euphorically about its
extraordinary merits. No piece of modern architecture that I
have ever seen has anything like such grace combined with
such spirited good humour. It made me laugh aloud in pure
pleasure at the splendid arrogance of the thing.

'You ought to meet Gene Baker. He did the interiors. He'd
love to hear you talk. Hey, Gene – '

For a man who had built Paradise, Eugene Baker seemed
oddly quiet and mousy. He was wandering shyly, alone, in the
labyrinth of his creation.

'All the plants are rooted in *Licha*. It's a synthetic soil-
substitute, better than real soil by far. Its nutritional value's
much higher.'

What about the brook? I asked. How many Baluchis did it

take to keep those pebbles watered?

'Highlighted polyurethane,' said Eugene Baker. 'Transparent film. Gives the illusion of water without the water.'

We crossed one of Mr Baker's synthetic streams and stood in the shade of one of his synthetic groves.

'I think it's right for Dubai,' he said. 'It wouldn't work anywhere else in the world, but it's right for Dubai.'

The Ruler's party had left the main building and were off inspecting the helicopter landing pad, the health clinic and the swimming pool. We followed them out. The façade on the back of the complex was dominated by a great golden labyrinth, set in relief into the sloping outer wall.

'What's it like working here?' I asked the man next to me in the crowd.

'Well . . .' he said. He wore thick pebble-spectacles, through which he gazed out doubtfully at a puzzling world. 'You see . . .' He sneaked cautious glances over both shoulders and dropped his voice to a conspiratorial undertone. 'Back home, I'm used to working in a place that looks like a profit-making enterprise. To be totally honest, I can't seem to get accustomed to working in a palace.'

'That,' I said, 'is probably just what the civil servants in Florence said when Lorenzo the Magnificent moved them all into Vasari's Uffizi.'

And for a moment, it seemed true. With the falling sun glinting on the labyrinth, and the flying black muslin of Sheikh Rashid across the court, the date on the Islamic calendar was exactly right: it was pure Quattrocento.

6

Arabia Demens

At Dubai airport I attached myself to a long queue of babbling
Yemenis who were waving air tickets at each other. Smaller,
darker and much scruffier than the Gulf Arabs, the Yemenis
had thrush-egg skulls and curiously knotty faces. They wore
plastic sandals, midi-length skirts and jackets which all appeared
to have once been the top halves of the cheapest and shiniest
Hong Kong suits. What, I wondered, had happened to the
trousers? I suspect that where Europe has butter-mountains
and wine-lakes, the great unnatural landmark of the Yemen is
a huge ribbed crag of trousers, like a pillar of black basalt.

In the Gulf, the Yemenis were taxi drivers, construction
workers, soldiers, roadbuilders, mechanics, rig hands. In the
hierarchy of labour they formed an upper working class of
semi-skilled men – a clear notch or two above the Baluchis,
Pakistanis and Bangladeshis, but far below the middle class of
Palestinians, Egyptians, Jordanians and Europeans. For two
and three years on end, they lived in huts and camps, posting
their wages back to their families in the Yemen. The queue I
had joined consisted of lucky ones; the end of term had come
for them, and there was a larkiness around the ticket desk
which reminded me of happy July mornings on the station
platform of the town where I had been at boarding school.
Like us, they had tin trunks in which their entire lives were
packed. Unlike our trunks, though, theirs were brilliantly
painted with suns, moons, flowers, and for all the ragging that
was going on they carried these trunks as carefully as if they

were made of glass.

The plane was like a cheerful country bus. We rattled on in the dark over the Empty Quarter while I gnawed a cold chicken leg and tried to concentrate on Thesiger's *Arabian Sands*. It wasn't the right place to read that book. Our flight was on almost exactly the same course that Thesiger and his companions had taken across the Empty Quarter in 1947, but the coincidence served only to stretch the thirty years between Thesiger's journey and my idle plane-reading into centuries. His Arabia seemed an impossibly far-off place.

I read: 'The Arabs are a race which produces its best only under conditions of extreme hardship and deteriorates progressively as living conditions become easier.' The man in the seat next to me shook a little pile of nuts into my hand. We laughed companionably. He was holding a toy giant panda on his lap, and made it squeak for me. Thesiger's party, meanwhile, was running out of water, and their camels were on the point of death.

> I looked round, seeking instinctively for some escape. There was no limit to my vision. Somewhere in the ultimate distance the sands merged into the sky, but in that infinity of space I could see no living thing, not even a withered plant to give me hope.

The bright chatter of the plane drowned the noise of the engines. It had turned – as almost any communal space in Arabia seems to turn – into a club. The returning Yemenis, giggly with excitement, crowded into the middle of the gangway, telling jokes which were greeted with peals and whoops. My fellow-traveller and I smoked each other's cigarettes, munched nuts and played with the panda. At the same time as Thesiger, exhausted, lying low for fear of bandits, at last reached the well at Khaba, our well-fed company, all in deliriously high spirits, touched down at Sana'a.

It was nearly midnight. After two months of living in the hot fog of the Gulf, I took one lungful of the thin Yemeni air and found it deliciously cool and dry. Sana'a is in the middle of a volcanic plateau nearly nine thousand feet above the sea. It's high up on the giddy top of Arabia, and when one steps out of the plane one walks on to what should by rights be sky. A walk of a hundred yards across the tarmac left me light-headed and short of breath. It seemed that I was the only passenger on the flight who had no one to meet me, for half the population of the city had turned out to press their faces against a flimsy barrier of wire netting, waiting to catch sight of husbands, brothers, fathers, sons. They made a noise like the chorus of a gaudy Italian opera, shouting out names of men they hadn't seen for months and years. Abdul Azziz! Ali! Mohammed! Jamal! Abdurabu! Ahmed! Ali! Tariq! Ibrahim! Mahdi! Mohammed! Jamal! Hamud! Husain! Everyone was kissing and hand-holding through the wire, and I wished that there had been a waiting face there for me. It seemed a long time since I had kissed anyone, but for the men in the arrival hall it had been very much longer.

They had kept in touch with their families through letters, of course; but the letters would have been written by scribes sitting on packing-cases in market squares and running off their standard epistles-for-every-occasion. Any wife to any husband . . . any father to any son . . . any husband to any wife. Particular details – a birth, a death, a disease – could be slotted in at the request of the sender: Jamal would know that he had a son whom he had never seen, and that he was a fine boy, for boys are always fine in Arabia; but as he scanned the faces at the wire, he might well be hard put to it to pick out that of his own wife, daringly unveiled for this extraordinary occasion.

In the crowd I saw a child with a panda. The boy looked bewildered and tearful as his father crouched in front of him, jogging the toy animal up and down on the concrete. Brothers and fathers hugged one another, their loosely tied head-dresses falling askew over their shoulders. I felt a trespasser on the scene: everyone who arrives at Sana'a airport ought really to be coming home, and the half-dozen or so of us who were itinerants shyly squeezed our way past these celebrations. Our presence was unnoticed and unseasonal.

The night outside seemed particularly black. I piled my cases into a taxi and asked the driver to take me to the Rowdah Palace Hotel. Someone in Bahrain had recommended it as the best hotel in Sana'a, and I had written from Abu Dhabi to reserve a room. We drove through two or three miles of bumpy total darkness and ended up at a single pool of light in a rocky courtyard, where a vulpine dog bayed at our arrival. The driver chucked a brick at it, and it went off to snarl at a safe distance.

In the lobby I found a Yemeni rolled up, asleep, in a blanket at the foot of a flight of stone steps. I had to jump up and down on the flagstones to wake him. '*Yallah!*' he moaned at me; Go Away.

'But I have a reservation – '

With a series of rather overtheatrical grunts and moans, he slowly came-to. There were no reservations, he said: I did not exist. To prove it, he stumbled off into a back office and brought back a box containing a postcard and four aerograms that looked as if the mice had got at them. None of them was from me. Their postmarks were all months old. Since, as far as I could see, the hotel was not exactly overburdened with guests, this didn't strike me as a conclusive reason for sending me back out into the night. Grumbling, wrapping himself deeper into his blanket, the man showed me a room.

It had walls of solid stone, four feet thick. It was decently, even prettily, furnished, but it still looked like a cell. It was the cell of a monk rather than a prisoner, perhaps, but it was a cell nevertheless. Casting my luck on an unlikely die, I asked the man if he could find some whisky for me. For the first time since I had woken him, he brightened. A sleepy grin widened his face.

'No whisky,' he said. 'No beer. No alcohol.'

It is, I suppose, not really an irony at all that prohibitionist Arabia's chief contribution to the world's languages is the word *alcohol*.

'Coffee, then? Can you get me some coffee?'

'Coffee sleeps.'

Sniggering faintly, he shambled off down the stairs to continue his own sleep. I did what I could to make myself at home, laying out my stock of books on the creaky table. Trollope and Wilkie Collins looked sadly out of place; Thesiger and Freya Stark didn't seem right either. Lévi-Strauss was merely intimidating. The only book which offered the prospect of good company and cheer was Evelyn Waugh's *When The Going Was Good*. Waugh had been to Aden – now the chief city of communist South Yemen – in 1930. I gloated over his description of the Yemenis with vindictive joy.

> They are of small stature and meagre muscular development; their faces are hairless or covered with a slight down, their expressions degenerate and slightly dotty, an impression which is accentuated by their loping, irregular gait.

That was the man downstairs. I would have liked to have been able to translate the passage into Arabic, inscribe it in poker-work, and hang it over the surly little bastard's head. Much consoled, I read on by the light of the bare overhead bulb. The Yemeni electricity supply seemed to be slightly dotty too. I could actually watch the current struggling uncertainly round the filament in the bulb, now dimming to a pale gleam, now building to a dangerously brilliant white. For moments at a time, the room went dark, then the guttering light would revive. The pages of *When The Going Was Good* were stained with red wine which I'd spilled on it at Ralph Izzard's house in Bahrain. That all seemed a very long time ago.

I woke, still dressed, to find myself lying in what seemed to be the end of a rainbow. The low window was a tracery of irregular holes cut in the stone, and each hole was filled with a fist-sized lump of coloured glass, staining the sunlight scarlet, purple, green and gold. It had turned me into a groggy pierrot. Dazzled, I went to the window and peered out of one of the holes from which the glass had gone. No one should catch their first sight of the Yemen before breakfast: it brings on vertigo and an alarming conviction that one must be suffering from some extreme disorder of one's vision.

The hotel was surrounded by steep towers of mad mud-Tudor. They looked like the surviving entries from an ancient sandcastle competition. Every square inch of their walls had been worked and decorated with casements, arches, gables, crenellations and rough friezes of whorls, lozenges and curlicues. They leaned and toppled dizzily, straining to the limit the crude materials from which they had been built. 'The arabesque,' I remembered from Dr Farouki's lecture in Doha, 'has no limit. It is denaturalized, destylized . . . a song of praise.' These towers were arabesques in mud and rough stone. I couldn't begin to guess their age. Some were in ruins. Some were evidently inhabited, with drying washing draped across balconies and battlements.

A woman, completely covered in a heavy purple shawl which made her look like a walking beehive, crossed the dusty square below me. A buzzard glided overhead. There were splashes and pools of vivid green: I registered cedars, cypresses, vines, figs. A pair of yellow dogs scrapped listlessly among some overturned petrol drums; a man on a mud turret was smoking in the sky; somewhere out of sight there was the shrill chirrup of a two-stroke engine; in all this busy elaboration of stucco, dust and greenery there was no visible logic, no point for the eye to rest. It was a landscape of commas and semi-colons – everything disjointed from everything else. Even on its distant fringes, the mauve hills were jagged, improbably streaked with green. The view from the window made my eyes turn and dart in their sockets like tropical fish; it was all too rich, too full of surprises. The thought that later in the day I would have to set about decoding this amazing stew of alien signs and symbols made me want to go back immediately to bed. I had three weeks ahead of me: judging from that minute or two spent squinting through a draughty hole in a window, it would take all my time just to make an inventory of the things one could see on one wall of one tower. The Yemen had been known to older travellers as *Arabia Felix* – the happy corner of fertility in a desert continent. But its fertility, and human ingenuity, looked as if they had run riot long ago and created an Arabia which was not so much Felix as Demens.

I set off gingerly in search of breakfast. After the dazzling confusion of the world outside my window, I was glad of the long dark corridors inside the hotel. Once it had been an imam's palace, and it was a forbidding, complicated tangle of stone archways and steep stairs. I saw that the man who had let me in the night before was still asleep at the bottom of one flight. I went up some steps which led to a blank stone wall, tried another lot, wandered through a tunnel and found a dining-room which disconcertingly resembled a suburban

Wimpy Bar, with bottles of tomato ketchup on plastic tables. I sat down with my back to the window, determined to get my bearings gradually. A man wearing a curved dagger round his waist like a codpiece asked me rather disagreeably what I wanted. I said that I would like some breakfast. He seemed to think that this was a very odd request indeed. Please, I said: it would be a great kindness if he would bring me some coffee and an egg. He scowled and fingered the hilt of his dagger. He repeated the word *egg* doubtfully. Yes, please, I said; I would like it boiled for five minutes. He walked backwards towards the kitchens, watching me all the time as if I was a dangerous madman.

The best part of half an hour went by, broken intermittently by the sound of distant giggles and scuffles. Then the man with the dagger came back with my breakfast. It was reasonably close to what I had ordered: a tin of Japanese apple juice and a very small, very dirty raw egg with a couple of chickenshitty feathers sticking unappetizingly to its shell.

'Boiled! Cooked! *Taha!*' I said. '*Taha!*' – and heard my own voice. It sounded quite lunatic enough to justify the man's worst apprehensions.

'It *can* be a bit tricky getting what you want here – ' Two Englishmen in identical denim safari suits had come into the dining-room. 'We've found the best bet is just to stick to tea. They make rather good tea, actually.'

I have never been so preposterously glad to hear the accent of Wimbledon and East Sheen. The Englishmen were obviously as disturbed by my appearance as the waiter was. Sweating profusely, ranting wildly in pidgin-English and pidgin-Arabic, I was not cutting much of a figure.

'Been here long?' asked one of them cautiously. I think that perhaps he suspected me of having just crawled out of a cave in the mountains: the Yemen is notorious for attracting reclusive crazies. The hills in the north of the country are probably full of bat-eyed Englishmen living on nuts and roasted crows – fugitive diplomats, one-time RAF officers and travelling brush-salesmen. I explained that I was only suffering from a mild attack of culture-shock, and showed the men my egg. I noticed that my hand was shaking. So did they.

They had been in the Yemen for a month — members of a United Nations commission on agriculture. They were conducting a survey on the grain-growing potential of the plateau, and I found that listening to them had much the same effect as swallowing two very strong benign tranquillizers. Wonderfully calmed, I found myself asking polite questions — over rather good tea — about maize and corn and barley.

'We can give you a lift to Sana'a a bit later on, if you like. We've got a Land-Rover outside.'

'But isn't this Sana'a?'

'No, no; this is Rowdah — just a village. Sana'a's another six miles down the road. Twenty quid, probably, if you take a taxi.'

All that confusion — and I hadn't even expended it on the right place. I felt cheated, lost and sweaty.

We drove out of Rowdah in the Land-Rover. The hotel had been a palace, and so, it seemed, had every other house in the village. The place was blocked solid with falling towers; in its heyday it must have been crawling with royalty. Half the palaces now, though, were just fields of dried mud and broken stones where goats, poultry and grubby children foraged in puffs of dust.

We passed a military barracks, with a twice-lifesize plastic tank perched on a rock, then a long desolate flatland of scrub which had been recently walled off behind a sign which announced it, in English, as 'The 26th of September Park'.

'Do they have a park for every day of the year, or is the twenty-sixth of September special?'

'I think it's the day of the Glorious Revolution.'

'Which one?'

'The last one.'

'They're dragging this country by the scruff of its neck into the middle of the fifteenth century — ' The remark was made in those heavy inverted commas which signal a standard cliché; it was the kind of remark which custom required one to make about the Yemen. I laughed politely, but it did not in fact seem to fit in at all with what I could see. After the endless construction sites of the Gulf, Rowdah and the outskirts of Sana'a looked like sites of idle destruction. Doors were falling out of walls; walls out of houses; houses out of streets; and whole streets seemed to be falling clean out of the city. If all enterprise in Europe had stopped dead in the middle of the Renaissance, and the whole edifice of civilization been left to quietly self-destruct, then London, Florence, Venice, Chartres and Amsterdam would look today much like my first impression of Sana'a. It was like driving at speed into an enormous bad cheese. The odd breezeblock building, the new street-lights which had been sunk awry into the mud sidewalks, the rough tarmac, neon signs, roundabouts and Pepsi-Cola hoardings did almost nothing to counteract the overwhelming sense that the place had gone rotten. Rot was in the air: it smelled of rotten wood, rotten meat, rotten clothes, rotten money. Sana'a was 'off'. Long after I had left the Yemen, I kept a one-rial bank-note in my wallet. It had gone soggy with handling, and it had acquired the authentic stench of the city. Back in London, paying for a bag of groceries at my cornershop, I was able to summon the Yemen like a genie just by opening the wallet and catching the powerful whiff of that one-rial note.

The agriculturalists dropped me off in the market square. They might, I felt then, just as well have set me down in the city centre of Purgatory. The smell, the glare and the shattering din of horns and motors made the insides of my head curdle. I had been told to expect the medieval. ('I *love* Sana'a,' said an enthusiastic lady in Abu Dhabi. 'It's just like going *right* back into the middle ages. It's the *real* Arabia.') I had not been warned of the Toyotas, the Datsuns, the Hondas and Chevrolets which ploughed through the narrow mud streets in swirling cauls of dirt, taking sides off walls and forcing people, dogs and cattle to run for their lives. None of the vehicles looked more than a year old, and many of their drivers looked not much older than their cars – scowling babies with their fists pressed permanently down on the buttons of their horns. 'Novelty' horns had hit the town: it was like listening to a mass rally of ice-cream vans, all playing different tunes in furious competition. I was nearly killed by a demented infant who mounted the pavement in his Toyota and blasted me with the first four bars of 'The Camptown Races':

> De Camptown darkies sing dis song:
> Dooh dah! Dooh dah!

And pedestrians added to the appalling racket by carrying loud transistor radios tuned to rival stations, as well as new tape-recorders which belted out Western pop songs, Arab dance tunes and the lovelorn bawling of The Lady.

> Gwine to ride all night!
> Gwine to ride all day!
> Bet ma money on de bobtail nag,
> Somebody bet on de bay!

At the time, I was in no fit state to meditate on things like the per capita Gross National Product of the Yemen. Had I been able to do so, the jangle of all this new expensive hardware might have puzzled as well as deafened me. For the last available figures show that the Yemen, with a GNP of $120 per person per year, is one of the dozen or so poorest countries in the world. It didn't sound it. Hurling myself into a wall of brown dust in order to avoid being run down by a truck with a nasty grin on the face of its radiator, I felt it wise to leave all questions of history, architecture, economics, politics and religion for later.

For the moment, I tried to restrict myself to making small, cautious moves. It wasn't easy. Throughout my trip the idea of the labyrinth had never been far away. I had seen labyrinths used again and again as decorative motifs; I had been inside consciously labyrinthine houses; the souks I had visited had all been constructed on labyrinthine principles; and I had sensed that the larger structure of Arab society was – unlike the vertical hierarchies of the West – a labyrinth too. Until now, though, the labyrinth had been little more than a useful symbol. Suddenly in Sana'a I was in the middle of a real maze. Its walls were oppressively high, its corridors narrow, its noise frightening. Wherever I turned, there were new riddles and contradictions. If I thought I was in one place, it turned out to be another. I was beginning to behave like a scared rat in a psychologist's maze – bolting into blank walls, jumping at shadows, and shouting obscenities at the drivers who seemed determined either to run me over or to send me mad. Sana'a was functioning exactly as a labyrinth should: it was a close protective hive for insiders; but for an outsider it was a trap with no apparent means of escape.

I was down to the whimpering stage when I asked a man if he knew where the British Embassy was. He said he would show me. He liked the British very much, he said; it would be a pleasure for him to accompany me. I followed him gratefully through a series of streets which were simply ditches of cracked mud lined with tall mud houses. The streets of Sana'a are paved with silver, in the form of hundreds of thousands of flattened soft-drink cans, as well as with rocks, garbage, flies and the small leathery corpses of dead rats. In the rainy reason, which comes in August, they turn into rivers, and are, presumably, washed clean of the year's accumulated filth; but this was March, and they had the ripe tang of a maturing culture rising from them. My guide scampered ahead of me, his skirt flying, bounding nimbly from crater to crater. We appeared to have recrossed our tracks several times before we arrived at a main road, where he pointed out the new street lighting and, immediately across from where we were standing, a Union Jack hanging limply on its flagpole. I thanked the man profusely. He offered me a cigarette and remarked that the English were a fine people with a long and honourable history. I felt sorry that I was such a poor specimen of my race.

He was carrying what looked like a large chunk of privet hedge wrapped in cellophane paper. Would I like some too? he asked. I thanked him but said that I would rather not accept, if he didn't mind. He stripped off the leaves from the top of one sprig and put them in his mouth.

'Yemeni whisky,' he said, grinning through green teeth. We shook hands, and I left him chewing his *qat* on the corner.

In the lobby of the embassy, I searched hopefully through the rack of pigeonholes for letters from home. There were none for me. I studied the notices on the board. There was going to be an Easter Service, three days late, conducted by a priest who was flying specially from Saudi Arabia for the occasion; English residents were asked to contribute generously towards his air fare. In the waiting-room, there were some old copies of *Encounter* and the *Listener*, and I found just the sight of their covers oddly cheering, as if I'd bumped into a gang of dull old friends. Taking time out from Arabia, I gutted their book-review sections. It seemed a funny, distant, enviable world, full of nursery niceties and nursery punishments. Margaret Drabble was being ticked off by nanny for being naughty and Paul Theroux was being handed a lollipop for being good. I got through two very cosy, very nannyish paragraphs about a novel by Iris Murdoch before I realized that I had written them myself. It was not a tone that I – or, for that matter, anyone else – could have managed in Sana'a.

I didn't want to leave the embassy. It was a nice, cool English place, and I prevaricated with the Indian clerk who kept on coming into the waiting-room and asking me my business. Indians are accustomed to guile and subtlety, and he eventually fathomed that I must have entered the building in order to make contact with the Head of Chancery. Nothing could have been further from my mind, but the Head of Chancery turned out to be a mild, kindly man who gave me coffee and said that he supposed that I wanted a 'briefing'.

'I really only came in for a breather, actually. I don't think I'm ready for a "briefing" yet.'

'Oh, good,' said the Head of Chancery, and invited me to dinner.

I left the embassy feeling buoyant and restored. The Head of Chancery had suggested a string of people whom I might meet, had made several telephone calls on my behalf, and had even managed, in the nicest possible way, to give me the 'briefing' that I thought I didn't want. Had it not been for the friendliness of Lord Buckmaster on that morning, I think I probably would have fled the Yemen on the next plane out. He supplied me with enough clues to make a start on finding my way around the maze.

From the Ministry of Information, I collected a copy of the Five Year Plan. From the Department of Tourism, I got a map of Sana'a which was a fine cobweb of wiggly lines – an intricate piece of graphic invention, it vividly conveyed the idea that the city was far too complicated and dense to be mappable. No landmarks were shown; none of the streets named. After several days of carrying this impressive piece of paper around the town, I came to the conclusion that a mistake had been made and that I had in fact been given the random scribblings of a deeply introverted and anally retentive child. At the embassy, I had learned of another hotel – the Dar Al-Hamd Palace. I walked out to it. It was a real hotel, with a telex machine chattering at the back of the lobby and a waiter carrying bottles of beer on a tray; and, yes, I could move in tomorrow.

I wandered back to the market square. It was now empty, dusty, locked in the dog-day torpor of a Yemeni afternoon. The few motor horns that were still left had lost their vicious edge, and I found a café where I bought a bowl of thin stew and a hunk of unleavened bread, and was able to sit in a quiet corner reading the Five Year Plan.

In my newly mellowed mood, it struck me as a very good plan indeed. I dipped my bread in the oily gravy and read up on the future of the Yemen before I knew anything about its past. The projects ran into hundreds, from paper bag factories and stone-crushing plants to campaigns against the desert locust, measures to combat tuberculosis and bilharzia, projects for teaching religion 'on a scientific basis', and 'Project to draw up an accurate map of Yemen'. New cities were to be planned and built; old ones to acquire garbage disposal systems, automatic telephone switchboards, public toilets, potable water, schools, docks, public gardens and – for Sana'a – a 'Sports City'.

> *Project of carbonate beverages stoppers factory*
> *Project of Al-Akel factory for underwear*
> *Project for the production of spaghetti and noodles*
> *Project to reactivate old mines*
> *Project to create a shrimp industry*
> *Project for buying seven emergency generators*
> *Project to buy two aircraft*
> *Project to build a National Theatre*
> *Project to print one hundred books on history, literature and meditation*
> *Project to record the Koran*
> *Project to build the Great Mosque*

Project to estimate the workforce
Project to consider family budget

The 'Projects' had the invigorating roll and sweep of heroic poetry. All of human life was there – from its undergarments to its religious beliefs. Nor were they to just be made fun of: they were simply putting down in black and white the oceanic scale of change which is required of any 'underdeveloped' country in making the transition to becoming a 'developed' one. Lots of countries have made that change; Yemen's Five Year Plan is a plainspoken list of the factors involved. It has all the limitless ambition of Islam – the same sublime cheek as the airy mud palaces which surrounded the café where I was reading, the same lack of scepticism that I had met so often in the Gulf.

Yet the first half of the document consisted of an evaluation of the Three Year Programme which the Five Year Plan had been designed to follow up. It was not a recital of triumphs; indeed, its frankness verged on the embarrassing.

3:6 *National Tobacco and Match Company: This company is suffering from strong competition, old machines, lack of spare parts, lack of maintenance and lack of skilled personnel.*

3:8 *National Printing and Publishing Company: A modern printing press was established but it was destroyed by fire at the end of the Three-Year Programme.*

8:1 *Ministry of Finance: The deficit continued due to costs of operations and investment expenses. Among the most important obstacles are the bulky administration, low productivity and the prevalence of smuggling.*

9:1 *Ministry of Education: Illiteracy is about 74·4% among males and 97·7% among females. There are, however, centres for adult education in literacy.*

10:1 *Ministry of Health: The health situation in Yemen is characterized by the spread of epidemic diseases (such as bilharzia, tuberculosis, malaria, etc), a low level of food and nourishment, poor knowledge of health and nutrition and the need for pure drinking water, sewerage systems and public cleaning services. Sixty-five per cent of the people live in shacks, caves or one-room houses.*

> 11:2 *Ministry of Awqaf: In spite of the tangible progress*
> *in this ministry, it is still far from the realization of*
> *its objectives. Its system is still inefficient, its*
> *property is fading away, and its revenues are decreasing.*

I called for another glass of tea to wash down the last of my bread. The two halves of the document faced each other in brute contradiction. Was it possible for the same authors to be responsible for the castles-in-the-sky of the 'Projects' and for the hardboiled realism of the 'Evaluation'? Yet the schizophrenia of the Five Year Plan was perfectly in tune with everything that I had seen during the last twelve hours. Extreme surliness: extreme friendliness. Extreme poverty: extreme wealth. The tumbledown streets, with the smell of death and starvation on them, were awash with brand-new luxury goods. Even the change from morning to afternoon involved a violent reversal. When I'd arrived, the place had been seething with manic, bluebottle busyness; now it was so inert that it was hard to imagine it ever stirring back to life. All round the square, in scraps of shade, in woody cupboards set in walls, under jumbo-sized umbrellas, the Yemenis were given over to chewing *qat*. Everyone in sight had his bunch of privet, with a wad of leaves as big as a cricket ball bulging in one cheek.

> *Project of planning major cities*
> *Project for roads and electrification in cities*
> *Project to number houses and streets*
>
> 5:1 *Ministry of Public Works: In most municipalities*
> *the Ministry failed to meet the needs of the large horizontal*
> *expansion of construction in cities due to increasing*
> *emigration to cities, lack of planning, inability to*
> *take care of community health, lack of administrative*
> *efficiency, insufficient equipment, low salaries, and*
> *disputes about the ownership of municipality land.*

The eyes of the *qat*-chewers were withdrawn and unfocused. Several days later, someone described the effects of *qat* to me like this: 'It makes you feel like big king: you think you can do *anything* – ' Perhaps the 'Projects' had been written during the afternoons, while the 'Evaluation' had been compiled in the

bitter reality of the mornings. Given the mare's nest of paradoxes in which they appeared to be living, it was no wonder
that the faces of so many of the Yemenis I could see looked like
reef-knots tied in flesh.

I paid my bill and walked to the centre of the square where a
group of taxi drivers were lounging against their cars. I wanted
to go back to Rowdah.

'Fifty rials,' said one man.

'Twenty,' I said. In most Arab countries, bargaining is a
way of establishing a social relationship. Both sides have time
on their hands, and buyer and seller get to know one another
as they haggle amiably over the price. That was not the way
in which things turned out to be done in the Yemen. The
man shrugged, transferred his wad of *qat* to his other cheek,
and spat in the dust at my feet. I tried the other drivers.

'Twenty-five rials? Will you drive me to Rowdah for twenty-
five?'

No one stirred.

'Please?'

'A hundred rials.'

'That is too expensive.'

The bulge of *qat*, repeated on the side of every face, looked
like a national malignant growth. A young man, who had
been standing on the outskirts of the group, came over. He
stood in front of me for several seconds before saying anything,
and when he did speak it was in very carefully rehearsed
English.

'You are an English man.'

'Yes.'

'I will drive you to Rowdah for twenty rials.'

'Thank you very much.'

'For you to speak English to me for the examination. For
me to speak English to you. It is the practice for which I drive
you. Do you understand me?'

'Absolutely. An English lesson to Rowdah.'

'That is correct, sir. You make my English to improve very
much for the examination.'

It seemed a fair deal. Hamud was a serious man: he gave the

same grave attention to his driving that he gave to his English. Wherever possible, he liked to give numbers to things. He was twenty years old. He had owned his taxi for seven months. In the mornings, he attended the Gamal Abdel Nasser Secondary School, and in the afternoons he drove his taxi. At school, he was number three in his class. Last year, he had been number four. Once, he had been number one. That was four years ago. He was also studying four subjects: he ticked them off on his fingers. Mathematics. Chemistry. Physics. English.

'If I make mistake, you speak, please.'

'You're doing very well.'

'Thank you, I am pleased.'

Hamud was not chewing *qat*. I asked him why not.

'I eat *qat* one day only of the week. That is good. For one day only, is good. For seven days, is very bad.'

We drove past a collapsing shack from which a man was selling Rothman's King Size cigarettes and balls of string. It was called the 'Filmustaqbal Stores' – the Stores of the Future.

The next day was a Friday, and I felt it looming grimly. I suggested to Hamud that since he wouldn't be at school next morning, he might like to continue our mobile English lesson, and drive me into the country.

'How many rials will you pay me, sir?'

'One hundred and twenty.'

'I wish to accept the invitation.'

'Do you learn your English from an Englishman, or is your teacher an Arab?'

'The country of my teacher is Egypt, sir.'

'In England, we don't call each other "sir". That is very old-fashioned. If I call you Hamud, you should say Jonathan. Or you could call me Mr Raban.'

'I understand, sir. Thank you.'

I felt that Hamud's resistance to the colloquial was based not so much on ignorance of common usage as on a positive dislike of its inexactitude. His formal manners were in accord with his taste for numbers. He seemed to find my own way of talking reprehensibly sloppy.

'I'll see you at nine tomorrow, then,' I said after we'd reached the hotel.

'Nine *a.m.*, sir,' he said severely, and drove off, counting his way through the gear-changes. I was afraid he was going to be a rather dour companion to spend a whole day with.

The hotel was empty. Climbing the stairs to my room, I felt giddy: the heat and the altitude had induced a mild dreamy lethargy in which walls and floors were uncertain quantities. Just under my rainbow window a child was riding a Suzuki motorbike in circles in the dust, playing his horn as he went.

Hitler has only got one ball!

I sat at the table and tried to write. The few sentences which I did manage to get down came out scrambled. My hand-writing had taken a turn for the worse since the Gulf, and the best that I could do in the way of grammar was a string of dashes – shaky parentheses which interspersed a series of unrelated and irreconcilable remarks.

But poor old Go-balls has no balls at all!

As the sun went down, I saw the flicker of Tilley lamps across the square. The electric light in my room had gone completely, and I took my notebook off with me to see what kind of night-life Rowdah had to offer.

There was a café: a couple of sheets of corrugated iron raised over a pile of rocks and one unsteady joist. It served. A pile of cardboard boxes labelled 'Mobil Heavy Duty Oil' kept the wind out on one side; and someone had pinned cigarette advertisements torn out of magazines on to the joist for decoration. Inside there was a rough table, a few benches, a tea urn, a hubble-bubble. Three men were playing cards, and I was dealt into the game without question as soon as I sat down with my glass of tea.

The rules were obscure; but three packs had been shuffled together, and I got whole fistfuls of aces, so I took my fair share of tricks on the basis of a dim memory of having once been dragged into a parish whist drive. The tea was pale and sweet, thickened with Carnation tinned milk – much like tea at the whist drive as I remembered it. My fellow players looked like pirates, with twists of greasy rag around their heads, and the silver hilts of their curved daggers crossed against their chests; but we sat there laying jacks on tens as sedately as a quartet of old biddies at a Hampshire village institute. The play was wordless: bulges of *qat* wobbled slightly in the men's cheeks as they hesitated over their cards, and the oil lamp above the tea urn popped and sputtered.

It was a good calm place, this sociable pool of light with the patter of cards on the table and the darkness closing round us. The man next to me passed me a sprig of *qat*. I shredded some leaves from the top of the stalk and tried munching them, hoping for visions. I have never tried chewing privet, but I imagine that there would be little difference between the tastes. After a while I spat the stuff out.

'You do not like *qat*?'

'This is the first time I try it. Another day, perhaps, with luck – ' I used the word *Inshallah*. It's a word which has been mocked too much by Europeans whose only acquaintance with Arabic is the triumvirate of *Inshallah*, *Bokra* and *Maalesh*. In fact, *Inshallah* nicely conveys the general unreliability of the world. It inflects the promises and expectations which it always follows with a proper degree of caution. After my first taste of *qat* I felt that a great deal of caution was in order.

'*Inshallah*,' said the man, and laughed civilly. His teeth must have been worth a small fortune. By the light of the Tilley lamp, his mouth looked like Aladdin's cave. 'All Yemenis like *qat*.'

It was my deal.

A fair number of the clues to Yemen's maze of contradictions were distributed within the bright circle cast by that lamp. More than fifty per cent of all Yemeni men were working abroad, in the Gulf and Saudi Arabia. The money they earned there was being sent home weekly to their families, and it was flooding the economy. One bank alone was receiving a million pounds a week in foreign currency – and few Yemenis used banks at all. Most of the money was coming in in wads of folded notes, posted from Dubai, Abu Dhabi, Jeddah, Riyadh. People could only guess at the total amounts involved, but they were huge and totally unregulated. Yemen was living on remittances. Although Saudi Arabia and the Gulf states were making large payments of aid to the Yemeni government, the money which the state had to spend was just a trickle compared to the vast quantity in the pockets of private individuals.

This remittance money was being spent hand over fist on goods from abroad. In the café where I was sitting there was hardly anything in sight which was not an import. The Japanese motorcycles parked outside, the transistor radio on a ledge of rock, the playing cards, the tins of milk, the jackets and sandals of the card-players, the glasses we were drinking from, the cellophane in which the qat was wrapped – everything had been bought from outside the country. The only objects which had been produced in the Yemen were the curved daggers and the qat itself.

The rest of Arabia had looked to the fertile soil of the plateau to provide a granary for the subcontinent; but the best soil was given over to the cultivation of qat. It was easy to grow, its price had more than quadrupled in two years, and farmers would not bother with maize, wheat, barley, when they could become millionaires on a few acres of qat. The drug – costing between five and eight pounds for a sprig sufficient for one man for one afternoon – was sopping up a large proportion of the remittance money; most men were reckoned to be spending about fifty pounds a week on qat. They were also getting through three or four packs of cigarettes a day, and many were buying two or three bottles of black-market whisky a week, at about ten pounds a bottle. (Qat keeps one awake; so one needs whisky to get to sleep.)

I had arrived in a very poor country which had been on a wild spree for the last two years. The Yemenis, whose main export, apart from Mocha coffee, was their own manpower, had been occupying themselves buying Toyota cars, Suzuki motorcycles, Hitachi radios, Sony television sets, Rothman's cigarettes, Johnny Walker whisky, and chewing qat. Their government had been unable to control this binge. While the families of the labourers abroad were blowing their pay-packets on luxury goods, the streets of Sana'a were still garbage tips, the structure of the city medieval. Families who didn't have cousins, fathers, husbands working in the Gulf were starving as inflation rose. If any proper balance were to be restored between the state and the individual, then every project in the Five Year Plan would have to come into being very fast indeed. Yet most of the skilled manpower which was needed to implement the Plan was out of the country; and the massive doses of foreign aid which the government was receiving represented only a fraction of the cost of the economic revolution which the country needed.

Yemén had turned into a 'client economy'. It had been terribly weakened by seven years of civil war from 1963 to 1970, when Saudi Arabian troops, supporting the royalist regime of the Imam, had fought Egyptian and Russian troops who supported the republicans. At the end of the fighting a shaky republican government had emerged and the Imam had been exiled to a London suburb. Yet these had been just the years when the oil-rich countries had been establishing their power. Yemen, isolated from the outside world, drained by the war, had become fatally dependent on their wealth. While states like Dubai and Abu Dhabi grew more and more princely, the Yemen was taking much of the strain of their success. Politically, it was still desperately volatile: Colonel al-Hamdi, its head of state since 1970, had been assassinated six months before I arrived. (Three months after I left, Ahmad Ghashmi, Hamdi's successor, was killed by a bomb brought to his office by a South Yemeni peace envoy.)

So we sat in the café, playing whist and chewing *qat*. The money which had paid for the *qat* had almost certainly been earned by a migrant worker a thousand miles away from where we were sitting. The gleaming petrol tanks of the motorcycles outside winked in the lamplight. The transistor radio, with its built-in cassette-recorder, was a handsome piece of Japanese precision engineering. What was Yemen's own was the air of glazed fatigue in which we played, the dirt which stuck in our throats, and the presence, everywhere in sight, of the makeshift, the gimcrack and the tumbledown.

Hamud was waiting for me outside the hotel at nine.

'I am here for twelve minutes,' he said.

There were blue rings under his eyes.

'I study Chemistry until three this morning. Then I do not sleep.'

I loaded my cases into the boot of his car. No day in the

Yemen could start better, I felt, than one which began with my checking out of the Rowdah Palace. Hamud, too, was in an oddly holiday mood. He was wearing a newly-washed robe and had his best dagger belted round his waist. He honoured Friday by relaxing his style of driving and making erratic forays into colloquial English.

'You want that we take women?' he asked.

'If you want, sure – ' I laid two dictionaries on the seat between us.

The women lined the side of the road to Sana'a. They were completely covered under half a dozen layers of grubby cotton-prints and woollen shawls, and looked more like laundry bundles than human beings. By this time, it did not strike me as a paradox worth noting that the most heavily veiled women in the whole of Arabia should be out hitch-hiking on a Friday morning.

Hamud braked the car to a near-standstill, wound down his window, peered, and sniffed.

'Very dirty woman,' he said, slamming his foot on the accelerator.

He repeated this manoeuvre four times in the course of half a mile. Finally he announced that all Yemeni women were dirty.

'It is not good for my car. They make a bad smell.'

I tried to tell Hamud about the Women's Movement, thinking he deserved a moral lecture. 'Yes, yes, yes,' he said impatiently. 'But your women wash. Your women do not smell. Here it is different.'

'What about when you get married?' I asked. 'Won't you want to marry soon?'

'I marry when I am twenty-eight. First, I study. Second, I work. It takes much money to buy a wife. I do not want cheap wife. I do not spend two thousand rials – I spend twenty, thirty thousand rials. It costs much to buy a good wife.'

One of the most important reforms carried through by Hamdi's administration had been to fix the maximum bride-price at three thousand rials (about £425). After the assassin-ation, Ahmad Ghashmi had rescinded the new law and the price of brides was now caught in the same inflationary spiral as the price of qat. This provided yet another incentive for young men to work in the Gulf and Saudi Arabia, in order to earn enough money to be able to afford a wife.

We were stopped at a roadblock manned by soldiers.

'Why this is, I do not know,' Hamud said. 'It is not usual.'

At a roundabout, a mile up the road, there was another. The soldiers looked tired. They peered cursorily inside the car and waved us on.

'In the morning, early, there were many, many . . . *dabbabat*, you know *dabbabat*?'

I looked it up in the dictionary. It meant 'tanks'.

'They make a long line. They go to the north, I think, to the mountains. I do not know what happens.' It was a matter for comment, but not for any great curiosity: Hamud was evidently used to military roadblocks and columns of tanks. He was more interested in finding a route which took him past the largest possible number of mosques.

Every few miles, between roadblocks, he would stop the car.

'I go to the mosque. You may come, please.'

At first I mistook this enthusiasm for visiting religious buildings for simple piety; at the second mosque, I discovered its real reason. Hamud was obsessed with washing himself. He loved the cavernous stone wash-houses with their leaden troughs of stagnant green water. He would douse himself, blow like a grampus, plaster his wet hair closely round his skull, and head back to the car.

'You wash too,' he said.

'I'd rather not, thanks.' Fed on scare-stories about bilharzia, I was probably excessively suspicious of that thick, jade-coloured water. It looked like a paradise for bilharzia snails, which begin by infecting the soles of one's feet and end up by destroying one's brain. My doctor in London had suggested that it would be a good idea to go everywhere in the Middle East in gumboots, just to be on the safe side. He would not, I felt, have approved of me taking a bath in the mosque wash-house.

'Why do you not wash? It is hot. You get dirty.'

'I am not a Muslim,' I said.

'It does not matter. You can wash.'

I stuck priggishly to my guns, more alarmed by my doctor's warnings than I was by the prospect of Hamud's wrinkled nose.

'You see,' I said, 'I am just like the women on the road.'

'No,' Hamud said seriously. 'You are more clean. You do not make such a bad smell.'

'Thanks.'

'You are welcome, sir.'

We drove out a few more miles across the plateau, with the road steadily rising ahead of us. The landscape was just rock – bare and cream-coloured, furred in places with grey lichen. Hamud stopped the car.

'I show you Wadi Darr.'

We climbed a small, ribbed peak. Hamud pointed down. We were on the lip of a sheer face of rock. Wadi Darr – the Fertile Valley – was nearly a thousand feet below us, a great stretch of vivid green with a steep little city of stucco towers at its head.

'Here is grown the best *qat* in Yemen.'

It was an intricate patchwork of smallholdings and irrigation ditches. I had not seen anything like so much green since I had left England. To the Arabs of the desert – to Sheikh Zayed with his passion for trees – Wadi Darr must have represented everything that their Arabia lacked. *Darr* means copiously flowing, productive, rich, lucrative, profitable. So it was.

'And all that is just *qat*?'

'The farmers grow some little corn. Enough for them and for their families. Otherwise it is *qat*.'

'Isn't that a terrible waste of land?'

'What means *waste*? The *qat* is the very best in the whole of Yemen.'

We went back to the car and drove down a zig-zag track into the valley. At the bottom was a single tree-lined street which was a small hell of musical horns. Yet another imam's palace was perched on top of a high crag, and the *qat* market was in full swing under its walls. Carts, donkeys, pick-up trucks were heaped high with the stuff. Cross-legged men squatted in the shadows selling off single sprigs of it. The amount of money which was changing hands was on a scale which would have impressed even Mahdi Tajir. Yet everyone looked like a pauper. The men who were selling the largest quantities of *qat* wore the dirtiest skirts and the most torn plastic sandals: the place was swarming with ragged millionaires. Hamud, in his white tunic and slicked-back hair, looked like the most prosperous man in town; the real rich men were all convincingly disguised as ruffianly beggars.

For about £8 I bought a modest armful of *qat*; enough to experiment with. Hamud scraped a leaf with his thumbnail, tasted the juice and said that it was a fair example of the best *qat* in Yemen. We walked on up to the top of the market where other stallholders sat under canopies of coloured cotton supported on crossed sticks: they were selling hunks of flyblown meat and a few wizened vegetables. One of the side-effects of *qat* is that it takes away the appetite. The sight of the meat, under a glistering frost of bluebottles, made me think that chewing *qat* might well be one of the most sensible precautions I could take during my stay in Sana'a.

'Now we go to the mosque,' said Hamud. While he busied himself with his ablutions, I took off my shoes and walked on the raised terracotta courtyard. The stones were as hot as a griddle in the sun, and I had to hop and skip to a patch of shade on the far side. Sitting on the balustrade and cooling my soles, I was able to look across the valley to other villages, set high up on jutting pillars of rock, their medieval skyscrapers spiralling like genies in the haze.

Every village was a miniature city. Perhaps the short stature of the Yemenis had given them their love of pure altitude, for even the smallest hamlet was a cluster of steep tenements. In other Arab countries villages are lateral in structure. Few houses are more than one storey high, and their arrangement on the ground expresses the complicated network of cousinship in which every building houses a single unit of an extended family. They are essentially communal places: the latticework of divisions within each household is much more important than the easily-crossable boundaries which separate one house from another. By contrast, the vertical villages of the Yemen suggested a taste for fortification and privacy which I had seen nowhere else in Arabia. They looked like communities of individualists and closed families. Many of them pre-dated Islam. In fact, many were not truly Arab villages at all. Long ago, when Yemen had a flourishing export trade, it had supplied the Levant with frankincense and myrrh; and one of the most important of all the ancient caravan routes connected

Sana'a with Jerusalem. Until 1946, the country had remained the home of a large number of Jewish merchants and craftsmen; and Yemeni architecture is a weird idiosyncratic mixture of the Arab and the Jewish. It was the Jews who had given the Yemenis their precocious talent for the urban, which the Yemenis, in their turn, had translated back into a completely original form of arabesque.

Hamud and I drove back up the side of the valley to one of these rocky village-cities. It consisted of just eight mouldering towers, bunched around a vestigial market square. There was a well, a pound of smelly donkeys, and half a dozen shops kept by stunted boys who were all ribs and knee-bones. It doesn't take much to set up shop in the Yemen. An old packing-case provides the basic building, and inside it the shopkeeper squats with a few packs of cigarettes, six or seven bottles of Cola, a tray of boiled sweets which have seen better days, and some battered tins of fruit and milk. Hamud and I between us stripped one shop of its entire stock of 'Seven-Up' and stood in the sun drinking fizzy pop.

'My head hurts. It is the studying which I do. Every night I study, to make myself an engineer. Every morning I have a big pain in my head. It is the Chemistry which is very hard for me. Do you know Chemistry?'

'No,' I said. 'I was no good at science at school.'

'It is very difficult.' Hamud sat down dolefully on a rock. He looked burdened by his own ambition. Hamud, like so many Yemenis of his generation, was desperate to better himself. In that village, sunk up to its axles in several centuries of dirt, poverty and inertia, Hamud's aspirations seemed to have everything stacked against them.

'Will you go to the university when you've finished school?'

'I would like. I would like very much. I hope – ' He rubbed his fist against his forehead. 'Many, many people want to go to the university.' He was evidently doubtful as to whether his brains could take the punishment he was meting out to them each night. He relieved his feelings by throwing a rock at a stray goat which scrambled, yelping, down a cliff of shale.

'*Yallah! Yallah! Yallah!*' I had the suspicion that the unfortunate goat was really a substitute for myself. I had dragged Hamud out to visit villages which only reminded him of the world he so much wanted to escape.

'Let's go back to Sana'a,' I said.

On the road, we were overtaken by a truck driven by one of Hamud's friends. It had a *Hitler-has-only-got-one-ball* horn, and it pulled up ahead of us with a great fanfare of *go-ballses* and *no-ballses*. We all piled out: Hamud's friend, Ali; Ali's cousin, Mahmoud; and a moustached dwarf whose name I didn't catch. Everyone embraced everyone else.

'You like whisky?' asked the dwarf.

'Very much,' I said.

He reached through the canvas side of the truck, and clinked one bottle against another.

'Whisky,' he said with a ferocious Quilplike wink. 'We have whisky,' and he patted the hot mudguard tenderly as if it was the rump of a favoured pony.

'It sounds good.'

'We all drink together. Everybody drinks. You drink, I drink – ' he raised an imaginary glass in the air. So did I.

'Cheers,' I said.

'Cheers – ' the dwarf practised the word doubtfully. 'Tchy-yas!'

Hamud and I were invited to go to Ali's house that afternoon, to chew *qat* with the family. Quite suddenly, the Yemen had come to seem an easy hospitable place to get around in.

'Cheers!' shouted the dwarf as we drove away. 'Cheers – ' I shouted back.

'It is not good to drink whisky,' Hamud said. His Furies were worrying him again. He had seemed a fish out of water among his happy-go-lucky friends, afflicted by anxieties and barbs of conscience which left him standing awkwardly on the edge of the jokes and the hand-holding. 'It is not good for study.'

Just outside Sana'a we passed the television station, on the top of a heavily fortified crag. Its car park was full of tanks with their guns trained on the road.

'*Dabbabat . . .*' I said.

'You learn Arabic quickly,' said Hamud. 'It takes much study.'

Ali's house was in the centre of a warren of junk, sleeping dogs and crumbling mud bungalows. Everything had gone to the colour of piecrust in the sun: burnt dogs, burnt clay, the burnt-out chassis of wrecked cars from which every last nut and bolt had been assiduously beachcombed. Hamud, worried for his springs, inched the car down a street of boulders and pot-holes. A lame dog lurched ahead of us. Too torpid to bother to stop and cock its leg, it leaked as it walked. Its thin trickle of urine dried the instant that it hit the dust. Hamud blew his horn at it, but the dog ignored him. It looked as if it didn't greatly care whether it lived or died. I made some spinsterly English noises about the miserable state of the animals in the city.

'The government likes to shoot dogs. That is good, I think, to shoot dogs.'

We took our bundle of *qat* and crossed the street to Ali's house. A front door opened on a tiny courtyard where the family kept their two goats and half-dozen chickens. A further door led to the room in which the men lived.

After the desolation of the street outside, the room seemed palatial in its comforts. It was warm and rainbow-coloured. Squares of brightly-patterned dress material had been tacked over the windows to filter the sunlight, which fell in splashes of lemon, red and purple on the carpets and cushions. A cluster of tall brass hubble-bubbles occupied the centre of the room, and there were silver trays with Thermos flasks of coffee and iced water, fingerbowls, ears of sweetcorn and packs of cigar-ettes. Beside everyone's cushion was a brass spittoon and a goblet of burning incense. The *qat* lay in a communal heap. We added our sprigs to this green Guy Fawkes bonfire, and I was formally introduced to the family.

The bearded grandfather made a little speech of welcome; brothers and cousins bowed and shook hands. I was shown to my cushion, and the *qat*-session began.

The solemnity of it, the coloured light, the churchy gleam of hammered brass and silver, reminded me of a communion service. Hamud taught me how to nip off the topmost leaves from each stalk, chew them, then store them in the pouch of my cheek. Gradually one builds up a fibrous wad of crushed leaves from which one sucks the juice through one's teeth. *Qat*-chewing parches one's throat; one needs draughts of coffee and water every few minutes, and I found that managing this acidic mouthful of dry hedge was difficult enough, without having to undertake the further rigours of making conversation.

Qat is the kind of drug which creeps slowly up on you from behind. I had just decided that it was having no effect on me whatsoever when I heard a shrill schoolgirl giggle and realized that I was the one who was giggling. There seemed, in fact, to be two of me. One fellow was crouched in a recess, soberly recording the details of the *qat*-session for his notebook; the other was skittish and voluble. This second man was trying to make a joke in Arabic – an enterprise which struck the first man as so vain and foolhardy that he felt mortified at having to listen to the attempt. The second man's main trouble was that he found it impossible to remember words that he had spoken only a second or two before. He found himself in the middle of a sentence without having the least idea of how he had arrived there or in which direction he was supposed to be going. This did not seem to matter very much, since he appeared to be getting on extremely well with a cousin who was studying 'the telegraph'.

'You like the *qat*?' Hamud asked.

'It doesn't have any effect on me,' I said, exchanging clothes with the cousin. He put on my jacket, I put on his tunic. He gave me his belt and dagger. When I tried to fasten the belt around my waist, the two ends were six inches short of each other.

'I am too fat,' I said.

'All Englishmen are fat,' said the cousin, whose own waist cannot have been more than eighteen inches in circumference. He unclipped a small holster from his belt and gave it to me: it contained a Czech automatic pistol with a full clip of slugs and the safety-catch off.

'We could go and shoot some dogs,' I said. The cousin laughed and put the safety-catch on before handing the pistol back to me.

'Let's go and shoot a dog – '

'You see, you like the *qat*. This is the best *qat* in Yemen.'

'There's a dog outside. We could shoot that.'

'This is the first time you eat *qat*?'

'It doesn't do anything for me. Why don't we shoot some dogs?'

The other me skulked in a corner, watching these goings-on with an expression of detached scepticism. He noted the new telephone installed in a whitewashed alcove. He observed that the flex of the instrument was tied up in a neat loop; it was attached to nothing. If you picked up the receiver, it would be like putting a shell to your ear: you might, with luck, be able to hear the sound of the sea. Some shaky black-and-white pictures were flickering on the portable TV, and a cousin was putting a tape of Arab music into a Hitachi radio-recorder.

I had emptied a whole Thermosful of coffee. The grand-father called to the women's quarters for more, and offered me a turn on the hubble-bubble. Sucking, chewing, giggling, idly watching the feet of the women passing behind the half-open door which led to their kitchen, I was reduced to a state of contented infantilism. Another Thermos of coffee was brought in by a tiny, scrawny child of three or four. No woman would enter the male quarters when guests were being enter-tained there, and small children were necessary go-betweens. The little girl went to her grandfather to be cuddled. She had a skin-disease of some kind on her face, and looked as if she was on the verge of malnutrition.

My more active self had forgotten his enthusiasm for shooting dogs and was planning a European tour for the cousin. The cousin had the chance of pursuing his study of the telegraph in Paris: nothing was actually fixed; as yet he was only a candidate for a scholarship, but on *qat* he was already there, and we were busy with sights and itineraries. He was going to be away for three years, and we were fixing trips to London, Florence, Monte Carlo and the Scottish Highlands. I felt someone jogging my elbow, and found it was me again; the sceptic in the corner had detected a flaw in the arrangements.

'What about your wife and your child? Will they go too?'

'No, they stay in Sana'a.'

'But won't you miss them? Is it good to go away for so long when you have a wife and a young child growing up?'

'My mother will look after my wife. She will be quite safe.'

'But won't you miss her?'

'Why? I am only going away for three years.' He shrugged. 'It is no time.'

'When do you leave?'

He looked suddenly vague. He tore off another handful of leaves from his branch of *qat* and sat chewing them for a few moments. 'Next month,' he said. 'Yes. I think I will go to Paris next month.'

Ali said: 'Perhaps I will go to Paris too. I would like to see the Folies Bergères. In Paris there are many things to do in the nights.'

'If you want a night out in Sana'a, what do you do?'

'Nothing. There is nothing to do. You cannot go out after ten o'clock. That is the law. There is one cinema. The seats are cracked, they show the same old film always. Two years ago, I go. Then one month ago I go again. The people were the same people, they sit in the same seats, the film is the same film. In Sana'a, they are narrow-minded, you see. It is not like Paris.'

As the afternoon drew out, the rhythm of the *qat*-session changed. The manic chatter petered out and everyone in the room became reflective, slow and inward. The only sounds were the trickle of the hubble-bubble and the footfalls of the women beyond the door. The inside of my own head was busy with distracted thoughts; it felt like a nest of cheeping baby birds, but I was in no mood for talking. Nor were my neighbours. They stretched vacantly out on the cushions, the pupils of their eyes as big as blackberries, the lumps of *qat* in their cheeks pulling all the skin on their faces sideways.

The old man was turning the pages of the only book in the room. He spent a long time on each picture, reading the details carefully as he scanned the page. It wasn't until he shifted his position that I saw what the book was: a tourist guide to the Yemen. The pictures he was studying so avidly had been printed by the cheapest kind of colour-process, and it had given them the livid vigour of very old technicolor movies. They showed the streets of Sana'a and the close-up faces of people who looked exactly like the old man himself. Perhaps the book was there because it really did include his photograph; or perhaps he liked it because the techniques of photography had given his own life the interestingly alien glaze of something fossilized and remote. I would have liked to have asked him, but by this time we were both sealed off from each other in bubbles of deep, drugged privacy. I would never have found the words that I wanted.

Ali said, 'You want to go to sleep?' He pointed to a stack of brightly coloured mattresses at the far end of the room.

No, I said; I was fine.

'This is good *qat*. The best.'

'Very good – I've enjoyed it very much. I would like to try it again.'

He switched up the sound on the television set. There were some pictures of dignitaries accompanied by martial music.

'This is the news – '

I listened for a mention of *dabbabat* and roadblocks, but there was only a list of tomorrow's official receptions. The minister of something was going to fly to Riyadh to meet the Saudi minister of something else. Then the martial music started up again over a jumpy shot of a man with a bad case of facial warts.

The old man, absorbed in his book, didn't bother to glance up. These announcements were not news – and if there was any news of importance, it would not come from the television set but be picked up in the street.

Hamud and I left. It was already dark, and I felt jittery and on edge. *Qat* produces a hangover which makes one feel altogether too alert for one's own good. Hamud's unusually careful driving struck me as dangerously fast and wild. When we reached the Dar Al-Hamd Palace, I got out my wallet to pay him.

'Please,' Hamud said. 'Yesterday, we were not friends. Today you are my friend.'

'Hamud, really, I would like to pay – '

'You are my friend, now, yes?'

'Yes – '

'Because you are my friend, you give me fifty rials more than what you say yesterday. I think that is right. For friendship.'

I gave him the extra fifty thinking it sad that if Hamud had to put a price on his own friendship he should value it at just

£7. Still, the Yemenis have a reputation for frankness and realism: if they assess the cost of friendship as half that of whisky, it's probable that they have sound economic reasons for doing so.

The hotel was full of prospectors. It had a telex machine and a line of electric porcelain fountains down the hall which looked like illuminated bidets; but in most other respects it was much like my idea of an inn in Nevada during the gold rush. Word had got around the world that there were 'flush times' coming in the Yemen, and the hotel was the headquarters of a curious bunch of fortune hunters.

Geologists sat around in the lobby during the evenings, muttering in corners about rock faults and soil samples. The dream of discovering a great Yemeni oil field haunted the country, and people were hopefully drilling holes in the sea bed off the coast, in the mountains to the north, and on the desert border with Saudi Arabia. One reliable authority on the subject took me outside the hotel in order to tell me, in a lowered voice, that the discovery had already been made, that Yemen was sitting on the biggest oil-well in the whole of Arabia, but that the government were keeping the strike secret; in the present economic and political situation they could not cope with the consequences of such an avalanche of new wealth. He told me where the strike had been made, and how the formation of the rock there exactly duplicated the geological structure of Saudi Arabia's richest oil field. For two days, I went around the city with a superior air, hinting to people that I knew more than I could tell. Then I met another reliable authority who explained the same theory to me in a loud voice, and said that it had been totally discredited more than eighteen months before.

There were other mineral prospectors, mostly lone entrepreneurs who were trying to fiddle their way into obtaining a concession to mine copper, iron, lead or zinc. They had their particular mountain staked out, and spent long days in the anterooms of government offices, jumping up and grinning furiously whenever they caught sight of a deputy minister.

These, though, were not the prospectors who most interested me. By far the richest and most accessible seam in the Yemen was the thick paper layer of remittance money – billions of rials of it. It demanded a bold, open-cast system of mining, and it attracted ingenious, far-sighted men for whom the Yemen was the last, and quite possibly the most lucrative, frontier. Business in the Gulf was dominated by corporations: for a single man or a small firm, it was nearly impossible to find an opening left in Kuwait, or Abu Dhabi, or Dubai. The Yemen was different. There were many wildcat claims, which turned out to be worthless after the investigation of a week or so, but there were also a lot of easy pickings. The corporation-men had barely heard of the country; it was still – just – the province of the sieve-and-pan brigade.

They looked like real prospectors: men with beards and bees in their bonnets, much given to talking in whispers and winks. They left the hotel at some impossible hour in the morning, long before I was up, and came back covered in dust in the late afternoon. They were cagey about exactly where they had been.

'Oh . . . went out to some villages . . . you know.'

The passenger-seats of their Range Rovers were stacked with old RAF survey maps. In the back of the car they carried cases of samples, spare parts, and heaps of schemes, reports, questionnaires and notions.

One man had struck it lucky with depilatory cream. For several weeks he had been travelling with an assorted batch of cosmetics. Since nearly all the domestic shopping in Yemen is done by men, he had found it difficult to rid himself of his stock of lipsticks, powder puffs and cakes of eye-shadow. Then, in a store in Hodeida on the Red Sea coast, he had made his great discovery. The shopkeeper had brushed aside everything else in his case and seized on a tube of depilatory cream.

'Apparently the chaps here are very keen on getting their wives to pull all their pubes out. They'd been using a mixture of honey and dried mud, and doing no end of damage to themselves. The one thing in the world they really wanted, it turned out, was a good brand of depilatory cream.'

So he had dumped the rest of his stock, telexed for a crate of depilatory cream, and was busy driving out to remote mountain towns and rescuing Yemeni womanhood from the agonies of dried mud and honey.

Perhaps the altitude of the plateau was going to their heads, but there was something glittery and manic about nearly all these men. There was an American who repeated over and over again: 'The Yemen's really going to be *something*. When Saudi Arabia's just a collection of ghost towns in the desert, this place is going to be *something* – just you wait.' He had been doing badly, I think, and was trying to mesmerize himself by chanting this prophecy at every passing stranger.

Two Germans, called Siegfried and Hoover, were engaged in a long and tricky deal with a disreputable-looking man in a filthy shift and torn sandals. Every evening he would shuffle into the hotel lobby, squinting and sticking to the shadows. Siegfried and Hoover would fly up like snipe at his entrance. Their talks with him rarely lasted for more than five minutes at a time, and they would return from these sessions of muttering in dark corners with identical changed faces. Either they were so woebegone that they couldn't bring themselves to speak until they'd got through half a bottle of whisky between them; or they came back cackling with euphoria. One night the deal was on; the next it was off. Every two days, Siegfried and Hoover announced that they were taking the next flight back to Hamburg – but they were still resident in the hotel when I left; and, judging by the form things were taking then, they are probably there now.

'He will decide tomorrow. He says he needs to think about it tomorrow, over *qat*.'

'He said that yesterday. He said that last week.'

'This man,' said Siegfried, 'he is like Pierpont Morgan.'

'He don't smell like Pierpont Morgan,' said Hoover.

'He comes to the hotel because he does not want anyone to know where he lives.'

'He lives in a hole in the souk.'

'A friend of mine from Hamburg – you know, he sold this man a cargo ship. The price was a million marks. This man pays cash; he keeps it under his mattress.'

'I bet the mattress makes a big stink.'

'We are like fish for him. Each time he pulls on the line he likes to make us wriggle.'

'Next Saturday, we go home. That is final. I am sick and tired. He is never going to make his mind up.'

'Next Saturday, we are *here*. Hoover is a big pessimist. Hoover needs a drink.'

Siegfried wore a black jersey with the word SKIPPER printed across his chest.

'Hoover does not need a drink. Hoover has a headache already.'

'Maybe he decides tomorrow.'

'Maybe, maybe, maybe – ' groaned Hoover, and had another drink.

The man with the boldest and most generous dreams was Harvey, a gigantic Lancastrian who had come out prospecting the territory for a firm which manufactured deep-freeze plants. In eight days, Harvey had fallen in love with the entire Yemeni nation. He wanted to be their Lord Jim. In the afternoons he held court: a booming hippo of a man, surrounded by four or five very small and fragile-looking Yemenis. He lectured them on the declension of their agriculture. He talked of how arid pastureland, when not properly husbanded, is fit first for cows, then for sheep, then for goats, and finally only for camels.

'You're bloody nearly down to the goat stage already,' said Harvey; 'and if you don't look out, you'll be down to camels in fifteen years.'

The Yemenis looked frightened, not so much by Harvey's words as by his hands, which roamed idly in the air as he spoke like a pair of hairy paddles. Harvey broke things easily: chairs, tables, glasses and Yemenis were likely to get accidentally smashed as Harvey's enthusiasm mounted.

'What are you doing about your topsoil? Bloody nowt!'

Harvey had plans for the Yemen. He was going to plant a forest to stop the topsoil from blowing clean off the plateau. He was going to irrigate the farmland. He was going to teach the Yemenis how to cross-breed cattle and develop new strains of maize and barley. In the course of an hour, the Yemen was Arabia Felix again: protected by Harvey's forests, Harvey's cows grazed on rich meadows next to fields of waving corn.

'I could do it, you know. I'd bloody love to do it. Give me a year or two, and the things I could do with this place . . . I could work bloody miracles with it!'

The Yemenis nodded politely, and tried to shuffle their chairs a little further out of Harvey's range.

He had worked as an agricultural consultant in Africa. He had raced camels in Socotra. He was constantly on the move, zig-zagging across the Third World, a huge, restless rolling stone. When he returned from one of his excursions into the hills, his hosts and guides looked dead-beat; Harvey, though, had an apparently inexhaustible reservoir of sheer animal energy and good humour. He once announced that he was known throughout Africa as the White Butcher. I didn't doubt it. In the Yemen, he had found a landscape which needed so much doing to it that even Harvey's enormous appetite for action might be slaked on it. Towards the Yemenis themselves he showed that stooping, clumsy tenderness with which very big people tend to treat very little ones. When he talked about the farmers whom he had met in the hills, he described them as one might speak of some heartbreakingly pretty girl. There was no colonial condescension in his manner. He was quite straightforwardly soppy about the Yemen.

'Last year, I was in twenty countries, always moving on. I've been doing this for twelve years now. I've never wanted to stop. I'm a next-plane-out man by nature. And do you know, today, for the first time, I suddenly got this settling-down feeling – do you know what I mean?

'We were up on this farm, talking to this bloody marvellous old geezer. It's just a little farm – you know, couple of cows, a dozen sheep, little patch of maize and this bloody great field of *qat*. I went round with the old man, he showed me everything. He showed me the ditch he was digging, and how he got the water from the well on to the land – and I thought, what I'd like to do, what I'd really like to do . . . I'd like to go and live with that old man on his farm. I'd build a dam for him. I'd plant some trees. I'd get a proper irrigation system going there. I'd show him how to cross-breed his stock . . . Christ, it'd be like a bloody little paradise.

'I'm not joking. I'm going to be back. You see.

'But aren't they nice people, though? Aren't they bloody lovely people?'

It was a few days before I did find out about the *dabbabat* and the roadblocks. From a friend in London I had an introduction to Ahmad, a young Yemeni with a degree in economics from an English university and a job in a government department. Ahmad was a member of a new generation of Yemenis. He was everything that Hamud might dream of becoming. For obvious reasons I can't describe Ahmad in much detail: but he was highly educated, he had acquired most of his social and political ideas during his stay in Europe, and he was an intense patriot. He picked me up in his car and we went for a long winding drive around the outskirts of the city.

'There was an attempted coup. It was led by a fool – an army officer in the north, an old supporter of Hamdi. He had no chance. He had a tiny section of the army with him, and some tribesmen. It was a total miscalculation.'

There was a fly buzzing torpidly against the windscreen. Ahmad squashed it with his thumb.

'They put him down like that. In one morning. He was an idiot.'

'They killed him?'

'No. He was taken prisoner.'

'Will they execute him?'

Ahmad laughed.

'No, they will send him to live in his country house.'

'Why was Hamdi himself assassinated?'

'Look,' Ahmad said. 'You are talking to someone who loved Hamdi. From other people you will hear other stories. I will tell you the official reason, so you can see how stupid it is; then I tell you the real one. They killed him, they said, because he was an immoral man. They said they found him with French prostitutes. In other stories, the prostitutes are Japanese. To anyone who knew Hamdi, that is an impossible thing – as a man he was not like that. I am afraid it is a typical thing that they cannot even decide whether these girls are French or Japanese. I think perhaps the people who make up these stories do not know the difference – they think France is somewhere in Japan, perhaps.

'The real reasons are many. There was the law he passed on the bride-price. That put many of the old conservative tribesmen in the south against him . . . it helped to create a climate. But that was not important, really. He was talking to South

Yemen. The Saudis were frightened he was going to reunify the two countries, so were the Americans. I think it was a Saudi-CIA plot which killed Hamdi.

'I think you cannot understand. The ordinary people loved Hamdi. There was an old woman in Taiz. She was just an old peasant woman. She knew nothing of politics. She had never been to Sana'a. For her, the world stopped in Taiz. But when Hamdi was killed, I saw her crying. She was crying over someone she had never seen. But she could *feel* Hamdi – she could feel what he was doing for the country, even though she couldn't understand. That is how very, very many people in this country feel. Hamdi is still loved. People will not forget him just because he is killed by some frightened men who tell lies about him afterwards.'

'Would you have liked to have seen Friday's coup succeed?'

'Of course not. I am a supporter of Hamdi. I am not a supporter of fools. This man had no brains.'

We drove down a dirt road and Ahmad parked the car on the edge of a dismal construction site of hanging dust, joists and ragged piles of breezeblock. Ahmad said that it was an important housing development. He caught the wrinkle of scepticism on my face.

'One has to begin somewhere. We have had just two–three years. But we have to repair the damage of centuries. You have seen the city! What we have to do is *enormous*. Sometimes I think it is impossible, but I have hope. We need all the people we can get. There are so few people with education, who can understand what needs to be done. I think that you come from England, you look at this and you think, "hopeless", yes?'

'In honesty, I suppose so. But I've only been here a few days. Sana'a strikes me as just being out of control. I don't understand how anyone can bring it back on to the road. You seem to be drowning in this flood of money. In England, we think we have problems. We go hairless when we get fifteen per cent inflation. We talk about rising prices and the housing shortage as if they'd reached crisis proportions. But if a British economist or politician came to Sana'a, he'd simply blow his brains out at the end of his first week.'

'We have a saying in Arabic,' Ahmad said. 'When the old

dog shits biscuits, then there will be change in the Yemen. The people we need are going to have to be very clever, I think. If you ask me, I say that it is not impossible to make old dogs do these interesting things; it is difficult, yes, but a man with a great deal of intelligence . . . he might come up with the biscuits.'

'Hamdi?'

'Hamdi pulls one biscuit from the wrong end of the dog – so they kill him. That is another problem we have to face in the Yemen.'

'What about *qat*?'

'*Qat* is a disease. We can grow out of *qat*. Many young men have stopped chewing it. I have a son of six. I hope that he will never chew *qat*.'

'Do you chew it yourself?'

'Occasionally, yes. I chew it on Fridays with my friends. But afterwards I dislike myself for it.'

I asked Ahmad if his wife wore the veil: she didn't. Nor did the wives of most of his friends.

'A lot of the girls now in the schools are refusing to wear the veil. They want jobs, some of them are able to go to the university. The Yemen is not strict like Saudi Arabia or the Gulf countries. I think it is easier for women here, once they have made the decision to change. They may have to quarrel with their fathers, but they do not come out against the whole society. It is possible to do your own thing here. People do not mind too much about what an individual does.'

'That may be a weakness as well as a strength.'

'If a few educated people do these things, then I think many people may follow quite soon.'

When Ahmad left me at the hotel he said: 'Please, I am telling you all this because I love my country. I don't expect you to love it, but I would like you to try to understand it. It is very difficult, I think, for someone from the West to understand. Either he sees a hopeless chaos, or he thinks it is all very pretty and quaint. I would like you to see that it is something else.'

I went up to my room to read and think. I was diverted by a sudden theatrical display of weather outside my window. For the last two months, there had been no weather to speak of at all. I'd grown used to the monotonous rise and fall of the sun, to alternating bouts of heat and cool, and to a night sky which looked like a planetarium – too clear and twinkling to be true.

At last something was happening. A Wuthering Heights wind was banging doors down distant corridors, and the tossing of dry branches outside my window almost drowned the orchestra of motor horns in the city. The air, charged with brown dust, was thickening to a dirty mauve, and the edges of the mountains showed like sharp cardboard cut-outs. A leaf-storm of buzzards was blowing about between the trees, with big birds (I had at first mistaken them for vultures) turning over and over in the wind.

There was a nearly continuous rumble of thunder in the mountains, with sheet-lightning high over the clouds twinkling like diamonds on a turned wrist. Yet this high-altitude bother was queerly impotent. One sensed a kind of angry constipation in it all, as if the atmosphere was straining to empty itself but having little success. I longed for it to rain. Crouched at the window, I was an excited fan of the storm-clouds, but feared that I was backing the losing side: against the stolid force of dryness and dust it seemed that they had little chance of doing much more than huffing and puffing and making irritable noises.

When the rain did come, it was at first just a few drops of blood squeezed from a stone. I could have done better by spitting on the ground. Then, for five minutes at most, there was one enormous splash, as dramatic in its effect as a burst dam. It blackened the earth and gave back a sudden vivid colour to the grass and trees and little allotments of vegetables and *qat*. It stopped with the same violent precision as it had begun, leaving the city amazingly changed. The dusty towers looked like pillars of melting chocolate, their white stucco friezes washed quite clean. For a moment, Sana'a even smelled fresh: I caught a faint trace in the air of spring blossom and new leaves before it was wiped out again by the old stink of carbon, dogs and garbage.

In a room on an upper floor of the hotel, someone was practising scales on a clarinet. There was a repeated snatch of

Mozart's Clarinet Quintet, fumblingly played, then more scales. It must have been one of the prospectors. For days I studied my neighbours in the dining-room, trying to spot the closet-clarinettist; none of them looked remotely musical. But it had been nice to hear the clarinet, trickling uncertainly down those scales and landing up in pools of bottom Ds and Es. Whoever it was, his sense of occasion, if not of musical timing, had been perfect. The clouds had turned to innocent twists of grey-and-gold cotton wool; the sun was going down in a honey haze behind them; and the clarinet followed it, hunting for notes deeper and deeper down the scale.

I sat in on an English lesson at the Gamal Abdel Nasser Secondary School. The Scottish instructor – one of three Britons employed in the Yemeni school system – was drilling the class in the difference between the 'present simple' and the 'present continuous'. There were twenty very thin, very eager boys aged between about fourteen and twenty-two. They were part of that tiny educated leaven in a country which has an illiteracy rate of ninety per cent, and they had tense, ambitious faces. They had been trained to compete continually against each other, so that the lesson turned into a kind of noisy greyhound race. The moment that the instructor was half-way through a question, his voice was drowned by shouts of 'Teacher! Teacher! Teacher!' and I lost sight of him behind the thicket of urgently raised hands. If a student began to stumble over an answer, the others fought to grab the question for themselves, bellowing for Teacher's attention. I once taught for a term at a comprehensive school in England: had the children in my class ever shown a small fraction of the enthusiasm displayed by these Yemeni students, I might have stayed in the job a great deal longer. They were ravenous for the good marks and certificates which would take them out of their villages and tenements, and they behaved as if every minute spent in the classroom could make or break them.

The drill centred on two oilcloth pictures which had been hung on the blackboard. They purported to represent a typical English family at home. In fact, they showed the same cosy, never-never land which I had seen so lovingly reconstructed in the British Club in Bahrain. It was (if a date could be put on it at all) 1951 in some idyllic Thameside suburb. Mr Brown was listening to a fretwork-fronted radio. Its loudspeaker was concealed behind an art-deco rising sun, and Mr Brown was no doubt hearing Alvar Liddell reading the news on the Home Service. The Browns' cocker spaniel was curled up asleep at his feet, his pipe was drawing nicely, and Mrs Brown, in her home-made gingham frock, was bringing him a cup of tea on a tray. There were antimacassars on the chair-backs; the aspidistra was on its stand; Winston Churchill was in his heaven and all was right with England.

The Browns struck me as a good deal more odd and exotic than the Yemenis; what the Yemenis themselves must have made of them I cannot think. Still, the Browns served well enough when it came to sorting out the difference between the present simple and the present continuous – even though the tense which they actually represented was the past nostalgic.

'What is Mrs Brown doing?'

'Teacher!'

'Teacher!'

'Ali – '

'She . . . iss . . . bringéd . . .'

'Teacher!'

'She *wass* bringéd – '

The instructor licked his finger and wrote on the blackboard. 'You mustn't forget your *i-n-g*!'

'Teacher!'

'Mohammad – '

'She wass bringing him some ti.'

'Now, what is Mr Brown doing?' The Scotsman's pointer rapped on the oilcloth in the direction of Mr Brown's mouth.

'He . . . iss . . . smocking his pip!'

'Good. Now then, Abdurahman . . .'

We eventually left the home life of the Browns. (It is worth saying, I think, that every English teacher I met in the Middle East deplored the teaching-aids with which he had been landed, and was no fonder of the Browns than I was.) The class went on to their textbook, *Living English For The Arab World*. This was decently practical in tone, and dealt with matters like building, farming and car maintenance. Today's chapter was about irrigation and hydro-electricity.

'Jamal, why must we water the soil?'

'Because the farms has crops. Because the crops must grows.'

'What does the dam do?'

'The dam . . . push . . .'

'Teacher!'

'Yes, Ahmed.'

'The water pushing, and it strongly. The dam pushing, and it strongly. All water push round dynamo and make electricity!'

'Very good. Now, what is this word "valley"?'

'It is a hole!'

'It is . . . tunnel!'

'Teacher! Teacher!'

On the dot of ten o'clock, the class broke for the door, piling round it like a rugger scrum. I found it hard to match up the ardour they had shown during the lesson with their evident desire to be out of the room as fast as they possibly could. Within a few seconds the courtyard below was noisy with motorbike engines.

'Why are they so keen to get away?'

'They don't want to miss the executions,' said the Scotsman.

On the blackboard, Mr Brown was still smocking his pip in his slippers. He looked terribly out of his element in the Yemen.

The executions had been taking place for three days. On the first day, I had gone to the main square and found what looked like a cheerful market going on. The only puzzle was that I could see no goods for sale. I pushed my way into the middle of the crowd and found two old men dancing and chanting. They were ragged, even by Yemeni standards, and each man had a drum which looked like a garden sieve, with a single skin stretched over a wooden frame. They twirled these drums on their forefingers, spinning them into the air and catching them on their finger-ends. With linked arms, they skipped round and round, grinning and singing.

I asked if any of my neighbours in the crowd spoke English. A Sudanese said that he did.

'Can you tell me what words they are singing?'

'They say, "We are having an execution today, we are having an execution today. This is a warning to all people not to do bad things. If you do bad things you will be executed too." Those are the words. It is a way of passing the message on, you see.'

The women and children had the best seats. They squatted in two parallel lines around a narrow concrete path where the old men were performing. There were people sitting on the tops of trucks, people in trees, people leaning out of windows, and people jumping up and down in the dust behind the crowd, trying to catch a glimpse of the spot where the condemned men were going to kneel, then be machine-gunned to death at point-blank range. It looked as if the women and children had placed themselves in a pretty hazardous position: sitting ducks for ricocheting bullets. In the second and third rows, babies were being held up in the air so that they could get a good view of the entertainment, and toddlers were perched on the shoulders of their fathers and brothers.

When an army truck drew up, a festive buzz of excitement went through the crowd. I left. My reasons for not watching were entirely selfish. I thought I had enough material for nightmares in my head without adding this particular event to my stock. When the shooting happened, I was as deep as I could get in the souk, taking photographs of old carved doors. Two hours later, I crossed the square on my way back to the hotel. The crowd had gone. A man was selling Polaroid pictures as mementoes. When he tried to sell me one, I pointed to my own camera; I had taken all the pictures that I wanted.

That afternoon I tried to find out who had been executed and why. The answers that I got are, I think, an interesting example of Arabian news:

There were three army officers.
There were five army officers.
They came from Hodeida.
They came from Taiz.
They came from Sana'a.
They were soldiers, not officers.
The crime had been committed outside their barracks in Sana'a.
The crime had been committed on the coast.
The crime had been committed in the north of the country, in a village.
The crime was the raping and killing of a thirteen-year-old boy.

This last point was the only common element in every story. The age of the boy never varied, nor did the details of his killing: he had been clubbed to death after an orgy of buggery.

In this contradictory tangle of information, one statement alone seemed totally suspect to me – the story of the boy. Its exactitude had the ring of untruth about it. It is possible that it really happened, but I doubt it. It's much more likely that it was a metaphor. One cannot publicly punish people for crimes which one cannot publicly announce: Hamdi had been killed for 'keeping prostitutes in his house' – a neat enough analogy for his dalliance with the communist south. 'Raping and killing a thirteen-year-old boy' sounded to me like another convenient figure of speech. It was a further example, if one were needed, of that insistent doubleness and ambiguity which is in the character of the language.

I wanted a more literal version of what had happened, and tried out my own theory on a Yemeni acquaintance.

'This story isn't true, is it? These were the men involved in the uprising last Friday, weren't they?'

Although we were in a private car, he winced at the loudness of my voice. There are things which one is supposed to know which should never be spoken of aloud.

'Please,' he said. 'We talk about anything, but we do not talk of politics. I think I cannot have an answer for that question. It is different from in Europe. Here people do not mind so much about a human life. So – someone shoots me, nobody minds. They see my body . . . they laugh. They pass by. So I do not say anything on that question.'

In the hotel, the executions gave the Europeans a nice opportunity to display their own skill at embroidery. One of the prospectors told me that he had seen the bodies hanging from lamp-posts, that the sky overhead had been 'black with bloody buzzards', and that the birds had been picking out the eyes of the dead men. I had just returned from the square myself, and I felt that my failure to notice this appalling spectacle might cast serious doubts on my abilities as a more or less professional observer; so I agreed that I had seen the bodies and the buzzards too, just to be on the safe side. Reality seemed so hard to locate anyway that it was much the easiest course of action to fall in with whatever fictions were going at the time.

I felt starved of news. There was, admittedly, one stall in Sana'a which sold old copies of *Newsweek*; but since all articles about the Arab world had been snipped out or mutilated (the words 'Saudi Arabia' alone were enough to bring the censor into action), the magazine was a sorry mess of cut pages and it had usually lost one, if not both, of the staples which were supposed to hold it together. When a party of engineers came up from Hodeida with a good radio, I was keen to see if we could tune it to the BBC World Service. We set it up in the hotel lounge and took turns in hunting through the forest of stations. We found a lot of Arabic, and even more tweeter and woof. There was a burst of Japanese, then some glottal clicks and stops which might have been Swahili; and then, out of a heavy drizzle of buzzes and whistles, an English voice came on.

'. . . another away win, Nottingham Forest retain their position at the head of the First Division. Chelsea . . .' The voice was lost in crackle, and we never found it again.

There is nothing more convenient when you are abroad than to find other people's customs 'barbaric'. It puts a useful distance between you and the country you are in. It bolsters your own sense of identity, and creates a kind of picture-frame through which you can view the funny goings-on of foreigners with a feeling of pleasurable indignation. Generations of Englishwomen have managed to keep the Italians in perspective by harping on the way in which they are beastly to cats and shoot sparrows for sport. In one or two Arab countries, including the Yemen, legal punishments take place in public. The number of occasions on which this actually happens is tiny; but it's true that if you wait long enough you may see someone being shot, amputated or lashed. My own feelings during the three-day festival of executions ran true to standard British form. The manner of punishment, and the way in which it was treated as an enjoyable circus by the townspeople, seemed horrible. I didn't want to stay any longer than I needed to in Sana'a. The place was infected by the executions. I found it dirty, frightening and inhumane.

I was jerked out of this state during a conversation with Ahmad. We were talking about the time he had spent in England as a student.

'There was one thing I could never understand,' he said. 'Near the college there was this big building for old men and old women – '

'An old people's home – '

'That is right. Is it usual in England for everybody to put their fathers and mothers in these homes when they are old?'

'Well, when they can't look after themselves any more . . . They have their meals provided for them and everything, and they have their own rooms . . .'

'These are sort of prisons for old people, these "homes"?'

'No – they're not prisons at all.'

'To me, this home looked like a prison.'

'But they can come and go as they please – '

'They have money?'

'Not very much, but, well . . . pocket money.'

'I think that is really the same as being in prison. Why do people get sent to these homes? Did they do something wrong? Do their families simply not like them any more?'

'Many of them go in voluntarily. They would prefer to be looked after. They can be nursed there, and there's always someone around to make sure that they're all right – '

'But why do their families not do these things? I think it is very strange. In England, old men and women do not get respect. I noticed it in the street. People push them about, and then they send them to these "homes". In the Yemen, it is different. People are respected because they are old. They are thought wise. Their families like to have the old people in the house with them. They ask them for their advice; it is thought an honour to have your father or your grandfather living with you. You know that I want a lot of change in the Yemen. But I do not think we'll ever build these "homes". That is not the kind of change that I would like to see happen.'

Several weeks later, when I was back in London, some Englishmen were publicly flogged in Saudi Arabia for distilling illicit liquor and selling it to the locals – a very serious crime indeed which, as far as the Saudis were concerned, combined

245

rank profiteering with blasphemy against Islam. A woman at a party was telling me that the Arabs were 'totally uncivilized'. I told her about the public executions in Sana'a, and then about Ahmad's puzzlement over old people's homes. 'God, how ghastly!' she said. 'What do you mean?' I said. 'Shooting people like that in the middle of the public square,' she said.

Abdurabu was a gentle fixer. He had his own telex machine and a business card which announced that he would go anywhere and do anything. He ran an import-export agency, he arranged introductions for foreign businessmen; anyone who wanted to buy a Range Rover, meet a minister, find a hotel room, dispose of a hundred tons of surplus steel or start up a soft-drinks factory went, first of all, to Abdurabu.

'This chap,' said one of the prospectors, 'knows everybody. The gentry come up to him and kiss him in the streets, and when you go out to the country, the peasants swarm round him as if he was their long-lost brother.'

I had met him when he was trying out samples of the Yemen Arab Republic State Cigarette. I lit one, sucked, and watched the entire cigarette crackle like a brush-fire up to the filter tip, where it threw out a few sparks and died.

'What is your opinion?' asked Abdurabu.

'Very good, except that it seems to have more nitrates in it than tobacco. If you cut down on the nitrates, it would be more of a cigarette and less of a firework.'

'That is interesting. Several people say that to me before,' Abdurabu said, and gave me a Parker biro in rolled gold.

'I can't possibly accept this,' I said.

'I have many of them. It is business.'

He was a thistledown man. He cannot have weighed much more than eighty pounds, and most of this was concentrated in his skull, so that he gave the impression of being a balloon of pure mind, insecurely tethered to the ground. When he was walking, which he did in a balletic style of hops and skips, I would almost swear that I saw both feet in the air at the same time for several seconds at a stretch. On two occasions, I sat at the same dinner table as Abdurabu. He ate only a few scraps of fish to feed his brain. He kept himself alive on air and overwork. Every day I would see him criss-crossing the city in his green Peugeot, working his way through a forest of appointments and assignations. He was always wearing a monogrammed Aertex shirt of startling whiteness. I think he must have moved too fast for the dust of Sana'a ever to settle on him; had I believed in extra-terrestrial visitors, I would have questioned Abdurabu very closely about his origins.

He had gone to university in Paris – so he said – and spoke English, French and German in much the same way that he walked; lightly and skippingly, leapfrogging over obstacles of syntax and vocabulary, singing out his sentences in a pure counter-tenor.

I had told him that I had found the old city a maddening din. My ventures into it had been timid and short. Every time I went into the souk, its mixture of deafening noise and indecipherable intricacy sent me into a panic state of high bad temper.

'Come,' Abdurabu said. 'I will show you *everything*.'

We drove down a street past lines of women walking in their shrouds. Abdurabu, still a bachelor at thirty, priced them for me. It wasn't a contemptuous exercise; he was pointing out the sad irony of the bride-price system.

'Thirty thousand rials! Pouf! Twenty thousand . . . you like to pay twenty thousand for her? There is cheapie. Ten thousand. I would not give ten. Ah! This one, you see? High class goods! Fifty, sixty thousand – very expensive. Now, how you like *her* – I get her for you for fifteen. Trade discount.'

'Highest I'll go is ten,' I said.

'Ten?' Abdurabu whistled in mock disbelief. 'Ten – and she has all her teeth? No deal.'

'Will you marry, Abdurabu?'

'Of course, I would like. It is not good to be alone. But I do not want to buy a wife; I want to marry her. In Paris, I lived with a girl. She was my friend. I would like to marry her. But she would not come to Yemen.'

'Would you like to live in Europe?'

'This is my city. I love my country. I do not leave, I think. But it is very difficult for me to marry a Yemeni girl. That is sadness for me.'

'What do single men do here? Are there prostitutes?'

'There are some women, yes, in the souk. But I would

not go. It is dangerous.'

'You mean, they've got VD?'

'It is not so much the question of the gonorrhoea; it is more the question of Security, you understand . . .?'

'There are a lot of Security men?' The only Security man I'd seen had been a slow-witted-looking fellow who hung around the hotel. His chief occupation appeared to be watching Bugs Bunny cartoons, with Arabic subtitles, on the TV in the lounge. He had however succeeded in getting a British business-man's pocket dictaphone taken to pieces in the police station; he had observed his suspect talking into what was clearly a radio transmitter.

'Of course. There is always Security. This is an Arab country.'

We left the car and walked into the labyrinth. Abdurabu led me through a succession of streets which were too narrow for cars, but were still noisy with men bullying their donkeys. Someone had parked his ox on a corner, and it stamped and bellowed, kicking up a small dust-storm. Abdurabu patted the solid lead which formed the corner of one house and said, 'This is so old . . . sometimes I think it must be the oldest city in the world.'

It was true that he knew everyone. He could hardly go ten yards without someone stepping out of the crowd to embrace him. His business interests were ubiquitous.

'One moment . . .' he said, dodging into an alley full of troglodytes in caves. It was choked with rancid smoke, and every man in it was beating some lump of metal to death with a sledgehammer. They chanted as they worked, but since everyone was singing and hammering in his own private time, the effect was an atonal cacophony of bangs and yells. It would have made a good soundtrack for a film of Dante's *Inferno*. The caves themselves were rough scoops, cut into the rock; the back of each one formed an open furnace, and its dripping pro-prietor squatted in front of the flames, beating out the molten metal on a stone anvil.

'These are Yemeni craftsmen – ' Abdurabu shouted at me. 'They make hings. Yemeni hings are most popular, famous and traditional.'

'I see – ' I said doubtfully.

'You have seen many Yemeni hings?'

'I'm not sure exactly what a hing is.'

'A hing! Hing!' carolled Abdurabu. 'You have door, door opens and shuts, on hings! – '

When I got used to peering through the smoke, it was remarkable to see how much violence and seeming chaos was dedicated to the production of such delicate and carefully-made objects. The hinges were lovely things; shaped like twin fleurs-de-lys, elaborately scrolled and patterned, they lay in heaps round the feet of the chanting troglodytes. Abdurabu had particular business in one cave, where the blacksmith sat like an early Christian martyr in the flames, chewing *qat* and stoking up his fire. Figures were shouted backwards and forwards through the smoke, another deal done.

'I get this man a new kiln,' Abdurabu said. 'I hear of one yesterday. I hear from someone that this man is trying to buy. I am in business for only one year and a half, so I must work very hard to find out everything that everybody wants. It is very difficult to start a business of one's own.'

'At this rate, you ought to be a millionaire in another year or two.'

'Yes,' Abdurabu said modestly, 'I hope so.'

Another friend intercepted him and invited us back to his house. Like Abdurabu, Husain wore Western dress – a smart boutique suit of silver grey and rainbow-striped shoes with platform heels. He too had studied in Europe; he'd done a course in electronics at Hamburg and worked as a technician for Cable & Wireless. His house was in the eye of the labyrinth.

'Husain says that from his roof you can see the whole city.'

We went in single file down a street which was just a dusty crevice, stepped over a few sleeping dogs, and arrived in a tiny square. The square itself was really a gloomy airshaft with a single eucalyptus tree growing at the bottom; it was surrounded on all sides by narrow towers set at odd angles to each other, and the spaces between them formed a web of narrow alleys like the one we had entered from. Most were dead ends. It was quieter than anywhere else I had been in the city; it seemed that even Yemenis might have difficulty in finding their way here. One can't get to the heart of the maze by Toyota, and the musical horns were mercifully distant, lost in the outer galleries of the system.

The inside of Husain's house was cold and dark. We climbed three flights of steep stone stairs to a bare little sitting-room furnished with a single rug and a few cushions. Puffing my way up, I thought how odd it was that every detail of the architecture of the place seemed totally out of proportion to the people who lived in it. Each stair was a good eighteen inches high – above knee-height for an average Yemeni man. Had they built these houses in the expectation that they were going to grow into giants? Was the scale of the city supposed forcibly to elevate the inhabitants? Husain and Abdurabu had gone at the stairs like mountain goats, skipping up from peak to peak. I lumbered behind, a gangling heavyweight with the sound of seagulls crying in my chest.

Husain stood at the door of his sitting-room, shouting orders into the bowels of the house. He wanted some bottles of Cola. He wanted his son to show to his visitors. The man in the Carnaby Street suit had suddenly switched into a traditional Arab father. There was a rustle on the stairs and a disembodied pair of hands projected the child into the room. The bottles of Cola came, in the same fashion, a moment or two later. We played with the boy for a while, then Husain got bored and shouted for his wife to come and take him away. Again the hands showed, and the child wobbled off towards its mother.

'I think we are lucky to find Husain in the street,' Abdurabu said. 'In this house, he could live for one year without going out.'

It was true. When estate agents describe residences as 'detached' or 'self-contained', they are using the words frivolously. Husain's house really was detached and self-contained. It had its own well and its own granary. Within its seven narrow storeys, a complete autonomous society was able to function, behind a front door thick enough to withstand a battering ram and honeycombed with ancient keyholes. Here a family could live, right in the centre of the city, in almost complete isolation from their neighbours.

In the Gulf I had seen that 'societistic' aspect of Islam which Dr Farouki had stressed so heavily in his lecture. It was a general rule that when I met someone in, say, Qatar or Abu Dhabi, I encountered first a code of manners and only secondly a person. The Gulf Arabs lived very much in public, and they had developed an intricate system of social rules which governed every aspect of their conduct. 'Etiquette' was of supreme importance to them – as it must be to anyone who lives much of his life in the open, among strangers. In that sense, the heyday of Victorian 'Society', or the great public theatre of the Elizabethan royal court, were close in spirit to bedu civilization: all three had based their social code on the idea that man's prime responsibility is to deal honourably and gracefully with strangers.

Husain's house was a vivid symbol of the ocean of cultural difference which divided the Yemenis from their bedu neighbours. Not only had the Yemen itself been isolated from the rest of the world for long stretches of history, but this isolation was visibly rooted in the separation of house from house, individual from individual. Every Yemeni I'd met had prided himself on 'doing different'. There was no code of manners to rely on. The Yemenis despised the protracted negotiations over a price which most other Arabs take such pleasure in, just as they despised good manners. One taxi driver, for instance, might drive me six or seven miles, then refuse to accept any payment at all because he 'liked the English'. The next would name a wild price at the end of the trip, and then throw my money in my face when I remarked that his rates struck me as being a bit on the high side. Waiters would either flick plates of food contemptuously sideways at one, slopping their contents half across the table, or sit down with one and rush, without any preliminaries at all, into a friendship. Sometimes I felt that I was liked, sometimes I knew that I was hated; in the Gulf these expressions would always have been masked behind the formalities of the code, in the Yemen they were naked. The only constant factor in my social encounters in Sana'a was this prickly individualism which combined the exaggerated machismo of the little man with a love of idiosyncrasy for idiosyncrasy's sake. It showed in the clothes people wore, in their personalized motor horns, in their architecture, in their faces.

Houses like Husain's went straight against the grain of Islam as the religion of public, communal life. In Sana'a, a man's house really was his castle; a tall, gloomy tower in which one might develop just about every conceivable kind of eccentricity. In these crumbling pillars of family privacy, Yemeni individualism had survived a lot of onslaughts already. People had locked their doors against Turkish rule. They had accepted only as much of Islam as happened to suit them. (In their determination to do different, the Yemenis invented the flattened dome to go over the top of their mosques.) Ten years ago, they had seen Egyptians, Russians and Saudis off their premises. Now they were facing an inflationary avalanche of foreign cash. Watching Husain bellow at his womenfolk, a king in his own musty domain, I suspected that the Yemenis might actually be more unscathed by all this than any outside observer might reasonably expect them to be. When crunches came, they holed up in their towers, chewed *qat*, spat, slept, and waited for a century or two for the fuss to go away.

We climbed up to the roof. It was like stepping out into the middle of a vast pop-up picture book. Away from the street, the whole city turned into a maze of another kind, a dense, jumbled alphabet of signs and symbols. The stucco friezes on the towers formed a continuous scrawl of handwriting all round one; the zig-zag pattern was, I realized, based on the shape الله, the word 'God'. There were other words, too; fragments of sentences inscribed in mud, stucco, brick and in the pinpoint work on wooden lattices. Yet where Allah reigned on the friezes, Jehovah had the windows to himself: the Star of David, recast in the shapes of leaves and flowers, was picked out on nearly every tower. The secular world chimed in with the heads of dogs, men, goats and camels, chiselled into whatever vacant patches had been left. A single decorative arch, raised in stone relief on the side of one tower, yielded: twin crescent moons surrounding a Star of David, carved water drops, lozenges, triangles, fleurs-de-lys, and some undecipherable calligraphic squiggles. Some shapes had been taken from nature, some from geometry, some from Islam, some from Judaism.

I had never seen a city which was so literally legible. It stretched all round my feet, an enormous code in three dimensions. If I half-closed my eyes, I almost thought that I could read it. The message didn't have a beginning, a middle or an end. If it had any structure at all, it was a crazy circular epic about colliding worlds. On the page-like walls of every house, the paradoxes were written up: religions clashed, the realms of nature and culture bled into one another, the domestic and the metaphysical were set in brute juxtaposition. The literate shaded into the pictorial, the pictorial into the literate. It was as if the entire city was conspiring to tell one that the world really is like a scrambled book. You could look at the walls of Sana'a for a year, finding more and more hidden meanings in them; you could read moral lectures from them; you could, no doubt, discover from them that Bacon wrote Shakespeare, that the world is flat, that spacemen from another planet conquered the Yemen a few millennia ago, that fluoride does terrible things to drinking water, that God was a mushroom, and that the world will end on 14 June 1987. With more reason, you might look at them for an hour and see that they coalesce into a single simple statement: that the world is infinitely complex, illegible, fraught with paradox, that it offers endless temptations to the gnostic to decode it, and that over the whole mad whirligig of contradictory meanings rides the endless looping signature of Allah.

On *qat*, perhaps, I might have been able to read some secrets from the rooftop. It is possible that on long, drugged, visionary afternoons, the city becomes articulate and talks with manic fluency to its inhabitants. As it was, I just felt brain-damaged by the effort of trying to take in this garble of symbols and oppositions. I wanted a further point of perspective: the mountains to the south looked like a good, clean, airy place from which one might take a longer view down over the labyrinth. I asked Abdurabu if it was possible to get up to the top of them.

'Once, yes. There is a road. But it is forbidden now. There are army things there . . . what is *dabbabat*?'

'Tanks,' I said.

'They make a fort there, I think.'

'I think that is not true,' Husain said. 'My father used to go to the mountains. He came back with bags of stones, and melted these stones, and made things from them. Copper. There is much copper there. That is why people cannot go now.'

'This is why they say that it is for army reasons, you see,' explained Abdurabu. I was getting used to the two-headed Arabic explanation by now, and it was only when I got back to my notebook in the evening that I noticed a small hiatus in the logic of this exchange. If you mean one thing, it is a point of moral principle actually to say something else.

'You have seen all that you want to see?'

'Yes, thank you.'

'We go down then.'

I was shown to the door on the roof first, as the guest. I had started on the stairs when Abdurabu touched my shoulder.

'No – first you must shout "*Yallah*".'

'Why?'

'That is to tell the women to go to their quarters.'

'Sorry,' I said. 'I can't. You do it.'

'*Yallah-ah!*' shouted Abdurabu. Deep down underneath us, there was a faint pattering and rustling, then silence.

'It is OK now. We go down.'

After the glare of the rooftop, the stairwell was a cold velvety black. On the fourth floor, a thin chink of light showed between a door and its jamb . . . a pair of eyes, a glimpse of a black veil over mouth and nose, and then the door was shut. I could hear giggles all the way down to the street.

As we walked through the souk, Abdurabu said, 'Husain is lucky. He has a good house. I would like a house like that. But it is very expensive. I must do good in my business.'

'How much does it cost to rent a house in the city?'

'For a family, perhaps three or four thousand rials a month.' It was about £500.

'That's for foreigners, though, surely, not for Yemenis?'

'No, that is for Yemenis. For foreigners, maybe more. You see why it is important for me to be millionaire.'

He picked his way lightly past a line of squatting beggars. Their skins were nearly black; they were Tihamas, refugees from the coast who lived in cardboard boxes and scrapes in the rock on the edge of the old city. At night I'd seen them sweeping the streets – making a pitiful display of shifting heaps of dirt from one place to another with brooms made out of a few twigs. I gave a couple of rials to a child with a pot belly and the creased face of an old man.

'*Yallah!*' said Abdurabu. 'It is not good. You should not give money. You give to one, they all come, then you have no more money.' As if continuing the thought, he said he would like to buy me a lace skullcap as a souvenir of our afternoon; looking at the Tihamas, I thanked him and said no, he had shown me things that I wouldn't forget, and that they were the most important souvenirs.

'I might lose the skullcap; I shan't lose the view from Husain's roof.'

'Ah,' said Abdurabu. 'Next year you come back, perhaps I have a house like Husain's – ' and he skipped in front of a Mercedes truck. It had been brilliantly decorated in Day-Glo paint; the Mercedes trade-mark of a circle enclosing three radial arms had been repeated over and over again in different colours to make a dazzling arabesque. As he tried to run Abdurabu down, the driver played *John Brown's Body Lies a Mouldering in the Grave* on his horn.

I slept badly, disturbed by the muezzins, my head rattling with confused images. A veiled nurse handed out contraceptive pills to Yemeni mothers at the Save The Children Fund Clinic; students at the English Department in the university teased out a poem by Edwin Muir –

> Oh then our maze of tunnelled stone
> Grew thin and treacherous as air.
> The cause was lost without a groan,
> The famous citadel overthrown,
> And all its secret galleries bare . . .

I had tried to persuade the students that Muir was using deliberately archaic images to create a mythological landscape outside the reach of history. It had been hard going, since the window of the classroom had looked out over the very landscape of crumbling turrets that Muir had imagined as an abstraction. A sign, pointing, as far as I could see, to a heap of rubble, stated: dR AL AnSi HaMUd OTOLARYNGOLO-

GIST. One Friday, there had been an eclipse of the moon, and the surrounding hills had glittered with bonfires lit by villagers who thought that Allah was punishing them for their sins by taking the moon away. I had attended the Easter Service at the residence of the British Ambassador. A side table had been converted into an altar. The room had smelled of blossom, polish and tobacco smoke. We'd sung,

> Alleluia! Alleluia! Alleluia!
> The strife is o'er, the battle done;
> Now is the Victor's triumph won;
> O let the song of praise be sung:
> Alleluia!

while the voices of the muezzins calling from neighbouring minarets had drowned out our feeble singing, and I'd looked through the ambassador's french windows on to an English lawn with daffodils and sweet peas simultaneously in bloom. There had been Dr Khibsi, of the National Institute of Public Administration, who was trying to introduce the Yemenis to the joys of April Fool's Day, and the view from the rooftop, with the city laid out like a mad encyclopedia.

When I woke at five on my last morning in Sana'a I felt stale and hungover. Too many jigsaw puzzles had got muddled up with each other, and I had spent the night trying to match pieces from the wrong pictures. Salisbury Cathedral, the Cottage Garden and the Laughing Cavalier had come together in a frightful mess of botched colour, and Sana'a seemed to have been lost somewhere at the back of the cupboard.

At the airport, the remittance men were saying goodbye to their families. In the acid dawn light they looked sad and shrunken. They had had to leave their daggers behind, but everyone wore an empty scabbard, bound with coloured raffia. Scrubbed, stripped of their *macho*, they sat in small, disconsolate huddles on their tin trunks, waiting for their flight to Jeddah. In a day or so they would be working in road-gangs, driving taxis, or getting jobs as longshoremen. In a week they would be posting money home. In a year, perhaps, they would be back, *Inshallah*. They would get the scribe to write. One man had his fists in his eyes. Another kept on turning a piece of paper around in his hand. I think it must have been the name and address of his Saudi employer; it was clear that he couldn't read it. Sitting in the departure lounge among these forlorn exports, glad to be on my way again, I felt that I was Sana'a airport's number one rat-fink.

7

Two Nations

When my flight to Cairo was called, I saw a large American lady struggling with a heap of photographic equipment in aluminium tins. She was wearing a home-made jersey which came down to her knees and which looked as if it had been knitted out of thick vegetable soup. When I went to help her with her things she said 'Bless you!' She meant it, too, for she was a Southern Baptist missionary returning to the United States after a tour of duty in the Middle East.

'For someone in your business, Arabia must be a fairly stony row to hoe,' I said. She agreed that there was little doing in the way of Conversions, but that what counted was Christian Example. The Southern Baptists maintained a string of clinics staffed by American doctors, and in a country like the Yemen (which has one doctor for every twenty thousand people) these mission clinics were doing a very important job indeed. Apparently, though, the doctors and the missionaries were not seeing eye to eye.

'It is very sad to have to say it, but there is Dissent. Some of our evangelists are not in a state of Harmony with some of our doctors . . .' She was having some trouble getting into her Yemen Air seatbelt; three or four Yemeni waists could have been comfortably fitted into the space needed for her own.

'Would you care for Literature?' she asked. She had brought a string bag of tracts to read on the plane.

'No thanks,' I said. 'I'm afraid I'm an agnostic.'

'I am myself a Flexible Christian,' she said. As if to demonstrate this concept, she rolled amply from buttock to buttock in her seat and finally pronounced herself settled and content with a little mooing sigh. I stared distractedly at a page of *Martin Chuzzlewit* while she sorted through her tracts to find her favourite. 'Are you sure you wouldn't care to read some of our Literature?' She rooted in the bottom of her string bag. 'This, for instance, I find very emotionally moving . . . Testimonies by Christians in Beirut?'

'No, thank you – really,' I said. After take-off, the plane banked sharply and the Yemen slid up into the window: pumice-stone streaked with veins and crevices of green. I remarked that for a Southern Baptist it must be a fine thing to have another Southern Baptist in the White House now.

'If I am honest with myself I have to admit that I harbour one or two Serious Doubts about Mis-ter Jim-my Car-ter,' she said, laying out the syllables of the President's name as if she was manipulating them at the end of a pair of tongs.

'How so?'

'It's my belief that Mis-ter Car-ter is sometimes inspired by Direct Revelation. But very often he seems to act without Revelation at all. I just wish he'd come out and say to the American people when he was acting on Revelation and when he wasn't. To tell the truth, I'm not even sure that Mis-ter Car-ter knows himself whether he's getting Direct Revelation or whether he's not.'

This struck me as the most succinct and plausible explanation of the behaviour of the great peanut farmer that I had ever heard, and I cherished it all the way to Jeddah, where we stopped to refuel.

I was within fifteen feet of Saudi Arabian soil and that, I felt, was quite near enough. Trespassing round the countries on its fringes, I had been constantly reminded of the presence of Saudi Arabia. It was the huge icy heartland of the Middle East. On the Gulf and in the Yemen I had seen the pressures exerted by Saudi money, Saudi religious orthodoxy and Saudi politics. The Saudi sphere of influence was comparable to that of any imperial power; except that the Saudis used rials where the Soviets, the British, the Austrians, the Turks, had used brute military force. When the Emir of Sharjah had started a casino, the Saudis had closed it down by paying the Emir as much money as he would have received every month from his casino, plus a handsome bonus. The Saudis had closed the one 'wet' restaurant in Qatar. In every country I had visited, there had been prowling Saudis, grave fatcats whose job it was to keep a weather-eye open for any sign of malcontents stepping out of line. It had been rumoured that the Saudis were behind the assassination of Hamdi in the Yemen; and the Yemenis whom I had met loathed the Saudis. They were the boss class of Arabia. When other Arabs talked about the Saudis, two persistent adjectives cropped up again and again: the Saudis were 'arrogant', and they were 'hypocritical'.

This was underdog talk. It did not in fact tell one anything much about the Saudis themselves; but the fact of their unpopularity was important – and catching. Sitting in the plane at Jeddah I felt that I was at the drawbridge of a castle belonging to a legendary ogre, and I was glad that it wasn't going to be lowered for me. Had I stopped in Saudi Arabia, I'm certain that I would have been totally surprised by what I saw. The stereotype-Saudi comes from the same mould as John Bull, the Beastly Hun and the Russian Bear; and individual Saudis smart just as keenly at this cartooned version of themselves as individual Englishmen, Germans and Russians have done.

What the stereotypes reveal is not a truth about national character but a truth about the injustice and arbitrariness of national power. The image of the Saudi in Arabia compares very closely with that of John Bull. Both are fat men. Both are given to expensive vices (Bull has his cigar, Saudi has his illicit Scotch). Both treat the lesser breeds with jeering contempt, exploiting other people's resources for their own ends. Unlike the unbuttoned and cheerfully vulgar figure of Bull, though, Saudi wears a public face of extreme and humourless puritanism. His mouth turns down at the corners and his eyes are narrowed in perpetual disapproval of an errant world; while in secret he drinks and fornicates. John Bull might have been a first cousin of the lovable Mr Pickwick; Saudi is more like Ben Jonson's ghastly puritan, Tribulation Wholesome. He is not loved, and like most unloved people, he has a chronic tendency to being misunderstood.

When the Saudi Arabian foreign minister visited Abu Dhabi

he had stood in the hatchway of his plane, waved at the television cameras, and announced: 'We are all one nation.'

An Englishman who lived there said to me, 'Actually it was just supposed to be a nice fraternal gesture of goodwill, but he came bloody near to causing panic in the streets. They were taking those words apart and putting them together again for weeks, trying to work out what the implications were.'

As we taxied up the runway, I looked out at Jeddah. Its pastel-coloured concrete blocks and naked eight-lane highways raced faster and faster behind the double glass until they turned into a pretty pink-and-yellow blur. Then we were up, making a beeline for Egypt across the Red Sea. Jetting in and out of places is a much abused form of travel, but every so often it gives one a charge as strong as a sniff of cocaine. Anyone who has ever been stirred by the idea of lighting out, splitting, hitting the road, must be excited by that moment in take-off when the plane takes a huge deep breath, gathers itself and hauls you out of town, leaving a derisive bubble of spent gas hanging in the sky.

My companion was buried in her tracts. Martin Chuzzlewit was having a hard time of it on his transatlantic crossing, and I was sipping sweet airline lemonade from a plastic glass. Judging by what I had seen of it, Saudi Arabia looked absolutely fine.

Dizzied by the flight, I seemed to have left my thoughts behind in other places, and at first I mistook Cairo for home. I passed through its miles of dun-coloured suburbs with the inattention one reserves for things which are so drearily familiar that it is an annoyance to notice them. It was the outskirts of Birmingham – the same tacky estates of municipal flats, the same tired, shuffling look of people who've got used to spending half their lives in queues.

'I speak English very good. I study English for eleven years,' the driver said.

'Yes, excellent.' I didn't feel much like talking.

'Your English is not so good, I think.'

'I've been away a bit.'

'You speak very strange.'

'Too quickly, you mean?'

'No, not too quickly. I do not understand you when you speak English, because you speak English bad, I think.'

It seemed likely. I asked him to find me a hotel – in Arabic.

'You do not speak Arabic very good.'

'Catch-twenty-two.'

'I do not understand.'

'Hotel-fondoq. Please-min fadlak. OK?'

'I study English for eleven years,' he said aggrievedly.

I took in without surprise the sight of boys and girls walking hand in hand on the pavements. Like the unveiled women, and the little, battered utility cars, they were a part of being home. The man riding a camel at the side of the road, though, must have been an optical illusion – a leftover image from somewhere else, a bit of Qatar or Al Ain snagged in the eye like a piece of grit. The tufted palms, which lined the streets like old upturned floormops, had a dismal civic air. They looked just as displaced in Heliopolis as they would on any English ring-road.

We went past a used-car lot; it said SHADY CARS, and jogged my memory. This wasn't England after all. Here 'shady' was a lucky, talismanic word to work into the title of a business, and not a frank confession of sawdust in gearboxes and switched-back milometers. But as we pushed deeper into the city, I felt that this really was a homecoming, there was so much to recognize. The sweating cliffs of stained brownstone; the ravines of clogged traffic; the blue fog of exhaust fumes; the rime of thick dust on office windows; the dead letters falling out of neon signs – Cairo was a postal district of that nameless metropolis of which I have always felt myself to be a ratepaying citizen. Old, top-heavy, slow, full of subtle sleights and corruptions, it looked and smelled like home. From the taxi window, I spotted cafés, bars, bookshops. As soon as the ride was over I could be out there, browsing through the shelves, perched on a stool with a glass in my hand, back to the old urban hunting-dog tricks of the hard stare and the bar pick-up.

Like every really big city, Cairo had created its own climate. The sun was up, the temperature was pushing ninety degrees, but down at street-level there was a thick comfortable gloom. The violet, bricky air tasted of the humus in which urban rats like me are at their happiest. In air like that, one can disappear from sight, keep secrets and have adventures. In the faces which passed the window, I recognized old friends. I liked their doughy pallor, the preoccupied look with which they were cutting out private routes through the crowd.

I was so lost in the pleasure of returning that I would gladly have spent the entire afternoon crawling down those one-way streets, through traffic lights that didn't work, past rusty arcades and promising alleyways. The River Nile, when we eventually broke through to it in a sudden glare of sunshine, seemed an affront. It was actually dotted with lateen sails. Kipling was right, as usual, when he wrote:

> The East is wherever one sees the lateen sail – that shark's fin of a rig which for hundreds of years has dogged all white bathers round the Mediterranean. There is still a suggestion of menace, a hint of piracy, in the blood whenever the lateen goes by, fishing or fruiting or coasting.

I didn't want to be in the East, though; I wanted to be at home. I was reassured a little when I saw that these lateen sails were being cranked up and down by the bargemen so that their boats could pass under the road-bridges. I hoped that the masts on Kipling's vessels didn't have hinges.

We found a hotel with a vacant room on the far side of Tahrir Bridge. The rooms at the front of the building faced out over the Nile; mine was at the back, and it had much the better view. I could look out over a football stadium, a tower which looked like the Eiffel Tower recast, minaret-style, in wickerwork, and several miles of apartment blocks and flyovers. Over a bottle of beer and a chicken sandwich, I watched a scrappy match in which two teams of schoolboys were taking turns to knock hell out of each other with a succession of own-goals. The styles of both teams closely resembled that of my local club, Chelsea. It was good to be back.

The Nile seemed to be the only real problem. To walk back to the city centre, I had to cross the river, and I had arrived in town on exactly the same day as the *Khamsin*, the hot sand wind which blows up from the desert. On Tahrir Bridge, I caught it full in the face. It was like the strong gusty breath of an old goat. It stank of innards, and it was hard to feel at home with such a rank and singular smell in one's nose. The sand itself was impregnated with this stench; it lodged in one's clothes, one's fingernails, one's ears, one's toes. After a walk across the bridge, one's own body was gamey with the odour of foreign parts. It was on my fingers – desert, camel dung, muddy little villages with buffaloes up to their knees in stagnant pools full of bilharzia snails, sweaty woollen shawls, wild tomcats . . . a rich concentrate of old Arabia. There is a perfume on the market called 'Araby'; it doesn't smell like that at all, but if there was any truth in names it should. Yet even the *Khamsin* was closer to home than I might have guessed. I looked it up in the dictionary, just to give a more precise definition to the whiff that came off my own laundry. It is a Christian not a Muslim wind, named after the fifty days that come between Easter and Whitsun. Whether this coinage meant that the Copts had laid claim to the thing, or whether the Moham-madans were just blaming the stink on the Christians, I don't know. I tried to find out, but the people whom I asked seemed to think it a very stuffy and academic question. It was just the *Khamsin*; it lodged in the interstices of their best Louis-Farouk furniture; it was the chief hazard of Cairo in the spring; and as for its religion, they didn't care whether it was Shintoist, Sikh, Taoist or Zen, it was simply a damned nuisance.

Smelling like a Christian, I went back to where I'd seen the bookshops. It seemed pure luxury to be up a crooked lane, turning over second-hand books with broken spines again. Admittedly, most of them had titles which fell short of my wilder hopes. I rejected *Diseases of the Urethra*, along with *Everyman's Ready Reckoner* and volume one of Prout's *The Law of Tort*; but at the back of one shop I saw there was a whole wall of old Penguins, ragged orange-backs printed on war economy paper and priced at one-and-six. I found a copy of Wilkie Collins's *The Woman In White* – twenty-five piastres. Elizabeth Taylor's *A View From The Harbour* cost twenty piastres. And then I came across what now seems to me to be the most illuminating discovery that I made in Cairo: a line of forty-seven copies of Disraeli's *Sybil: or The Two Nations*. No one had touched them for years. They were veiled in a uniform film of dust. Someone in the 1940s, perhaps, had put Disraeli on the English Department syllabus, and *Sybil* had dribbled back here to roost in ones and twos until the shelf was full. I selected a copy from the middle of the line and shook a miniature *Khamsin* of sand and dirt out of its pages. At twenty piastres, it proved the cheapest comprehensive guide to Cairo that any visitor could possibly obtain.

I joined the afternoon crowd trudging round the circular walkway over Tahrir Square. It was starting to get dark, and the trams were making blue flashes on their wires. The walkway was packed solid. I went round and round it, carried along with the pack, missing my exit. It was a queer crowd to be in, too. I kept on being reminded of a place or a time that I couldn't quite locate. Everyone, it seemed, had the same deadened look of frayed gentility and shredded nerves. I had fallen in with a whole class on the move. Their suits were worn to a bluebottle sheen, their shoes cracked, their collars and cuffs had been broken by too many years of ironing. They carried scuffed cardboard briefcases, and a quite improbable proportion of people were wearing the sort of spectacles which make the eyes behind them magnify and swim in their lenses. If all the leaving certificates and diplomas and degrees which had been awarded at one time or another to this crowd could have been piled into a bonfire in the centre of the square, the flames would have been visible for miles. Somewhere in the crowd there were hidden hustlers, voices which found one's ear; but it was hard to connect them with a particular face.

'Hi, how ya doin'?' The accent had been copied, inaccurately, from gangster films.

'Fine,' I murmured, trying to spot my interrogator. He turned out to be obvious enough – his Afro hair and yellow open-necked shirt made him look positively freakish in the company we were keeping. But he kept behind me, and the movement of the crowd carried us both along, so that it was hard to get a square look at his face.

'You come along with me? You like the unusual. I got the unusual. I fix anything you want . . .'

'I'm only interested in the usual, thanks.'

'The usual! The usual! Boy, you come to the right guy. You want the usual? You want usual girls?'

'No girls, thanks – '

The voice came suddenly close. 'Fuckin' British! All da fuckin' same!' And he was gone, hunting for another soft mark in the crowd.

He was soon replaced by another voice. 'Hello. Welcome to Cairo. You want woman?'

'No – '

'OK, wiseguy – '

Then there was the old-fashioned approach, soft, mocking. 'Sahib? . . . Sahib?'

'I'm not a sahib.'

'Sahib – one minute, please . . .'

'Go away!'

'Sahib . . .?'

Round and round and round we went, Cairo's threadbare, circumambulant clerisy. Apart from the hustlers, everybody looked tired, educated and hungry. There were six exits from the walkway, but the invisible seventh was the one that really counted – the exit which led out of Egypt altogether, into Saudi Arabia, Abu Dhabi, Kuwait, Qatar, Dubai. The Egyptians I had met three months ago had made it off this walkway, and it was easy enough to imagine them back here in the crowd. I remembered the way they had looked on the Gulf: harassed, chain-smoking men who were courting early coronaries and hanging on to jobs which paid them ten to twenty times the salaries which they might expect to earn at home.

A hundred Egyptian pounds a month is reckoned to be a good wage for a man with a doctorate working in the Civil Service. An Egyptian pound is worth about seventy-five English pence. In Abu Dhabi, the same man might make ten to fifteen thousand pounds sterling a year. So the walkway round Tahrir Square was packed with the unlucky ones, the ones who were waiting for a letter or an interview, and the ones who simply liked their city too much to think of leaving it, and who were prepared to put up with wearing shirts with turned collars and shoes which let the sand into their holey socks.

It was only when I was back on the bridge taking the full

blast of the *Khamsin* that I traced the nagging half-memory which the circling crowd had triggered in my head. It was of an England which I barely knew – the England of the Attlee government, just after the war. The trams belonged there. (Though in England they were never quite so packed and people didn't have to cling precariously to their outsides as Cairenes did.) The clothes, too, fitted the period – the hand-me-downs and demob suits and shapeless garments bought from jumble sales. It was the faces which brought back the image of the 1940s most vividly: I might have seen them in old copies of *Picture Post* with its grainy photographic studies of London street scenes after the blitz. They looked, in a phrase from the time, 'whacked'. They too were exhausted by a long war. They'd had too little to eat, they slept in fits and starts. I'd seen the same stiff shabby gentility in people of my parents' generation: the air of trying one's best to put a good face on things, the attitude of those who know that they are down on their uppers but who are trying their damnedest not to show it.

They belonged, in the world that I came from, to the age of Woolton loaves, ration books, clothing coupons and whalemeat steaks. Even the hustlers fitted the image of Flash Harry black marketeers – men in zoot suits and co-respondent shoes who traded in nylon stockings and contraband sausages. If Cairo really was a version of home, something peculiar had happened to the clock.

The hotel lift carried me up twelve storeys and three decades on. The dining-room was half-filled with a party of English package tourists. Today they had returned from a trip down the Nile, and tomorrow they were going to see the pyramids and the Sphinx. From a wine list which offered Cru de Nefertiti, Cru de Cleopatra and Cru des Ptolemies, I chose the Ptolemies, who turned out to be white and sweet. My fellow-diners and I had come at Cairo from different angles, and we'd arrived at different places. They'd flown from Gatwick to the land of Pharaohs, while I had made a homecoming of sorts from Sana'a. I felt a little envious of their Egypt. It was a place where one climbed the pyramid of Cheops to watch the sunrise and held hands in the tombs and saw *fellaheen* and camels and mummies and the funeral mask of Tutankhamun. I would have liked to have gone there myself, but from where I was sitting it sounded too faraway a country for me to reach.

Soldiers were on guard outside the abandoned film-set of the Cairo Trade Fair. They lined Tahrir Street; bored men leaning on rifles under the palms. Even by moonlight one could see the bad fit of their battledress and that embarrassed, shanghaied look of the draftee. Everything about them said plainly that they weren't really soldiers, that someone else had made them put on their uniforms, and that they were tired of the masquerade. One by one they politely barred my way, asked me what time it was and whether I could spare a cigarette. I apologized; I was a pipe-smoker, I didn't carry cigarettes. They shrugged. *Maalesh*. Just their luck. And returned to their palm trees to count away the minutes of their guard-duty.

I was on my way to the casino at the Nile Sheraton. I wanted to hob-nob with the quality at the roulette tables, and I'd been told that the Sheraton was the best place to catch the super-rich shaking out the contents of their wallets.

'You will need your passport,' the desk clerk at my own hotel had said, 'to prove you are not an Egyptian.'

'That's bad, isn't it? You mean you can't go there, but a Saudi can?'

'That's good. It means only the fools can throw their money away.'

The Sheraton was holding a birthday party for itself when I arrived. A pretty girl in a sash which announced that she had been Miss Sheraton of 1974 gave me a glass of champagne, and a band of bagpipers wearing dishdashas with scarlet overtunics marched through the lobby playing 'The Campbells Are Coming'. They were followed by what looked like a religious procession of some kind. A dozen men in surplices were holding flaming brass incense burners with which they surrounded another four men who were acting as pall-bearers to a giant chocolate cake.

'It is very pretty, I think,' said Miss Sheraton 1974 a bit doubtfully. 'Now I must go to be in the photograph.'

All the Miss Sheratons surrounded the cake. 1974 had been overmodest: 'the photograph' was on the scale of a napalm bombing raid. The girls, the priests, the pall-bearers, the cake and the bagpipers were whited-out in a prolonged guttering flash, as thirty or forty Saudi camera-buffs came in for the kill. The Nikons, Hasselblads, Yashicas and Pentaxes involved in the operation would alone have raised sufficient money to pay for the beginnings of a sizeable airforce. The real enthusiasts had three or four of these objects strung round their necks at once, and executed a form of fan dance with them, keeping them in constant motion as one came up to the eye, blazed away, and was instantly replaced by the next camera on the circuit.

1978 blew out the candles on the cake. She looked in real danger of being charred to a cinder by the explosion which attended this act. The pipers started in on 'Auld Lang Syne', and I fled to a downstairs bar to give my ears and eyes a rest. It was empty except for a Cairene who had dropped in for a beer on his way home.

'Do you like this sort of thing?' I asked. The pipe band was now on its way downstairs. It was going to leave no part of the hotel untouched by its hideous groans and skirls.

'I? No. I think the noise of fighting cats is better. It is something that the Saudis like.'

'Why is it that Arabs are so keen on bagpipes?'

'*Saudis*,' he said, correcting me. 'I think it is because they like very big things. If they have a noise, they want it to be the biggest noise.'

They'd got it, too. Now only a thin partition-wall separated us from the band and we had to shout to make ourselves heard over the top of 'Scotland The Brave'.

'I know England! I have been to Epsom!' yelled my companion at the bar.

'Why did you go to England?' I called back.

'Medical reasons!' he shouted. 'I have treatment!'

'I shall need treatment too! The bagpipes are making me deaf!'

The band started trooping down to the basement floor, leaving us in relative peace.

'The hospital in Epsom is very good.'

'If the Saudis can have so much fun in Cairo,' I said, 'why is it, do you think, that they bother to come to London?'

'Because London is a symbol. It is the capital of Europe. It is a place where you take the whole family, because it is historical. I think that is why. If a Saudi businessman goes to New York, or goes to Geneva, he goes alone, with a secretary. It is for business only. If he goes to London, he takes his wife, his children, everybody – to see this symbol. Cairo, yes, is fun. He drinks, he gambles . . . there are girls. But it is not symbolic. London is the big symbol. The biggest.'

'Like the sound of bagpipes – '

'I think this is bad for Cairo. Here people are very poor. They do not have money to spend. They see the Saudis – spend, spend, spend, every minute they spend more money. For an Egyptian, this thing is a hurt to his pride, you know?'

'That's pretty well exactly what people feel in London.'

'They have more money in London than in Cairo. It should not make them feel so bad.'

He went home. I went up to the casino, flashing my passport to prove that I was a fully accredited fool with foreign currency at my disposal. Egyptian pounds are not accepted in exchange for chips. 'We only take real money,' said the cashier when I tried offering him some of his own notes. I had a fifty-dollar bill which I had earmarked for an emergency, and passed it across the counter.

'I want it in one-dollar chips, please.'

He looked at the single bill, looked at me, and sniggered.

'English, right?' He'd met my type before. He counted out a nice big stack of red chips, and as I was gathering them up he leaned forward and said, 'Hey, I hope you come lucky!' It was a sudden, queer little flash of fraternity between two under-dog nations. I think it would have really made his day if I had managed to knock the stuffing out of a couple of Saudi millionaires at blackjack with my measly fifty dollars.

I went down into the pit and watched the run of play at a roulette table. The petrodollar was the basic unit of currency, and it was the blunt language of the petrodollar in which the game was conducted. There was no croupier-French here: it was 'No more bets', not *'Rien ne va plus'*.

I usually like casinos. I have happy memories of making small losses at Monte Carlo, Venice and Besançon; at each place the loss was a worthwhile price to pay for becoming a temporary member of an absorbingly interesting society. At the Nile Sheraton, it was altogether different. There were no women at the tables, and the atmosphere in the room was more like that of a board-meeting of directors of some public-utility company than that of the chamber-opera which I'd seen in European casinos. A game of roulette needs at least one widow on a spree, one shaky loser on pills, one ravishingly stupid blonde *coiffeuse*, one tattooed sailor and one flinty professional gambler to make it come really alive. The game I was watching looked stone-dead. Most of the players were either Saudis or Kuwaitis. Their dark business suits were identical, so were the heavy gold watches on their wrists. There wasn't a single flicker of anxiety, excitement or greed in sight. They looked as if they were merely killing time, and might just as well have been playing patience.

One man did have a system which was new to me. He saturated the entire board with chips – a little heap on every number. It was costing him a few hundred dollars a game to have the pleasure of seeing a great tower of chips pushed back to him every time, while the croupier raked home the even larger sum which the same man had invested on all the numbers which hadn't come up. Of all the expressionless players, he looked like the man who was coming closest to actually enjoying himself. With each game he could savour the twin pleasures of being a winner and a loser, while at the same time he could demonstrate his total indifference to the trifling matter of financing his indulgences. One thing, at least, was certain: he wasn't in it for the money.

My own system worked on much the same theory, if on a drastically reduced scale. I bet on alternate games; and each time I placed one dollar on *Noir* and another dollar on the same block of four numbers. This technique does not make one the most popular figure on the table; but it does mean that, with very little money indeed, one can remain for hours on end as a fringe-participant in the game. My pile rose to sixty dollars, dropped to thirty-five, then stabilized at around forty. Just occasionally, the ball would seem to get snagged around my block-of-four, and I would get tempted to go in for something more adventurous; but then the ball deserted my numbers, and my chips dribbled back to the croupier in modest ones and twos.

At any one time there must have been about a hundred thousand dollars in play. This was backed up by several times that sum in heaps of chips around the table. There was still a constant traffic in paper money. At the end of each game, more rials would come out, and the croupier would reach for them with a long-handled spatula which folded the notes and dropped them into a sort of pillarbox mouth at the head of the table. The inside of the table must have been solid with money. I tried to count the stuff as it disappeared into that mouth, but there was too much of it and it was dispatched at too great a speed. I wished I'd been a cigarette smoker: a lighted butt, casually dropped into the aperture under the croupier's elbow, could have sent a fortune up in smoke.

The Nile Sheraton is by a bridge over a backwater of the river which turns Gezira into a long sprawling island. At two in the morning, I stood on this bridge and lit my pipe. Bored half to death by the dull business of the roulette table, I had tried to lose in order to have an excuse for leaving. For an hour, I had done my best to rid myself of my little cache of chips, but they had kept on coming back to me. Eventually I blew the lot – thirty-six dollars' worth – on my birthday number of fourteen. The ball, to my relief, landed up somewhere in the twenties, and I had quit the game.

The current here was slow and oily. It was a natural place to tie up for the night, and there were half a dozen shark-nosed dug-outs anchored under the bridge. On one of them, a fellow-insomniac was brewing tea by the light of a Tilley lamp. His cabin was just a plank laid over the stern of the boat, and he looked cold in his thin burnous. As he warmed his hands at the little glow of charcoal under his tin kettle, he looked up. His expression wasn't friendly. I felt properly rebuked for being a tourist.

I walked back to my hotel down Tahrir Street. The guard had changed. I had no cigarettes. It was going to be a long wait till morning.

Overcharged with this new city, I found it hard to get to

sleep. I tried reading Elizabeth Taylor. In England, I am an addict of her books, but in Cairo her world seemed at once too provincial and too exotic to be believable. *A View From The Harbour* was set in a seaside town in the West Country in 1947. I did my best to follow the lives of people called Bertram and Prudence and Mrs Wilson and Mrs Bracey; it was no go – they were impossibly remote. I put the book down and tried *Sybil* instead. That was much more to the point. Disraeli's thunderous prose fitted the small hours of Cairo to a *T*, and I swept through the first hundred pages in a heady rush.

'Well, society may be in its infancy,' said Egremont, slightly smiling; 'but say what you like, our Queen reigns over the greatest nation that ever existed.'

'Which nation?' asked the younger stranger, 'for she reigns over two.'

The stranger paused; Egremont was silent, but looked inquiringly.

'Yes,' resumed the younger stranger after a moment's interval. 'Two nations; between whom there is no intercourse and no sympathy; who are as ignorant of each other's habits, thoughts, and feelings, as if they were different dwellers in different zones, or inhabitants of different planets; who are formed by a different breeding, are fed by a different food, are ordered by different manners, and are not governed by the same laws.'

'You speak of – ' said Egremont, hesitatingly.

'THE RICH AND THE POOR.'

I had tried to read *Sybil* once before, when I was a student, and had found its version of Victorian England too melodramatic and theoretical; I couldn't connect it with any society that I knew. One day in Cairo, though, had given the book the force of vivid documentary. By the time that I fell asleep, Disraeli's noblemen were wearing white robes trimmed with gold, and his mean industrial streets – the 'close courts and pestilential culs-de-sac' swarming with their 'infinite population' – smelled of the *Khamsin*.

The High Council of Arts, Literature and Social Sciences was in a wide street of Palladian stucco houses. If one turned a strong sun-ray lamp on Cheltenham and scattered a few tons of sand over the place, one could turn it into a passable replica of Gezira. There were few people about. It had the perpetual-Sunday-morning air of expensive suburbia, and it was easy enough to find the High Council of Arts by its cracked stucco and peeling paint. One way of dealing with intellectuals is to strand them conspicuously among their betters, and the High Council of Arts looked like a gangling bookish creature in broken shoes caught up, to its bewilderment, in the middle of the smart set.

The house had been designed for an elegant salon-life of standing lamps, ottomans, thick carpets and cut flowers. When it had been requisitioned for the intellectuals, it must have been stripped bare. Now it was a draughty shell, with lino on the floors, institutional green paint on the walls, tubular stacking chairs, and the general air of a bankrupt prep school. Bits of its plaster dados and cornices had fallen out, and no one had swept up the pieces. Its golden-section windows gave the view over the garden an interestingly impressionistic effect; through the smeared and dusty glass it was possible to make out what might have been palms and bougainvillea. I felt more like a prospective buyer of the place than a visitor. An estate agent would have made a great deal of its 'potential', and I found myself involuntarily refurnishing it in my head, my footfalls echoing in the empty stairwell.

The intellectuals looked as if their tenancy of the building was dreadfully insecure. They camped out in corners of rooms that were too big for them, with trestle tables manoeuvred into whatever position would catch the few patches of grubby sunshine that were going. A poet lived in a disused ballroom. A critic and playwright had cornered a relatively snug scullery. A man who was introduced to me as 'the only writer of science fiction in Arabia' had his quarters somewhere up in the decrepit fo'c'sle of the house. I had said that it would be nice to meet 'some writers'; and the director of the Council rustled up a scratch crew for me by calling in on just a few of the doors nearest to his office. For all I know, the house may have harboured hundreds of writers, scratching up in the attics, cudgelling their brains in empty boudoirs and talking to the deathwatch beetles in the lofts.

We went to the 'Committee Room' to talk. A bronze bust on a plinth had been turned to face into the fireplace, so that one could only see its hollowed backside.

'Who is that?' I asked.

'That is President Nasser,' said the poet.

'Why is he back to front?'

'Ah, you see the Sharia Committee had a meeting here last night. They have demanded that we remove President Nasser from the house. At present he is just turned to the wall, but I think the Sharia Committee will soon have him taken away.'

'Why do they want him out?'

'Two reasons. If the first one fails, then they use the second. The first is, Nasser was a socialist. We must not have statues of socialists in the building. The second is a religious reason: Islam prohibits representational images. So the Sharia Committee has us in its pincers. I am afraid that Nasser will not be here for very long.'

'But Cairo's full of statues. Everywhere one goes there's another statue.'

'There are statues and statues. Cairo isn't full of statues of Nasser.'

The poet himself looked ill. His face was prematurely creased, and the sallow bags of skin under his eyes were cracked and papery.

'I'm sorry,' I said, 'I don't read Arabic, and don't know your work, but I'd very much like you to tell me about it. What are you working on at present, for instance?'

'I do not write poems any more. The last book of poems I wrote was eight . . . nine years ago. It is very hard now. If you write a poem, they say, then you must write your poem about the Five Year Plan, or something like that. What do I do, in conscience? I stop writing.'

'And yet you can say this to me freely in this room – in a government building?'

'Oh, yes, we have "freedom of speech",' he said sadly. 'But freedom of writing is something else. Freedom of publication is something different again. We can talk like this. That is good.

It is "just talk". So long as it remains "just talking" it is harmless. That is what the state likes – it likes writers to just talk.'

'And you don't mind me publishing this in England in my book?'

'I think that it is good that it should be published. But it won't be published in Cairo.'

The other two writers had nodded their agreement with him when he was speaking. I asked the writer of science fiction to tell me about his work.

'My last book is about a world under the sea. It has its own minerals. Enough wealth. It would like to live peacefully by itself, but there are two other worlds fighting over it. They want these valuable minerals. They are very powerful, these worlds, they have very advanced technologies, they have much money, they need the minerals of the world under the sea, and they make war over them. It is a war-of-the-worlds book, you see.'

'And the world under the sea caught between two great powers is really Egypt?'

'No, it is imaginary. It is a world that I make up in my imagination.'

'But it is a political metaphor – '

'It is not political, it is science fiction.'

'Perhaps, though, you are free to say things in the form of science fiction which you couldn't say in a realistic novel?'

'Yes, I think a writer of science fiction is free, because his world is all in his imagination.'

'Policemen,' said the poet, 'are not clever men. I think it is good that they don't understand metaphors.'

The playwright, however, had not been so lucky. He had written a trilogy called 'The Clown and His King'. Its plot was oddly like that of the play by Abdel Rahman, the Qatari writer, about the king, the princess and the singing donkeyman. It too was 'folklore', but the policemen had spotted its real identity under its historical disguise. The trilogy had been published, but the plays were forbidden performance.

'How is it that your plays can be published but not performed?'

'Because everyone can watch and listen to a play – people who cannot read and write can understand. But very few people will read it. My writing, you see, is very concreted and aggressive.'

The fugitive writers, squatting in this musty shell of a great house, were the last, sad survivors of Cairo's liberal intelligentsia. Until very recently, Cairo had been the intellectual centre of the Arab world. It was the city where powerful ideas were hatched and discussed; Cairene novels, Cairene political journalism, Cairene poetry and Cairene theatre had set the standards by which writers in Baghdad, Damascus, Algiers and Khartoum had measured themselves. The men I was talking to had grown up in an intellectual climate in which a writer from, say, New York, London or Paris would probably have felt more or less at home. They insisted on still speaking as if the climate hadn't changed. Their talk was deliberately incautious. They didn't want to be 'dissidents', and they were waiting until the last possible minute before accepting the fact that they were moving fast into that cold paranoid world of bugging devices, imprisonment and *samizdhat*. I think they knew what was coming. Five weeks after my conversations with them, Sadat passed a 'measure' which brought Egyptian censorship into line with that of the most hard-headed Eastern European states; and editors and journalists who had published 'unconstructive' criticisms of the Sadat regime were jailed in a purge which aroused curiously little interest in the West. At the time, Sadat was being lionized as the peacemaker of the Middle East, and it would no doubt have been awkward to make much of the fact that his great Peace Initiative was providing him with an excellent excuse to tighten the screws of what was already a totalitarian regime.

On this particular morning, though, there was at least a chink of freedom still showing. The talk was angry and unbuttoned. The turning of Nasser's bust to the wall was a symbol of what was in the air. Nasser himself had been no great champion of intellectual freedom, and defending *his* right to remain in the Committee Room appealed to the writers' sense of irony. They would make their show; the Sharia Committee would win; but they were used to standing on the justice of lost causes, and Nasser's bust was a nice test-case.

We talked about the things which had brought about the

crack-up of Cairo intellectual life.

'There are few people left now. Those of the Left went in 'seventy-three. Many of them are now in Iraq, some in Algiers, some in Beirut, a few in Europe. Others went to the Gulf and Saudi Arabia, where they could earn a lot of money in the universities or the ministries of information. It was very easy to leave. Some of my friends had to go; the others went because the carrot was too big to resist.'

'You cannot have an intellectual life if you can't meet other people, if you can't talk. In Cairo, that is becoming physically impossible. The city is one big traffic jam. To find a taxi, to go to work, to find another taxi, to come home – that takes the entire day. There is no leisure for talk. Sometimes, I think they make these traffic jams deliberately – to prevent us from ever meeting each other. If you want to stop the exchange of ideas, make a nice big traffic jam: no one can get to the meeting, no one talks, there is no "subversion". It is easy, you see.'

'We cannot live near the centre of the city. It is impossible for an Egyptian to rent a house here. On this street we are in now, you look at every house – Saudi, Saudi, Saudi.'

'What all the intelligentsia are asking – the one big question: how can we have a state independent of Saudi and Saudi finance?'

'Do you think that's possible?'

'I have to believe it. Otherwise, things are hopeless. It is not just Saudis renting our houses, there is something else. It is a new conservatism. You know, girls whose mothers have never worn the veil – today some of them are going behind the veil for the first time. Or the power of the Sharia Committee . . . that is a new thing. This is what "Saudi" means. This is what happens because we are dependent.'

'But surely Egyptian women are the most liberated in Arabia?' I asked. 'I've seen hardly anyone wearing a veil. I know of university professors who are women here. Isn't there a Women's Movement? Aren't there women writers?'

'I think Liberation means something quite different here,' the poet said. 'For most girls the freedoms are very small, they are not really freedoms at all. It is the freedom to wear make-up, the freedom to have a boy-friend, the freedom to be seen holding hands . . . It's not the *angry* freedom of the West. It's not the freedom which makes people write. I think we are a long way from seeing a women's novel of the kind you have in England or America.'

I told him about my conversation with Ayysha Sayyar in Dubai – about the secret novel in the locked drawer.

'I think the women in the Gulf may be in a better position to write than women are here.'

For any writer, though, the ground was stony. Nearly a hundred and forty million people speak Arabic, yet even well-known Arab novelists cannot hope to sell more than three to four thousand copies of their books.

'For most people it is difficult just to read a newspaper. Many cannot read at all. They do not care about culture. What have they to do with books?'

'Who can afford to read books, anyway? In Cairo, you have a salary of sixty pounds a month; a book costs two pounds. How can you justify that to your wife and children? Or a seat in the theatre – it costs four pounds. Most Egyptians who would like to go to the theatre cannot go. It is too expensive. So: the Egyptian theatre is not for Egyptians.'

'I tell you the sad thing. Here in Cairo, we are surrounded by culture. Everywhere you go there is culture. But it is ancient. There is too much lag of time between it and us.'

As I left the High Council of Arts, the playwright said: 'There is one place where people meet. The Café Riche. You should come. It is a very poor café, you see; that is why it is called the Café Riche.'

The switchboard operator sat in her booth in the hotel; a patient lady with a heavy, pharaonic face. Her apparatus was ancient and vastly complicated. Lights flashed on and off, plugs were pushed in and yanked out: the technical dexterity required to make one telephone call was immense. Given a number to dial, she would smile sadly, take a deep breath, and bury herself in her machinery. The expression on her face during these operations was painful to watch. She looked like an airline pilot trying to land a jet in thick fog with two engines gone and the navigation system dead. Usually she failed: the call would stall, overshoot, or just break up some-where in the wires. Occasionally she succeeded, and if one held the phone close to one's ear, one could hear faint, squawking, metallic sounds which sometimes resolved themselves into words. At best, it was like getting a bad line to the moon.

I had heard that Jan Morris was staying at the Mena House Hotel, out near the pyramids, and I hoped that we might meet up for a drink or a meal.

'Oh dear, that is a very difficult number for me. Very difficult. But I will try.'

She did, and failed. After twenty minutes of terrible exertion she said: 'I am sorry. It is no good. I shall never reach the Mena House.'

'How do you tell "difficult" numbers from "easy" ones?'

'I have experience,' she said wearily. She held my hand: after perhaps a dozen joint assaults on the Cairo telephone system we had developed the natural intimacy of people who have had shared sufferings.

'Please, my dear,' she said. 'You must understand: Cairo is all out of connections.'

'It is broken.' It was a universal explanation. The telephone system was 'broken'; the air-conditioning was 'broken'; the Semiramis Hotel across the river was 'broken'; the meters on the taxis were 'broken'. It was like living in a house where cups fall off their handles when you pick them up, where every light bulb blows when you switch it on, where the vacuum cleaner coughs gobbets of dust over the carpets it is supposed to sweep, where legs fall off chairs, beds collapse, ceilings are not to be trusted and the plumbing is a maze of burst pipes and blocked drains. In this respect, it was not so unlike living in my own London flat. It requires a certain philosophy to accept breakage on such a massive and continual scale, but once one has adjusted to the idea that nothing is likely to work, and when you find something that does, it is an occasion for a modest little celebration, one can be happy enough.

Most of these breakages came about through overuse and simple tiredness. Too many people in Cairo were too exhausted to care any more. Things dropped easily from their hands and smashed. Some of the breakages were deliberate – like the taxi meters whose insides had been wrecked by the device of feeding them on little chips of wood.

I did have one ride in a taxi which was working on its meter; it cost barely a pound for a trip of nearly ten miles, most of it through heavy traffic. The price cannot have paid for much more than the petrol. Its driver, a fatally honest man, must have been living on air. Another driver, a cheerful realist, explained the system to me:

'Look, the government fix the prices. They fix them so they can go to the Saudis and the IMF and say, "You see, we have solved the problem. We have stopped inflation. Everything in Cairo is very good. Cairo taxis are very cheap. We have things under control, right?" OK – you know how they do this? They fix the prices for thirty years ago. Then was the cost of the car, the cost of gas, the cost of living. The fare they fix is a government lie. If I go on the meter, in one year I would lose my car, my house, my living. So when the government fix the price, what do I do? I fix the meter. It is "broken".'

Jan Morris and I did manage to meet. By taking long drives out to each other's hotels, leaving notes in pigeonholes and making the best headway that we could against the sluggish tides and crosscurrents of the city we succeeded in arriving at the same time at the same open-air café on the Nile. Just to be sitting at table among the mosquitoes with glasses of Stella beer seemed to me to be a triumph of generalship: a combination of foresight, hard work, high tactical skill and immense good luck.

As James Morris, she had lived in Cairo on a houseboat in the 1950s. James Morris had been *The Times* correspondent in the Middle East, and before that he had worked in a news bureau. Jan Morris, commissioned by *Rolling Stone* magazine, was revisiting Cairo for the first time since she had changed gender, and she was nervous about what Jan might see in James's city.

'I'm so frightened of going back to places and finding that I liked them better as I was than I do as I am.'

'So how does Cairo look?'

'It was such a relief this morning. I walked across from the hotel and climbed up a bit of the pyramid of Cheops. I got exactly the same feeling that I remembered – and I'd been dreading that it would look all wrong. But it wasn't, so I was able to breathe again.'

'It would have been quite interesting if the expression on the face of the Sphinx had turned into an idiot grin or a dirty leer.'

'Don't – ' said Jan Morris, anxious not to tempt fate.

'It all must have been so different anyway, when you were here last. Two wars ago – or is it three or four? No Saudis, presumably . . . Don't you find the city itself has changed so much that it's difficult to find your own landmarks in it?'

'Well, you see, I feel that *I*'ve changed so much more than Cairo has that it's really rather hard to tell.'

'What happened to your houseboat? Is it still here somewhere?'

'It sank,' she said.

I told Jan Morris about getting caught in the crowd on Tahrir Square.

'I think everyone is frightened of Cairo. I am. I always have been. It's partly why I love it, I think, because it scares me. You feel the power of the mob here almost more than anywhere else I know. One word from a leader, and you feel they could turn *murderous*.'

'Most people look to me too depressed and tired to be up to murder.'

'Oh, I don't think that's so. If there's any real change that I've noticed, it's that people look so much happier. I think it's changed for the better, if anything.'

'I find that hard to imagine.'

'The people I've met in the last day or two seem *much* brighter and more hopeful than I remember them. It shows on almost everyone's face.'

'We've hit the city from different angles.'

I was cheered by her sensibleness. Egged on by Disraeli and my conversation with the group of Cairene writers, I had been drifting into a vein of gloomy gothic. Jan Morris was quick and crisp. She was a proper traveller, with the traveller's gift for swimming in the stream without drowning in it; while I was a natural candidate for drowning. In her sensible jeans and sensible blouse and sensible headscarf she was like some enviable, distant female cousin whose ability to cope with the world is always putting the rest of the family to shame. I wondered if James Morris – whom I'd never known – had been an altogether more obviously haunted and muddled figure, and whether the 'happier' look of the people of Cairo was really more a reflection of the difference between the temperaments of James and Jan than it was a measure of a change in the city itself.

Jan, at any rate, was an island of air and lightness in a place that I found suffocatingly dense and heavy. I liked listening to her talk. She spoke in an eager alto, with a trace of dry rust around its edges, leaping from emphasis to emphasis, alighting for a second on a word in italics, like a chalk-hill blue in a meadow of dogroses. I lunched with her one day, at an outdoor restaurant near Giza. On the far side of the palm grove where we were given a table, a small boy was steering a wooden plough behind an ox. A man was riding a camel along the edge of a ditch bordering a paddy-field, and the sandy, corrugated pile of the Great Pyramid was somewhere just over my right shoulder.

'*Isn't* this nice?' said Jan Morris. '*Doesn't* it remind you of Cipriani's on Torcello? *Don't* you adore Cipriani's?'

The answer to both questions had to be no, but I did adore the way she put them and I felt sincere, unstinting admiration for the carelessly artful style with which she had made herself at home in this singular and alien landscape.

I found the Café Riche. It was up a street off Tahrir Square; a deep, friendly grotto with smoky walls and shadowy tables. Its punkah-fans had been broken long ago. Their blades were puckered and warty with beads of condensation, and they hung over one's head like huge limp starfish. It was a good, private place to talk and drink. I liked its aniseedy smell and its air, even at noon, of living by its own clock, which was always set somewhere in the argumentative small hours. It was, admittedly, haunted by security men, but they tended to stick to the terrace outside, where they sat on rush chairs making a great show of being engrossed in the small print of *El Akhram*.

Magdi, the playwright, was there when I first visited the place. He had an essay on Anouilh's *Antigone* in that morning's paper.

'You would like to read?'

'It's miles beyond me, I'm afraid.'

'I will translate for you. Here – ' he tapped the top of the column, 'I define the difference between the classical hero and the modern hero. Here – ' I looked at the impenetrable, pretty ripple of calligraphy across the page, 'I make the conditions of the modern hero. By modern, I mean after Ibsen. This says, "the modern hero is the hero who is in direct antagonism to the state". Here I show that the ideal modern hero is Che Guevara, and here I show you who are the modern heroes of the drama. The heroes of the modern drama are your Jimmy Porter and Antigone. I do not count the Absurd Drama. It is not of relevance.'

'I've always thought that both *Look Back In Anger* and *Antigone* were really sentimental plays. Anouilh, particularly. He's surely dealing in pathos rather than serious antagonism to the state? I think he likes to give his audience a good cry – he certainly doesn't send them out of the theatre to man the barricades.'

'But in my essay I analyse the modern tragic *situation* of Antigone.'

'Perhaps *Antigone* reads better in Arabic than it does in English or French; you can get the situation without having to swallow the sentimental language.'

'I do not read it in French. In Arabic, I read Antigone as a hero like Che Guevara.'

'And you can publish this in the newspaper? You talk about censorship, yet you can write this without being censored?'

'This,' said Magdi, 'is a dramatic-critical essay. It is not a political essay. There is a lot of difference.'

I caught the eye of a girl sitting at a table diagonally across from us. She was turning the pages of an old Tauchnitz Library edition and listening to our conversation. She looked deeply sceptical. She had good reason. A few weeks later, the editor of the paper we were studying was jailed for sedition.

The road to Giza is a gimcrack, Egyptian version of Las Vegas. By day, it is a dead scrubland. Tangles of neon tubing, blackened in the sun, are strung out on poles over the cabaret-joints. For two miles, there is nothing to see except this brutish filigree of neon, lath and tar-paper. There is the flap of torn plastic awnings and shreds of faded coloured bunting. Even the Cola stalls are abandoned. The pyramids are buried up to their knees in trash. When I first saw them, they looked curiously at home. This was racketeer-territory, and the crooks who run the seedy empire of clubs and dives along the Pyramids Road are a long way from being pharaohs. But there is something about the pyramids which is calculated to warm the cockles of the heart of any thoroughgoing gangster. It is easy to imagine Al Capone or Ronnie Kray being moved to tears by the sight of the Great Pyramid. Every single enormous block of it tells you that Mister Big was here.

Its shape, too, has a gangsterish simplicity. Cathedrals, mosques, castles feed the eye with detail. They invite one to exercise one's curiosity and intelligence. The Great Pyramid invites one to do nothing except acknowledge it. You can take it in in a flash from the window of a passing car. Its image sits somewhere at the back of your head for days; then you return, to study it at length. It is exactly as you glimpsed it; no more, no less. Its sole interest lies in its size. It is a simple-minded megalomaniac's dream come true. All the subtlety of engineering which went into its construction – the levelling of the ground, the dizzying calculus of stress and weight and proportion – was dedicated to the service of a fantasy so crude that a human vegetable could have conceived it. It exists below the level of reason. Its contempt for money, labour, time, materials, its blind disregard of limitation or compromise, could be matched by any psychopath in a locked ward for the severely subnormal. All the Great Pyramid does is stand between you and the sun, like a mindless giant with his thumbs locked in his hip-pockets, saying, '*OK?*'

No wonder that all the petty hoods and con-men of the city have gravitated to the ground around the pyramids. They were there, on a smaller scale, when Kinglake went to Giza in 1834 and narrowly escaped being murdered in the tombs. His remarks about the Great Pyramid deserve to be inscribed in neon and set on a conspicuous post beside the thing.

The truth seems to be, after all, that the Pyramids are quite of this world; that they were piled up into the air for the realization of some kingly crotchets about immortality – some priestly longing for burial fees; and that as for the building – they are built like coral rocks by swarms of insects – by swarms of poor Egyptians, who were not only the abject tools and slaves of power, but who also ate onions for the reward of their immortal labours! The Pyramids are quite of this world.

Anyone labouring half-way up the masonry of Cheops, and putting himself in a state of mind receptive to Inspiring Thoughts, would do well to remember those onions.

The pharaohs have the day pretty much to themselves; but after sunset, when the pyramids turn to blocky shadows, the fast operators down on the Strip come into their own. Miles of sleeping neon snap awake. In the afternoon, they were just a meaningless jungle-gym of wires and tubes; as the evening settles in, they burst into articulacy. GIRLS! they shout: GIRLS! GIRLS! All the open-sesame words start flashing at once: MANHATTAN! PARIS! GO-GO! DANCING! PIGALLE! EXOTIC! GIRLS! NITE! The sidewalks thicken with hustlers, attentive, helpful men who park cars and trade in flesh of every conceivable species and gender.

I went there late one night with Essam, a young taxi driver whom I had hired for a long, safe, talkative ride the previous day. Like so many people in Arabia, Essam moonlighted between identities. He was a taxi driver, he was a student of electrical engineering, he was a shop assistant, and he was an accountant in a cousin's business. At first, he had been reluctant to take me to the Strip.

'Please, I know . . . You want a girl; you will ask me to find you a girl – I have this so many times before. I do not want to find anyone a girl. It is very bad for me.'

'I don't want a girl. I just want to see the clubs.'

'The people who go to the clubs want girls.'

'Well I don't.'

'You make me this as a promise?'

'Yes.'

'I take you then. But I cannot find you a girl.'

On the drive out, he said: 'Yesterday, I read something in a magazine. I think it is very funny, but you would not like it.' He giggled.

'What was it?'

23

'I think I must not tell you. Perhaps it makes you angry. No. No, you would not like it.'

'Stop being such a stick, Essam. What was it?'

'It was nothing.'

'All right, it was nothing. What do you think of the weather today?'

Essam smirked.

'I think it make you have a very bad temper . . .'

'Warm for the time of year, is it?'

'We have in Cairo a famous man who writes for the newspapers. Every week he has an article in this magazine. Yesterday, he say something about the English people . . . What I tell you now, that is what this man says, you see?'

'Yes – '

'He says, "In my life, many times I have seen the English people throw money and Arab people go down in the dust for this money . . ."'

'Scrambling for it,' I said. 'We say "scrambling for money" in English.'

'Scrambling. So this man says, "I did not expect ever to see the day when the Arab people would throw the money and the English people would go . . . scrambling in the dust for it. Now I have seen this day come." That is what he says. Now, I think, you are very angry with me.'

'I think it's pretty funny actually. It's perfectly true.'

'You are making a joke with me?'

'No.'

'I think that really you are angry. You do not like me to tell you this.'

'I like it very much. I want to put it in my book.'

'It does not hurt your pride?' He had the mildly concerned expression of a doctor who has tapped a reflex and failed to elicit the faintest tremor of response.

'No – why should it?'

'I think the English people do not like to be told these things.'

'I think we ought to be told them at every possible opportunity.'

'That is strange,' Essam said.

'Anyway, it's not Egyptian money that we're scrambling for; it's Gulf and Saudi money.'

'Ah . . . Saudis . . .' His face saddened as he remembered that Egyptians were doing their share of scrambling too. For a moment, he had been up among the paymasters; and I was sorry that I had spoiled this happy image by my remark.

We drove out past the pyramids to Sahara City. At what Essam said was 'the best' nightclub, a few thousand men in suits sat in a vast barn watching a floorshow somewhere in the far distance. I said that I would prefer something rougher and smaller; so we returned to the Strip. The entire district had been rebuilt in the last year. On the nights of 18 and 19 January 1977, in the middle of the Cairo food riots, an angry crowd, armed with flaming torches, had swarmed up the Pyramids Road. They had burned and looted thirty-seven of these joints. The blaze must have been as fantastic a spectacle as the Great Pyramid itself. To the people of Tahrir Square on their dingy salaries, the Pyramids Road has always been a source of hurt and offence. Enraged by the ocean of money which was pouring through the clubs, and by the arrogance of their crook-millionaire proprietors, the crowd had tried to bring the whole flashy empire down in a splendid climax of purgative fire. It hadn't worked. The mob could burn the clubs, but they couldn't burn the supply of money which had created them. All they had done was to snip off the top growth of a deep-rooted weed. Within a few weeks the clubs were back, as busy, rich and nasty as they'd ever been.

It was a slow shunt down a mile or so of this spangled convolvulus.

'I know this club. It is good, not too expensive,' Essam said. It looked like all the others. Floodlights and neon lent a meretricious splendour to a ramshackle, one-storey hut of the kind that two men and a boy might reasonably put up in a week consisting largely of tea-breaks.

At Essam's insistence, I paid off a hustler on the street.

'It is wise. Without you pay, we come back, and my car is gone. Or it has big dents and there is no glass in the windows.' As parking tickets go, the price was cheap at one Egyptian pound.

I suppose that I'd been hoping for something really memorably repellent. I was disappointed. Essam's good taste had led me to what must have been the most staid club on the Strip –

either that, or the night life of Cairo is not half of what it is cracked up to be. The atmosphere was much like that of a 'smoker' in a college refectory. There was hardly a girl in sight. The audience was Saudi; perhaps a hundred and fifty men in robes and head-dresses, sitting at bare tables with bottles of Dimple Haig and stick-packs of Craven A cigarettes. Essam and I drank Jolly Cola and listened to the band.

The musicians were bored session men. They sounded as if they were playing in their sleep. They'd seen all the acts before, and it showed on their faces. I kept my eye on a drummer with a death-mask face. He sat through songs of heartbreak and lust, through the unveiling of a dozen women's bodies down to bare flesh, through the endless thrust and ripple of hips and pelvises going through their ritual mummery of intercourse and climax, without one twitch of an eye or a lip. Perhaps he was counting sheep or going through his tax returns. Two things, for certain, were not on his mind: he wasn't giving a second thought to either sex or music.

Essam turned out to be a stern critic. As the stream of women came on to the rostrum to sing, strip or dance, he assessed their talents for me.

'This one is no good . . . This one is very bad . . . This is one of the best dancers of Egypt; I have seen her many times before . . . This one is not bad . . . This is good, this one is very good – I have not heard her sing before . . .'

Of the dancers, Essam thought the fattest ones the best. One woman with a vast midriff was able to animate so many different parts of it at once that it looked as if she was keeping a whole farm of tame white mice trapped somewhere between the layers of her skin. I watched, fascinated, as they scampered in all directions between her navel and her pubis.

I was far too absorbed in the technical ingenuity of this operation to be in the slightest degree aroused by it. Indeed, the applause which greeted each act was of the sort one hears at televised horse trials; it was the discreet clapping of jaded connoisseurs, not the excited roaring of men whipped up to a pitch of unbearable excitement. As at the El Nile Club in London, the acclaim which counted most was money. Someone would start with a fistful of rials chucked at the stage, then a competition would break out between the tables, with each group trying to outdo the others as they hurled bigger and bigger wads of notes at the dancer. The most successful performers finished their acts in a violent leafstorm of paper money. They trampled it underfoot, it got caught up in their hair and the bangles round their necks, it cascaded over their oiled bodies and stuck to their breasts and thighs and stomachs.

One beautiful, very slender girl was quite different from the rest. She stripped down to her pants and went into a series of vivid grinds, clicking a pair of finger-castanets and spread-eagling herself in the air. She moaned and shuddered, her body gave a final, long, ecstatic writhe, and she was out of her fit, twirling on the rostrum like a spinning top. A muscle of my own stirred in wistful sympathy for her.

'Isn't she lovely?' I said.

'This is a very bad dancer,' Essam said, and took a contemptuous swig of Jolly Cola. 'I do not know why they have her. She is no good at all.'

The girl picked up a few measly rials from the floor and left the stage. All the vigour she had put into her act had gone. As she put her arms up to her breasts she looked pitiably exposed. I wished that I could have followed her out and told her that I, at any rate, thought that she'd been marvellous.

The dancers alternated with singers. Essam translated for me. A maudlin howl, delivered by what looked like a mountain of candyfloss, but was actually just a large Egyptian woman in more pink chiffon than was good for her, turned out to be an old travelling-companion of mine – a lyric mercilessly immortalized by The Lady.

'She sings "Lailah". That is "night". She says she will give all her life for one night in your arms . . .'

'I'd never get them round her.'

'She says that if you are far or near, she is close in her heart to you.'

'I find that a dreadful thought.'

'She asks her God to be close to all her lovers. I too think this is a silly song.'

The evening came to a curious climax at about one in the morning. Another enormous woman had been wailing on about how her lover had been taken from her by a rival, when a tableful of men started to chant, ' "Saudia!", "Saudia!".

"Saudia!" ' The call was taken up across the room. The singer nodded at the band, took several cubic feet of cigaretty air into her lungs, and brought out a noise of such explosive volume that it deserved to be measured in megatons rather than decibels.

'This is the national song of Saudi Arabia!' Essam shouted into my ear.

'What are the words?'

'Our God is One! Our Way is One! . . .' I lost the rest in the hubbub. For the whole club was now singing along. I was worried about the flimsiness of the building, which seemed all too likely to suffer the same fate as the walls of Jericho. Everyone was clapping and stamping and singing, breaking off only to throw more rials at the singer, who was now wading through a surf of banknotes. She had to sing 'Saudia' four times over. During her last encore, a pair of handsome black Egyptian cats, their tails high in the air, strolled through the band, picked their way disdainfully through the money on the rostrum, and left the club. Essam and I followed them shortly afterwards. I felt distinctly miffed. I had come to wallow in whatever pits of depravity Cairo had to offer, and had ended up in a revival meeting.

'Are most of the clubs like that?' I asked Essam.

'Some are not so good. That is a good club.'

Driving back into the city, Essam said: 'I was very much afraid tonight. I think you want me to find you a girl. I have this before. The Saudis and the Kuwaitis, when I take them to this place, they always say, "Now you must find me a girl." I am a Muslim. In my religion, when a man has sex with a woman the man pays for his sin. The woman pays also. But the person who brings them together pays for the man *and* the woman. So you see it is very bad for me to do this thing.'

The streets were empty; the cliffs of the city were a dense matt black. I thought of the girl whose dancing had been so little liked, and for a while I was sorry that Essam was a creature of moral principle. It was a lonely passing thought, and I can't think that a night with a prostitute in Cairo would have been of much comfort; but my hotel room seemed suddenly very chilly and very foreign. I was aching to be home.

*

Sarhan was a nearly permanent resident of the Café Riche. Whenever I went there, he was at one table or another. Years of serious drinking had given his face a blurry look, like a gouache painting which has been lightly wiped over with a wet cloth, and he talked with an angry rattle in his throat. He was a critic. The Egyptian papers in which his work was published had been closed down, one after another. Now he just managed to support himself by writing articles for magazines published in Baghdad, Damascus and Beirut, but there was nothing hangdog or defeated about him. He treated his own hard times with bellicose humour, and even when he was dead drunk he could out-talk me in a rapid English full of weird vowels with which Sarhan had decorated the language in order to make it a uniquely personal possession. His long *e*s and *a*s were like the trinkets which other people hung around the insides of their cars.

'When I talk English to you,' he said once, 'I sound pretty damn funny, hey?' It was a statement of pure pride. It would have been a low bourgeois concession for Sarhan to sound anything other than pretty damn funny in any language under the sun.

We were three-quarters of the way down a bottle of whisky when Sarhan set his best trap for me. We had already spent a couple of hours fencing amiably over trifles.

'Your book . . .' he said, wagging a stubby finger at me. 'It is a study of the role of the intelligentsia in the Arab world.'

'Well, no . . . not exactly. I'd like to try and say something about – '

'I make a distinction! I make the distinction between the *intelligentsia* and the *intellectual*! Yes. The *eentyleegentsiiaye* and the *eentlylay-eektiial*! What do I mean?'

'I don't know yet. Do you know what you mean?'

'Yees!' hissed Sarhan. '*I* know, but you don't. What *do* I mean?'

'The intellectual is a man alone; the intelligentsia is a class . . .?' I tried hopefully.

'Fop, fop, fop, fop!' he said, sloshing more whisky into both our glasses. 'Look! There is no understanding, without you understand the *context*!'

'OK, what's the context?'

'That is what I ask you! Dear God! What is the *context*?'

'Sarhan, I do not know the context. So you tell me.'

'You are not alone,' he said.

'What's the mystery about?'

'Ah, the mystery! The mystery! Now, see, we have a *mystery*! Now we get some place! I must take a leak.' He stood up, toppling, and glared down at me. 'There is . . . no . . . understanding . . . the role . . . of the intelligentsia . . . of the . . . Arab world . . . *without you understand the context.*'

'Sarhan, I have taken that point!'

He leaned on the table, spilling his own glass. He ignored the spreading pool of whisky on the table.

'Now I tell you. In the Arab world, the intelligentsia *has no context*!'

As he went off to the lavatory, he shouted it again, to the broken fans, to the café cat, to any lurking members of the security police who might be within earshot.

'In the Arab world, the intelligentsia has no context!'

No context. Out of connection. Broken. Breakage and discontinuity had become the essential structural features of all I saw in Cairo. In the mornings I took to walking in the old quarter between the Bab Zuweila and the Bab El Futuh, hoping to find some centre of gravity in this bewildering mass of shifting ground. All I found though was another city, set at a tangent to the rest, quite out of connection with the other Cairos in which I was living at the same time.

Stepping through a gloomy archway, one passed from the racket of trams and horns and the whole exhausting chaos of the Cairo office-day into a labyrinth of narrow mud streets and stooping houses hiding behind carved wooden lattices and ornate grilles. It was a walk of ten yards at the most. It might just as well have been a journey of several hundred miles. Cars gave way to donkey carts, cardboard briefcases to cane baskets shaped like birdcages. The oddest transition was one of dress. On the other side of the archway, it had been mid-morning; moments later, it seemed to be bedtime. There were no frayed shirts and threadbare suits here. Everyone was in grubby pyjamas or long nightshirts. The women, with heavy, protuberant faces, were hooded, but not veiled, in black silk shawls. With the smell of the spice souk in one's nose, and the sound of wooden cartwheels banging through the rutted streets, it was tempting to imagine that one had broken through into the 'real' Cairo.

It wasn't, of course. This was simply another cell in the honeycomb. The Islamic passion for order and division, for categories and screens and veils, had in Cairo entered into a form of marriage with the peculiarly Egyptian obsession with school-leaving certificates, diplomas and degrees. The arch through which I passed was exactly the same kind of lattice as divided male from female or meat from vegetables. Its function was to keep separate one mass of people with pieces of paper and letters after their names from another mass of people who were without these passports. It marked the boundary between the certificated and the uncertificated. It would have been nice to discover the antique heart of the whole city still beating in the picturesque squalor of Allah Street. The real lesson which it had to teach was more banal: it made me understand that people who have BAs do not wear pyjamas on public thoroughfares at eleven in the morning.

It was a good place to be a tourist, though. Jan Morris had told me of a splendid café half-way up the crumbly main street. Sitting on a bench outside, under a wooden balcony of extraordinary intricacy and dereliction, one could drink fine Turkish coffee, suck on the hubble-bubble, and enjoy all the lazy pleasures which go with having nothing to do in the shade while the rest of the world trundles sweatily past in the sun. These were truant mornings. If the cells and divisions of the city held any proper place for me, it wasn't here. I should have been revolving with the crowd of other graduates round Tahrir Square, or slugging it out in drunken talk at the Café Riche. Allah Street was a pretty nowhere for the eye to wander in and the head to clear. I sent home picture-postcards of it, saying that I was having a lovely time and wished everyone was here.

It was only the thought that it would be good to be out of the sun for a while which led me into the mosque across the street. It was as cold as an English January. Its clammy darkness was so thick that a jellyfish might have found enough moisture there to swim in. Everything dripped. Every arch and pillar in the place was leaking an icy perspiration from its pores. Stumbling on the wet flagstones, I found my way to a bit of darkness which was fractionally paler than the rest. What little light there was had come from a latticed window set so high up in the dome that the light was old and worn by the time it had reached the level of the floor. One could watch the beam dying as it made the long trip down, and when one stood in its feeble remains it smelled already dead.

Calling this building a mosque at all had been a Mamluk euphemism. It was a sultan's tomb, and his mausoleum had squeezed out the area of worship into a mean corner. Screens of carved rosewood, thirty feet high, had been raised round his corpse, and they had been inlaid with mother-of-pearl and chips of coloured stone and ivory. The thing was like a giant Damascene chest. In relation to its size, a man's body would have been a tiny trinket, lost somewhere in the dust at the bottom of the box. I tried to peer through the tracery of the outer screen. There seemed to be more screens inside – boxes within boxes, of – I suspected – ever increasing richness and elaboration.

Up till now, Dr Farouki's lecture in Doha had stood me in excellent stead. It had explained the meaning of a great deal that I had seen on my trip. This, though, was a real puzzler.

'Death is both natural and innocent. It is not a punishment or a tragedy. Concern with funerary affairs is absent from Islam. The Prophet said: "You must not weep or cry over your dead." '

That, at any rate, was Dr Farouki's line. Yet in the As-Sultan mosque I was looking at the dankest, darkest, most splendid piece of pure necrophilia that I had ever seen.

It is true that of all the commandments of the Prophet the one about funerary rites is probably the least regarded. There are fine mausoleums throughout the Arab world, and the mourners I saw following the coffins of their dead were crying with, if anything, less restraint than the muffled sobs which attended the last funeral I went to in a London cemetery. The tomb of the Prophet himself, at Medina, is an object of pilgrimage for Muslims. So Dr Farouki had been stretching things a little. One could see, though, that the general principle did stand: most Islamic graves are far plainer than most Christian ones, and when Muslims do build mausoleums they avoid making them too obviously grandiose in style – except in Cairo.

In Cairo, there is hardly a mosque which is not also a 'funerary complex'. Its tombs are beautiful, gigantic and forbidding. More money and craftsmanship has gone into them than into almost anything else in the city. Cairenes are much obsessed by death. Perhaps they couldn't live in the shadow of the pyramids without being infected with a pharaonic taste for preserving corpses and putting up memorials. The magicians and necromancers for which the city used to be famous are still there. (Cairo is the only place I've been to where, in the course of a few days, three different middle-aged women asked me if they could see my palm to read my life-line. I said I wasn't interested in being told what they saw there. They shook their heads forebodingly, and I have been expecting the worst ever since.) Sitting on a cold pediment in this dripping sepulchre, I thought for a moment that maybe I had stumbled on the heart of the city after all. The appalled satisfaction with which Cairo seemed to contemplate its own impending death, as its arteries clogged up, broke down, and fell out of connection, made it a front-running candidate for being the necropolitan capital of the world.

In the Café Riche there were saucers of white kidney-beans on every table. Naguib, a painter, was feeding them to the scrawny little cat which always hung around the drinkers, croaking for titbits. Something had happened to its throat, I think. It couldn't miaou, but instead it managed a kind of musical wheeze which suggested that despite being half-starved it was somehow getting through three packs of cigarettes a day.

Naguib was cuddling it. Patches of orange fur alternated with stretches of bare grey catskin. 'It is a very dirty cat . . . a *filthy* cat,' he said. These were words of praise. He put his forefinger to the cat's mouth. All the fur had gone around her blunt nuzzle, and she was running short of teeth and whiskers. She sniffed Naguib's finger and wheezed.

'Maybe she bites me, and I die – *mad*!'

Naguib's masters were Ingres, Gauguin and Van Gogh. He scratched a living by working as a cartoonist for a newspaper, but spent most of his day working on paintings in his studio –

paintings which would never be exhibited.

'I cannot have an exhibition,' he said. 'No, of course.'

'Why not?'

'Look, I tell you what I do. In my studio, I have six pieces of canvas. That is all my work. It is there on six pieces of canvas. Sixty paintings. How is that?'

The Café Riche liked riddles.

'Each time I make a painting. Perhaps it takes two months, or three, or something. Then I ask some friends, a few people – people from here, like Sarhan. We have a bottle of whisky. They look at the painting. They say what they think. They go. Then I begin another. I take this . . . grey paint . . . you know?'

'Primer?'

'That is correct. I paint all over my painting – ' He carelessly wiped an imaginary paintbrush in wide sweeps to and fro in the air. 'I wait for it to be dry. I paint another painting. So there is all my work. Six canvases. On every one, eight, nine, ten paintings, one on another. On every one, there are *years*. That is my work. But no one can see it. Even I.'

'Does it really have to be like that?'

'Look – ' said Naguib. 'This is a false demo-cracy! *Free? Free? Free?* Yes, you are free to talk, free to write, free to paint, *but* . . .' He imitated a censor snipping things out of a paper with a pair of scissors. His fingers went snip-snip-snip in widening circles round the tabletop.

'It is a sign of your humanity,' Naguib said, smiling.

'What is?'

'Talking to drunken men. You talk to me. I am a drunken man. It shows humanity.'

I pointed at the level of the whisky in both our glasses. 'It's the democracy of the bottle.'

Naguib laughed. He fed another kidney-bean to the cat.

'I think she is perhaps the filthiest cat alive,' he said admiringly.

I happened on the Gezira Zoological Garden when I was walking back one morning from the High Council of Arts. It was a neat, fenced civic park with rocky grottoes, shrubberies and tree-lined walks; a place for nannies and lovers. Students came here to read and picnic on the lawns. Boys and girls were amiably intertwined on the park benches. It was a pleasant home from home. I tried talking to the mynah birds, but they were not giving interviews. I tried reading *Sybil* on a bench, but the pages blazed too brightly in the sun. I prowled the gravelled walks, and found myself drawn into a treasure hunt. At each junction of the paths, there was a notice saying 'To The Aquarium'. The park authorities appeared to disagree violently about the location of this place, since all the signs pointed in different directions. I had time to kill, and was prepared to dedicate the entire morning, if necessary, to finding the aquarium. I was redirected back on paths I had taken ten minutes before; eventually I fell back on the old labyrinth tactic of taking only left turns, and rapidly arrived at what looked like a potting shed.

Inside, it was as black as the As-Sultan mosque, but an attendant shuffled out from a cubbyhole and took my arm.

'You want to see?'

'Please,' I said.

'One minute . . .' I could hear his sandals flapping on the stone floor. Then he switched on a couple of bare bulbs. It took a moment or two for my vision to adjust. As soon as I could see where I was, I felt that the discovery of the aquarium would have justified any number of contradictory signs and retraced paths. It was a real treasure-chest of glories.

The centrepiece was a stuffed shark. Its back had been broken in several places, and stuffing was leaking out of its sides, giving it the incongruous homeliness of an old sofa. A stuffed alligator was pinned up on a wall; its thick varnish had gone black and viscous with age. A Victorian collection of butterflies and insects had been propped in glass cases against another wall. Every exhibit had lost wings, legs, scales, antennae, bits of thorax – and these fragments had collected in dusty mounds at the bottom of each case. There were two stuffed seals, oddly bulgy and crooked, like pantomime horses. One prominent case contained a peculiar, pinkish jigsaw puzzle. After a bit of study, it was possible to make out legs and shells. Further thought revealed that a man in search of a hobby to keep him occupied during the long winter evenings might just conceivably assemble all these pieces to make a pair of lobsters.

The attendant plucked at my arm. There was a further room

– the aquarium itself. It was not just any old aquarium either. It looked more like the den of a mad poisoner. The shelves of the room were lined with druggists' jars, and every jar was packed solid with dead fish. The jars had been filled on much the same principle as the seating arrangements in a Cairo tram: their contents had been piled in, higgledy-piggledy fashion, without respect to genus, species, habitat or anything else. Fish from the sea and fish from fresh water enjoyed in death the same solution of formalin. Their colours had gone long ago; now their corpses had blended to a uniform creamy-white. I spotted eels, mullet, perch, sea-horses, barbel, carp, sardines, bass, groupers – all stirred up together into a grue-some fish pie. The room was high with the thin stink of their preservative.

I gave the attendant a pound. For such a comprehensive little tour of Cairo, it seemed the smallest tip that I could reasonably offer.

Lunching in the Café Riche, I met Nadya. She taught at Cairo University for a salary of thirty pounds a month, and I'd had an introduction to her from a friend in London. She was in bad shape when we met. For the last three days she had had no sleep, and her nerve-endings showed in her trembly hands and her dry bark of a voice. As soon as I saw her, I felt apologetic for pressing her to make a date with me, and said so.

'No, no – it is a distraction for me – that is good.' She lit a cigarette; the flame from the match juddered erratically around the smouldering tip. Her eyes looked old. 'So, are you seeing more of Cairo than the façade?'

'I'm trying to – '

'I think it's difficult for you. If you live in a hotel, you are part of the façade.'

By Western standards, Nadya's politics were those of a moderate social democrat. By Cairo standards, she was a member of the extreme Left. She had the habitual sideways squint of someone who expects official eavesdroppers round every corner. In many ways she was lucky. She had an academic job – however tiny the salary that went with it – when many of her friends were unemployed. Her family had money. She herself (she had separated from her husband) was 'liberated' to a degree that would have been unthinkable anywhere else in the Arab world. Yet she wasn't a spoiled radical of the American or European kind. Her clandestine political life was something she had taken on involuntarily, as a burden, not an indulgence. She was not a revolutionary.

Like the writers I had met, Nadya saw the Saudi grip on Egypt as a terrible stranglehold. 'It is just beginning now, but in the summer Cairo is saturated with Saudis, and the wealth they bring simply strengthens the façade. They have created a whole new class of people. People who work in the hotels and the services now earn four and five times as much as middle-class people who work in offices or industry. A waiter makes more money than a professor. It is an intolerable strain for a country to bear, this. Every year, the inflation is worse, and more and more Egyptians simply cannot afford the necessities of life. We are soon reaching a stage, I think, where waiters and people who drive taxis will be the only ones who can afford to live in this city. And just on a personal level, the Saudi presence has made life here so much worse than it was two or three years ago. If you are a single woman, you are assumed to be for hire – they think you must be a prostitute. This extends . . . it turns everyone, men and women alike, into prostitutes. This is how Cairo is becoming.'

She saw Sadat's Peace Initiative as 'a diversionary tactic'.

'Of course everyone wants peace. I do not think, though, that many people here believe that it will happen because Sadat went to the Knesset. I think he went in weakness. It was because things were so bad here – this was after the food riots, the burning of the clubs and everything – that Sadat needed to divert people's attention. Now he is a "world statesman". He has become a hero in the West. But he is not a hero in Cairo. I think it is just like President Nixon – when things get so bad at home that you can't do anything about them at all, you try Foreign Policy. With luck, people will forget the awful mess at home. I think the kindest thing I can say about Sadat is that perhaps he is buying time. But how he can solve these problems, God only knows. I am afraid, though, that Begin is not a fool. *He* knows why Sadat comes to the Knesset. I think he just plays cat-and-mouse with him. But in the meantime . . .'

She gestured at the jam beyond the café door.

Two members of Nadya's family had already left Egypt and were working in Europe. I asked her whether she would follow them.

'It was possible for them. I don't think it is possible for me. This is my home. I stay here. It is as simple as that. I think one has to stay, even if one is only staying on to fight things.'

She looked burned-out. Her bones showed through her skin. 'I am sorry,' she said. 'Perhaps it's just because you've caught me at a bad moment that I talk like this.'

'Perhaps I've just caught Cairo at a bad moment,' I said.

'I hope that is true. I would like to think so,' said Nadya, shakily lighting a new cigarette from the butt of her last one.

There were fairy-lights hanging in the trees of the Tahrir Pleasure Gardens, and a little fairground set in a clearing among the palms. There were never many people there. In the mid-evenings, a few Saudi servants, in dishdashas and kaffiyehs, kept it just ticking over; but it had the air of a party at which almost none of the invited guests had turned up. However alluringly it twinkled through the fronds, however loudly came the music from the loudspeakers in the trees, the passers-by on Tahrir Street ignored it. Perhaps the entrance fee was too high, or they were on their way to other, less innocent pleasures. Whatever their reasons for staying away, their absence gave the fair a desolate charm.

Its handful of customers were a grave lot. They strolled, in muted groups of three and four, past its stalls. They took turns to ride on the ghost train. They drove the dodgem cars slowly and carefully round the perimeter of a circuit no bigger than an average-sized living-room. They were at great pains not to bump into each other. This seemed very odd to me: real roads in Arabia tend to be like dodgem circuits; but the one dodgem circuit I saw was being treated with as much caution as if it was a real motorway under black ice.

I tried throwing coins into a saucer. They slid out. I shot a ping-pong ball off the top of a jet of water ten times out of ten, and was saddened to discover that I hadn't won a prize. The girl who ran the hoopla stall grabbed my wrist as I was passing.

'My name is Magda. I like you very much.'

She wanted me to throw rings round five-pound notes.

'I like you, too, but I don't want to play. I've played this game before.'

'Please – Dollink!'

'Sorry – '

'Dollink – I love you!'

Her hold on my wrist was like a clamp. With her other hand, she began gently massaging my fingers and palm.

'I love you so much, dollink . . .'

It all seemed a bit too sudden. I quite enjoyed having my hand held, though.

'I'm sorry,' I said.

'What is your name, dollink? My name is Magda.'

'My name is King Khaled,' I said.

'Dollink!' she said, letting go of my hand suddenly. 'You do not tell me true!'

I crossed the fair to the conjuror's tent. Most of the squat rush chairs were empty, but the conjuror's little audience was solemn and attentive as he went through his repertoire of tricks. It was more like a poorly-attended evening service in a city church than an entertainment.

The conjuror was doing mysterious things with playing cards and pound notes. For each feint, he received a small, polite ripple of applause.

'Haukus . . . boaukus!' he said, announcing every new transformation. I was as interested to discover where 'hokus pokus' came from as I was in the reappearance of the ace of spades or the missing banknote. The 'hokus' bit comes from the root meaning to change, transmute and to deceive by artful means; while 'pokus' comes (I think) from 'boq' – to play a fanfare on a trumpet. So the magicians of Egypt have made their contribution to the stock of international language. It was nice to learn that every conjuror at every children's party the world over spoke Arabic, almost certainly without knowing it.

The conjuror pulled a string of squawking doves from his mouth. I had seen his tricks before, and so had his audience. We clapped them discreetly, more, I'm afraid, in recognition of old dull acquaintances than in any spirit of surprise at his skill.

I left his tent. There were girls wandering round the gardens trying to sell nuts from trays, and rather too many small boys trying to persuade one to stand on their weighing machines. Even if a whole trainload of weightwatchers had descended on the fair, these boys would have been hard put to it to stay long in the business.

At Tahrir Bridge I found myself in the middle of a furious commotion. The traffic was blocked solid. The crowd bulged on the sidewalk. Horns were blaring. Soldiers and policemen were charging round in all directions, waving rifles and machine-guns and slapping at stray pedestrians with night-sticks. I wondered for a moment if another food riot had broken out.

The conjuring trick which followed was a piece of pure Egyptian magic. Somehow, the bridge was miraculously emptied. There were no cars, no crowds — nothing except a line of soldiers with their guns held upright in front of their noses. It had happened in the space of five minutes. For the first time since I had been there, Cairo went dead silent.

Then a motorcade of outriders and limousines came whooping over the bridge. As the second of the cars went by, I saw Sadat's face, impassive behind the bullet-proof glass. He disappeared, in stately solitude, into the depths of Gezira. The wail of his escorting sirens faded. Moments later, the city was back to normal; a vast, deafening, angry impasse.

It had been like the passing of a lonely ghost. I wondered whether the president's rides through Cairo were always like that. Did he look out of the window of his limousine each day and see only an empty, lamplit city of saluting guards? And when he read in the newspapers about that other place — the stricken cosmopolis of overcrowding, blight and disconnection — did he imagine it to be a fiction, cynically invented by the enemies of his regime?

Carried along in the swarm over the bridge, tasting the *Khamsin*, I envied the president's singular view of the city. For a few seconds, Cairo had been as quiet and ordered as a well-kept grave.

8

The Rock Garden

I had been wary of coming to Jordan. I hadn't liked the look of its Gross National Product. At less than five hundred dollars per head of the population, it made the country one of the poorest in Arabia. I had spent the last six weeks travelling among the poor relations, and I had caught their dispirited anger like 'flu. It is bad to be penniless anywhere, but there is a special poverty which comes from living cheek-to-cheek with millionaire neighbours. In the Yemen and in Egypt it was impossible not to associate the smell of the stale air on the streets with the stink of failure, envy and hatred. Almost everyone I got to know in these countries raged at their fatal dependence on their rich cousins. Both places had been sapped by long, recent wars; but I felt that the fighting had actually hurt them less, if anything, than the terrible prosperity of Saudi Arabia, Libya and the Gulf states. *That* was bleeding them dry of their own best talents. It was reducing them to the status of servants. When the master of the house called family prayers, they stood meekly in line at the back of the drawing-room, shuffling uneasily in their uniforms and second-hand suits. The Yemenis and the Egyptians were the ragged-trousered philanthropists of the Middle East. They were building the palaces and keeping the canapés circulating at the parties. Their own cities had once been the great centres of civilization in the region; now they were doffing their caps and going on all-fours in the service of their new masters. The injury which had been done to their pride was huge.

If it was possible to detect feelings like hurt and anger and humiliation in tables of statistics, then they glared out from all the figures I had seen about Jordan. With Saudi Arabia on one side and Israel on the other, it was strategically positioned to suffer most from the twin goads of war and economic servitude. Israel had lopped off the whole of the west of the country in the 1967 June War. Three years later there had been twelve days of civil war in Amman, when King Hussein's troops had confronted the Palestinians. Alice, that pillar of common-sensical English empiricism, would have had every reason to expect Jordan to combine the different miseries of Jamaica, Northern Ireland and 1940s Britain. It was a client-state, it was shaken by civil unrest, and it was on a narrowly suspended war-footing with the country across the river. Looking-Glass House, though, was constructed to confound the logic of Alice.

I had arrived in Amman after midnight, when the city was just a hilly twinkle of lights. When I woke, the view from my window was a brick wall, inches away from the glass. Breakfast was served in a basement. The Philadelphia Hotel was evidently doing its best to save its visitors from actually seeing Amman until they had been suitably fortified with food and sleep. I had, in any case, lost most of my eagerness to dash headlong into new places, and was quite content to sit for an hour over coffee, looking at the *Jordan Times*. I had not read a newspaper since I had left Dubai. I'd been living in a closed world of rumour and gossip, and Sana'a and Cairo had completely blotted out whatever might have been going on elsewhere on the globe. For all I knew, the pound could have dived out of sight, even of economists armed with telescopes. Britain could have declared war on Iceland, and New York been abandoned as a place unfit for human habitation. None of these things appeared to have happened. The world was much as I had left it. There had been more fighting yesterday in Beirut. The United States had announced that it would supply arms to both Israel and Egypt. These arms, an American spokesman had said, were to be used only for purposes quite unconnected with any hostilities which might once have divided the two countries. They were, indeed, very peaceful arms, and their presence was calculated to enhance even further the general state of blissful harmony now prevailing in the Middle East.

'There's glory for you!' 'I don't know what you mean by "glory",' Alice said. 'I meant, "there's a nice knock-down argument for you!"' 'But "glory" doesn't mean "a nice knock-down argument",' Alice objected. 'When *I* use a word,' Humpty Dumpty said in a rather scornful tone, 'it means just what I choose it to mean – neither more nor less.'

My eye slid from the Humpty-Dumpty talk of the American spokesman to a paragraph further down the page. The literary critic, F. R. Leavis, had died. The paragraph listed his books and noted his 'seminal' contribution to the study of English Literature. It seemed an odd piece of news to come across in the *Jordan Times*, and I felt that I was now in possession of two key facts about Jordan: its per capita GNP was $460 a year, and it was a place where the death of a Cambridge critic went on record alongside the war in Beirut and all the other afflictions and upheavals of the Arab world. To anyone trying to travel in Arabia with a minimum of factual luggage, I would commend the second of those facts as much the most significant of the two.

Primed to expect almost anything now, I walked down the steps of the hotel loggia into Switzerland. Amman was a mossy, alpine rock-garden. Its folded hills were packed solid with little stone chalets, but these houses looked more as if they had been quarried from the rock than built on it. They took their colours from the surrounding stone: pink, lime-green, oxide-blue, pale, creamy grey. If one squinted for a moment, there were no houses at all, just a pastel-coloured abstract of rocky outcrops and crevices. Every crag and knobble held a stunted tree, like a Japanese *bonsai*. There were little cedars, baby olives, and eucalyptus trees growing at queer angles on rosy pinnacles of bare stone. A shaly patch of waste ground at my feet was bright with periwinkles and daisies. The hills were cross-hatched with zig-zag streets and twisty mountain paths. Even the air was alpine – bright and biting, without a trace of that putrescent smell which I had thought was an essential ingredient in every Arab city. It all looked so dinky and bijou that I thought I had overshot my target, and landed up in a province far beyond the range of the book I was trying to write. Minarets . . . there must be minarets . . . I looked for them, and found a few hidden away in the crooks of the hills, where they looked quaint and curious, like picturesque relics of some old superstitious sect. The Roman amphitheatre in front of the hotel looked more at home here than the mosques. It was an exact replica of the one at Fiesole where I'd spent a long dull evening the previous summer watching an American mime troupe tell the entire history of the Wobblies in floodlit silence. In Amman, I was back on my summer holidays.

In holiday mood, I rented a forsythia-yellow Datsun. It was only when I got to the small print at the bottom of the rental-form that I was reminded that this was still Arabia. 'This rental agreement,' I read:

and its relating terms and conditions are drafted in bilingual text: Arabic and English. In the event of any dispute arising in connection with the meaning of words, expressions or sentences, this rental agreement and its relating terms and conditions, or differences between the two texts, the Arabic version will prevail.

I knew what that meant. The depths of ambiguity which it is possible to plumb in making an insurance claim in Arabic are legendary and terrible. If ever Henry Kissinger or Jimmy Carter or any of the other hopeful Western statesmen who have drafted Middle Eastern peace treaties had once tangled with an Arab insurance policy, they would be less sanguine about their proposed solutions. The treaty may be in plain English, but it is the Arabic version which prevails. In my own case, I offered up a short prayer that no dispute would be arising, and drove my Datsun so carefully that old ladies on bicycles were prone to overtake me on hills.

Gingerly prodding at the accelerator, in breakneck second gear, I roamed up the Jebel Amman, the nearest, biggest and richest of the seven little mountains which make up the city. I found Rainbow Street, bright with boutiques, jewellers', craftware curio shops and the sort of stationers' where you can buy only deckle-edged 'At Home' cards and amazingly expensive buff-coloured scented notepaper which looks as if someone has knitted it out of painted horsehair. The street itself was full of amazingly expensive buff-coloured people. There were more Gucci bags on show than there are around Sloane Square; more Dior dresses than on Bond Street. The men had blow-dried hair and wore Italian crocodile-skin shoes. Everyone passed in their own fragrant bubble of personal cologne. Feeling distinctly poor and smelly in this exalted company, I stood for a while looking in a bookshop window. The 'books' it sold were of a piece with the street; gigantic art-works, bound in tooled leatherette and inset with gold leaf. Most people's coffee-tables would have collapsed under their weight, but they may have been useful weapons for stunning sheep. Two women were talking at the entrance to the dress-maker's shop next door. Their conversation was in rapid Arabic. Their voices were pure Kensington. When they parted, they kissed.

'Ciaou!' one called.

'Ciaou!' carolled back the other.

They looked to me as if they were managing remarkably well on $460 a year. Nor, for that matter, did they look the slightest bit like people who would be interested in hearing of the death of Dr Leavis. Fearing that a dispute might arise if I got one scratch on the new yellow paint of the car, I drove it into the middle of a stony, flowery meadow, where it blended nicely with the broom and was a good fifty yards out of harm's way. Walking back through the long, thin grass, I disturbed a real Arab in a head-dress and burnous. He was eating sand-wiches and drinking from a can of Double Diamond. I had nearly stepped on him.

'*Ahlan wa sahlan*,' he said politely. Hello.

'*Ahlan wa sahlan*,' I said, picking my way over the top of his solitary picnic. I waited for him to say 'Ciaou!' as I left, but he didn't.

At the 'First Circle' (all of Amman's neat little roundabouts are called 'circles', and they all have numbers; its social life consists of moving in circles from circle to circle), I stopped in at a vinyl bar. A boy was sweeping a spotless floor, harrying out specks of invisible dust. When I slopped a teaspoonful of beer from my glass on to the table, he had a Kleenex there the moment that the beer made contact with the Formica tabletop.

'Sorry,' I said.

'Do not worry,' he said. I had not in fact intended to worry, but the gravity of his reassurance did alarm me. Moving my glass cautiously to one side, I settled down to my notebook.

This place might be Lucerne. It could, at a stretch, be taken for the smart, hilly bit of Berkeley, Calif. – though, on second thoughts, Berkeley's *much* scruffier. Met an Arab in a field: he must have got there by parachute. People who go around endlessly sweeping up floors make a curiously accusing sound with their brushes. They literally make you feel like dirt. The only nation I've ever been tempted to feel really racist about are the Swiss – a whole country of phobic handwashers living in a giant Barclays Bank. But Swiss Arabs! Even the beer tastes of soap. I think I may be here under false pretences. *The Middle East Yearbook* must have missed a couple of noughts off that GNP figure – or something, though God only knows what.

I walked up the road to the Third Circle, where I collected a couple of postcards which were waiting for me at the British Embassy. A young attaché let me into the back-stage area of the building through a complex series of bomb-proof steel doors.

'What's all this for?' I asked, still thinking I was in Lucerne.

'It's the Palestinian Situation,' he said. I went up to his office for a 'briefing'. 'You have to remember,' he said, starting his preamble, 'Jordan is a very poor country . . .'

I looked out of his window at the landslide of pastel villas.

'That's going to be the hardest thing of all to remember,' I said.

Half an hour later, back on the First Circle, I paid a call on the British Council, and had another 'briefing' in the office of the deputy-representative.

'Jordan isn't a poor country,' he said.

'Ill-founded rumours seem to be the lifeblood of this part of the world. I suppose that's just another one of them.'

'What I mean,' said Peter Skelton, 'is that "being all right" is *the* Jordanian habit of mind.'

That sentence continued to ring in my head for the next fortnight. The more I saw of the country, the truer the sentence seemed. I felt lucky to have it in my possession, and grateful to Mr Skelton for giving it me on my first day.

'By the way,' he said, 'did you see our bullet-holes when you came in?'

'No,' I said.

'We've only got a few,' he said modestly. 'You should have seen the USIS building up the road. They shelled that so badly that the whole thing had to be demolished.'

'Well that's one form of cultural criticism.'

'I think it was more in the nature of an accident, actually. They just happened to be in the line of fire.'

'It'd be nice to think that the Palestinians had just been reading F. R. Leavis.'

'He's dead, you know,' he said.

'Yes, I know. I read it in the paper.'

Zig-zag down a precipice, and up another pink and yellow hill: it was a roller-coaster city – an exhilarating place to drive in, as one left one's stomach behind in the valley and got it back again as one topped the next peak, with Amman changing colour at every bend. On Jebel Webdeh, I found the Department of Culture and Arts. Three young men with luxuriant moustaches (I remembered that I should send Major Barza a postcard; I'd landed up in his home-town) were carrying in a succession of enormous canvases. I had said that I would like to see some examples of modern Jordanian painting. As they started to fill a large room, I was beginning to regret the request.

'That's . . . interesting,' I said. It looked, in fact, like a bad cultural car-smash. One part of it belonged to the kind of sentimental genre-painting which is sold in chain stores and whose plastic surface mimics the brushwork on real canvas; another bit of the same painting was inspired by Byzantine icons; while yet another related to the arabesque of mosque floors. It was not so much a conscious commentary on its sources as a brain-damaged victim of them. As painting was stacked on painting, I got accustomed to their earnest imitativeness. Some had been smitten by Monet, some by Salvador Dali; together, they composed a crude parody-history of the major movements in modern European painting. When they tried

to deal with specifically Arab subjects, they dealt with them
through the eyes of sentimental strangers, so that painters
who had known bedu life depicted it in the manner of an
adventurous Victorian lady with a watercolour sketchbook.
They were so appallingly bad that there was an element of
desperate heroism in their badness. It was as if their artists
were having to rehearse the entire history of painting at hectic
speed, before finding themselves as painters in their own right.

'I am very interested,' I said, 'in the way your painters seem
to relate to the European tradition . . .' and spent a long time
scraping out and filling my pipe. I owed my hosts more than
this for all the porterage that they had done on my behalf.
I was saved by the arrival of Mohanna Durra, the one Jordanian
painter who has an established reputation in Europe and the
United States. We had in fact been using his office for this
impromptu exhibition. He came in, took one look at the garish
kaleidoscope of violent colours and bad ideas, blenched and
said, 'I need a cigarette fast.'

'Mr Durra will talk with you,' I was told. We were left alone
in the room.

'What *is* all this about?'

'I wanted to see some modern Jordanian painting,' I said.

'Good God.' He clenched his cigarette between his teeth. I
noticed that the ashtray on his desk was full of stubs which had
been bitten clean through before the cigarettes themselves had
been allowed to burn more than a third of the way down their
length. This *macho* impatience with things showed in his
manner, too. He bit off the ends of his sentences before finishing them, letting an exasperated wave of his hand take care
of the final clauses. He had the haste of a boy. Every so often
he would touch his skull where his black hair was going thin
on the crown; this seemed to cause him both irritation and
astonishment, as if he had reached the age of forty by some
overnight mistake. In the course of five minutes he could pass
from a state of extreme animation to one of inert boredom and
back again.

I told him about the book I was writing.

'You mean you are making an inventory of the chaos?
Isn't it just chaos? Don't you find it chaos? Look at the way
people dress here – a kaffiyeh . . . a tie . . . a jacket . . . a dish-

dasha . . . Oxford shoes! A chaos! Or what an Arab does to a Lamborghini, say. He buys this car . . . it has been perfectly well designed to be complete already. He destroys it! He covers it in fur, he hangs bangles all over it, and then he gives it a name – a woman's name! I ask you! Chaos!'

'Or a painting like that . . .' I pointed to the car-crash of different styles.

'Please, I am nursing a hangover!' He looked at his watch. At least five minutes had gone by since he had entered his office. In Durra's accelerated time-scale that was roughly equivalent to an entire morning.

'Come back to my house, have a Martini. We'll talk better there – '

'But you've only just got here. I don't want to drag you back the moment you've arrived – '

'People work too long in offices. You can get coronaries that way. It's a terrible thing to spend a whole day in an office.'

I was supposed to follow him in my car. I kept on catching the flash of his rear window as he disappeared over the next hilltop. Three mountains and twenty corkscrew bends later, I caught up with him in a traffic jam.

'Sorry,' I said. 'Were you trying to lose me?'

'No,' he said. His cigarette was cocked between his teeth and aimed at the sky. 'I don't believe in wasting time. I like people to move *fast*.'

Durra's house was a villa on stilts, high up above the city. It would have made a good perch for a hawk, with Amman laid out below it like an undulating field full of rabbits and mice. The drawing-room walls were hung from ceiling to floor with Durra's paintings. He too had raced through half a dozen different periods, but every painting had the stamp of the man on it. (Later, in other houses in Amman, I unfailingly picked out the Durras on the walls; their moody brilliance was un-mistakable, however much their styles and subjects varied.) They were smoky portraits with Rembrandt lighting; crowded interiors, full of people caught in mid-gesture, like impressionist snapshots of parties loud with arguments and affairs; hawk's-eye landscapes in which valleys and mountain ranges were kept firmly in their place by the arrogantly sweeping brush-work on the canvas. His latest paintings looked, at first glance, like abstracts; angular slabs and sections of pale colour which interlocked with each other in a crazy-paving of knife-edged lines. I saw that they were perfect representations of my first view of Amman. The colours were those of the rock – the same streaky rose, yellow, blue and grey. The slabs and lines and angles mapped the city.

'It is too easy to be a "Jordanian painter",' Durra said. 'We have far too many Jordanian painters. No one risks anything by it. I think one has to take risks. The standards that count aren't the standards of Amman. You have to risk yourself by the standards of London or New York or Paris or Milan. All right, perhaps you fail. But you have to prove you're not a coward. There are too many cowards about.'

A Saudi Arabian family was staying at the Philadelphia Hotel. In the early evenings, I would see them in the lounge, studying maps and guidebooks. Every morning they would get into their car – women at the back, men at the front – and drive off to visit another ancient monument. I had watched them going in a crocodile up the terraces of the amphitheatre, and had bumped into them again in the museum of folk history.

One day I spoke to the eldest son of the family. He said they lived in Riyadh. They were on holiday in Jordan because it was very historical. They were going to see the mosaics at Madaba tomorrow; yesterday they had been to the Roman city of Jerash. Later in the week, they would go to the temple at Petra.

He spoke no English, and my Arabic only stretched as far as discovering his itinerary. I wished we could have talked more. After all the complaints I had heard about Saudi philistinism and vulgarity in Cairo, this modest, studious family with their passion for archaeological sightseeing seemed to me to be people I should meet. They looked a great deal more interesting than the cold playboys at the Sheraton casino.

I asked Selim about the Saudi family. Selim worked for the radio station in Amman; and I'd been introduced to him in a café, when he'd promptly offered to give up his Friday holiday to accompany me to the Dead Sea. It would be his pleasure, he said. He would like to talk to me about writing, because he also wanted to write. So we had made a date and set off early in the morning, before the rest of the city had woken up. I told Selim about my fellow guests.

'Yes, we have many Saudis here. I think they are the nice ones. The ones who just want drinking and nightclubs go to Cairo. The ordinary people, though, like to come to Amman.'

'I'd never thought of Saudis as people who went round ruins with guidebooks.'

'I think all Arabs are homesick for culture, you understand? They remember things like old Arab philosophy, and Arab mathematics. But it is all so long ago. They want to find it again. Now they have money, big cars, big houses, but they have lost this culture. So they feel homesick, and then they go to places like Petra and Jerash.'

Selim waved at the streets on either side of us. 'This is a poor part of Amman. This is where poor Palestinians live.' It looked just ordinary to me. The houses were small, but they were better than shacks.

'Perhaps I've just been blinded by what I've seen in other parts of Arabia, but I can't see it. When you go to the poor quarters of Qatar or Dubai or any of the really rich states, there are people living in cardboard boxes and oil drums.'

'People are poor here in a different way. You will see.'

We drove up into the mountains past tidy fields of spring wheat, green vineyards and olive groves. Above the green belt, we came into a Durra landscape of pastel rock, folded over on itself in queer shapes like a tousled blanket. Convoys of trucks were coming up the steep road from the Dead Sea valley, heaped with crates of oranges, melons, tomatoes and cabbages. The camouflage-netting which had been used to tie down these loads was made of too wide a mesh to prevent the trucks from leaking their cargoes as they climbed uphill. The road was spattered with squashed fruit. Tomato juice trickled like blood down its culverts, and I kept feeling the tyres of the car crushing small pulpy bodies under their treads.

'You see they have two number-plates, one over the other? They come from the West Bank. At the border they must change from an Israeli plate to a Jordanian plate.'

There were bedu encampments at the side of the road: airy,

divided tents, with camels, goats, sheep, sometimes a very old, very battered Dodge pick-up.

'Could we pay them a visit?'

'They are not always so hospitable. It can be dangerous. We can ask them for water if you want, but I would sooner not do it. They just have started to come out here, I think. These are their summer quarters.'

The ways of the bedu were as foreign to Selim as they were to me. He was slight, moustached, serious; a city man with a university degree for whom Jordan outside Amman was another country. We were both tourists here. Selim sat in the passenger seat, wrinkling his eyes at what he saw from behind his dark glasses. In his smart Italian checkered shirt and Levi's, with a small leather handbag on his knee, he looked as conspicuous in this landscape, among his fellow-countrymen, as a bedu sheikh in full regalia might look in Dorset.

We stopped at a village to buy a kilo of oranges and some Pepsi-Cola. We drank the Cola sitting in the shade of a vine which had been trained over an awning of corrugated iron. High up on a post, far out of the reach of anyone except a giant, was a bleached postbox. I remarked that the people of this village must be very tall. The proprietor of the shop explained that the reason why the postbox was so far up was because it was extremely valuable. The government paid him five dinars a month to keep the box there. The postal van had not called at the village for years; all mail was now collected from another village, four kilometres up the road. But the money for his box kept on coming in. If it was lower down on the post, people might put letters in it, then he would have to take the box to the government, since he didn't have a key to open it, and his sixty dinars a year might disappear. We drank to this happy arrangement. The shopkeeper asked Selim whether it might be a nice gesture to paint the postbox for the government; Selim's advice was to let well alone.

An old man sitting opposite us had been eyeing my tobacco tin. He said that it was a very fine tin. He himself kept his tobacco in an old cellophane sachet. It must, he said, be a very splendid thing to be able to buy tobacco in a tin. We did a swap. I put my tobacco in his sachet; he put his in my tin. The shopkeeper refused to take any money for our drinks and oranges: we had talked, and it would be dishonourable for him to accept payment.

As we got back into the car, Selim said: 'Now you have seen a poor man. The one who asks you for your tin.'

The road steepened further. Behind almost every crag, now, there was a tank or a field gun. Tangles of barbed wire rolled through the wild flowers. Selim pointed to a blue shadow on the far side of the valley. 'There is Jericho,' he said. We passed the sign which marked sea-level, and drove on down to the lowest point on earth.

One of the odder features of this journey, and one which made the descent seem like something out of legend, was a dramatic change in the skin colour of the people. At the top of the hill, we drove through a village where everyone was white. Fair and blue-eyed, they looked like Swedes. In fact they were Circassians. They had been dispersed from their homeland at the same time as their neighbours, the Armenians, and had settled along the Jordan valley where they farmed, inter-married and generally kept themselves to themselves. As we got close to the Dead Sea, though, a few miles down the road, we came to a village where all the people had black African faces.

'I do not know why this is so – I think perhaps it is the heat . . .' Selim said without conviction. Jordanians tend to a certain reticence on the subject of the Nubian slave trade.

From Circassia to Nubia, from white to black, from the mountain to the valley, from quiet farms to all the apparatus of war, from alpine air to thick tropical heat – the road to the Dead Sea was overloaded with meaning, like the road of a pilgrim in an allegory.

We missed a turning, and landed up at a frontier post in the middle of a brackish marsh. The guard was slow-moving in the sun. His heavy battledress was darkened with sweat. He asked for a cigarette, steadied himself on the car to cough, and wearily directed us back. Across the river there was another pill-box, and the wink of binoculars. We were on the turn of April into May; already the temperature in the valley was over a hundred degrees. The soldiers fighting in this sector in the June War must have been half-dead with torpor. I found that a walk of just a few yards in that salty, standing heat left me exhausted. Within a few minutes, everything in the car that was made of metal had become too hot to touch.

We found the 'Beach Club' on a marsh at the north end of the sea. It looked more like a military installation than a holiday place, and so, in a sense, it was. Salt and sun had killed the colours of its slides, swings and dodgem cars. Its gardens were dotted with sick little palms, and people were drinking beer under torn awnings on the concrete patios.

'This is new,' said Selim. 'Before 'sixty-seven, we went over there – ' he pointed across to the shaded western coast of the Dead Sea. 'It is nicer. The beach there is better for bathing.'

Certainly no one in their right mind would have wanted to bathe here. To reach the sea itself one had to cross a hundred yards of salt flats. They were in a state of continual noisy flatulence, gurgling and squelching beneath the terrace where we were sitting. A few dead tree trunks stuck out of them, and the sea beyond was a bilious green.

By all ordinary standards, the Beach Club was not only situated at the lowest point in the world, it was also some ultimate rock-bottom in the whole ugly hierarchy of seaside resorts. But the standards which were at stake here had nothing whatsoever to do with those of Clacton or Coney Island. Taking a glass of beer at the Beach Club was a political action – one which called on considerable reserves of both pride and good humour. The holiday-makers were putting on a spirited piece of theatre. The line of Israeli command posts stretched just half a mile away across the marsh. *Our* Friday, though, wasn't going to be affected by *that*. Children would play on the swings; parents would doze over their papers, set up muddy beach picnics, and take snapshots of each other sitting upright in their bathing costumes in the treacly sea.

Selim pointed out the landmarks of occupied Jordan: Jerusalem up on top of the mountain, and beyond it Bethlehem and Hebron. We couldn't actually see these places, but they were there somewhere in the haze. The beer was as warm as cocoa, the view stretched no further than the Israeli lines, the salt flats were passing gas, but we were *being all right*.

'It is better in the winter,' Selim said, 'but I think it is still a good place to come. You like it?'

'Yes,' I said. 'I really do.'

He glanced over the morning paper which had been left on our table.

'I think this will interest you, perhaps.' He showed me the leader in Arabic. 'The King is setting up a consultative committee. It is not a democratic parliament – these are people who will be appointed by the government. Anyway, the headline here says "A Step In The Right Direction". Do you think it is interesting that every time there is a new government policy, they always have the same headline in the paper – "A Step In The Right Direction"?'

'It surprises me, really. After Egypt, Jordan seems so much more of an open society. I would have thought that the press here would be much freer to make criticisms of the government.'

'That is true, so long as it is just a domestic matter. If there is a particular minister, for instance, who is responsible for the building of something – he may be criticized very fiercely. But if it is national policy, then it is always a step in the right direction. There are no wrong directions to take. Until last year we had a paper in Amman, I thought it was very good. It was called *Rumours*. It was a satirical paper, you know? One week, they make a big announcement, a huge headline . . . "The Prime Minister Is On Holiday" . . . they want to say he is doing nothing, you understand? The next week, the paper is closed down. So it is free and not free. It can be hard to know when you cross from the one to the other.'

A few days later, Selim wrote a newspaper article himself, based on an interview with me. He read me the text, and I was interested to hear that I too was saying that everything was a step in the right direction. It turned out that the only thing which was not, in my opinion, a step in the right direction was the Balfour Declaration. Indeed my loathing of Mr Balfour appeared to be the one thing in my life which clouded an otherwise entirely sunny existence. Listening to Selim translating his article, I only wished he had been right.

We crawled back up the mountain road. On a little grassy plateau in the middle of nowhere there was a restaurant called simply 'Paradise' – a large, tacky, open-air joint with plaster arches and Lebanese rock music on the loudspeaker system.

Everything in sight had been draped with loops and ribbons of fairy-lights. In the afternoon sun they looked like so many strings of blackened sausages.

'This must be a Palestinian restaurant,' Selim said.

'How can you tell?'

'No Jordanian would dare to open such a place. He would not have the imagination.' He called a waiter over. Yes, the proprietor was a Palestinian. 'You see?' said Selim. 'I am right. I think one must be observant to be a writer.'

We ordered kebabs and a bottle of rosé wine. I inspected the label on the bottle. It had come from a Trappist monastery in Jerusalem.

'So we are drinking Trappist wine in a Palestinian restaurant,' I said.

'What you see in Jordan is often not "Jordanian" at all. The Palestinians are the big-city people. They know about night-clubs and restaurants; the Jordanians know very little of these things. Then there are the Lebanese. They all came to Amman in 1970, when things became too bad in Beirut. You know Rainbow Street? That is all Lebanese. Before it was just little shops, very dark. The Jordanians do not know about shop-windows and boutiques, they do not have a feeling for that kind of style. So the Lebanese bring this *chic* to the city. Who-ever heard of boutiques in Amman before the Lebanese came? No one. I think we are lucky to have these people: they teach the Jordanians things we could not learn by ourselves.'

Across the dry garden, a large Palestinian family was eating Friday lunch. More heavily built than any other Arabs, with fleshier, paler, more distinctively urban faces, the Palestinians put me in mind of another place altogether. We could have been at Blooms Restaurant in Whitechapel on any Sunday afternoon: the same faces, the same crowding of the generations around a single table, the same serious banter. Outside the Middle East, it can be hard to remember that Jews and Palestinians come from the same patch of Mediterranean ground; many of them have grown up in the same cluster of city streets. It is only recently that the Palestinians have had to learn the old, bitter Jewish lesson of living in exile and becoming a feared people in the countries which they have adopted as second homes. It seems to me to be one of the cruellest historical ironies that it should be the Jews of Israel who have created the new Pale which has turned the Palestinians into the Wandering Jews of the postwar world. In Jordan, as in the Gulf, I kept on hearing Palestinians spoken of in exactly the same terms as Europeans used to describe Jews. They were 'clever', 'artistically talented', 'very good at business': these were not compliments; they were the seeds of a resentment which any European must spot with alarmed recognition. The most shameful thing in his own recent past started with words like that. If and when the Middle East goes through the same kind of economic crises which Europe suffered first in the 1870s and then in the 1920s and '30s, will the Palestinians escape the paranoid tide of loathing which engulfed the Jews? Families like the comfortable, prosperous people at their table in the 'Paradise' restaurant look terribly like the potential scapegoats of some unspecified future of hard times.

Selim took me back to his house in Amman. His father formally welcomed me on the balcony. He was wearing a kaffiyeh on his head. '*Arabiya!*' he said, pointing to it. But his family had come from Circassia. His grandfather and his great-grandfather had worn another kind of head-dress; he wound his hands round his skull to show me. His father had taken to the kaffiyeh; he too. 'Now you see I am an Arab,' he said with some pride.

'I would like you to see my library,' Selim said. His room was small and barely furnished; it might have been a quarter in a soldiers' barracks, except for the single bookcase in which Selim kept his library double-parked, one row behind another on each shelf. He read in English, French and Arabic; and the library had a happily-used look, with markers and turned-down pages and broken spines. His taste was wide and promiscuous. I picked out a copy of Muriel Spark's *The Hothouse By the East River*.

'I did not get to the end of that one. I read another book by her which I like very much – *The Girls of the Slender Means*. But in that one there are many things I do not understand.'

I shared his feelings about the more recent works of Muriel Spark.

'So there are people in England, too, who find her difficult?'

'Many people.'

'That is interesting. I think that in England everybody finds her books very easy.'

'I don't think anyone would say that.'

'You are giving me hope,' said Selim.

His favourite book – the most marked, turned-down and broken-backed – was *A Tale Of Two Cities*. 'But it is only in Arabic, I am afraid. Every year I think I will try to read it in English, and then I go and read it in Arabic again.'

'Do you think that the times which Dickens writes about in that book are a bit like the times in the Middle East now? Is that why you like it so much?'

'It is possible. Perhaps, I think so, but there are many differences.'

He had *Lady Chatterley's Lover* – hidden in a back row.

'There are many words in that book which I do not understand. Lawrence uses long words.'

'In England, he's mainly famous for using short ones.'

'Long words,' Selim said, emphatically. 'I cannot read it because I have to look at the dictionary too much.'

I found Margaret Drabble's *Jerusalem The Golden*.

'I have a very bad time with that book. I read it again and again, but I never get more than to page twenty. It is not about what it says on the cover. It is not about Jerusalem at all.'

'No, the title comes from an English hymn. There's a line in the hymn which says "I know not, oh I know not, what social joys are there . . .", and the book is about these "social joys", in London not Jerusalem. It's really about the pop scene in London in the 1960s.'

'I think you must be right. I tried to read it as a book about Jerusalem, and I did not understand it at all.'

We went out on to the balcony. Selim's mother brought us glasses of mint tea. The sun was beginning to settle down prettily into the folds of the hills. Selim pointed out the bullet-marks on the corners of the house and told me about the fighting in the city in 1970.

'It was a very bad time. The Palestinians had their own check-points all over Amman. They had some hills to themselves, and they were giving people passes and permits to cross the city. You could not go anywhere without a Palestinian pass. They were training their soldiers openly. There – ' he pointed over the garden wall at what looked like a scout hut on the patch of waste ground beside the house, 'that was a Palestinian base. They were teaching young boys how to fire rockets there, every evening.

'When the fighting came, it was terrible. We went down to the bottom of the house for twelve days. We had a radio. That was our only contact with the outside world, but the stations were always being cut off, we kept on having to switch to find another station which was working. We just had to sit there, listening to the noise. We heard rockets, mortars, shells, machine-guns; it went on all day and all night. I thought this house must be the only house in Amman which was still standing. I was sure the whole of the rest of the city must be destroyed. That was when I tried to read that book about Jerusalem – '

'Margaret Drabble – '

'Yes. I took only two books with me. That was one of them. It did not make sense to me. When the fighting was over, and we came upstairs, I was *amazed*. The streets were still here. There were some houses gone, but most were as they had been before. They were just all chipped by bullets.'

Sipping mint tea and watching the sunset, I listened to Selim as if he was telling me a folk-tale about some ancient historical event. It was hard to believe that all this had happened only a little more than seven years before. The bullet-marks, though, on every wall and gable I could see, were still fresh.

'How on earth does Amman now seem so quiet? It's so neat and comfortable and well-swept that one would never guess that you'd gone through a civil war.'

'The people have the *will* to forget that it happened, I think. It is something that everybody does – the Palestinians and the Jordanians too. It is will-power only. And I think that we succeed. We have forgotten it. But one thing is odd. No one puts plaster or anything over the bullet-holes in their houses. There – ' he put his finger in a deep chip behind my head, 'my father would not fill that in. So perhaps we have to remember in order to forget.'

My meeting with the Durras was the beginning of a paper-chain of invitations to parties. Every evening, in some villa on one hill or another, there was a party. At each one there was somebody who was giving a party the following night, and everyone was invited. So evening after evening, we went to the same party. The hills and the villas changed, but the occasion remained the same. The routine was simple: for three hours one was supposed to drink as many cocktails as one could manage, then at eleven o'clock the household servants wheeled on a buffet, which we savaged before reeling home. The party seemed to have been going on for several years at least, and it had acquired the ritual quality of a church service. It was conducted in several different languages at once. It reached its inevitable nightly climax when angry wives flung car-keys at their husbands, and fat men suddenly started turning their backs on the people they were talking to. It was designed to keep all old wounds permanently opened while at the same time it afforded the maximum of opportunity to inflict new ones.

Sitting next to Gabriela Durra on one of these identical evenings, I began a sentence by saying, 'Surely, in a city of nearly a million people . . .'

'No! No! No!' she said. 'You don't understand! Amman is not a city of a million people, it is a city of a hundred couples!'

There were other people besides me who were on the fringes of the hundred couples. Ricardo was one of them. Every night he looked fractionally more wasted and ashen than he had done when I had last seen him. We got into the habit of meeting in corners. Ricardo had not been long in Amman, and the Party still shocked him. He had come from a city where the rich have to live in conspicuous austerity in order to avoid the attentions of the terrorists of the Red Brigade; each night in Amman was making him more angry and incredulous.

'I have never seen, without a Hollywood picture, such things!' He pointed at a wall. It had the usual selection of pictures on it. 'Picasso! Braque! Matisse! All these on a wall in one man's house!'

'They say it's a poor country, too.'

'How can they live like this? Have you seen the camps? Where live the Palestine people? Have you been?'

'Not yet, but I'm going – '

323

'It is terrible. I could not believe . . . And up here, this money, money, money! This waste! And the poor people, just one mile in distance . . .'

Faced with Ricardo's moral rage, I felt shifty. He was looking at the city from the perspective of Milan; I had come there from the much more obviously glaring inequities of the Gulf, the Yemen and Cairo – and I had to confess that I was enjoying myself and was not nearly as shocked as perhaps I should be by what I saw in Amman.

'They want you to see only the gold! You must lose your way, go nowhere, and then you will see the country as it is!'

'That's exactly what I've tried to do in every country that I've been to.'

'You must not stay here.'

'Why do you keep on coming to the Party, then, Ricardo?'

'I hate it. But I must go.'

'Why?'

'Because, if I do not accept, people begin to say "Where is Ricardo? Up to what does Ricardo get?" Then begins the talk . . . when begins the talk, then people tell terrible things . . . so I go. Now – no time for thinking, no time for reading. All I can do is drink. Tonight, tomorrow, every night. The same drink, the same people. All for stopping the talk. It is terrible for me.'

At the end of each evening, there always appeared to be a sofa with three large, heavy-lidded men sitting on it. Their paunches and moustaches matched. They drooped over their liqueurs like Easter Island statues, wordless, vacantly digestive. Perhaps they were the audience for whose benefit this whole lavish, long-running cavalcade had been put on; or perhaps they were its theatrical angels. At any rate, the only signs of life they ever showed were the uniform, thin trickles of smoke from their three Havana cigars.

Cairo had been all out of connections. Amman appeared to consist of nothing but connections. My attendance at the Party had been noted by other people, and it was earning their disapproval.

In the afternoons, I had taken to going to Noha Batshon's

little gallery at the Intercontinental Hotel – a shadowy jackdaw's nest of bedu coffee pots, folkweave carpets, hubble-bubbles and paintings. It was warm with hammered brass and scarlet rugs, and Noha herself was a gentle, serious woman who liked to take strays under her wing. She acted as an honorary aunt to a gang of young painters whose work she sold, and she was constantly surrounded by her real nieces and nephews; there were always children perched up stairs or huddled in among the treasure-trove of coffee pots and pewter bowls. The gallery was her salon. Her young men squatted about on the floor like rabbits, drinking tea and trying to persuade Noha to hang their pictures in different places. I liked joining them for an hour or so each day.

'I hear you've become a member of *Le Tour D'Amman*,' said one of the painters.

'I didn't know it had a name. Anyway, I'm not a member. I couldn't afford the subscription.'

A grave middle-aged lady in fishnet stockings said: 'I am afraid that you meet only dreadful, unrepresentative people in Amman. You meet only the people who drink and show off their money.'

'You should meet real people.'

'They are real people,' I said. 'What do you want me to do? Go whoring after bedu tents and the simple life? The fact that the Jebel Amman is rotten with millionaires seems to me something that's really worth exploring. What I want to know is how they've got their money when Jordan is supposed to be so poor. In Cairo, they get it from the Saudis. But these people aren't living off Saudi rials. Where is it coming from?'

'It comes from property, some from building.'

'This is nearly all since 1970.'

'When the Lebanese came from Beirut, the price of houses went up. People who had inherited a plot of land here and there suddenly found they could develop it for millions of dinars.'

'And the rebuilding after the Palestinian troubles here . . . There were contracts going in all directions. It was a big pot of honey. Everybody got sticky fingers.'

'Some of these people are just Lebanese crooks. I hope they

will go back to Beirut.'

'You ought to see the *real* Amman. You will not find it at these parties.'

I wasn't so sure. Nowhere was the Jordanian habit of 'being all right' so conspicuously on exhibition as at the Party. The partygoers had done well out of the troubles of Beirut, then they had done well out of the troubles of their own city. Their knack of coming out on top of things fitted in exactly with the bravura gesture of the Beach Club, with Selim trying to read Margaret Drabble while shells were bursting over the top of his house, even with that curious report of the death of F. R. Leavis. Everywhere I went in Jordan, I met a determined ebullience, a refusal to be done down by anyone; it was the kind of place where people were always whistling, whether or not they had anything to whistle about, and if they did have something to whistle about, then they crowed like crazy. After Sana'a and Cairo, it was very good to hear someone whistling for a change.

I tried taking Ricardo's advice and spent a long day driving nowhere. East of Amman the land was flat; miles of brown shale, telegraph poles, and hitch-hiking soldiers. I went where the soldiers wanted to go. A sergeant said he lived in Mafraq, so I drove to Mafraq, slotting the car in among the army convoys which appeared to be the only other users of the road. Spiralling puffs of dust came off the desert, but no genies materialized at their tops. A single brightly-shawled woman, tending a flock of goats near the road, assumed a weirdly disproportionate importance in this empty landscape. From horizon to horizon it was a dull burnt-ochre; the vivid chemical colours of a shawl blazed in it with the brilliance of a great monument or a forest fire. The towns were nondescript; the villages just clumps of beehive mud-huts, the same dun colour as the desert. As I drove further north, I could see the beginning of rolling dunes to my right in the far distance; the start of the great Arabian desert of crescent hills of sand which sweeps across a thousand miles from Syria and Iraq to the Yemeni mountains.

A signpost pointing up an empty road said 'Baghdad'. Had there been the ghost of a chance of getting a visa at the Iraqi border, I might have taken it; to have spent so long in Arabia without once being alone in that heroic desert of the travellers' tales seemed like a piece of culpable absent-mindedness. 'But didn't you just *love* the desert?' people said when I came home. Embarrassed, I would try and shift the conversation to the splendours of the skyscrapers of Abu Dhabi or the aquarium of dead fish in Cairo, and I would watch suspicion gather in the eyes of my questioners. If I hadn't stood on the top of a great dune and been inspired by the beauty of those endless, empty shapes scooped out by the wind, then I hadn't really been to Arabia at all.

Perhaps there was truth in what their eyes said. At the junction with the highway to Baghdad, I took the timid left turn and not the adventurous right. I nudged the border with Syria and headed for a range of green mountains. Shale steadily gave way to thin grass, grass to flowers, flowers to a sudden amazing burst of liquid colour. The landscape was alight with it. It was a kaleidoscope of new blossom. Finches and redstarts dipped and flittered through the overhanging trees. The roadside was thick with poppies, irises and wild lupins. There were groves of hibiscus, and tangles of rockroses on the limestone crags. This was, perhaps, just twenty miles from that other Jordan of dust and stones. Climbing into the hills towards Jerash, with the green valley dropping away down to the River Jordan, I caught the full force of the words 'Promised Land'. Before, they had always made up a dim metaphor. When the Israelites were led, on foot, through the Sinai desert to this extraordinary patch of fertile ground, they must have thought that they were quite literally entering a paradise on earth.

Little lakes, caught in the crooks of the hills, were silver spoons. There were terraced farms all the way up the mountainsides, an intricate patchwork of scarlet, green and gold. The rock itself looked painted; a watercolour wash of violet and rose pink, broken by splashes of jagged black where queer caves yawned just a few feet over my head. At the time, sharpened by the drive through the desert, I thought it was the loveliest place I had seen in the world.

No wonder that it had been so fiercely fought over. This was Gilead, given to Machir, son of Manasseh. 'They saw the

land of Gilead . . . the place was a place for cattle.' The highest
compliment that Solomon could pay his darling's hair was to
compare it with 'a flock of goats, that appear from Mount
Gilead'. For Jeremiah, it was the land of balm – if there was no
balm in Gilead, then the world had come to a hopeless pass.
When the Lord threatened the royal house of Judah, he said
'Thou art Gilead unto me . . . yet surely I will make thee a
wilderness, and cities which are not inhabited'. Throughout
the Old Testament the name of Gilead is synonymous with
fertility and civilization. Its inhabitants were as much to be
envied as any oil sheikh sitting on his millions. With the great
crush of the desert pushing in on three sides, and the wandering
tribes scratching a bare living out of dust and shale, this
teeming Eden must have impressed unfortunate outsiders as
one of God's grossest ironies. Even now, when the wealth of
the Middle East had shifted from crops to oil, from the greenlands to the desert, Gilead was rich. I stopped at a farm which
was a small family market-garden. The farmer showed me
the quality of the soil, crumbling it between his fingers, and
pointed out the things he was growing – grapes, aubergines,
oranges, wheat, barley. His whitewashed stone cottage might
have been a wealthy man's holiday house in the Cotswolds. He
could have prepared much the same feast which Shobi,
Machir and Barzillai mounted for King David when he
arrived in Gilead:

> They brought beds, and basons, and earthen vessels, and wheat,
> and barley, and flour, and parched corn, and beans, and lentils,
> and parched pulse, and honey, and butter, and sheep, and
> cheese of kine, for David, and for the people that were with him,
> to eat: for they said, The people is hungry, and weary, and
> thirsty, in the wilderness.

The farmer did offer me refreshment, but it was not on the
scale of David's feast; it was a welcome bottle of warm Pepsi-
Cola.

The nature of envy hasn't changed since Old Testament
times. Checking through the references to Gilead, I noticed
the mounting resentment with which its wealthy farmers
were regarded by the later prophets. Jeremiah sounds a

warning note; in Hosea, hostility to the people of Gilead comes to an angry climax:

> Gilead is a city of them that work iniquity . . . they commit lewdness . . . there is the whoredom of Ephraim, Israel is defiled . . . Is there iniquity in Gilead? Surely they are vanity!

I recognized that tone of voice instantly: it was exactly the way that the Cairenes had talked of the Saudis, and the Jordanian middle class of the Jebel Amman millionaires.

The Party that night was at Mr Mango's, and for dessert there were mangoes standing in cut glass goblets. As we stood upstairs, spooning the soft fruit into our mouths, Mr Mango charged up from below, a rotund whirlwind, the points of his beard and whiskers flashing.

'Stop!' he shouted. 'Stop! That is me you are eating! Me! Me! Me!'

'Welcome,' said Ahmad Abbadi. 'You are most welcome. Welcome.' He showed me into his office at police headquarters, and offered me a box of chocolates. He looked like a body-builder. His pectoral muscles rippled under his shirt and his biceps were the size of vegetable marrows. He had been born a nomad, living on dates and camel's milk, going barefoot to school, and herding the family goats, camels and sheep. Now he was a major in the police, he edited the *Police Gazette*, he had an MA degree in anthropology, and the telephone on his desk rang every two minutes. He had made a long, strange crossing from one culture to another, and his pride in himself was at once innocent and overwhelming. 'I am a bedu,' he said. 'There are two civilizations. There is the material civilization, and there is the spiritual civilization. The bedu man is the highest peak of the spiritual civilization.'

He showed me his thesis. 'This is read by everybody at your Oxford University.' In it, he had traced the patterns of settlement and nomadic migration of the bedu tribes of Jordan as they zig-zagged between the greenlands and the desert. I wanted to ask him, though, about his own migration. How had it been to make that journey from the desert to this office?

'You must understand. For the bedu man, everything i possible. There is no difficulty. Look here – ' he picked up a copy of the *Police Gazette*. 'I am the editor of this magazine . . .'

I was beginning to get a little restive. The idea of the bedu *Ubermensch* was no more appealing than that of the Saxon *Ubermensch*; and it seemed that I was in for a long lecture on Abbadi's racial superiority. He pointed to a page of print.

'Here is an article that I write. You see – this says "by Major Ahmad Abbadi". That is correct, yes? Now. This page here. This is you. This is the man of the city.'

'I don't think I quite follow – '

'This here! This page . . . this . . .'

'Print.'

'You are correct, sir. This page of print. This is you. There is no space to write more. You see, the page is *full*. You cannot put more print on without making mess. Now. This – ' he picked up a blank piece of jotting-paper from his desk. 'This is the man of the desert. The bedu man. He is open. Anything may be written on him. To him, all experience is possible. I give you an example. The bedu man loves news. He wants to know all that is going on in the whole world. This is very traditional. Wherever he goes, to trade, at the caravanserai, he questions everybody he meets. News goes from person to person. Now the bedu has a radio. He listens all the time, to every station, to Cairo, to London, to Amman, to Damascus, to Jerusalem. Now the bedu will know more of Carter and Brezhnev than the man of the city. It is because he is open, like this piece of paper. You must understand, sir, the bedu is very *human*, especially to his children and his women.'

The bullishness of Abbadi's manner was peculiarly Jordanian. What he was saying, though, corresponded exactly with what I had seen and heard on the Gulf. I did not care very much for his description of me as a blackened page of the *Police Gazette*, but his metaphor of the blank sheet of paper did ring true. The extraordinary capacity of the bedu to adapt themselves to massive changes of circumstance was visible on every street and building in Abu Dhabi and Al Ain. I asked Abbadi if he had been to the Gulf states. He had, and loathed them.

'There, they move too fast, with too much money, to the material civilization. And then you get the problems, of drinking, of fighting, of going after women. All this I have seen. Here in Jordan, the bedu is different. He is a much better man. He moves very slowly, very carefully, with much knowledge. The material and the spiritual slowly *bend* to each other – you understand?'

'But what happens to the next generation? How are your own children growing up?'

'I have no children yet. I am only thirty-two years old. That is very young to be a major. When I have children, I will go to live in a village, outside Amman. I teach them to live on dates and camel's milk. I make them go barefoot. I make them *hard* like me.' He tightened a bicep to show me what he meant. 'In the winter, we live in a simple house. In the summer we go to the tent . . .'

'Do you honestly think that's possible? How can you go from an office like this, with a car, a colour TV, a city flat with electric light, back to the desert? To do that you have to turn history on its head.'

'Of course it is possible. I am a bedu. This is my tradition.'

There was an odd moment in our conversation, when Abbadi was trying to explain to me that Islam was the 'spine' of Arab culture. Not knowing the word in English, he took the blank sheet of paper and drew a picture on it. It was laborious work. His pencil moved slowly and erratically over the page. Then he turned the paper round and pointed at the spine of the 'man' he had drawn. A two-year-old child could have made a better stick-man. One arm came out of its stomach, the other out of its neck; its legs came from equally dissimilar sources. Abbadi was clever; he had written an important postgraduate thesis; he was the capable editor of a magazine; but he couldn't draw a stick-man. Apparently there was no convention in his head for representing the simplest human figure. It was not surprising that Jordanian painting showed every sign of having to start from scratch.

I mentioned this to the salon of young men at Noha's gallery.

'You have been to see Abbadi? That man is a *nut*! The things he does to the poor bedu in that thesis!'

It seemed that I couldn't put a foot right with them. I was hoping that they'd congratulate me on meeting a real person.

It was only after I left Jordan that I realized that when they talked about 'the real people' they were referring to themselves; at the time, I would never have guessed.

I had passed the Palestinian camps before. From the road, they did not look shocking places. They were dense estates of bungalows, with steep mud streets full of goats and children. Every highway out of Amman had a camp somewhere along it – a straggly terracotta of breezeblock, chipboard, corrugated iron, concrete and brick. Many of these houses were painted in the same pastel rock colours as the buildings in the city. They were bright with roof-gardens; olives and cedars grew in the spaces between the bungalows; and by whatever muddled standards I had acquired during the course of my trip, they looked to me like modestly prosperous small towns. Each time I drove past a camp, I remembered Ricardo's horror and failed to match it with even a flicker of pity or outrage on my own part. The camps looked makeshift, but they gave away no clue that their inhabitants had lost one jot of self-respect. The roof-gardens alone, with lines of well-pruned plants in pots, showed pride. Housing estates of tower-blocks on the outskirts of English cities are far more dismal places; their broken windows, spraygunned walls and vandalized trees are public announcements of the anger and defeatedness of the people who live there. The Palestinian camps looked as if the refugees, too, were determinedly *being all right*.

There were a quarter of a million refugees living in the camps in Jordan, and the Relief and Works Agency of the United Nations administered them, running schools, clinics and refectories. I was taken by an official of UNRWA to visit Marqa Camp, five miles outside Amman. On the ride out, I felt that the occasion was fringed with a mixture of absurdity and embarrassment. I was sitting in the back of a new, white, chauffeur-driven Chevrolet Impala. My camera and notebook were laid out on the seat beside me, and I felt more like a goggling tourist than at any time since I had arrived in Arabia. I had wanted, as far as was possible, to be a fly on the wall, an eavesdropper; at Marqa Camp it seemed that I was being cast in the role of the charity-minded lady from the Big House on a morning's conducted tour of the local slum.

Through no merit of my own, it didn't turn out that way. Marqa Camp was not a slum and it allowed no opportunities at all for pitying condescension of the kind which I had felt had been set up as my expected response. Like the rest of Jordan, it was run on a shoestring economy, but it was a brisk efficient place in which people were making do as best they could on whatever means they had available. There were few men of working age on the streets; most had jobs in Amman. There was the ordinary morning air of a commuter suburb. It was true that some of the houses were just one-room tin shacks; but there were others, built of brick, with shady court-yards and gardens. I had supposed that being a refugee condemned one to being a member of a single depressed class. That was evidently quite untrue. Some people on the streets were shawled peasants; others were comfortable middle-class ladies – executive wives out shopping or taking the dog for a walk. When we left the car, I caught a glimpse through the window of one large corner-house, and saw bookshelves, standing lamps, cut flowers on a table.

I was shown over the clinic. A red-haired doctor was in charge. He talked to me while a stream of patients shuttled in and out of his room. He said that he was sorry that he must work as he talked, but that the clinic was badly understaffed, and I could see how many mothers and children were waiting outside.

'Are most of the illnesses that you are treating serious ones?'

'Most, no. Most are the usual things: bronchitis, diarrhoea, 'flu, measles. The drainage system of the camp is not very good. In winter, when there is a lot of rain, diseases tend to spread. There is some tuberculosis, but it is rare. The real problem has been to talk people into coming regularly for check-ups. We have ante-natal classes, and we encourage women to come back to the clinic with their families every two or three months. We are trying to move from being a car-repair shop to preventive medicine. I think we are succeeding, but it takes much propaganda, and we are doing it on very little money.'

A middle-aged woman came in. Her eyes hurt, she said, and she found it difficult to see things. The doctor examined her.

'This is exactly what I mean. This is serious. She has

trachoma. I think she perhaps has come just in time, but I am not sure. If she had come three months ago, then it would be different. But to see a case of trachoma is not very common. It is your lucky morning, you see.'

'Is it her lucky morning too?'

'Perhaps. I hope so.'

In another room, two nurses were giving children injections.

'We are using all the vaccine we can get. Our immunization programme is still a little primitive – we are not able to reach everybody.'

'Who does?'

'There is more urgency here. The conditions of the camp, particularly the drains and the closeness of the houses, make life very easy for germs. We are in a bad position to face an epidemic. One must always cross one's fingers . . .'

I looked through a heap of record-cards of patients. They consisted of long lists of diseases which the patients didn't have. There were rarely more than one or two ticks among the long columns of crosses. Bilharzia – negative. Syphilis – negative. I came across an occasional diagnosis of typhoid and tuberculosis. In 1976, there had been an outbreak of cholera in Jordan, but it had been controlled and no refugee suffering from the disease had died.

'In Gaza, there is a problem with polio, but not here.'

When I left the clinic, the doctor said: 'I hope to see you again – in Jaffa, Palestine.'

At the girls' high school, I sat in on an English class. The girls were in a uniform of blue denim tunics, black trousers and white headscarves. They seemed smart and eager. It was a first-year class, based on strict drill and, as in Sana'a, an oilcloth picture hung on the blackboard.

'Where is the tree?'

'The tree is by the river!'

'What is this?'

'That is a tractor!'

There was, I was glad to see, no sign of the Brown family, no smocking pips, cocker spaniels or fretwork-fronted radios.

The school ran on a shift system. The afternoons were re-runs of the mornings, with another set of children getting five hours of daily education; while in the evenings there were adult literacy classes.

'You mean this building is actually idle between about midnight and seven in the morning?' I said to the headmistress.

'Perhaps we come to that. I think then they will have to find another headmistress, though.'

I asked if the teachers weren't exhausted by the hours they were working. I had taught in a school myself and knew how taxing the job was.

'It is different. It is much easier here, I think, for the teacher. I read of schools in England. I think there all the children are very naughty, the teacher must run and shout all the time. You have seen what it is like here; it isn't so difficult, I think.'

We crossed the street to a prefabricated hut where supplementary rations were being given to the children of the poorest refugees. In the half-dark, with the glint of foil bowls of gruel down the long line of tables, this place did seem in keeping with what I had expected of the camp. There was no poverty, though, in the ambitions of the children themselves. Two boys of nine or ten attached themselves to me when they heard me speaking English; they wanted to practise on me.

'When you are a man, what job will you do?'

'I be teacher.'

'I be doctor.'

They were possible ambitions, too. Many of the Palestinians I had met on the Gulf, the entrepreneurs and technocrats who were largely responsible for running Doha and Abu Dhabi, had started out in refugee camps. The doctors and teachers at Marqa Camp were refugees themselves, and the camp schools had a high record of getting students into technical colleges and universities. It was not too improbable that a hungry-looking child with his bowl of slop and paper cup of skimmed milk might land up at the Massachusetts Institute of Technology or the London School of Economics. The pressure to make out was intense.

Walking down a street of concrete steps we met a red-eyed, crook-backed old man who said that we could come inside his house. It was a single room, bare except for a pair of bedrolls, an old wooden trunk, some pottery waterjugs and a thin carpet spread on the cement floor. The old man said that he came from Hebron, and that he believed he was 135 years old. Perhaps 134 or 136; he couldn't quite remember. He hoped some time to return to Hebron. His house there was not like this, but these were temporary quarters.

'I am very lucky,' he said. 'I have a young wife.'

As we left him, his wife came in, carrying water and a bag of oranges. She looked as if she was somewhere on the wrong side of eighty.

I was still puzzled by the immense difference between one house and another at the camp. Surely the people who had cars, courtyards, houses with many rooms, could afford to live elsewhere?

'The fact that they are in the camps is a declaration of political status. They may be quite wealthy men with jobs in government or business, but they live in the camps as a declaration of their Palestinian identity. Often there comes a conflict. If a man is a doctor or a lawyer in Amman, for instance, and he wants to give dinner parties and so on, it may be hard for him to invite people to his house in the camp. Then he will move – when his professional status becomes more important to him than his political status.'

The Palestinians in Jordan had been granted dual citizenship. They could retain their status as registered refugees, while at the same time they enjoyed the same political and social rights as other Jordanians. Some ministers, and many directors of government departments, were Palestinians. The director of the Ministry of Information, Peter Salah, was a Christian Palestinian. 'This dual citizenship started in Jordan,' he said, 'but I think it must happen elsewhere. The pressure is too great to resist. Even in the Gulf states, I think, it will happen eventually.'

'When I was in the Gulf,' I said, 'I felt the place was just swarming with migrants. Very few people had any long-term interests in the countries they were working in. Palestinians particularly. Yet the Palestinians were the people who were most likely to stay there for the rest of their lives.'

'Of course that's right,' Salah said. 'Dual citizenship is something that must be in the interests of these countries themselves. It is not just "Palestinian" pressure which will make it happen; it is the need for continuity. And continuity is the one thing that the whole of the Arab world is badly lacking.'

Leaving Marqa Camp in the white Chevy, I still wondered whether I was suffering from some form of traveller's trachoma. There were many people in Amman who saw the refugee camps as terrible places. I agreed that the historical events which had turned the Palestinians into refugees were terrible; but I could not see that the camps themselves were squalid or degrading. Some people in the city – Palestinians, especially – did share my view. I asked Peter Salah whether he thought I was being blasé and insensitive about the camps: he said no. It has occurred to me since that Marqa Camp might have been a showpiece, that what I saw was only the whiting on the sepulchre. I doubt it, though. UNRWA was in deep financial difficulties and desperate for more money. Had the organization wanted to rig what I saw of their work, they would surely have taken me to the worst rather than the best of their camps: when I tried questioning the people who thought the camps were ugly and inhuman, they were irritatingly evasive. They did not name anything that they had seen at Marqa, or Irbid, or Jebel El-Hussein. They talked instead about millionaires who collected precious stones and hung Matisses on their walls; they gestured at Rainbow Street, and the cocktail hour, and the property boom.

'That is not the point!' I said.

'You are being deliberately blind!' they said.

They may have been right.

The telephone rang in my room. It was Mohanna Durra. He hadn't been at the Party the previous night.

'Well?' he said. 'Was it a good *performance*?'

The Party really was a showpiece. It demanded to be judged by purely theatrical standards. It had actually been a good performance. A door had been open to the garden, and at midnight a man called Victor had come in from the moonlit olive grove playing an accordion. He had started with moaning Arab tunes, each note stretched as if it was on an inquisitioner's rack. He moved on to Czech folk dances, then to American pop, and finished up with 'Viva La Spania':

> We're off to sunny Spain!
> Vi-va La Spaan-yaa!

Musically speaking, it was the precise equivalent of the painting I had seen on my first day in Amman: a car crash. East smashed into West, the past into the present, the serious into the kitsch.

The Party was roaring out –

> We're going to catch that Costa Brava plane!
> Vi-va La Spann-yaa!

I was crouched under a Roman bust of some emperor or other with a tumblerful of Scotch. I wasn't singing, nor was the woman on the other side of the bust.

'I think this is a bad life that we lead,' she said. 'We cannot talk, we only drink.'

Noha Batshon said that she would like me to see the plot of land she'd bought. It was just half an hour's drive from the city, and it would be beautiful in the evening. She locked up her gallery and we drove out on the road past Jebel Webdeh. At the top of the hill, there was an extraordinarily ugly building. It looked like a bank designed by a manic-depressive: it was marble-fronted, with columns of blue-grey concrete and barred windows. It was the Security Headquarters, and in 1970 it had been the place where Palestinian guerrillas had been interned. Like the bullet holes in the houses, the building was kept as a reminder and a warning. It was known as 'The Blue Hotel'. People of cruder sensibilities called it 'The Toenail Factory'.

As we went past it Noha remarked, 'The head of security now is such a tall beautiful man. Every woman falls in love with him. It is impossible not to.'

'Perhaps that's the first law of efficient dictatorship. Always appoint a really good looking head of security.'

'Sometimes I think you are cynical.'

We went up into the mountains, another balmy, Gilead landscape. Noha's plot was on a bluff at the top of a rutted track. On the far side of the valley the hills were striped with terraced farms, and there were cattle grazing in the fields below. Up on the bluff, though, it was a pretty wilderness of brambles, rocks and wild flowers in the tufty grass. A few fragments of an old stone wall showed that someone once had lived here before.

'It's a lovely place for a house,' I said.

'You like it? I am glad. It is nice, I think, to live in a country like Jordan where there is still virgin land, but which is not savage.'

She had brought a tape-measure with her. I held one end of it down on a rock, while Noha unrolled it to a clump of thistles.

'Here, I make the kitchen.'

The sun was going down fast. The light we were standing in was thick and buttery. Below us, the valleys and crooks of the hills were turning into inky pools.

'Here . . .' Noha went from bare rock to bare rock. 'I have my drawing-room. You see, I have a view over the valley. From the bedroom too. I think that is nice, don't you?'

She measured out her future on the ground in the failing light. The tape-measure would not stretch to the end of the hall. The bathroom was in the middle of a patch of prickly broom. Noha wrinkled her eyes at the sunset.

'I think I am going to be very happy here,' she said. 'Don't you?'

9

The Biggest Souk
in the World

The taxi driver who took me to Ammān airport remarked, at the first set of traffic lights we came to, 'Here I make accident.' At the next crossroads but one, he said, 'Here I make accident also.'

'Please don't make an accident with me. I'm going home.'

'Today, I go very safe, very slow.'

'Good.'

'Where you go to?'

'I'm flying to Beirut, then catching another plane to London.'

'Ah, Beirut. Once it was good. Now it is very bad. I think all *Arabya* is bad now.'

I wondered if it might be possible to tell him the story of the curate's egg, but decided that neither of our languages was up to it.

I had champagne with my breakfast as we flew over Syria, with the Mediterranean showing through the gaps of the mountains of Lebanon. In the transit lounge at Beirut, I read in the paper about the fighting in the city the previous day. There was a suburban road running just beyond the airport car park: it was thick with ordinary-looking people in ordinary cars going to work in an ordinary way. The only odd thing I noticed about Beirut that morning was that a rather pretty female attendant was supervising the use of the men's urinals.

Taking the bus out to the London plane, I saw the patches on the runways where old bomb craters had been filled in. The insistent normality of the airport, with its free glasses of lemonade and souvenir embroidered coasters, had much the same spirit that I had seen in Jordan. MEA, the Lebanese national airline, was 'being all right'. It had kept its flights on schedule through eight years of intermittent civil war. Its staff had to be nicer to its passengers than most aircrews bother to be, since people were understandably nervous about touching down in the middle of a war zone. They had given me a free ride, and I am under an obligation to drop the name of MEA somewhere in this book; but this particular paragraph would have slipped in anyway. The calm of Beirut airport gave me an inkling, at least, of how Amman had survived the Palestinian confrontation of 1970, and of how Lebanon itself might, with luck and grace, survive its own current horrors. When I had set out from London, I had intended to stay in Beirut. That was impossible. I had wanted to write about the tensions of Arabia; but I was not going to become an amateur war correspondent.

I read over the pile of notebooks I had collected over the last fourteen weeks. The words seemed less interesting than the incidental mementoes which had been picked up in their pages: the stain from a slopped cup of thick coffee in Dubai, a dried leaf of *qat* in the Yemen. It was in the Yemen notebook that I found John Saunders. He was a lecturer in English at Sana'a University, and he'd spent the last seven years teaching around the Middle East. He spoke almost no Arabic, but was a convert to Arabia. He had told me how he dreaded going back to England.

'I could never live there now. Three weeks at a time is as much as I can take. It's extraordinary how difficult and frightening it can seem, going home. Last year I went back — there was some family business to settle. I found it incredibly hard to deal with the simplest things. I dreaded going out to the supermarket. If I turned on the television, that yell of advertisements seemed designed to just batter one down. Once you get into Arabia, it gets you. You'll find that, you know. When you go back to London the shock will hit you. There's far more culture-shock involved in going back than there is in coming out. Coming out, you expect it; going back, you don't, and it comes at you like a wall. You'll feel it, too. You're bound to.'

What did hit me was the silence of London. The roll of traffic down the M4 from Heathrow seemed like a funeral cortège after the hooting din of every Arab city. There was a sleepy placidity in the way we shifted lanes all the way along the Cromwell Road, without a single horn being sounded. Home was a grave, staid place.

It was May, and I had come back just as the first of the summer Arabs were showing on the streets around Earls Court. I caught the fright in their eyes. Families huddled tight together as they made the dangerous plunge into the crowd. This crowd wasn't sociable and open as crowds in Arabia are; it was a cold mass of people keeping themselves to themselves behind glazed, indifferent eyes and heavy body-armour. In Arabia, one walks in the crowd; in London, one walks through it. Where in Dubai, for instance, everyone was constantly catching each other's eyes, here eye-contact was ritually avoided as if every stranger was a potential enemy.

On the Earls Court Road I saw a young Qatari whom I had met at the Industrial Training Centre in Doha. He had the look of a single-handed yachtsman managing a difficult passage in a heavy sea. His white robe was blowing out behind him in the wind, and his head was moving in a jittery series of side-ways jabs at the air.

He was staying with his family in a hotel on Nevern Square. Yes, he liked London very much. He did not go out much. Today he was going to buy a radio. It was good, because he had cousins staying at another hotel on the Cromwell Road. They visited each other every day, his family and his cousins; otherwise they spent most of the time in the hotel. He had been on the Tube once. That was very difficult.

I had felt much the same fright in Doha. I knew what it was like to be a nervous trespasser on someone else's culture; except that the Qatari had much more excuse for his alarm then ever I had.

'Here there is much thiefs. My friends have many things stole. They lose all their money.'

The unfriendly crowd harboured pickpockets and thugs. The Qatari had no sense of what New Yorkers call 'sidewalk craft': he was marking himself out for attention, sticking close to walls, catching strangers' eyes. His exotic costume made him a natural target for any mugger on the look-out for a victim. He and his family, he said, never went out after dark; that would be very dangerous, wouldn't it? For him, sadly, it would.

This was the beginning of the season, too, for 'Arab stories'. 'Arabs' (their nationalities were hardly ever mentioned; Qataris, Yemenis, Saudis, Egyptians were all lumped in together under the same opprobrious title) were shoplifting. Their purses, when they were caught, were invariably stuffed with disgraceful amounts of money (money which, in fact, they usually dared not leave behind in their hotels for fear of having it stolen). There were stories about their rudeness to decent English shoppers, stories about their 'barbaric' behaviour in their own countries, gleeful stories about their lapses from the sanitary straight-and-narrow in public places. Anti-semitism against Jews had been outlawed, but anti-semitism against Arabs had become a licensed national sport. It seemed ugly and frightening, the more so since hardly a single voice was being raised to check it. No one bothered to point out that the Arabs were much more stolen-from than stealing. No one voiced the dull truth that very few Arabs – even very few of the Arabs who were staying in London – had nearly as much money as the Fleet Street journalists who poured such envious, moralizing scorn on them.

I caught this Arab fear of London. It was outweighed for me, as for them, by an exhilarating sense of the grandeur, freedom and solidity of the place. There was for a start the sheer quantity of news. For the first week or two that I was home, I was dazed by the daily flood of it. To see issues of policy once again debated in public in a climate of continuous argument seemed an extraordinary liberty. I watched the Prime Minister being attacked on television and for a moment, forgetting myself, I thought *that man's gone too far* and saw jail sentences and forced exile. I spent whole mornings reading the papers, wallowing in scandals, rows and savage criticisms. In the countries I had visited, hardly a single paragraph of the front pages of *The Times* or *Guardian* would have been allowed past the censor's scissors, had those papers been in Arabic and dealing with domestic Arab affairs.

More important even than the quantity of news was the quantity of commodities. I could not take in the dazzling mass of goods on show. Knightsbridge and Oxford Street were heaped with them. Harrods was a treasure house of fantastic toys. I spent an afternoon there, wandering between floors, feeling a childish wonder at the glory of the place. Arab shops have their things arranged in plain piles; here every counter was a theatrical set. Artful positioning and subtle stage lighting gave an exaggerated, dramatic life to the most ordinary object. Even a ballpoint pen was placed so as to excite the prospective buyer in a display of seductive commodity-striptease. London was the biggest, most tantalizing souk in the world.

The most powerful of all the qualities of the city, though, was the gravity I had first felt when I had been driven from the airport in the silent traffic. One could feel it in the buildings and sniff it in the air – the reliable weightiness of a place which is all continuity and gradual change. The hugger-mugger architecture of London, with Georgian rubbing shoulders with Victorian Gothic, Pont Street Dutch, Edwardian commercial and 1960s glass, had that unmistakable reassuring quality of an old, well-lived-in family house. Change in Arabia has come in whirlwinds; in London it had happened as an infinitely gradual geological process, with layer slowly building on layer. On one's own street one could see all the fossils of one's ancestors preserved in the rock.

This, surely, was what had drawn the Arabs to the city. Selim had said, 'All Arabs are homesick for culture.' Almost everyone had talked about the fatal lack of continuity in their own countries. I think that perhaps I did, briefly, see London through Arab eyes when I felt that it was like the church in Philip Larkin's 'Churchgoing':

A serious house on serious earth it is,
In whose blent air all our compulsions meet,
Are recognized, and robed as destinies.
And that much never will be obsolete,
Since someone will for ever be surprising
A hunger in himself to be more serious,
And gravitating with it to this ground,
Which, he once heard, was proper to grow wise in,
If only that so many dead lie round.

My Arab neighbours were now no longer like Martians at all.
I could understand scraps of their language; on a handful of
occasions I was able to act as an interpreter when people got
into difficulties in my local shops. I was in a position to begin,
at least, to ascribe motives and particular identities where six
months before I had only seen an undifferentiated mass of
strangers.

Many of the Gulf Arabs were waiting for hospital treatment
in London. They had been flown over to Europe under
government health schemes and were kicking their heels in
Earls Court, hanging on the day when they would be admitted
to a clinic. They had been given a living-allowance of ten to
fifteen pounds a day, and they were spending their time in a
self-contained bubble world of Arabia-in-exile. Unused to
foreign food, they were cooking their own meals on gas-rings
in their hostels and hotels, or going out to the falafel- and kebab-
houses on the Earls Court Road. Their local newspapers were
on sale outside the Tube station. The network of cousinship
gave them a makeshift, threadbare society. For everyone who
was in London for a month or six weeks, there was a cousin or a
cousin's cousin who was here on an industrial training course –
an old British hand who could shepherd them through the
hazards of this big alarming city.

Earls Court, in fact, was much like the British Clubs which
I had seen on the Gulf; it afforded a rough facsimile of home.
Between the hotel, the kebab-house, the Arab newsagent's,
the Oriental grocery and the Arab cinema, it was possible to
forge a temporary life which much resembled the one they had
left behind. The British expatriates in the Gulf had not been
very intrepid in their exploration of their host countries; nor

were most of the Arabs in London. An expedition to the Museum of Science and Natural History in South Kensington was their equivalent of the visiting businessman's trip to the gold souk or the dhow harbour. Like the expatriates, they were tiptoeing so lightly over the top of an alien culture that their feet barely touched this foreign ground.

They were not rich. They didn't shop in Knightsbridge and Bond Street. They went to Woolworths, Marks and Spencers and the British Home Stores. Unless he was a member of the ruling family, or a prosperous entrepreneur with a clutch of agencies, a man from a small, oil-rich Gulf state might have about eight thousand pounds a year at his disposal. This sum would include his housing allowance, his car allowance and his salary. By English standards, that is modest wealth; by American ones it is genteel poverty. It is certainly not the stuff that the dreams of the leather-clad prostitute on the Earls Court Road were made of.

In Earls Court, the economic pattern of Arabia was repeating itself in miniature. Gulf and Saudi money was creating a web of service-industries which were manned by people from the poor north-west of the peninsula. The groceries, the clubs, the kebab-houses, the Halal butchers, were run by Palestinians, Jordanians, Egyptians, Syrians and Lebanese – the skilled upper-servants of the Arab world.

There was another, brutish service-industry which had grown up around the Earls Court Arabs. This was a product of native British enterprise. Gangs of thieves were systematically working the hotels. One singularly nasty racket involved the use of a girl who would claim that she had been raped by an Arab, threaten to call the police, then get her male accomplices to strip the man's room of money and valuables. Unable to speak English, knowing that they would make no headway with the authorities, the Arab victims submitted to this trick and didn't dare to make any formal complaint.

What puzzled me most was the continued willingness of such people to come to London. It was a far more dangerous city than any they had known at home. How did they face the obvious dislike which was being shown them by the British? Several months after I had returned from my trip to Arabia, I was talking to a Palestinian woman who had lived in London for several years. I said that in Arabia I had met with infinitely more courtesy than any Arab could hope to encounter in London; how did the Qataris and Abu Dhabians manage to deal with the wall of cold dislike with which they were faced in England?

'They simply do not see it,' she said. 'They think that English people are very polite. They respect the English and believe the English like them. You see, you have to understand the language very well, you have to be extremely sophisticated, before you notice the anti-Arab feeling here. These people don't read English newspapers. They don't see the cartoons. They just don't know about these things.'

'But surely every English person they meet must reflect some of this antagonism? Don't they just notice it on the street?'

'No, they don't. The English are so unexpressive. They don't show their real feelings. If an Arab asks somebody to show him the way to a station, an Englishman will give him directions. So they think the Englishman is very friendly and helpful. It's quite different in Paris. No Arab wants to go to Paris now. A Frenchman speaks with gestures . . . he shows his dislike with his hands. But the Englishman's hands do not move when he talks. It is only in the nuance of the voice that he gives away what he actually feels; and most Arabs, unless they are very well educated, cannot hear this nuance. *I* hear it. I see the cartoons. I read the newspaper stories. But the man on the Earls Court Road knows nothing of this. He thinks the English love him. He is frightened of the criminals, of course, but he thinks that ordinary English people are all very polite. He has this idea of the "English gentleman". Because he cannot speak the language, he thinks that everybody is very stiff-upper-lip on the surface but kind underneath.'

'I think that's sad and shaming.'

'No, I think he is lucky to have these illusions. I only wish I could have them myself.'

One after-image lodged in my head and wouldn't go. The morning after I had returned to London, a friend was driving me up Park Lane. As we went past Hyde Park I heard cannon fire. I looked out across the traffic to see a lot of men in red coats and cocked hats charging across the park with muskets.

Their guns flashed, and little puffs of smoke settled in the misty air under the trees. I leaned half-way out of the car window to see more of this extraordinary spectacle. The only thing that seemed in any way ordinary or familiar about it was a small group of men in dishdashas and head-dresses in the watching crowd.

'What on earth is that?' I said.

My friend didn't even turn her head to look. The battle of Waterloo, or whatever it was, wasn't worth the effort of a glance.

'Oh,' she said indifferently. 'It's just the Queen's birthday, isn't it?', and made a right into Brook Street.

Fontana Paperbacks

Fontana is a leading paperback publisher of fiction and non-fiction, with authors ranging from Alistair MacLean, Agatha Christie and Desmond Bagley to Solzhenitsyn and Pasternak, from Gerald Durrell and Joy Adamson to the famous Modern Masters series.

In addition to a wide-ranging collection of internationally popular writers of fiction, Fontana also has an outstanding reputation for history, natural history, military history, psychology, psychiatry, politics, economics, religion and the social sciences.

All Fontana books are available at your bookshop or newsagent; or can be ordered direct. Just fill in the form and list the titles you want.

FONTANA BOOKS, Cash Sales Department, G.P.O. Box 29, Douglas, Isle of Man, British Isles. Please send purchase price, plus 8p per book. Customers outside the U.K. send purchase price, plus 10p per book. Cheque, postal or money order. No currency.

NAME (Block letters)

ADDRESS
